WOMEN'S EMANCIPATION AND CIVIL SOCIETY ORGANISATIONS

Challenging or maintaining the status quo?

Edited by Christina Schwabenland, Chris Lange,
Jenny Onyx and Sachiko Nakagawa

D1612795

P

First published in Great Britain in 2017 by

Policy Press
University of Bristol
1-9 Old Park Hill
Bristol
BS2 8BB
UK
t: +44 (0)117 954 5940
pp-info@bristol.ac.uk
www.policypress.co.uk

North America office:
Policy Press
c/o The University of Chicago Press
1427 East 60th Street
Chicago, IL 60637, USA
t: +1 773 702 7700
f: +1 773-702-9756
sales@press.uchicago.edu
www.press.uchicago.edu

© Policy Press 2017

British Library Cataloguing in Publication Data
A catalogue record for this book is available from the British Library

Library of Congress Cataloging-in-Publication Data
A catalog record for this book has been requested

ISBN 978-1-4473-2478-2 paperback
ISBN 978-1-4473-2481-2 ePub
ISBN 978-1-4473-2482-9 Mobi

Cover design and image by Hayes Design
Front cover image: Clifford Hayes / www.hayesdesign.co.uk
Printed and bound in Great Britain by CMP, Poole
Policy Press uses environmentally responsible print partners

Dedication

The editors would like to dedicate this anthology to the memory of Martha Farrell, who worked tirelessly throughout her life for the emancipation of women. Her career spanned 35 years in informal education, gender mainstreaming, gender equality and policy advocacy. She worked for Participatory Research in Asia (PRIA) in India for 19 years alongside her husband, Rajesh Tandon, PRIA's founder.

Martha Farrell's contributions included training grass roots women leaders alongside work on gender awareness and mainstreaming, ensuring that policies on the prevention of sexual harassment were implemented within organisations (starting with her own organisation, PRIA). Her PhD research on sexual harassment in the workplace has been published by Uppall (2014) as *Engendering the workplace: Gender discrimination and prevention of sexual harassment in organisations.*

Her work can therefore be seen as covering the span of topics our anthology is addressing: the need to counter discrimination wherever it is experienced, within organisations as well as in the wider society.

Martha Farrell was murdered by terrorists in Kabul, along with 13 other aid workers, on 13 May 2015. She had been in Kabul to provide training on gender issues for the staff of the Aga Kahn Foundation. Her life, and so sadly, also the manner of her death, are emblematic of the challenges facing all of us who want to create a more equal society, free of gender discrimination and oppression.

Christina Schwabenland, Chris Lange,
Jenny Onyx, Sachiko Nakagawa
February 2016

Contents

Images, figures, maps and tables

Images

Figures

Maps

Tables

About the authors

Cawo Abdi is an Associate Professor of Sociology at the University of Minnesota and a Research Associate at the University of Pretoria, South Africa. Professor Abdi's research areas are migration, family and gender relations, development, Africa and the Middle East. She has published on these topics in various journals and is the author of a book, *Elusive Jannah: The Somali diaspora and a borderless Muslim identity*, University of Minnesota Press, 2015.

Charisma Acey is Assistant Professor of City and Regional Planning at the University of California, Berkeley. Her work in West Africa, Southern Africa and Central America focuses on environmental governance, poverty reduction, and access to basic infrastructural services in urban and peri-urban settlements. Recent and ongoing research includes fieldwork in Ghana, Nigeria and Uganda exploring informal service providers, gender and access to water and sanitation, and sustainable household-scale alternative energy solutions. She earned both her PhD in Urban Planning and Master's in Public Policy from the University of California, Los Angeles Luskin School of Public Affairs.

Annie Dussuet is a sociologist. As a Senior Lecturer at Nantes University, she is habilitated to direct research (HDR), is a member of the Nantes Centre of Sociology, Centre Nantais de Sociologie (CENS) (CNRS FR 3706). Her research concerns work and gender and how public and private spaces are articulated. Her major publications deal with domestic work (*Logiques domestiques*, L'Harmattan, 1997), homecare services (*Travaux de femmes*, L'Harmattan, 2005), nonprofit organisations (*L'économie sociale entre informel et formel*, PUR, 2007), health and ageing at work (Revue de l'IRES, no 78, 2013), conciliation of public/private in women's lives (*Local welfare policy making in European cities*, Springer, 2015). Her interest is currently redirected to working conditions in associations, spatial mobility of the elderly and gender discrimination.

Sally A East has worked within the charity sector for more than 20 years. Having qualified in practice, specialising in charities registered in England and Wales, Sally then worked within small and large charities across the globe, including Amnesty, British Council, British Heart Foundation and currently, Police Now, where she is Operations and Finance Director. Her passion for knowledge has motivated her to gain a second doctorate, her thesis entitled: *Flexible working in charitable organisations: an exploration of barriers and opportunities*. In the autumn of 2015 Sally was selected from 850 candidates as 'a leading woman in the charity field by Top Female Executives' (*Charity Today*, 2 September 2015), and was Finalist for the UK Financial Director – Public Sector (2016) Business Finance Awards. Sally utilises her expertise focusing on change management, finance and governance.

Elena Elia is a social and institutional communication expert, and her main fields of expertise are related to health communication, social policies and third sector organisations. She's been teaching sociology of communication and third sector and social services at the University of Florence. Her activities focus on consulting, planning and training, with a special focus on participatory processes.

Érika Flahault is a sociologist and Assistant Professor at the University of Maine, Le Mans, France. She is a member of ESO (UMR 6590), CNRS (National Centre for Scientific Research) and ANEF (National Association of Feminist Studies). Her research interests are: women's position and part in associations; professionalisation in the nonprofit sector; single women: space and time relations, identity building and destinies; social alternatives. Publications linked with the book: Érika Flahault, Annie Dussuet, Dominique Loiseau (dir), 2013, Cahiers du genre, 'Associations féministes: reproduction ou subversion du genre?', no 55 and Érika Flahault, Henry Noguès, Nathalie Schieb-Bienfait (dir), 2011, L'économie sociale et solidaire: Nouvelles pratiques et dynamiques territoriales, Presses Universitaires de Rennes.

Gesine Fuchs is a Lecturer at the Department of Social Work, Lucerne University of Applied Sciences and Arts. She holds a PhD in political science from the University of Hannover (Germany). In her work she is mainly concerned with the question of how we can achieve comprehensive and sustainable democratisation of societies. She specialises in political representation, comparative politics, law and politics and policy analysis. Her research projects include comparative studies on legal mobilisation for equal pay by social movements and on gender equality policies in Switzerland, Germany and Austria. She is co-editor of the feminist political science journal *Femina Politica*. See www.gesine-fuchs.net.

Eva Maria Hinterhuber is Professor of Sociology with a focus on gender studies at the Rhine-Waal University of Applied Sciences

(Germany). She holds a PhD in Comparative Political Sociology at the European University Viadrina Frankfurt/Oder (Germany). Her fields of expertise are political sociology; democracy, transformation and civil society; religion, migration, and integration; peace and conflict studies; gender studies; with a regional focus on Eastern Europe. She is co-editor of the feminist political science journal *Femina Politica*. Among other publications, she recently published a book on women's voluntary engagement in social civil society organisations in Russia.

Fabien Hildwein is a PhD candidate at HEC-Paris, in the Management and Human Resources Department, under the supervision of Professors Eve Chiapello and Joëlle Evans. He is studying how an activist group expresses its claims, interacts with media organisations and how activists are recruited and mobilised by the group. His research interests also include organisational discrimination and feminist perspectives on management.

Rochelle Keyhan is the Director of Feminist Public Works. After five years of involvement with the Hollaback! movement, both as board member for Hollaback!, and founder/director of HollabackPHILLY, she left in November 2014 to run Feminist Public Works. As Director of Feminist Public Works, Rochelle handles the organisation's programming, educational curriculum and speaking engagements. Rochelle is bar certified to practice law in Pennsylvania, and is a practising attorney in Philadelphia focusing on women's issues and nonprofit legal assistance. A graduate of UCLA (English and Women's Studies), Rochelle received her JD from Temple University's Beasley School of Law.

Chris Lange is currently engaged in the nonprofit management and social work of a faith-based organisation in Beirut, Lebanon. She is a social worker by profession and has a doctorate in political science from the Free University of Berlin, worked in third sector research as a freelancer and taught at the Alice Salomon-University of Applied Social Sciences and other universities in Berlin, Germany. She is co-founder of the Affinity Group of Gender of the International Society for Third-Sector Research (ISTR).

Aura Lounasmaa completed her PhD in the Global Women's Studies Centre in the National University of Ireland, Galway, in 2013. Her research examines the activism of women's rights-based and faith-based organisations in Morocco. Aura is a Lecturer in the School of Social

Sciences and the Graduate School, University of East London, and a Research Fellow at the Centre for Narrative Research. Her research interests are feminism, women's activism, human rights and women and Islam. Aura has acted on the board of Sibeal, an Irish postgraduate feminist and women's studies network, and in several feminist student and civil society organisations. Aura also holds a Master's in Economic Science in European Economic and Public Affairs from University College Dublin.

Anne Namatsi Lutomia is a PhD candidate in Human Resource Development at the University of Illinois at Urbana-Champaign. She holds a Bachelor of Education degree in French and Secretarial Studies from Kenyatta University, Kenya, and a Master's degree in Nonprofit Management from Hamline University in Minnesota. Her research interests span international research collaborations, leadership, learning, labor mobility, Kenyan feminisms, other mothering, the archive and nonprofits organizations. Her work has been published in *The Nonprofit and Voluntary Sector Quarterly*, *Feminist Africa*, *Transnational Social Review*, *Journal of Gender & Cultural Critiques*, *BUWA! Journal on African Women's Experiences* and *Kenya after Fifty: Reconfiguring Education, Gender, and Policy*. Her dissertation seeks to understand the case of an international scientific research collaboration network based in the US and Benin. She has extensive work experience in NGO and nonprofit sectors in Kenya and the US and serves on nonprofit boards in both countries. She is a budding poet and photographer.

Blaire MacHarg is a graduate of the Master's of Public Administration programme at DePaul University, where she specialised in International Public Management. She received her Bachelor's degree in Political Science specialising in International Studies with a minor in French from Arizona State University. Blaire has a background working in universities, government and the private sector. Blaire currently lives in Chicago where she works in the finance industry as an anti-money laundering professional.

Gareth G Morgan is Emeritus Professor of Charity Studies at Sheffield Business School, Sheffield Hallam University and for 17 years he coordinated the University's Centre for Voluntary Sector Research. He has supervised a number of doctoral dissertations analysing charity issues and led various research projects in the sector including studies for the Charity Commission. He is the author of five books and a wide range of journal articles. He has a keen interest in issues of gender equality and equality law over many decades and has been actively involved in a number of voluntary organisations working in this field.

Sachiko Nakagawa is a Japanese researcher on social enterprise and social inclusion and especially focuses on work integration social enterprises (WISEs) for people with disabilities. She gives many presentations and publishes many papers in international conferences, international journals and books edited by foreign researchers. She is an active member of the International Society for Third-Sector Research (ISTR) and EMES European Research Network, and also a partner of the International Comparative Social Enterprise Models (ICSEM) project, which Jacques Defourny and Marthe Nyssens coordinate with EMES European Research Network. She was the coordinator of the Affinity Group on Gender of ISTR for six years, between 2008 and 2014.

Jenny Onyx is Emeritus Professor of Community Management in the Business School at the University Technology Sydney (UTS). She is Co-Director of the Cosmopolitan Civil Societies research center, and former editor of *Third Sector Review*. She is particularly concerned with issues of advocacy, social capital, volunteering and civil society, and has published widely in these fields.

Ruth Phillips is an Associate Professor in the Social Work and Policy Studies Program and the Associate Dean for Postgraduate Research in the Faculty of Education and Social Work at the University of Sydney, Australia. Her research and publication activity includes social policy, third sector studies and feminism. Ruth has been an active member and contributor to the International Society for Third-Sector Research (ISTR) for the past 15 years and was an editor for Australia's leading third sector journal *Third Sector Review* for five years until 2015, when she resigned from that position after being elected to the ISTR Board.

Inés M Pousadela is a Policy and Research Officer at CIVICUS: World Alliance for Citizen Participation, a researcher for OGP's Independent Reporting Mechanism in Argentina, and an Associate Researcher at the Institute of Communication and Development (ICD) in Uruguay. She holds a PhD in Political Science (UB, Argentina), a Master's degree in Economic Sociology (IDAES-UNSAM), a Bachelor's degree in Political Science from the University of Buenos Aires, and two Photography degrees (Montgomery College, USA). For the past decade she has alternated between academic research in

Latin American Studies at American University (CLALS), Brown University (BIARI Program), Georgetown University (CLAS) and the University of Maryland (LASC), and independent political consultancy with NGOs and international organizations.

Raquel Rego is a Portuguese sociologist. She has a PhD in sociology obtained in 2007 at the Université Lille 1 (France) and at the ISCTE-IUL (Portugal) with 'praise and distinction unanimously'. She has worked at SOCIUS-ISEG, and is currently a Research Fellow at the Institute of Social Sciences, University of Lisbon. Her research activity has been focused in the area of associationism and volunteering, industrial relations, corporate restructuring, professional regulation, among others. She is a member of the Portuguese team of EurWORK from Eurofound and a board member of the IRENE network.

Dorothy Owino Rombo is an Assistant Professor of Child and Family Studies in the Department of Human Ecology at the State University of New York, Oneonta. She holds a PhD in Family Social Science from the University of Minnesota, twin cities. Her research interest is on the ecological predictors of the wellbeing for vulnerable populations: women, children, immigrants and international families. With a minor in family policy, analysis of public policy is another scholarship of interest. Having lived most of her life in Kenya before migrating to the USA, Dorothy has roots that drive her passion for exploring solutions to challenges experienced by Kenyans and beyond. She has published work that focuses on policy analysis, family strength and feminist analysis.

Brenda Nyandiko Sanya is a PhD candidate at the University of Illinois, Urbana-Champaign. Her dissertation, 'States of discretion: black migrating bodies and citizenship in the United States', is an analysis of immigration law and court cases, in which she locates Black Africans in the long trajectory of African American migrations. She received her Master's in Gender/Cultural Studies at Simmons College in Boston, where she researched the constitutional rights of Kenyan women and civic engagement through emerging technologies. Her writing has appeared in *Feminist Africa, Left History, Transnational Social Review, Policy Futures in Education, in Mobilized Identities: Mediated Subjectivities and Cultural Crisis in the Neoliberal Era*, and most recently, in *Kenya after Fifty: Reconfiguring Education, Gender, and Policy*.

Christina Schwabenland is a Reader in Public and Voluntary Sector Management at the University of Bedfordshire. She has a doctorate in voluntary sector studies, has published two books on voluntary sector research, *Stories, visions and values in voluntary organisations* (Ashgate/ Gower, 2008) and *Metaphor and dialectic in managing diversity* (Palgrave, 2012). She is currently researching diversity management in the voluntary sector, and her work has been published in *Human Relations*, *Organization* and *Culture and Organization*.

Masako Tanaka is Associate Professor of Faculty of Global Studies at Sophia University in Tokyo. She teaches International Cooperation Studies, South Asian Regional Studies and Gender and Development. Her main works focus on roles of different actors in development aid and citizens' movements. She has been working as a development practitioner and engaged in various civil society organisations, both in Japan and in Nepal, for two decades. Her recent doctoral thesis was about a case study of evolutional process of a trafficking survivors' organisation in Nepal.

Marco Tavanti is a Full Professor of Nonprofit Management at the University of San Francisco and Director of the Master of Nonprofit Administration. He is founder of the World Engagement Institute (WEI), President of the Sustainable Capacity International Institute (SCII) and served as expert advisor for the Somalia Strategy Forum (SSF). His field is international sustainable development and global civil society. He is author of *Sustainable Human Security* (2014), *Las Abejas: Pacifist resistance and synthetic identities in a globalizing Chiapi* (2003) and editor of the *International Journal of Sustainable Human Security*. He serves as international consultant expert for numerous NGOs, CSOs, IGOs and specialised agencies for the United Nations.

Annette Zimmer is Professor of Social Policy and Comparative Politics at the Institute for Political Science at Münster University, Germany; she gained her doctoral degree in Political Science in Heidelberg (1986), habilitation in Kassel (1995), and is Local Associate for the Johns Hopkins Comparative Nonprofit Sector Project, Visiting Professor of German and European Studies at the University of Toronto, Canada, Visiting Fellow at the American Institute for Contemporary German Studies at the Johns Hopkins University, Washington DC, President of the International Society for Third-Sector Research (ISTR) from 2015 to 2017. She is a member of the Board of the German Political Science Association (2000–09) and of the Advisory

Board for Civic Engagement of the German Federal Ministry for Family and Youth/Government (1998–2009); she is on the editorial boards of several relevant journals and co-editor of a book series on civil society; her focus in research lies on voluntary associations and nonprofit organisations in various policy fields, including the arts and culture, social services and sports.

Acknowledgements

We would like to express our appreciation and gratitude to all the contributors who have worked with us throughout the last four years. Also, thanks to the wider membership of the International Society for Third-Sector Research's Affinity Group on Gender (AGG), from where this anthology originated, and who have been very supportive throughout. Very special thanks to Annette Zimmer for suggesting that the AGG could take on this task, and for contributing the Foreword to the anthology. Without her belief in us we would never have even begun!

Christina Schwabenland
Chris Lange
Jenny Onyx
Sachiko Nakagawa

Foreword

Annette Zimmer

Congratulations to the editors and authors of this volume. The articles provide an interesting and highly informative overview of the state of the art as regards the nexus between civil society research and gender studies. In contrast to many books and articles on women's issues, this volume highlights the topic of emancipation. What does emancipation mean? And what distinguishes emancipation from empowerment? How does emancipation work on a structural as well as on an organisational level? With a very special eye on gender equality the encompassing framework of women's emancipation allows the investigation of both the broader political and social context as well as the working environment and the societal context for women. Christina Schwabenland, Chris Lange, Sachiko Nakagawa and Jennifer Onyx have carefully edited the 16 articles collected in this volume. They tell a fascinating story about the difficulties, struggles as well as the options and opportunities of women's organisations and groups to either get a step ahead or, on the contrary, to struggle with significant problems and difficulties on their way to emancipation. Many of those who followed this book project from its very beginning at the ISTR conference in Siena in 2012 know about the difficulties and barriers to getting an innovative and encompassing approach accepted by publishers and up off the ground. It is an approach which builds on two, unfortunately for publication purposes, very distinct streams of research – civil society and nonprofit research on the one hand and gender studies on the other hand. Furthermore, up until now very little has been published that builds on these two distinctive research traditions. Finally, a focus on empirical work and on the study of organisations is not very common in the area of gender studies, which is one that tends to be very theoretical and by and large arguing from a more or less 'western perspective' of the developed world. Against this background, the editors of this volume, indeed, took the risk of discovering new frontiers of civil society and gender research. The outcome of their adventurous endeavour proves that they were right to take the risk of addressing a fascinating topic from a new and innovative perspective.

A foreword is not the right place to provide an overview of all the topics addressed in this volume or even to provide a deeper insight into specific issues. However, a very personal point of view from my side might be allowed. Indeed, I highly appreciate the in-depth discussion on mainstream neoliberalism. The reluctance to join the crowd and follow mainstream approaches constitutes a common point of departure of many articles of this volume. A case in point constitutes the highly critical discussion of 'empowerment' serving as a synonym of women getting ahead in many official documents and in political discussion. The article by Ruth Phillips clearly indicates that women should be careful. For sure, empowerment constitutes a very individualistic approach and hence leaves current economic, social and political structures untouched. However, if the grand design of the current social and political structures is not going to be changed, there is very little hope that 'empowerment' will indeed serve as an avenue towards women's emancipation. At the same time, many of the articles collected in this volume draw our attention to the fact that in the media and in the social sciences women's activism is very often reduced to a single issue, a one-off event. Quite a number of the articles of this volume take a very critical stance on this by highlighting the embeddedness of specific events of women's activism and their broader societal context. In some cases, the authors show that 'the event' is closely connected to a specific culture and tradition. That's why a specific form of women's activism – such as the performances of the Russian punk rock group Pussy Riot – is understood quite differently in its original context. As Eva Maria Hinterhuber and Gesine Fuchs highlight, Pussy Riot has to be located within Russia's new political protest movement to which the women's group added 'a new protest culture with a religious dimension'. Indeed, it is a common feature of the articles collected here that they provide background information that generally is not put up front by classical articles in the social sciences. However, thanks to this background knowledge we are able to see the so-called larger picture and to perceive risks as well opportunities for women and for societies at large.

A further case in point are the articles discussing current developments on the shop floor. For sure, employment has been a significant tool for women's emancipation since the nineteenth century. However, as clearly indicated by a number of authors, today's managerialism definitely has a strong impact on the female labour force. As we all know, women's work by and large translates into cheap labour or even labour without any pay. Current fiscal constraints and the difficulties of public financing put many of those nonprofit organisations and associations that constitute the main shop floor for women under tremendous stress. The organisations react to these challenges by constantly reducing salaries or by changing working conditions. 'Flexibilisation' has turned into the economic term, which is used for shadowing the deterioration of working conditions in many parts of the world and particularly in those areas where the majority of the workforce are women, such as the social service industry.

A further merit of this volume is that it provides insights and examples of women's activism all over the world. In contrast to many other books focusing on gender issues, this collection of articles and reports does take globalism seriously. You find articles focusing on current developments in Africa, Asia, Latin America and of course Europe and Russia. Last, but not least, it is great fun to dig deep into the volume. Some articles clearly show that women's activism is not what we call in German a 'sour beer affair'. Instead, there are many ways to make your point with the goal to bringing women's emancipation ahead. Again, a textbook example provides the article on the French female activist group *La Barbe* that builds on the strong tool of humour. Wearing false beards at CSO's assemblies and thanking the company for its success in not letting women into the inner circles of management, *La Barbe* unmasks the absurdity of many companies' politics. Indeed, this is a sad story, but it is nevertheless fun to read how women are becoming more and more innovative and in touch with culture in order to make their argument. I am sure those who will read the articles of this volume will definitely profit as much from the reading as I did. In sum, this book deserves careful perusal.

ONE

Introducing the anthology

*Christina Schwabenland, Chris Lange, Jenny Onyx
and Sachiko Nakagawa*[1]

Introduction

We know that through the organisations of civil society ordinary women have done extraordinary things to challenge oppression locally, nationally and across the globe. We know that they have achieved many successes, and have developed outstanding entrepreneurial activities. Yet this story remains largely untold until now. Women are at the heart of civil society organisations (CSOs). Women come together to run activities, provide services, establish local networks and raise funds; studies suggest that women are more philanthropic than men and make up the majority of volunteers (Themudo, 2009). Yet research into civil society organising has tended to ignore considerations of gender. The rich history of activist feminist organisations is rarely examined. It is time that changed.

We also know, however, that sometimes organisations find themselves drawn into colluding and reproducing the structures that maintain women in positions of marginality and systemic disadvantage. That is why we must also question our collective achievements. If we are to advance theory and to develop strategies into the future, we must also be concerned with critiques of organisational processes, dynamics and activities as well as success stories.

In this anthology, we identify some of the issues and lessons that arise from the various case studies presented, primarily from a grounded empirical analysis, exploring the multiple sites of domination and struggle and the respective challenges of working inside as well as attacking from outside oppressive institutions. We specifically focus on the role of CSOs and return to the challenging question posed by the title. To what extent are CSOs able to challenge the oppression and domination of women at a local, national and international level? To what extent do CSOs actually find themselves working in ways that are themselves discriminatory and therefore perpetuate the status quo? In order to examine these questions, this anthology brings together current research on CSOs and their involvement in the emancipation of women. The anthology contains contributions from researchers and activists working in many different parts of the world, and includes work on new and emerging issues as well as perennial ones. How do CSOs make use of social media? What is the effect of the growing significance of religion in many cultural contexts? How do they respond to the impact of environmental degradation on women's lives?

Theoretical frames

Our anthology brings together two bodies of literature, which have generally been treated separately; that of research into civil society and its organisations, and that of feminist research into organisations. In this chapter we begin by setting out some of the key theoretical developments that have informed research in these areas and then discuss the overlapping and conflicting areas of interest. We conclude by presenting our conceptual schema for exploring this overlapping terrain and demonstrating how it is developed through the contributions of the individual chapters.

Civil society organising: current and emerging research agendas

Research into civil society organising is a relatively new, albeit rapidly growing field. The Association for Research on Nonprofit Organizations and Voluntary Action (ARNOVA) was founded in the US in 1971 (Horton Smith, 2003) and the International Society for Third-Sector Research (ISTR) in 1972 (www.istr.org). Horton Smith reflects that at the time of ARNOVA's inception:

> my reading of the literature on voluntary or common interest associations indicated two virtually opposite but complementary empirical conclusions: One was that such phenomena were also the direct topic of research by some scholars in many other scholarly disciplines and professions than sociology ...the other was that there seemed to be no interdisciplinary or inter- professional efforts to integrate the study of associational and volunteer phenomena, which I began to term 'Voluntary Action Research' (VAR). There were no relevant interdisciplinary scholarly associations,

no such conferences, nor scholarly journals, nor research institutes dedicated to VAR. (Horton Smith, 2003, 459)

Early scholarly research into CSOs, not as yet constituting a discipline of its own, tended to draw primarily on political science, and to a lesser extent on sociology or management literature for inspiration and approaches. Not surprisingly, early concerns were with the nature of civil society itself, alongside debates about its function. Foley and Edwards distinguish two, somewhat conflicting streams: the first, drawing on de Tocqueville, 'puts special emphasis on the ability of associational life in general and the habits of association in particular to foster patterns of civility in the actions of citizens in a democratic polity' (Foley and Edwards, 1996, 1). The second, inspired by Gramsci, sees civil society as a space in which 'social domination and power relations are contested' (Sanger, cited by Hinterhuber, 2014, 9). These two contrasting conceptualisations of civil society constitute what Foley and Edwards describe as a 'paradox' or tension that is unresolved, and continues to influence both researchers and policy makers, and determines the problematic that runs throughout this anthology.

Out of these contrasting understandings have emerged a number of related research interests. A major concern of much CSO research is that of democratic engagement and the enacting of citizenship (Kenny et al, 2015). These studies investigate the extent to which involvement in associational activity, primarily through volunteering, helps to foster social capital (Onyx and Leonard, 2000; Rochester et al, 2010; Kenny et al, 2015) and promote 'active citizenship' through which local groups create bonds of neighbourliness and also hold democratic institutions to account. The 'social capital' strand of research received an injection of enthusiasm (and funding) following the success of Robert Putnam's work on democracy in Italy (1993), in which he concluded that local government functioned more effectively in areas that had a strong tradition of associational activity – although the nature, or even direction of these causal links is still debated (Jochum, 2003).

The more conflictual understanding of civil society has inspired a contrasting body of work on social activism, social movements and community development. Bock (1988) suggests that social movements are caused by tensions or even crises in a given society; their role is not to support democratic institutions and to strengthen existing societal conditions but to challenge and even fight them. Thus, social movements arise out of a perceived need for social change while community development-based volunteering tends to be more concerned with building social cohesion and better meeting the needs of communities.

Not surprisingly, researchers looking at civil society *organisations* are also likely to focus their attention differently, depending on what they understand their purpose to be. So, for example, one strand of research on accountability focuses on accountability to funders and policy makers while others look at accountability to the community (Leat, 1990). Under the increasing influence of neoliberal ideologies, there is pressure for civil society organisations to become social enterprises and adopt internal management systems that are more 'businesslike'. Thus, as Dart notes: 'moral legitimacy of social enterprise can be understood because of the consonance between social enterprise and the pro-business ideology that has become dominant in the wider social environment' (Dart, 2004, 419). In contrast, other researchers, particularly those concerned with community development, investigate mechanisms for participation and community control, seeing those as means of operationalising the organisations' mission (Rawsthorne and Howard, 2011; Taylor, 2007).

Social movement theorising also seems to be distinguished by these two broad strands; Mayo (2006) identifies a 'rational actor' approach, that assumes that people mobilise around identified areas of self-interest (primarily economic and political, such as the union movement), and what she describes as the 'new social movements' approach which places greater emphasis on issues of identity, ideology and social and cultural reproduction. Mayo suggests that rational actor approaches are useful for providing insights into contextual pressures that threaten the survival of a movement and its responses while political processes involved in new social movements are helpful in addressing the ways in which movements mobilise within a particular context and how they 'frame' issues, and develop 'repertoires of contention' (Mayo, 2006, 72).

Of course representing a huge variety of work through such a binary schema is over-simplistic: the extraordinary diversity of the sector is a strength but also a source of conceptual challenges. This may, at least partially, account for the enormous amount of work devoted to definitions, boundaries and relationships (for example, a recent edition of *Voluntary Sector Review*, November 2013, had five articles on this topic). Some of this work focuses on the boundaries between and relationships with the other two sectors, public and private, or state and market. Other studies explore inter-sectoral relationships such as those between the voluntary and community sectors, advocacy and service providing organisations, member-led versus 'top-down' (Tanaka and Rego, Chapters Nine and Eleven, this volume). Some of these studies are concerned with a drive for purity; 'real' voluntary organisations as opposed to 'hybrid' (Evers, 2005; Billis et al, 2010; Rochester, 2013). The literature on social movements also reflects differing views about the boundary between social movements and social movement organisations, Della Porta and Diani (1999) holding that movements are distinct from formal organisations, while Mayo (2006) suggests that the boundaries between them are more fluid. Another key distinction between the two kinds of social movements (the 'rational actor' approach and the 'new social movements' approach) refers to their mode of operating, with new social movements such as the World Social Forum, and the feminist movement itself, preferring horizontal, networked forms of organising rather than vertical (hierarchical) structures (Kenny et al, 2015).

Feminist organisation studies: current and emerging research agendas

Much of feminist theorising until relatively recently arose out of second-wave feminism in OECD countries and the women's liberation movement(s) of the 1960s and 1970s (Belsey and Moore, 1997; Lewis, 2014). Early concerns were focused on the material injustice, and the demand for equal rights for women, for example, the right to vote, the right for equal employment and wage opportunities, the right to equal access to education. An early concern was with problematising the division between public and private/domestic space, arguing that such divisions were not innate, but political constructions ('the personal is political') that perpetuated women's segregation in the home, and restricted their access to the public sphere as 'natural' (Hinterhuber, 2014). Feminist theorising examined the underlying patriarchal structures of society and how these perpetuated unequal rights and access to resources. Of concern was the nature of paid and unpaid work inside and outside the home; the extent to which the family was to be understood as an institution, women's role within it and whether it was itself a part of civil society.

Fraser (2013) traces the trajectory of western feminism through this initial focus on the *redistribution* of resources and labour, both economic and domestic, turning then to a shift in western feminist academic scholarship to deeper concerns with *recognition* which have concentrated more on the ways in which understandings of gender are constructed, reified and challenged. Much of this work takes its inspiration from Simone de Beauvoir's famous interest in the processes of 'becoming' woman and has been developed by writers such as Kristeva, Irigaray and Butler. It is de Beauvoir's proposition that the understanding of gender as socially constructed, fluid and mutable (as opposed to the more 'essentialist' view that gender is inherent, biologically determined and 'natural') that has shaped most current feminist research. It also explains why the focus of this research is on the processes through which such constructing occurs and can be disrupted and challenged; the 'doing and un-doing' of gender (Nentwich and Kelan, 2014). Two primary sources of investigation are, therefore, 'discourse' (because language constructs meaning) and 'the body' (through which gender is realised and inscribed). West and Zimmerman (1987; 2009) suggested that gender is achieved in interaction, and involves 'being *accountable* to current cultural conceptions of conduct becoming to – or compatible with the "essential natures" of – a woman or a man' (West and Zimmerman, 2009, 114). For West and Zimmerman social structures and hierarchies are critical in shaping these cultural conceptions, with pressures on women to conform to such external demands. However, the poststructuralist understanding subsequently developed by Butler places more emphasis on the notion of performativity by women themselves, summarised by Nentwich and Kelan as 'the process through which gendered subjects are constituted by regulatory norms that are restrictive and heterosexual' (Nentwich and Kelan, 2014, 123).

There are several commonly made criticisms of this body of work. One is that much of what is written is very inaccessible because of the level of abstraction and the complexity of the language used. Second, although it has become very sophisticated in philosophical terms it has moved a long way from engaging in women's day-to-day experiences and practical concerns. While it may well provide some insights into why women continue to perform as gendered subjects to their own disadvantage, they give little practical guidance as to how to prevent violence against women, for example (and can even be seen as a justification for 'blaming the victim'). The activist edge that was strong in the earlier phase of the women's movement is blunted. A third criticism is that this western dominated 'turn' in feminist theorising has not adequately represented the experiences of women in the Global South, themselves also profoundly heterogeneous (Mernissi, 1991; Mohanty et al, 1991; Mohanty, 2003). Even more concerning, the dominance of western feminism may have acted to silence their voices from the on-going debates. Omvedt (2004), for example, identifies a number of significant differences in understandings about the nature of women's oppression and by extension, different trajectories and imaginaries of emancipation. Spivak (1994) famously contends that the voice of the 'subaltern' (in Gramscian terms) can never be heard if mediated through western constructed frames of reference.

Turning to the field of organisation studies, early feminist theorising argued that bureaucratic organisational structure perpetuated institutional forms of dominance and subordination (Ferguson, 1984). According to Ferguson's analysis it is both the case that feminist discourse is antithetical to the discourse of bureaucratic control, and that it is impossible for women within bureaucracies to resist the imperative of domination and control. Women in senior positions then come to reproduce the very structures of inequality that they struggle to overcome. The alternative feminist organisational structures developed during the 1960s and 1970s had the following characteristics in common, as summarised by Bordt:

1. authority is distributed among all members;
2. leadership is a temporary role assumed by each member through the rotation of chair or facilitator position;
3. decision making is participatory;
4. division of labour is minimal and specific tasks are rotated among individuals;
5. information, resources and rewards are equally shared among all;
6. power is conceptualised as empowerment rather than domination;
7. the process of organisation is as valuable as the outcome;
8. social relations are based on personal, communal and holistic ideals.
   (Bordt, 1990, 4)

These forms of feminist, collectivist organisations were subsequently critiqued as being impractical, ineffective and counterproductive. In particular, power inevitably becomes centralised into an informal elite, an oligarchy that is unaccountable to any wider or higher authority, thus producing 'the tyranny of structurelessness' (Freeman, 1975).

Gherardi's (2003) review of feminist organisation theory identified three research agendas: women in organisations and management (more related to the focus on redistribution), organisation theory as gendered knowledge practice, and the study of the processes of gendering as they occur within organisations (recognising that organisations are not neutral but sites where gender dynamics, and even understandings of what it means to be a man or a woman are reproduced, sometimes resisted, sometimes transformed). Thus, much feminist organisation research is focused on deconstructing and problematising the *internal* dynamics of organising, rather than the external actions of the organisation.

Overlapping and contrasting concerns

One overlapping concern between CSO research and feminist research is the question of whether emancipation is achieved through making existing structures and institutions more accessible to women (the 'redistributive' approach) or whether emancipation can only be achieved through a radical deconstructing and remaking of those very structures. Hence, the nature of organisation and organising, and questions as to whether these processes reify existing oppressive practices and definitions, become centrally important. In the NGO literature this debate is reflected in the critiques of differing approaches to development and in particular, the ideological shift in policy from the 'women in development' (WID) agenda (characterised by policies aimed at integrating women into existing development programmes) to the 'gender and development' (GAD) approaches (ostensibly aiming to challenge the structures of male/female power relations, yet in practice working primarily at the level of the individual (Phillips, Chapter Two, this volume; Mayo, 2006)).

Another interesting area of overlap is the shared, albeit somewhat distinctive interest in Gramsci's political theory. While the CSO literature has taken up his conceptualisation of civil society as a space which struggles for hegemony are contested, feminist writers, especially from the Global South, have been inspired by the postcolonialist 'subaltern' histories project, which aims to reclaim history from the perspectives of the most marginalised (Gramsci appropriated the word 'subaltern', originally used to refer to the most junior military personnel, the 'cannon fodder' and extended it to refer to any oppressed group) and Spivak's contribution to it in her much quoted essay 'Can the subaltern speak?' (1994). Spivak's question carries a symbolic role, beyond the actual lines of her argument, representing the invisible and unvoiced, and the challenges of responding to their situation more broadly.

While the idea of an underlying tension between challenging or maintaining the status quo is clearly relevant to our concerns, it is striking how little civil society research regards either the civil society 'space' or the organisations themselves as gendered. There are, of course, exceptions such as Odendahl and O'Neill (1994), Parpart et al (2002), Howell and Mulligan (2005), Hagemann et al (2008). More recently, Hinterhuber's recent literature review (2014) on gender and civil society makes an important contribution. However, it is also the case that women's and gender studies in the field of political and social sciences have 'addressed "civil society" as a research subject only to a very limited extent' (Phillips cited in Hinterhuber, 2014, 2).

Where the literature on CSOs and women's emancipation does overlap is in the work on social movements. Bock (1988), for example, focuses on the study of women's movements in the context of theories on social movements.

Furthermore, some of these studies are interested in problematising not only the aims and aspirations of social movements but also their structures and forms of organisation with Jordan and Maloney (1997) noting that social movements are not all characterised by non-hierarchical and participatory styles of organising. However, in the literature on civil society organisations more generally 'organisation' is rarely deconstructed or critiqued in relation to gender. To the extent that the internal processes or organisations are examined it is primarily in light of their effects on the mission, or driving purpose (Hasan and Onyx, 2008).

Therefore, to briefly summarise: feminist organisation studies literature tends to focus on the core problematic of organisation itself, while CSO literature is more likely to concentrate on the ways in which organisations seek to influence the political, social and/or economic environment. However, within each of the two bodies of literature we have also identified several areas of shared concerns. The first is the ideological debate between the more liberal approaches that underpin calls for redistribution and for the inclusion of women versus the more radical approaches that seek to deconstruct the prevailing power relations that maintain women in marginalised positions, even when the numerical representation of women is increased. The second area of overlapping concern is the heavily western orientation of much of this literature and the importance of incorporating insights from the experiences of women's organising beyond these narrow confines. A third concern regards the effects and consequences for women of the increasingly dominant and global phenomenon of neoliberalism.

Nancy Fraser's collection of essays (2013) provides a useful analysis of the particular tensions and crises that have provided the context for more recent manifestations of women's organising by presenting an analysis of the trajectories of western feminism situated within the context of the growth of neoliberal capitalism. Fraser approaches the topic from a feminist perspective but in her analysis she raises some relevant concerns about the role of CSOs that overlap with Mayo's analysis of social movements. In particular, both Fraser and Mayo highlight what Fraser describes as a 'disturbing coincidence' that the shift in ideological emphasis (characterised by Fraser as the movement from redistribution to recognition, and by Mayo as the movement from the WID to the GAD stance) accompanies the international growth in neoliberal strategies that have had profoundly negative consequences for women. Particularly relevant to our concerns are their suggestions that CSOs have been, at least to some extent, complicit in these developments. This has happened primarily because CSOs have moved into the space vacated by the retreating state.

This move has been welcomed by some but heavily critiqued by others. In support of their arguments that CSOs have contributed to the growth of neoliberalism, Mayo points out that while there has been a significant increase in the role and influence of CSOs during this period, this has accompanied a growing dependence on women for providing social services, who previously might have been employed by the state (with long-term contracts and secure salaries) working in CSOs (on either a voluntary basis or on a steadily declining rate of pay and insecure working conditions). Fraser's critique focuses on the role of micro-credit. She argues that 'micro-credit has burgeoned just as states have abandoned macro-structural efforts to fight poverty, efforts that small scale lending cannot possibly replace' (Fraser, 2013, 222). This has happened, in part at least, because 'counter-posing feminist values of empowerment and participation from below to the passivity-inducing red tape of top-down etatism, the architects of these projects have crafted an innovative synthesis of individual self-help and community networking, NGO oversight and market mechanisms' (Fraser, 2013, 221–2). This challenge, that CSOs have contributed to, or at least been complicit in, the growth of neoliberalism, and with consequences that have been deleterious for women, warns us against complacency, and requires us to ask, if neoliberalism is itself a source of oppression, how is it to be challenged and resisted?

Emancipation as a standpoint to challenge domination

Fraser's (2009) thesis is that the second-wave feminist critique of an androcentric, state-organised capitalism wove together economic, cultural and political dimensions of gender injustice, although it also paved the way for post-Fordist capitalism: feminist cultural critique and identity politics prevailed over socio-economic critique. Fighting androcentrism with grassroots organising and anti-hierarchical rhetoric went well with the neoliberal ideas of horizontal team capitalism and the envisioned liberation of individual creativity and had the effect of further undercutting of the family wage ideals. These moves together unwittingly provided a key ingredient of neoliberalism, namely the dual earner model. A focus on labour market participation prevented the re-conceptualisation of care work. Finally, neoliberal anti-etatism dovetailed with feminist critique of the paternalist welfare state; progressive ideas of citizen's empowerment in civil society legitimated retrenchment and marketisation. Accordingly, Fraser asks whether there is 'a subterranean elective affinity between feminism and neoliberalism' (Fraser, 2009, 114).

Fraser's response is to strengthen the notion and significance of emancipation. Emancipation is different from empowerment, though both are sometimes used interchangeably and both can have positive implications for women. Empowerment is about giving (or taking) power or authority to women, individually or collectively. But emancipation is broader; to emancipate is 'to free from restraint of any kind, especially the inhibitions of tradition; to terminate paternal control' (Macquarie dictionary). Emancipation as a focus is useful if one wants to develop an expanded and non-economistic understanding of capitalist society (Fraser, 2013, 226). She recalls Polanyi's analysis of 'The Great Transformation' from the 1930s. Polanyi analysed the history of capitalism with a double movement, historical tendencies of marketisation on the one hand and social protection on the other. He distinguished two possible relationships of markets with society: markets can be embedded (historically the norm), that is, linked to non-economic institutions involving restraints and interventions, or they can be dis-embedded, that is, free from extra-economic controls (as in neoliberalism). Polanyi associated embedded markets with social protection and saw it as positive; however, the core of the feminist critique of the welfare state is that many institutions of social protection are oppressive, selective, sexist or outright racist. At the same time, marketisation can be liberating, yet also oppressive. Emancipation thus can line up with marketisation or with social protection. Radical feminists of the second wave leaned towards marketisation, not always intentionally, whereas socialist feminists tended to favour social protection and the transformation of the mode of protection.

These thoughts lead Fraser to the conclusion that Polanyi's double movement has to be complemented with emancipation – a standpoint from which one fights domination from wherever it stems: 'emancipation is to scrutinise all types of norms from the standpoint of justice' (Fraser, 2013, 233). Emancipation is a third movement between marketisation and social protection and the relations between two movements are mediated by the third. In this sense, social protection fights against tendencies within emancipation, which are eroding solidarity; yet emancipation attacks 'public hierarchy' and oppressive forms of social protection, as well as oppressive forms of marketisation, as in the case of care work.

Fraser cautions against adopting over-simplistic analyses that swing between the two polarities of presenting the freedoms of the liberated market as the solution to over-weaning state dominance on the one hand, and the benevolent state as the guarantor of protection against the depredations of the uncontrolled market, on the other. She points out that neoliberal capitalism and state protectionism have both provided opportunities for women. However, they have also reified dominating and oppressive structures and traditions. She argues instead, for an analysis that 'avoids reductive economism but also avoids romanticising "society"' (Fraser, 2013, 230). Fraser's suggestion is to position emancipation as a third, and equally incommensurable category and as a standpoint from which domination can be identified and challenged from wherever it is manifested, noting that 'emancipation aims to expose relations of domination wherever they root, in society as well as in economy' (Fraser, 2013, 233).

It is our intention to use this notion of emancipation, as an aspiration and a standpoint, as the underlying structuring principle of this book. Emancipation, in Fraser's understanding is a positioning from which other systems/institutions/practices can be critiqued. Omvedt (2004) reminds us that emancipation means different things to different women and in different contexts and we recognise that the trajectories of feminism and neoliberalism Fraser maps and critiques are not manifested in the same way in different parts of the world, where feminist organising is not specifically against the state nor against the market but against the prevailing hegemony. Neoliberal forces (from the west) certainly have had an effect, but that is added to pre-existing cultural forces of domination. In most if not all societies the relationship between women and men is imbedded in traditions, habits, regulations shaping the role and position of women and men in these societies. Therefore, culture and traditions, including religion, are categories that also deserve serious examination as they can function as systems of oppression.

The genesis of the anthology

The idea for the book originated in a discussion between members of the Board of the International Society for Third-Sector Research (ISTR) and the Affinity Group for Gender (AGG), which has been convened on a voluntary basis on behalf of ISTR since 2002. The AGG brings together researchers who are specifically concerned with promoting, highlighting and supporting research into CSOs and women's emancipation both within ISTR and beyond. A call for chapter proposals was circulated through the ISTR network as well as through gender studies/feminist and organisation research channels. Forty-four abstracts were submitted and the final selection was made taking into account geographic spread and the extent to which the proposed chapter would add either new understanding or greater nuance to already existing knowledge.

The breadth of activities discussed within these chapters is impressive and demonstrative of the scope and diversity of the field. We include chapters on emergent social movements, CSOs that are heavily reliant on the internet for organising, women's groups and generic groups, campaigning and advocacy organisations, grassroots associations and service providers operating under government contracts. However, despite our good intentions, we are aware that there are some significant gaps. Several authors had to withdraw as other commitments competed for their time. Some important themes were identified by the editors, but no proposals were submitted to develop them. Efforts were made to commission chapters on important topics and these were partially successful, but not completely so. We are particularly aware of the lack of contributions from the Middle East, except for Morocco, despite women's significant involvement in the 'Arab Spring' alongside their increasing vulnerability as these events have unfolded.[2] There is also nothing on China. However, we do have contributions focusing on Asia (Nepal), Russia, Africa (Nigeria and Kenya), South America (Uruguay) and Europe (the UK, France, Italy and Portugal) as well as two studies taking a global perspective.

We have chosen to include a wide range of issues in the anthology because gender relationships permeate all realms of life for individuals and sociological groups as well as providing the genesis and focus for many organisations. In order to attract the interest of innovative and unconventional contributors we have deliberately left the definitions open of what we acknowledge are very contested terms for feminists working within civil society. The field of CSO research is redolent with studies on definitions; of the sector (non-profit or non-government; community or voluntary or development) and of its organisational forms (social movements, associations, enterprises, networks, charities, charitable businesses, the list goes on). Similarly, feminist researchers debate the distinctions between empowerment and emancipation alongside the differing theoretical and political stances inherent in the use of the categories of 'woman' and/or 'gender'. The authors presented here occupy a range of views about whether, for example, social movements are organisations, and whether voluntary and non-governmental; or whether empowerment and emancipation are interchangeable terms or represent important distinctions. We hope that within each chapter the particular stance of the author(s) is clear. While we have not imposed any framework of our own on our authors' conceptual framework, we, as editors, do explore some of the theoretical implications of these terms in this and the final chapter.

Structure of the anthology

Our anthology will therefore be focused around these different understandings of emancipation, how domination is to be resisted and how emancipation is to be achieved through organising. Therefore, although each of the chapters contains these dual emphases, in the first section we present chapters that are more outwardly focused and in the second section we include chapters that look inward, at organisations themselves. Drawing from the literature reviewed above we have identified three different understandings of organisation; organising as a means to an end, organising as the manifestation of alternative values and imaginaries and third, organisations as institutions that reify and maintain oppressive understanding of gender and role.

Phillips' chapter complements ours, and is therefore included in the introductory section, because her research directly concerns these differing and competing understandings of emancipation and empowerment, underpinned by an international empirical study of women's organisations. Her chapter is driven by concerns about the failure to achieve gender equality on a global scale and leads her to explore how women's NGOs identify (or don't) with these different paradigms of emancipation. Her findings highlight important limitations of the 'empowerment' paradigm, arguing that it has lost much of its transformational potential.

Overview of the first section

This section contains contributions that focus primarily on women's activism, how it is to be achieved and how domination is to be resisted through organised collective action. The first two chapters, by Elia and Keyhan, written from a practitioner standpoint, describe the emergence of two new networked movements, one in Italy with very open-ended concerns and aspirations, the other worldwide and focused primarily on street violence/harassment. As described by the authors, these movements manifest very contemporary attributes including sophisticated use of the internet and reflecting concerns of representation and multiple interpretations of experience. The second two chapters provide case studies of two radical activist groups, both of which appropriate cultural symbolic resources and deploy them in highly sophisticated ways. Hinterhuber and Fuchs analyse the Russian activist group Pussy Riot, which aims to challenge, disrupt and widen the space for public expression while *La Barbe's* activities, discussed by Hildwein, are more focused on the absence of women in the world of work. The technologies employed by each of these groups rely on the disruptive power of parody.

These chapters are followed by Pousadela's discussion of the campaign to legalise abortion in Uruguay from a political perspective with emphasis on women's participation in political processes. The section concludes with a chapter that exemplifies Fraser's appeal for analyses that take emancipation as a position from which to identify and critique domination in whatever institutional structures it manifests itself: Acey explores women's activism within the Niger Delta region and employs an ecological perspective to highlight the inter-relationships of the many agencies involved and their implications for women's increased participation and choice.

Overview of the second section

The second section focuses on organisations: CSOs whose primary purpose is women's emancipation, CSOs run by women and women working in mixed CSOs. The chapters are arranged so as to bring out some of the underlying problematics.

The first two chapters explore the potential for intermediary organisations, conceptualised as 'incubators' by Tanaka and 'meso'-level organisations by Tavanti et al. Tanaka's 'incubators' draw on feminist imaginaries and construct the role of the organisation as that of nurturer, while the risks and possibilities of cultural domination are also noted in Tavanti et al's analysis.

Difficulties faced by organisations working with competing understandings of feminism are taken up by Rego and Lounasmaa. Rego studies women's leadership in emergent Roma associations in Portugal, exploring the ways in which women fashion models of leadership that are rooted in cultural norms and values which, while problematic in certain ways, provide contrasting models to the more elitist approaches of infrastructure organisations. Lounasmaa, however, focuses on tensions between 'faith-based' and 'rights-based' organisations in Morocco, highlighting the importance of each place in maintaining a sense of difference even when sharing many concerns and aspirations.

The next two chapters look inwardly, interrogating processes of gendered organising within CSOs. The approaches these authors take have most affinity with the body of work of western European feminist organisation studies, exploring how the undoing and re-doing of gender is reified within patterns of organising. Their specific interests are in the kinds of jobs available to women in CSOs (Dussuet and Flahault) and more specifically in flexible working (East and Morgan).

The section concludes with a case study of *Maendeleo ya Wanawake*, the longest standing women's organisation in Kenya. Lutomia et al are highly critical of *Maendeleo ya Wanawake*'s operating processes and achievements but their critique is wide ranging and brings together many of the themes addressed earlier on. This chapter, like the one by Acey that concludes the previous section, draws on alternative models of feminism to provide a critique that encompasses multiple standpoints.

Finally, in the concluding chapter, the editors draw out and summarise the insights into the key problematics afforded by the contributions in this book. We believe that this is the first anthology to attempt such an overview of the part played by civil society organisations in the ongoing battle against the oppression of women. We highlight the wonderful diversity of events and perspectives and strategies across the globe, yet all expressing an amazing energy and common concern to reject domination. We know that the work is not finished, and we hope that the lessons learned from these cases can help activists and researchers alike to focus on future strategies. But above all, we wish to honour what has been achieved.

Notes

[1] Thanks to Eva Maria Hinterhuber and Gesine Fuchs for the summary of Nancy Fraser's arguments, which we have incorporated into this chapter.

[2] The Issam Fares Institute for Public Policy and International Affairs at the American University of Beirut is undertaking a study of the gender dimensions of the Arab Spring but even preliminary findings will not be completed in time for inclusion in this anthology.

References

Belsey, C and Moore, J, 1997, Introduction: The story so far, in C Belsey and J Moore (eds) *The feminist reader: Essays in gender and the politics of literary criticism*, 2nd edn, Basingstoke: Macmillan

Billis, D (ed), 2010, *Hybrid organizations and the third sector: Challenges for practice, theory and policy*, Basingstoke: Palgrave

Bock, U, 1988, *Androgynie und Feminismus: Frauenbewegung zwischen Institution und Utopie*, Weinheim Basel: Beltz Verlag

Bordt, R, 1990, How alternative ideas become institutions: The case of feminist collectives, *Program on Nonprofit Organizations, PONPO, working paper 159*, New Haven, CT: Yale University

Dart, R, 2004, The legitimacy of social enterprise, *Nonprofit Management and Leadership* 11, 4, 411–24

Della Porta, D, Diani, M, 1999, *Social movements*, Oxford: Blackwell

Evers, A, 2005, Mixed welfare organizations and hybrid organizations: Changes in governance and provision of social services, *Journal of Public Administration* 28, 9–10, 737–48

Ferguson, K, 1984, *The feminist case against bureaucracy*, Philadelphia, PA: Temple University Press

Foley, MW, Edwards, B, 1996, The paradox of civil society, *Journal of democracy* 7, 3, 38–52

Fraser, N, 2009, Feminism, capitalism and the cunning of history, *New Left Review* 56, Mar/April, 97–117

Fraser, N, 2013, *Fortunes of feminism: From state-managed capitalism to neoliberal crisis*, London: Verso

Freeman, J, 1975, *The politics of women's liberation*, New York: David McKay

Gherardi, S, 2003, Feminist theory and organization theory: A dialogue on new bases, in C Knudsen, H Tsoukas (eds) *Oxford handbook on organization theory*, pp 200–36, Oxford: Oxford University Press

Hagemann, K, Michel, S, Budde, C (eds), 2008, *Civil society and gender justice: Historical and comparative perspectives*, Oxford: Berghahn Books

Hasan, S, Onyx, J (eds), 2008, *Comparative third sector governance in Asia: Structure, process and political economy*, New York: Springer

Hinterhuber, E, 2014, Time to tango! Bringing civil society and gender together, *Working paper no 3*, Zentrum fur Europaische Geschlechterstudien, Institut für Politikwissenschaft, Westfälische Wilhelms-Universität, Münster, Germany

Horton Smith, D, 2003, A history of ARNOVA, *Nonprofit and voluntary sector quarterly* 32, 3, 458–72

Howell, J, Mulligan, D (eds), 2005, *Gender and civil society: Transcending boundaries*, London: Routledge

Jochum, V, 2003, *Social capital: Beyond the theory*, London: NCVO

Jordan, G and Maloney, W, 1997, *The protest business*, Manchester: Manchester University Press

Kenny, S, Taylor, M, Onyx, J, Mayo, M, 2015, *Challenging the third sector: Global prospects for active citizenship*, Bristol: Policy Press

Leat, D, 1990, Voluntary organisations and accountability: Theory and practice, in H Anheier, W Seiben (eds) *The third sector: Comparative studies of nonprofit organisations*, Berlin: Walter de Gruyter

Lewis, P, 2014, Postfeminism, femininities and organization studies: Exploring a new agenda, *Organization Studies*, 35, 12, 1845–66

Mayo, M, 2006, *Global citizens: Social movements and the challenge of globalisation*, London: CPSI/ Zed Books

Mernissi, F, 1991, *The veil and the male elite: A feminist interpretation of women's rights in Islam*, New York: Basic Books

Mohanty, CT, 2003, *Feminism without borders: Decolonizing borders, practising solidarity*, New Delhi: Zubaan

Mohanty, CT, Russo, A, Torres, L (eds), 1991, *Third world women and the politics of feminism*, Bloomington, IN: Indiana University Press

Nentwich, JC, Kelan, EK, 2014, Towards a topology of 'doing gender': An analysis of empirical research and its challenges, *Gender, Work and Organization* 21, 2, 121–34

Odendahl, T, O'Neill, M (eds), 1994, *Women and power in the nonprofit sector* Chichester: Jossey Bass

Omvedt, G, 2004, Women's movement: Some ideological debates, in M Chaudhuri (ed) *Feminism in India*, New Delhi: Kali for Women

Onyx, J, Leonard, R, 2000, Women, volunteering and social capital, in J Warburton, M Oppenheimer (eds) *Volunteeers and volunteering*, pp 113–24, Sydney: Federation Press

Parpart, JL, Rai, SLM, Staudt, K (eds), 2002, *Rethinking empowerment: Gender and development in a global/local world*, London: Routledge

Putnam, R, 1993, *Making democracy work*, Princeton, NJ: Princeton University Press

Rawsthorne, M, Howard, A, 2011, *Working with communities*, Deerfield, IL: Common Ground

Rochester, C, 2013, *Rediscovering voluntary action: The beat of a different drum*, Basingstoke: Palgrave

Rochester, C, Ellis Paine, A, Howlett, S, 2010, *Volunteering and society in the 21st century*, Basingstoke: Palgrave Macmillan

Spivak, GC, 1994, Can the subaltern speak?, in P Williams, L Chrisman (eds) *Colonial discourse and post-colonial theory: A reader*, pp 66–111, New York: Columbia University Press

Taylor, M, 2007, Community participation in the real world: Opportunities and pitfalls in new governance spaces, *Urban Studies* 44, 2, 297–317

Themudo, NS, 2009, Gender and the non-profit sector, *Nonprofit and voluntary sector quarterly* 38, 4, 663–83

West, C, Zimmerman, DH, 1987, Doing gender, *Gender and Society* 1, 2, 125–51

West, C, Zimmerman, D, 2009, Accounting for doing gender, *Gender and Society* 23, 112–22

'Empowerment' as women's emancipation? A global analysis of the empowerment paradigm and the influence of feminism in women's NGOs[1]

Ruth Phillips

Introduction

Forty years after the second wave of the women's movement forced ideas of women's emancipation and women's equality onto the agendas of many governments and of key international development institutions, we should be able to declare that we have a world largely devoid of gender inequality. However, no such claim can be made, as in absolute terms, the majority of women in the world are still unequal to men in social, civic, political, legal, economic, personal or cultural spheres. Although in most rich democracies women can point to substantial improvements in their status as citizens and as partners in more equal intimate relationships, no single country can claim to have achieved gender equality.

This chapter recognises women's NGOs as key players in emancipatory action for women. Keck and Sikkink (1998) have demonstrated that despite much early feminist action having been initiated by white middle-class women, the internationalist nature of these actions contributed to building important networks of women across the world. This networking built early platforms for women's campaigns to achieve equality. Despite the well observed limitations of western feminisms and feminist activities (Mohanty, 2004, 17–42), the emergence and contribution of grassroots, national and international women's NGOs has been most rapid and crucial in developing countries, where they have played a significant role in addressing women's emancipation from a personal to a political level (Leonard, 2003, 87–90).

This chapter will first establish the current extent of gender inequality from a global perspective. Second, it will provide an overview of the ways in which gender equality has been adopted as a policy framework. Third, the chapter will raise key theoretical issues related to the empowerment paradigm, and finally it will present findings from a global study, exploring the relationships between gender equality policy and practices and women's emancipation. The chapter aims to answer this key question: to what extent are the ideas and policies that are framed by empowerment as a practice and as an emancipatory concept central to gender equality programmes within women's NGOs around the world? To explore this question, the chapter draws on findings from a global online questionnaire, conducted between 2011 and 2013. The study focused on how gender equality was understood, what programmes were implemented as well as the identification and influence of feminist theories and practices in activities aimed at gender equality. Findings were based on 283 questionnaires completed by women's NGOs from across the world. The data illuminates the complexity of the contemporary women's emancipation agenda and provides insight into how women's NGOs currently identify with feminism within their activities. In the discussion of the data, and responding to the key debate raised in the introduction to this anthology, the impact of neoliberalism on, and via the discourse of empowerment is also raised in relation to what women's NGOs do, and how they perceive their role as activist organisations working for women's emancipation.

Women's global inequality

Women's non-governmental organisations (NGOs) are and, arguably, have always been central to women's emancipation. The women's movement, which has been behind the formation of women's NGOs, has played a pivotal role in women's emancipation across many national contexts. It has been able to mobilise autonomous pressure on the state to respond to demands and force women's equality demands onto public agendas (Htun and Weldon, 2012). Across the world, but particularly in developing countries, NGOs function as the important formalised agents for social change for women, this occurs at the grassroots level where women's services and support are offered and provided as well as at the policy and advocacy level where the broader objectives of the women's movement are placed on the public agenda both formally through government and informally through public voice, protest and social media (Leonard, 2003; Jad, 2009). The key role of NGOs as the praxis between feminism, gender equality policy and women's emancipation from domination is why women's NGOs are the central focus of this discussion.

To contextualise the contemporary need for women's emancipation, it is not difficult to profile the depth and nature of women's inequality across the world. Gender equality data is widely collected and global communications widely and rapidly report high profile incidences of oppression. Research reports and news of such incidents are circulated through both mainstream and alternative, more localised media.

Research clearly demonstrates that even in countries where women have achieved relative equality, vital general conditions must exist. For instance, findings in a key global study conducted over four decades by Htun and Weldon (2012) identified a distinct characteristic of countries that have successfully introduced comprehensive policies to combat violence against women. They found that instrumental aspirations such as getting more women into governments, increased economic growth, or political parties being avowedly friendly towards women gaining power are not key factors. However, 'the autonomous mobilization of feminists in domestic and transnational contexts' is the key to successful policy responses to violence against women (Htun and Weldon, 2012, 548). Such autonomous mobilisation of feminists is a particularly important component in developing countries, where grassroots mobilisation is critical and where poor marginalised women are in greatest need of gender equality (Orock, 2007, 94). For example, Orock argued that in much of Africa, inequality is deepening along gender and class lines as gender equality for 'ordinary', rural women and for women working outside the formal sector is ignored (Orock, 2007, 94).

Gender equality policy

Gender equality policy and programmes in development have been in place since the 1970s, however, there is no strong evidence of widespread success. As concluded by Kilby and Crawford, despite the widespread adoption of gender equality programmes, 'implementing such programmes has proved challenging' (Kilby and Crawford, 2011, 6) although there has been 'some progress' in the fields of education and health. This view was also supported by a worldwide study that found that although gender equality is strongly supported across the big majority of the countries surveyed, the commitment to gender equality is weakened when challenged by issues such as a dip in the economy in which case the respondents felt that men should be given preferential treatment over women (Pew Research Center, 2010, 2). According to Orock, despite many African governments adopting gender equality policies, this adoption has become a politicised process for gaining funding. Unless there is political leadership or advocacy for gender equality from government ministers, gender equality programmes end up being 'a springboard for a few elite women to move up the hierarchy and enhance their professional qualifications' (Orock, 2007, 93).

Despite the apparent failure of these gender equality policies, most governments, particularly in the west, have adopted them, investing in programmes to achieve gender equality and funding international gender equality programmes as part of their foreign aid commitments. However, for most of the world, it is civil society organisations that are responsible for carrying out the on-going gender equality agenda.

Women's specific status and role in development has been a key focus of wider development policies since the 1970s. The so-called 'women in development' (WID) approach, informed by liberal feminism, emerged and became dominant in development approaches at the height of early feminist demands for social justice and equity for women in the 1970s (Miller and Razavi, 1995). However, WID focused on the allocation of development resources to women based on economic efficiency arguments about what women could contribute to the development process rather than what women needed from the development process (Miller and Razavi, 1995, 2). 'Women and development' (WAD) grew from neo-Marxist feminists' critique that highlighted the role of women's labour and the invisibility of women's work as part of what had to be addressed by development (Hirshman, 1995) and was an alternative as it challenged the WID approach. Postmodern feminists subsequently challenged both approaches. They argued that both the WID and the WAD approach universalise the experiences of women, thus ignoring intersections between race, class and gender (Parpart, 1995). Owing to such challenges, 'gender and development' (GAD) became the dominant approach and has been central to debates about gender equality ever since (Parpart, 1995). Under GAD, policies directed towards women emerged that aimed to challenge socially constructed gender roles and became more focused on the redistribution of power between men and women (McIlwaine and Datta, 2010).

It is within the GAD approach that gender equality and empowerment discourses have become prevalent. Feminists from developing countries criticised the tendency of western feminisms to generalise the experiences of women, thereby excluding the differences between women of diverse cultural identities and their distinct experiences of being women (Caughie, 2010, 7). The GAD approach allowed for recognition of intersections between cultures, racial identities and social and economic status. And, what is important for many cultures, men were not excluded from the GAD approach.

McIlwaine and Datta (2010), however, suggest that challenging the power relations between men and women, inherent in the GAD approach, was resisted by mainstream development practitioners. Also, they argue that for some feminists the move from women's strategies to gender strategies was seen as a retreat from feminism and a 'loss of the feminist edge' (McIlwaine and Datta, 2010, 370–1) because GAD did not call for strategies to effect the explicit transformations of social and political structures such as the shift from a needs-based analysis to a rights-based analysis (McIlwaine and Datta, 2010).

Most important were the debates and developments that challenged the hegemony of dominant western feminism. These resulted in the emergence of diverse feminist theories and approaches, particularly in developing countries. They opened up spaces from which all women could speak – a key strategy of post-colonial feminism (Phillips, 2011) – and were also intrinsic to the growth and development of grass roots women's movements in developing countries.

Women's NGOs have played a central role in all of these development strategies (WID, WAD and GAD) as evidenced by their recognition by the United Nations as key deliverers of development policies and programmes. The United Nations Millennium Development Goals (UNMDGs) are the first comprehensive set of global social policies. UNMDG 3 promotes gender equality and empowerment of women (UN, 2013). However, it has been criticised for using an understanding of empowerment that fails to recognise the way that power is used to oppress women. Furthermore, there is a strong anti-institutional feminist criticism of 'NGOisation': the process whereby women's NGOs were formed as agents of neoliberalism and as part of neoliberal restructuring of the democratic state, set up to replace the state's fundamental duty to afford basic rights and freedoms to women (Bernal and Grewal, 2014). They are regarded as the 'illegitimate offspring of feminism' (Hodžić, 2014, 245). This is aligned with a southern criticism from African feminists who challenge the empowerment paradigm and 'have argued that the situation of women in Africa cannot be addressed by prioritising gender alone' (Hodžić, 2014, 235).

Feminism, empowerment and the 'empowerment paradigm'

This chapter makes a distinction between the wide range of feminist definitions and understandings of empowerment as a process of emancipation and the prevailing use of the term as an instrumentalised concept that is predominant in development policy. As Batliwala describes, empowerment has become a 'magic bullet for poverty alleviation and rapid economic development rather than a multi-faceted process of social transformation, especially in the arena of gender equality' (Batliwala, 2007, 561). For Rowland this concept of empowerment is non-feminist. Feminist notions of empowerment recognise that power, in this context, must be understood within the 'dynamics of oppression and internalised oppression' (Rowland, 1995, 102). Understanding power in this way means that groups are oppressed when they lack the power to participate in formal and informal decision-making. Therefore, empowerment must be seen as more than opening up access to decision-making, it must also include processes such as consciousness-raising and capacity-building in order to assert power to act and to challenge oppressions (Rowland, 1995). An understanding of empowerment that fails to see power within the dynamics of oppression has become the dominant framing of gender equality in the UN as well as in wider global, national and local policies. Feminist agendas and the process of women's emancipation have been lost or become unachievable. This dominant paradigm is imposed from external institutions on NGOs, and as a result, NGOs activities fail in their efforts to achieve women's emancipation.

The distinction between the feminist concept of empowerment and this more instrumentalised policy discourse rests on the extent to which power is taken into consideration. Allen, arguing from the feminist perspective, suggests that empowerment and domination are indivisible; empowerment cannot be understood in a vacuum and must be conceptualised in relation to domination (Allen, 2008, 164). Therefore, a critical theory of power must strive to illuminate not only domination and empowerment, but the complex relations between them (Allen, 2008, 164). Allen also suggests that successful resistance to domination, in both a systematic and structural sense, is unlikely to occur through the empowerment of individuals and that 'some sort of collective action or struggle also seems necessary' (Allen, 2008, 164). This is not only a key theoretical claim and point of debate between structuralist and postmodern feminisms, but equally relevant to an analysis of feminist practice prioritising individual empowerment over structural reform.

Sahay suggests that 'the process of empowerment is both individual and collective, since it is through involvement in groups that people most often begin to develop their awareness and ability to organize to take action and bring about change' (Sahay, 1998, 220). Allen distinguishes between 'power over', 'power to' or 'power with' (Allen, 1998). Empowerment and resistance fit into the 'power to' conceptualisation of power, which Allen defines as 'the ability of an individual actor to attain an end or a series of ends' (Allen, 1998, 34). In this understanding of empowerment, power is perceived as self-efficacy. 'Power with', which combines individual capacity with collective action, is closer to that described by Sahay (1998) in which empowerment is a process, therefore not something that can be taken up individually or given to people.

The 'empowerment paradigm' seen as a merely individualised transformative rather than a structurally challenging concept fits well with the shift away from the feminist discourses that dominated the claims for women's emancipation and equality from the 1970s to the late 1980s. The dominance of the term 'gender' over that of 'women' in the GAD agenda, alongside GAD's emphasis on market development, has resulted in a neoliberal appropriation of empowerment as a label within gender equality programmes and development policies. This dynamic concerns key feminist development scholars and practitioners (Kabeer, 2005; Smyth, 2007; Batliwala, 2007; Einspahr, 2010). The dominance of this limited notion of empowerment, referred to here as the 'empowerment paradigm', represents a shift away from speaking about women's oppression. Therefore, it is a central issue in the relationship between women's emancipation and the role of women's NGOs.

This chapter argues that in the contemporary context, a social change-oriented understanding of empowerment has been lost in many policy contexts. Instead, the individualist empowerment paradigm has become more influential. Policy and programmes for gender equality often fail to recognise relationships between empowerment and domination. Within the UNMDGs and other national policies the intrinsic need for collective action in order to achieve real gains in equality has been left out of global gender equality objectives. In her analysis of UNMDG 3, Kabeer reinforces this perspective:

It is through the mobilisation of women as women but also as workers, mothers, and citizens that the international community can ensure that the MDGs speak of the needs and interests of half the world's population. Building this collective capacity of women in all spheres of life to participate and to hold authorities accountable is thus the only basis on which the world's policy makers can keep the promises that they have made on the issue of gender equality. (Kabeer, 2005, 23)

For example, the UK Department for International Development refers to empowerment as 'individuals acquiring the power to think and act freely, exercise choice, and fulfil their potential as full and equal members of society', and further states that it is also about 'negotiating new kinds of institutions and, incorporating new norms and rules that support egalitarian and just relations between women and men' (as cited in Smyth, 2007, 584). This definition includes a reference to an egalitarian relationship between men and women. However, Smyth notes that this definition sets out processes in terms that are very general and that the implementation of empowerment as a policy goal is likely to become outcomes oriented or instrumental (Smyth, 2007, 584–5). Such an understanding of empowerment contrasts with Allen's (2008) conceptualisation of empowerment as resistance or as a transformative strategy for change. Perhaps one explanation for the increasing dominance of this more limited understanding of empowerment is that by failing to recognise obvious structural impositions against women's freedoms and equality, the status quo of patriarchal power in many societies is maintained and resists feminist demands.

This chapter argues that the individualistic empowerment paradigm is also a dominant policy and practice framework within NGOs (Hashemi et al, 1996; Fonjong, 2001; Magar, 2003; Jafar, 2007; Kilby and Crawford, 2011; Bernal and Grewal, 2014). The study discussed below demonstrates the dominance of the individualistic empowerment paradigm within governmental and international institutions, which are also the most likely majority sources of funding for NGOs. However, as empowerment is measured in various ways by funders and programme developers, it is also likely to be understood in various ways. Magar suggested that empowerment may be understood as 'individual capabilities, group capabilities, resources and achievements (achievement of autonomy, agency and awareness of legal rights necessary for empowerment)' (Magar, 2003, 513). In a study of women's NGOs in Bangladesh eight indicators were identified including mobility, ability to purchase small and large items, economic security, decision-making, political and legal awareness and participation in protests (Hashemi et al, 1996, 638). In Fonjong's research about NGOs in Cameroon, empowerment was measured by adopting the UNICEF empowerment framework of 'welfare, access, "conscientization", participation and control' (Fonjong, 2001, 224). Empowerment was also highlighted as a key approach in CARE Australia, defined as the sum total of changes needed for a woman to realise her full human rights – the interplay of changes in agency, structure and relations (Kilby and Crawford, 2011, 34).

In 1994, Wieringa suggested that there is 'no consensus among those who advocate the empowerment of women as a crucial element in the development process' (Wieringa, 1994, 833), and indeed, the lack of consensus on empowerment still seems to hold strong in the contemporary development context. Rowland suggested that most frameworks for understanding power strive to appear neutral because they ignore the question of how power is 'actually distributed within a society' (Rowland, 1995, 101). It is not surprising then that men's domination of women is unrecognised or unarticulated in the contemporary women's empowerment paradigm, as demonstrated in the discussion earlier. Recent feminist scholarship further claims that, in general, most empowerment approaches are limited as they only meet women's practical needs rather than developing challenging gender roles that can be seen as strategic challenges to men's domination (Moser, 1993; Fonjong, 2001, 224; Walby, 2005; Jafar, 2007; Einspahr, 2010).

The gender equality outcomes of economic programmes, such as micro-financing, are of a particular focus in this debate as such programmes are burdening already poor women and are rarely successful in changing their overall equality status (Hashemi et al, 1996; Izugbara, 2004). Further, as Feiner (2011) points out, such programmes are often run in countries that are under pressure to impose structural adjustments to their economies, resulting in reductions in basic welfare support. Therefore, for women with families to support the small loans that are meant to replace welfare support fall short, often leaving them indebted in ways that they hadn't been before (Feiner, 2011, 3). The micro credit debate highlights a central criticism of the empowerment paradigm, which is the expectation that vulnerable people should empower themselves, without acknowledging structural inequalities and 'systemic oppressive forces' (Anderson, 2000, 227). This debate also reveals its alignment with neoliberalism. The example of micro financing leads to a questioning of the sustainability of the empowerment paradigm (Ashford, 2001).

Research findings: gender equality policy and practice in women's NGOs

Methodology

The key purpose of the global online questionnaire on 'Understanding Gender Equality in Women's NGOs' was to accumulate data that reflected women's organisational perspectives. Key criteria for selection of the NGOs invited to participate in the study were their independence of government, that they had no relation to the UN (other than as funder), and their identification as a women's NGO. This meant that the larger, generalist NGOs that also have gender equality programmes, and the largest funded projects from the UN as well as official donor aid, were not included in the study.

The underlying principle of collecting data from women's NGOs was to 'listen' to their data and to build knowledge from them as an iterative resource for social policy analysis of gender equality across the world. The research also provided an opportunity to explore the importance of feminism in the current global context. Responding to a direct question about their objectives, 240 of the 283 NGOs (that completed the survey) indicated that 'gender equality' was one of their key objectives, only 16 indicated that it was not.

A key objective of the research was to gain a widespread sample from all regions of the world. For some countries, only one or two women's NGOs were identified or had viable email addresses, and were invited to participate. In other countries, up to 50 or more organisations were invited to complete the survey. The survey was translated into French, Spanish, Italian, Korean and Japanese. The translated versions were sent to NGOs that hosted their websites in those languages only, along with the choice to complete the survey in English.

To keep the survey instrument as quick and simple as possible, identification was only by region (as defined by the OECD). However, an unexpected outcome of the survey was that many of the NGOs that completed the survey also responded directly, keen to identify themselves, express support for the study and gratitude for the invitation to participate. This provided data to show how widespread the national diversity of responding NGOs was, as set out in Table 2.1.

Table 2.1: Range of known countries in which NGOs were based (* = 8 or more) (63/N=283)

Region (OECD)	Range of known countries that have responded (strong response*)
Africa	Burkina Faso, Botswana, Cameroon, Democratic Republic of the Congo, Ethiopia, Ivory Coast, Kenya, Nigeria, Rwanda, South Africa, Sudan, Tanzania, Uganda, Zimbabwe, Zambia
Arab States/ Middle East	Israel, Lebanon, Palestine
Asia and the Pacific	Afghanistan, Australia*, Bangladesh*, Cambodia*, China, India*, Indonesia, Japan, Malaysia, Nepal, New Zealand, Philippines, Thailand, South Korea*, Vanuatu
Europe and the Commonwealth of States	Belgium, Bulgaria, Croatia, Czech Republic, Denmark, England*, France, Greece, Hungary, Italy*, Ireland*, Kosovo, Latvia, Norway*, Slovakia, Spain*, Scotland, Spain, Sweden, Turkey
North America	Canada, USA*
Latin America and the Caribbean	Argentina, Chile*, Colombia, Honduras, Jamaica, Nicaragua, Uruguay, Venezuela

The majority of responses were from Europe and the Commonwealth of Independent States (90), the second largest group was from the Asia Pacific region (84). There were 39 responses from North America, 33 from Latin America and the Caribbean and 30 responses from Africa. This reflects a global spread and a balance between developing and advanced economy nations. The majority of NGOs identified themselves operating on the national level (146), the second largest group was that of community based NGOs (85), and international NGOs accounted for 51 of the sample. International NGOs were mainly situated in Europe (26) and North America (19). The majority of respondents identified their NGO as secular (non-religious) and their funding profiles show a high level of support from government grants and independent fundraising, as is detailed in Figure 2.1.

Gender equality and empowerment findings

The findings of the survey revealed a strong framing by the dominant empowerment paradigm but also showed – somewhat at odds with this policy framework – a highly rights based aspiration to achieve gender equality, alongside a commitment to challenge domination. As Table 2.2 shows, the promotion of human rights for women was the most common activity amongst the participating NGOs. This was followed

Figure 2.1. Funding sources of women's NGOs that responded to the survey

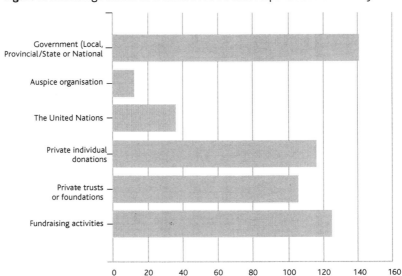

by advocacy for women's citizenship rights, political campaigning for women's rights and women's community development. These activities are all collectively organised and focused on women's relationship to power in their societies and communities. However, 40 per cent of the NGOs also indicated individual empowerment as an activity, perhaps reflecting the aims of the programmes women's NGOs are funded to run.

The NGOs' activities were analysed as individual interventions or as broader social change programmes. It was evident that even though the majority of NGOs identified as feminist, many activities appeared to conform to the individualistic empowerment paradigm rather than a social/structural change activity that requires collective action and challenges the way power is exercised. However, the activities most often indicated by the NGOs reflect the collective aims of social change. Although all of the activities listed in Table 2.2 were carried about by NGOs, the table reflects the rank of those indicated most often as one of the activities conducted, in the order from most often indicated to least often. The first eight activities are highlighted as they represent structural rather than individual activities and services. For example, the promotion of human rights for women implicitly recognises that they are currently not free from oppression and that they do not have equal human rights. Therefore, to engage in this activity requires challenging the way social power is exercised in a society or community. This is in contrast with programmes such as

Table 2.2: Women's NGO activities and services

Q3. Which of the following does your organisation provide?
Promotion of human rights for women
Advocacy for women's citizenship rights
Political campaigning for women's rights
Women's community development
Individual empowerment
Conducting work training programmes for women
Educating men about women's equality
Providing assistance for grass roots women's organisations
Services for women who have experienced sexual violence
Grass roots activist training
Running adult education programs for women
Legal counsel for women
Women's health services
Providing employment assistance for women
Provision of basic needs for women and their children
Women's maternal and reproductive health services
Micro financing for women
Financial assistance for women
Emergency relief for women and their children
Provision of women's refuge housing from domestic violence
Services for refugee women and their children

employment assistance or refugee services, which target individuals. If such services are part of a wider programme of emancipation and lead to a comprehensive transformation of the position of the women they assist, then such activities can be part of an emancipatory agenda. However, the 'NGOisation' criticism (Bernal and Grewal, 2014) suggests that such an emancipatory agenda can be overshadowed by a more institutional agenda, dominated by a neoliberal framework.

We cannot generalise from this data about the global tendencies of women's NGOs. We can, however, compare them to the questions asked in the survey about different types of feminist thinking or practice. The responses indicate a high level of support for empowerment feminism. This may reflect different understandings of empowerment (as discussed earlier) or it may reveal a tension between what is expected from empowerment practices on the one hand, and the wider global social policy objectives on the other. For it is the wider global social policy objectives that appear to dominate women's NGO activities, which, based on policy examples such as the UNMDGs, tend to emphasise individual empowerment to the exclusion of strategies that challenge domination. It also may reflect an important necessary contextual engagement for feminist activity, where there are no other opportunities for feminist action for women's emancipation.

The gender equality objectives that reflect an anti-domination paradigm are also demonstrated when asked about the most effective ways of measuring national improvement in gender equality, as reflected in Table 2.3.

Table 2.3: Views on the best way of measuring gender equality improvements

Q14. The best way to measure national progress on gender equality is by measuring improvements in (in order of best to least)	
Equal rights for women under the law	1
Reducing violence against women	2
Reducing women's poverty	3
Women's participation in work	4
Girls' participation in school	5
The proportion of women in formal government	6
Women's access to public resources regardless of social class	7
Maternal health	8

Figures 2.2 and 2.3 provide a breakdown of the different levels of operation of NGOs (local, national and international) and their responses to the question of what they understand gender equality to mean (Figure 2.2) and what best leads to gender equality (Figure 2.3). Figure 2.2 indicates a strong, rights-based focus to social, economic and political equality as well as demonstrating that national women's NGOs have a strong, complex and multifaceted understanding of gender equality.

Figure 2.3 shows that a majority of NGOs (60 per cent) indicated that all of the strategies in the list should be pursued. However, there was also a wide range of additional comments in relation to the question of what best leads to gender equality.

Figure 2.4 organises these responses according to the different levels of organisation: community, national or international. The comments could be interpreted as reflecting a sense of failure, which might be attributable to the shift from identifiable feminist strategies

Figure 2.2: What gender equality means for NGOs: cross-tabulation with the level of operation (n=282)

Please indicate what 'gender equality' means for your NGO
(Please tick one or more response)

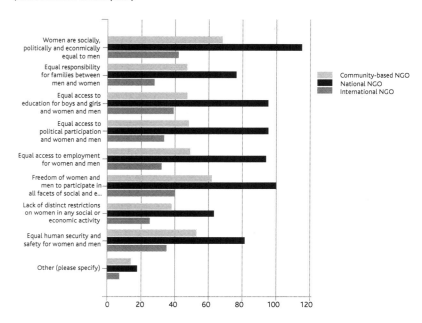

Figure 2.3: What best leads to gender equality: cross-tabulated with level of NGO operation (n=282)

Which of the following best leads to gener equality
(Please tick one or more response)

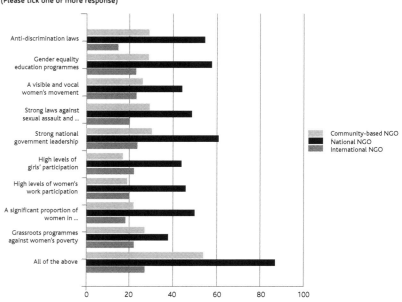

toward 'gender equality' strategies. For example, from a community-based NGO: 'Rename and reframe the goal from "gender equality" to women's rights then when the goal is clear the response can be clearer'. And from an international NGO: 'No efforts have managed to produce equality yet so nothing is "best".' There were also some strong comments that recognised the power and domination nexus, 'naming and shaming of men's organizations and institutions that undermine women e.g. religious extremists', and 'advocacy and outreach with religious leaders to challenge discriminatory or misogynist interpretations of religious texts and rules'.

These additional comments demonstrate the influence of empowerment paradigm alongside a highly critical, strongly emancipatory feminist agenda that recognises power and domination as key issues. Religion plays a role in cases where it undermines equality. In the study responses, 30 NGOs indicated a religious affiliation, 254 identified as being secular or non-religious.

Feminism in women's NGOs

To the question whether an NGO identified as feminist, the majority (69.5 per cent) responded in the affirmative (either 'yes' or 'sometimes') with only 27 per cent not identifying as feminist. There were also a small number of 'other' responses including comments such as: 'as a sex worker organization we are blamed for being feminist and non-feminist in equal measures'; 'we believe in the equality rights of all women and although we work in an anti-oppression, anti-racist, feminist framework we do not use the term, because a number of the women we serve are very marginalized'; 'neither feminist nor patriarchal, always in terms of gender equity'; and 'given the commitment of our organization for women and girls and therefore its leaders, which are made mostly by women, our organization is always described as a feminist'. Community-based NGOs were most likely to identify as feminist (75 per cent) whereas international NGOs had the least proportion of affirmative responses (63 per cent).

To include a question asking about identification with a specific feminist theory or politics is potentially problematic. One concern is that such a question might alienate some respondents, but overall the respondents appeared willing to identify with the range of possible feminisms. In order to address the diversity of the respondents' ideas or experiences with feminism, there was an opportunity to respond in their own words. Although most of the categories of feminism included in the questionnaire were primarily drawn from scholarly

Table 2.4: Other comments on means of achieving gender equality of local, national and international level NGOs

Additional means of achieving gender equality as part of 'other' responses:		
Community-based NGOs	National NGOs	International NGOs
Women empowerment through cultural activities	The parity laws and quotas	Changes in economic policy that affects women's lives
A change in the mind-sets	Assistance to women in the field of rural development and food security	A proliferation of women's media to help change public perceptions of women
Naming and shaming of men, organisations and institutions that undermine women, eg religious extremists	All of the above because women are side-lined in Cameroon implying more opportunities to be offered them if gender equality must be assured	No efforts have managed to produce equality yet so nothing is 'best'
Free safe and legal access to abortion and contraception	Women need to organise themselves and to be a driving force for change, for impact on policy and actions at all levels in society	Community activism; social norm change work
Rename and reframe the goal from 'gender equality' to women's rights, then, when the goal is clear, the response can be clearer	Independent of the sex of the person, both men and women have equal rights and are equally capable of making decisions in the social, familial, political, economic and cultural. A just and democratic society is one that provides equal opportunities regardless of sex, realising that both men and women are in the same conditions to exercise leadership and citizenship, abolishing all forms of discrimination between the sexes and ensuring that it takes out with solid, concrete policies that promote the development of women and men in equal conditions	Integration of feminist orientation in mixed social movements, strong laws and international standards against other forms of gender violence such as prostitution, not only those named above, as laws shift public opinion
Early childhood education on gender issues	Changing attitudes, training the staff of the justice system, and of the public, implementation of the law	And secular state government
Political interest and great economic development	We think that all of the above are necessary, but to all of them apparently a strong women's movement is a condition. (Even if there would be a significant proportion of women in government, without gender sensitivity it may not bring much to women.) Strong enforcement (and accountability to do so) of any good laws is also necessary	
	Advocacy and outreach with religious leaders to challenge discriminatory or misogynist interpretations of religious texts and rules	

and/or theoretical feminisms; liberal, Marxist, post-colonial and so on, this was justifiable because they are used in research literature on feminism in development and women's policy contexts. However, the category of 'empowerment feminism', drawn from an analysis of the websites of women's NGOs, reflects a more practice-based orientation. In the analysis, 'empowerment as a policy framework for gender equality programmes' dominated. Based on these responses, empowerment feminism is not seen as exclusive of other feminist influences, thus further adding to the complexity of what is meant by empowerment or its diverse formulations, as discussed earlier.

Figure 2.4. Responses to what types of feminism inform the NGO's activities, by level of NGO

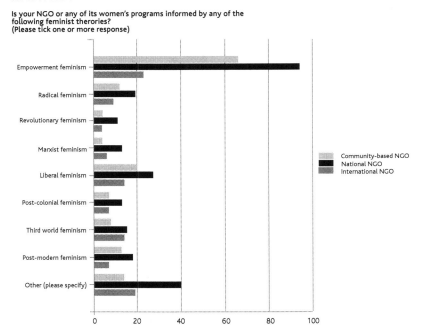

There were 73 'other' responses to this question, which elicited a wide range of comments. There were also some objections to the question as being overly theoretical or abstract for practitioners. Some additional types of feminisms were put forward such as Islamic feminism, anarcho-feminism and libertarian feminism. A national NGO based in one of the ex-Soviet states added the following comment:

I don't think we can say that any of our programmes or the NGO is directly informed by any of these. We are struggling partly with issues that were on the agenda in the west in the early 70s, partly by what everybody struggles with at the moment, partly by the aftermath of state socialism (eg our judiciary is comprised of mostly women and yet, if it has any effect at all, it has a detrimental effect on women's access to justice, or in socialism almost everybody held a job, had income, etc). We take what we can use from any of these theories (not so much post-modernism, I guess), and use it. (Survey Response No 50, 2011)

Some responses highlighted empowerment as the basis of the feminism of the organisations in question, while others described it as a practice, for example: 'empowerment of women' and 'empowerment is an important method for our organisation'. Of key interest is the correlation between the responses of those NGOs, that chose 'empowerment' feminism and their identification with feminism overall, as illustrated in Table 2.5. A large proportion (45 per cent) of those respondents who indicated 'yes' or 'sometimes' to the question concerning the influence of feminism on their NGOs did include empowerment feminism as influential, but quite a large proportion (36 per cent) of feminist NGOs did not.

Overall, 65 per cent of the NGOs identified empowerment feminism as being adopted or at least influential in their practice. The second highest single theory adopted was liberal feminism with 22 per cent of the NGOs selecting this category.

The research indicates the high importance of feminism within NGOs. It also indicates that feminism is not only a strong influence, but provokes complexity in debate and identity at both theoretical and practice levels. The data demonstrates that empowerment is a dominant framework in both specific gender equality programmes as well as in the thinking of feminist NGOs. This suggests that the ways in which empowerment is understood and applied continue to be diverse. It may be, however, that the aim of many women's NGOs to address domination is not supported by the more narrowly defined idea of empowerment in wider policy and programme goals. Many of the comments and responses of the NGOs indicate the desire to counter domination but this does not emerge as part of the individualistic empowerment paradigm or how it appears to be understood.

Table 2.5: NGO identification with feminism: cross-tabulated with identifying empowerment feminism as a practice or influence

Is the term 'feminist' used to describe your NGO? Cross-tabulation with empowerment feminism Yes No			Empowerment feminism		Total
Is the term 'feminist' used to describe your NGO?	Yes	Count	82	36	118
		% within empowerment feminism	44.8%	36.4%	41.8%
	No	Count	37	34	71
		% within empowerment feminism	20.2%	34.3%	25.2%
	Sometimes	Count	55	23	78
		% within empowerment feminism	30.1%	23.2%	27.7%
	Never	Count	4	2	6
		% within empowerment feminism	2.2%	2.0%	2.1%
	Other (please specify)	Count	5	4	9
		% within empowerment feminism	2.7%	4.0%	3.2%
Total		Count	183	99	282
		% within empowerment feminism	100.0%	100.0%	100.0%

In relation to global social policy objectives, further data in the study show a split between NGOs in their views on the effectiveness of the UNMDG 3 (which, as discussed earlier, has an instrumental model of empowerment and gender equality as its key policy goals for combating poverty). The data shows that 155 agreed that UNMDG 3 was an effective means of combating poverty, but 67 disagreed. Although not a majority, this indicates a significant critical perspective on the broad UN gender equality/empowerment agenda. This finding also supports earlier criticisms of the UNMDG 3's application of the more individualistic empowerment paradigm with its focus on needs rather than rights (Moser, 1993, 74; Fonjong, 2001, 224; Walby, 2005; Jafar, 2007, 257).

The means of measuring the impact of UNMDG 3 are highly instrumental, based on numerical outcomes of the number of girls in schools, women in parliaments and so on, without any detailed qualitative or multi-dimensional indicators of the outcomes (UNMDG, 2012). The position paper written by Bond for International Development (which represents 370 UK based international NGOs) comments:

> ...it is of concern that the strong language in the Outcome Document on tackling gender inequality is not followed through with concrete outcomes, indicators and commitments to new resources. Nor are there robust accountability mechanisms in place to monitor progress in women's empowerment, making it possible that rhetorical commitments to putting women at the heart of development will evaporate in practice. (Bond for International Development, 2011, 14)

The overly simple index of gains also relies on governments' willingness to provide numerical statistics, but such numbers do not help to account for the quality of the education received or the power of women in parliaments to exert any influence. There are also no official multi-dimensional analyses of these outcomes, especially in relation to women's economic, social and political equality and to combating violence against women (Bond for International Development, 2011, 14). This presents the strongest evidence in this study of the neoliberal capture of the dominant empowerment paradigm and the lack of an emancipatory feminist agenda at a global level. Further, the anti-institutional criticism of women's NGOs is also is applicable in this context. This argues that they are actually working against feminist aspirations because where they find themselves taking over the role of the welfare state their existence 'is deeply connected to neoliberalism and privatisation' (Bernal and Grewal, 2014, 302). This concurs with concerns raised by the editors of this anthology in the previous chapter, where they acknowledge a level of complicity between civil society organisations and the growth of neoliberalism.

Conclusion

The study discussed above was prompted by the fact that 40 years after the so-called 'second wave of feminism' in the west, there is no evidence of women's emancipation worldwide. The key aim of the research was to build knowledge to assist in understanding why there has been so little progress on a global scale. Based on this study, women's NGOs have not lessened their focus on achieving these goals, nor their recognition of women's inequality. There are, however, some doubts about the efficacy of the empowerment paradigm in terms of improving gender equality. The data from the study identifies some frustration and distancing from this gender equality approach, especially in the qualitative comments, often reflecting an on-going commitment to what some may consider to be out-dated feminist theories and/or practices. Indeed, the entire thrust of this chapter could be read as a call for a return to more radical feminist approaches, which may be the only way to address the relationship between power and domination so well-articulated by Allen (2008) in her theorisation of feminist concerns with power. This call would have significant implications for the understanding of gender concerns, that so strongly influenced the shift in development approaches from the WID/WAD to the GAD framework; especially, as GAD was seen as a way of recognising the construction of dominance of one gender over another (McIlwaine and Datta, 2010).

Although there are thousands of women's NGOs operating from the grassroots up to the international stage and there is widespread endorsement of the idea that there should be gender equality, the gains are insufficient for women to become truly equal to men on a global scale. A clear message from women's NGOs is that the transformations required for gender equality must occur at a structural level; all women must have equal rights that are inclusive of human, civil, political, legal, social, welfare and economic rights. For many women in rich democracies such rights are available, but access to such rights is uneven, with certain groups of women continuing to be excluded from the benefits of the gains made by women's movements of past decades. Therefore, in countries where there is not a vocal and demanding women's movement that represents women who are economically, culturally or socially marginalised from the grass roots upwards, it is even less likely that widespread emancipation from inequality will take place.

A critical appraisal of the current dominance of individualistic (which this chapter proposes is non-feminist) empowerment as a process to gain gender equality calls for global social policy to recognise how the intersection of various exclusions and oppressions lead to domination. For example, poor women are often caught in an ethnic or social framework that regards them as holding a lower status. This results in their domination by men. Therefore, challenging the existing dominant policy agenda, as exemplified by GAD, is central to women's emancipation. This challenge must target the 'soft' or individualist use of the 'empowerment paradigm' as well as the neutering effects of the concepts of 'gender' and 'gender equality'.

Notes

[1] An earlier version of this article has been published as Phillips, R, 2015, How 'empowerment' may miss its mark: Gender equality policies and how they are understood in women's NGOs, *Voluntas*, 26, 1122–42, doi: 10.1007/s11266-015-9586-y

References

Allen, A, 1998, Rethinking power, *Hypatia* 13, 1, 21–40

Allen, A, 2008, Power and the politics of difference: Oppression, empowerment and transnational justice, *Hypatia* 23, 3, 156–72

Anderson, J, 2000, Gender, race, poverty health and the discourses of health in the context of globalization: A postcolonial feminist perspective on policy research, *Nursing Inquiry* 7, 4, 220–9

Ashford, LS, 2001, New population policies: Advancing women's health and rights, *Population Bulletin* 56, 1, 1–45

Batliwala, S, 2007, Taking the power out of empowerment – an experiential account, *Development in Practice* 17, 4/5, 557–65

Bernal, B, Grewal, I (eds), 2014, *Theorizing NGOs, States Feminism, and Neoliberalism*, Durham, NC and London: Duke University Press

Bond for International Development, 2011, UK civil society analysis of the UN MDG Review Summit 2010, *Position paper*, London: Bond (UK network of NGOs working in international development), www.bond.org.uk/data/files/Bond_MDG_Summit_Analysis_2011.pdf

Caughie, PL, 2010, Introduction: Theorizing the first wave globally, *Feminist Review* 95, 1, 6–9

Einspahr, J, 2010, Structural domination and freedom: A feminist perspective, *Feminist Review* 94, 1, 1–19

Feiner, S, 2011, Europe: Beware of banks bearing micro-loans for poor, *Women's Enews*, www.womensenews.org

Fonjong, L, 2001, Fostering women's participation in development through non-governmental efforts in Cameroon, *The Geographical Journal* 167, 3, 223–34

Hashemi, SM, Schuler, SR, Riley, AP, 1996, Rural credit programs and women's empowerment in Bangladesh, *World Development* 24, 4, 635–53

Hirshman, M, 1995, Women and development: A critique, in M Marchand, J Parpart (eds) *Feminism, postmodernism development*, pp 42–55, London and New York: Routledge

Hodžić, S, 2014, Feminist bastards: Toward a posthumanist critique of NGOization, in V Bernal, I Grewal (eds) *Theorizing NGOs, states feminism, and neoliberalism*, pp 221–47, Durham, NC and London: Duke University Press

Htun, M, Weldon, SL, 2012, The civic origins of progressive policy change: Combating violence against women in global perspective 1975–2005, *Perspectives on Politics* 106, 3, 548–69

Izugbara, CO, 2004, Gendered micro-lending schemes and sustainable women's empowerment in Nigeria, *Community Development Journal* 39, 1, 72–84

Jad, I, 2009, The NGO-isation of Arab women's movements, *IDS Bulletin* 35, 4, 34–42

Jafar, A, 2007, Engaging fundamentalism: The case of women's NGOs in Pakistan, *Social Problems* 54, 3, 256–73

Kabeer, N, 2005, Gender equality and women's empowerment: A critical analysis of the Third Millennium Development Goal, *Gender and Development* 13, 1, 13–24

Keck, M, Sikkink, K, 1998, *Activists beyond borders: Advocacy networks in International Politics*, Ithaca, NY: Cornell University Press

Kilby, P, Crawford, J, 2011, *Closing the gender gap: Gender and Australian NGOs*, Final report submitted to Australian Council for International Development (ACFID), ACFID Research in Development Series Report No 2, Canberra: ACFID, https://acfid.asn.au/sites/site.acfid/files/resource_document/Closing-the-gender-gap.pdf

Leonard, M, 2003, Developing countries, in G McCann, S McCloskey (eds) *From the local to the global: Key issues in development studies*, pp 76–94, London: Pluto Press

McIlwaine, C, Datta, K, 2010, From feminising to engendering development, *Gender, place and culture: A journal of feminist geography* 10, 3, 369–82

Magar, V, 2003, Empowerment approaches to gender based violence: Women's courts in Delhi slums, *Women's Studies International Forum* 26, 2, 509–23

Miller, C, Razavi, S, 1995, From WID to GAD: Conceptual shifts in the women and development discourse, *Occasional paper* 1, United Nations Research Institute for Social Development (UNRISD), United Nations Development Programme, Geneva: United Nations

Mohanty, CT, 2004, *Feminism without borders: Decolonizing theory, practicing solidarity*, Durham, NC and London: Duke University Press

Moser, C, 1993, Gender planning in the third world: Meeting practical and strategic needs, *World Development* 17, 4, 1799–825

Orock, RTE, 2007, Gender equality – whose agenda? Observations from Cameroon, *Development in Practice* 17, 1, 93–7

Parpart, J, 1995, Deconstructing the development 'expert': Gender development and the 'vulnerable' groups, in M Marchand, J Parpart (eds) *Feminism/Postmodernism/Development*, pp 221–43, London, New York: Routledge

Pew Research Center, 2010, *Gender equality universally embraced, but inequalities acknowledged*, Pew Research Global Attitudes Project, Washington, DC: Pew Research Center, www.pewglobal. org/2010/07/01/gender-equality

Phillips, R, 2011, Response: Postcolonial scholarship in social justice research, in L Markauskaite, P Freebody, J Irwin (eds) *Bridging scholarship, policy and practice: Methodological choices and research designs for educational and social change*, pp 157–66, Heidelberg, London, New York: Springer

Rowland, J, 1995, Empowerment examined, *Development in Practice* 5, 2, 101–7

Sahay, S, 1998, *Women and empowerment, approaches and strategies*, New Delhi: Discovery Publishing House

Smyth, I, 2007, Talking of gender: Words and meanings in development organizations, *Development in Practice* 17, 4–5, 582–8

UN (United Nations), 2013, Goal 3: Promote gender equality and empower women, *United Nations Millennium Development Goals*, Geneva: UN, www.un.org/millenniumgoals/gender.shtml

UNMDG (United Nations Millennium Development Goals), 2012, Gender Chart 2012, *The Millennium Development Goals Report*, Geneva: UN, http://mdgs.un.org/unsd/mdg/Resources/Static/Products/Progress2012/MDG-Gender-2012.pdf

Walby, S, 2005, Gender mainstreaming: Productive tensions in theory and practice, *Social Politics: International Studies Gender, State and Society* 12, 3, 321–43

Wieringa, S, 1994, Women's interests and empowerment: Gender planning reconsidered, *Development and Change* 25, 4, 829–48

Section One

Organising for emancipation

Se Non Ora Quando? ('If not now, when?') The birth, growth and challenges of a new voice within the feminist scenario in Italy

Elena Elia

Introduction

This chapter explores whether, and how, civil society organisations act in favour of women's emancipation by critically analysing the *Se Non Ora Quando?* ('If not now, when?') movement in Italy. The name of the movement was taken from the title of a famous book by Primo Levi, Italian author and concentration camp survivor, who was in turn inspired by a well-known rabbinical saying: 'If I am not for myself, who will be for me? And when I am for myself, what am "I"? And if not now, when?' However, the full name, *Se Non Ora Quando?* was soon shortened (at first informally, then also in official communication) to SNOQ, which has become the trademark for the movement's actions and a stable part of the identity of the movement.

SNOQ was chosen as the subject for this contribution because it represents one of the most relevant feminist phenomena that has emerged in the Italian public scene in the last few years, and also because of its specific characteristics. SNOQ represents an example of civil society challenging the status quo, in this case regarding the emancipation of Italian women. SNOQ also demonstrates that a movement can grow into a formal organisation that is able to operate at the national as well as the local level; it is well coordinated and has local committees enjoying a high level of autonomy. The chapter will also critically assess the capacity which the movement has developed from its first public initiatives to the point where it can make a difference to the lives of Italian women.

To do so, the chapter will analyse SNOQ by focusing on the themes that demonstrate the specificity and uniqueness of the movement, and by highlighting its relationship with other significant feminist initiatives in Italian history. Among these themes are the movement's presence throughout Italy's territories, its organisation and management structure, its relations with the media, its agenda setting, its political relations at the local and national level and its relations with other movements, both those that are openly feminist and those that are not. The capacity of the movement to steer public debate and influence public life will also be addressed by reconstructing its actions as well as by analysing its internal and external achievements.

Methodological note

The present study has been carried out mainly through participant observation and document analysis. The author was actively involved in the earlier stages of the movement and its initial activities, thus allowing for a close observation of SNOQ from the inside and a thorough analysis of its dynamics and decision-making processes. From this analysis the author has attempted to develop 'a holistic understanding of the phenomena under study that is as objective and accurate as possible' (DeWalt and DeWalt, 2002, 92).

Document analysis (Corbetta, 2003) was also subsequently used to broaden the analysis by examining two other features of the movement; first, its self-representation as narrated through the movement's national website (www.senonoraquando.eu); and second, the media narratives built around the movement and its actions. In order to reconstruct these perspectives, the internet as well as national and international newspapers were chosen as the main sources of information.

Italy: 'the land that feminism forgot'[1]

At the end of 2010 Italy was facing political, social and economic challenges. The nation's economy was close to bankruptcy. In the latest edition of the *Global Gender Gap Report* the country was ranked 74th out of 145 countries (and 21st among European ones) Women's employment rate was 26 points lower than men's (thus widening the gap between potential GDP and actual GDP by as much as 7 per cent) while their presence in managerial positions in boards of the over 28,000 companies with at least €10 million in annual revenue was below 14 per cent (Banca d'Italia, 2012).

One example of the discrimination still facing women in employment was the repeal of National Law 188, the law against 'blank resignation' whereby employers would force employees to sign a blank resignation letter as soon as they signed their contract. The letter would then be dated later on if the employee got injured, had an accident, was no longer needed or got pregnant, thus enabling the employer to fire them without repercussion. The law was approved in 2007, but in 2008 it was then cancelled, thus depriving employees with a legal means of protection.

Furthermore, the chronic lack of social services in a traditional, family-centred country such as Italy left the burden of care for children and the elderly to their families, and primarily to the female members. According to the National Institute of Statistics, domestic violence alone caused 156 deaths in the year 2010 (ISTAT).[2] Finally, Italy's position in the World Press Freedom Index of 2010 at 49th place was very low (and among the EU founder counties only preceded by France, which was ranked 44th) because the country was 'still dealing with some major interference in media activity by their political leaders'.[3] It is fair to assume that this comment was alluding to the then Prime Minister Silvio Berlusconi's entrepreneurial activities, which included running private television networks that were considered largely responsible for the humiliating representation of women in the media. It is against this background that the SNOQ movement was born.

The birth of the SNOQ movement

The SNOQ movement owes its inception to a mass public gathering in Italy held on 13 February 2011, when over a million women (and many more Italian women around the world)[4] of different ages, classes and socio-economic backgrounds came together in some 230 public squares and answered the question 'If not now, when?' with a resounding 'Now!'. This action came about in response to the appeal that had been circulating on the internet by Italian intellectuals and public figures from the end of January. The appeal highlighted the necessity of exposing the condition of the Italian women and to contribute to its improvement. The English version on the SNOQ movement's appeal reads as follows:

> The great majority of women in Italy are working both inside and outside the home, they produce wealth, they look for a job (one out of two succeeds), they study and make sacrifices to assert themselves in their chosen profession, they take care of their relations and look after children, husbands and aged parents. Quite a few are engaged in public issues, in parties, in trade unions, in enterprises,

in organisations and in voluntary services with the aim that the society they are living in might become richer, more civilised and welcoming. They have consideration and respect for themselves and for liberty and dignity achieved by the women who built our democratic nation, worthy of mention on occasion of the 150th Celebration of Italian Unity. This rich and important life experience is being obscured by the image of women constantly and indecently represented as bare objects of sexual exchange, in newspapers, advertisements and television programmes. This is no longer bearable. A widespread attitude offers to young people the idea of reaching glamorous goals and easy money by giving up their beauty and intelligence to the one in power, who is willing to pay back with public funds and positions. This way of thinking and the consequent behaviours are polluting social life and the models of civil ethic and religious awareness. Inadvertently we crossed the bounds of decency. The model of man–woman relations exhibited by one of the highest state authorities deeply affects our lifestyles and culture justifying detrimental behaviour to women's dignity and to the institutions. Those who want to keep silence, support, justify and reduce the on-going events to private matters, should take responsibility also in front of the international community. We are asking all women, without any distinction, to protect the value of our dignity and we are telling to men: If not now, when? It's time to prove friendship to women.[5]

The charge that the then Prime Minister, Silvio Berlusconi, had paid money for sex with an underage prostitute may have provided the final provocation but this only followed months of debate about the representation of women in television and in commercials, the abuse of their (often naked) bodies in order to sell products and services and the concomitant diminishing of their dignity, all of which only added to the difficulties that Italian women were facing on a daily basis. An example of one contribution to this on-going debate was the release in 2009 of Lorella Zanardo's film 'Il corpo delle donne' ('The body of women', www.ilcorpodelledonne.net/english-version/), a documentary on the representation of women in Italian television, and followed by a book with the same title. Discussions and debates on the issue were still continuing in 2011, alongside the perception that even with the release of the film and the ensuing public response, there had, nonetheless, been little change.

Initially, the appeal of *Se Non Ora Quando?* received some criticism from Italian feminist organisations as well as from individual women who considered it to be too focused on the public representation of women and on sexual scandals, and neglecting wider concerns about the more general struggles which women face.[6] The promoters were also accused of being too radical, snobbish and insensitive towards women who resort to their bodies to make their way in the world. Nicchiarelli wrote:

> Let's not take to the streets against other women: let's take to the streets also for prostitutes, all of them, or better, let's take the streets with the prostitutes, and not only those who are on the Ardeatina, but also those who go to the mansions to sell themselves to rich old men to buy Gucci sunglasses. Rather than asking for solidarity or 'friendship' with men, let's ask ourselves, as a feminist movement, 'How did we come to this point?' (Nicchiarelli, 2011, www.unita.it, author's translation)

Different versions of the appeal were also created. These were tailored to specific needs and relevant concerns, but they had the effect of diluting the original call to action, and changing its focus as it had initially been directed to men as well as women. Fragmentation, controversy, even open opposition are typical in the history of the feminist movement in Italy (Lussana, 2012), and not only from men, but also from women, whether feminist or not. Therefore, given that context, encountering these reactions in 2011 was not so surprising.

Nevertheless, the appeal, and the subsequent associated internet discussions which followed in the days preceding 13 February, triggered an enormous response. Activist groups from all over the country organised local rallies to be held on the same day, thus creating one of the biggest feminist mobilisations ever in Italy, as the national and international media coverage of the rally testified.[7]

Political parties and trade unions, even those who had helped 'in kind' in the organisation of the rallies, were asked not to use their own symbols and flags. The movement wanted to remain neutral in order to be more to be more inclusive and to encourage participation from people from all walks of life who supported the mobilisation's *raison d'être*.

Growth of the movement: from the first ID card to the first national event in Siena

The success of the event of 13 February raised expectations. To respond to these many of the groups which had organised the rallies all around Italy, including those that were more spontaneous, formed local committees. These groups managed to maintain the energy aroused by the national mobilisation by linking it to ongoing initiatives concentrated on local issues as well as those being planned to commemorate the forthcoming International Women's Day on 8 March. They acted autonomously, but used the name of the new movement, which was growing both in terms of numbers and of the range of activities and participation. No central coordination took place although the original group that had promoted the mobilisation at the national level, named itself *Comitato Se Non Ora Quando?* and continued working as the national point of reference.

The next stage in the movement's evolution was an initiative taken by this committee to create an 'ID card' for SNOQ that would function as a draft of the movement's 'identity' and its *modus operandi*. The document set out the 'qualifying and original characteristics' of the movement, which were to apply to both the national and the local committees:

- liberty, strength and autonomy for women in all fields;
- engagement of all different women's associations and professional associations of women;
- personal loyalty to the movement required from women coming from political parties and unions;
- political, cultural and religious plurality;
- special attention to young women and young men;
- use of 'across-the-board'[8] and pluralistic language.

Only committees complying with these principles could call themselves part of the SNOQ movement. Political parties and other associations would not be allowed to use its symbol or logo. Political symbols, and those referring to unions, would be kept out of SNOQ committees, while efforts would be made by each committee to encourage the participation of *all* women.

These principles were widely accepted across the peninsula. Several local committees developed them further, writing their own ID cards setting out their specific aims, strategies and principles. This idea of giving the newly created organisations a set of rules and principles was seen by the National Committee as a way into building relationships among members, which included women from all ages, political and social backgrounds, and coming to the movement with very different ideas of what it should or could be. For example, long and harsh discussions took place about whether the term 'feminist' could be used to define the movement. This term was a familiar part of the cultural and political background of the older women, but was perceived as awkward by the younger ones, many of whom would have never have called themselves 'feminist'. Language became an issue in a broader sense too, because a completely new form of communication had to be created to find common ground, to include and not exclude and, in the end, to make working together possible.

In May 2011 the National Committee issued a new call-to-action. All local committees were invited to a national gathering to be held in Siena on 9 and 10 July. The purpose of the meeting was for these local committees to get to know each other and to start defining a national political agenda. Participation at this gathering was overwhelming. The small city of Siena was, literally, invaded by hundreds and hundreds of women from all over Italy. They attended the 'conference' held in an open public garden, which provided some refuge from the hot summer sun. Women of all ages, different in social and cultural background, economic status and political engagement seemed to instantly become friends by sharing their thoughts in five-minute-long public speeches or on papers hung on a cotton thread like clothes left to dry in the sun. Many women from political parties (both left and right) and national trade unions also attended, but their welcome within the event itself soon became more controversial. If they spoke, they were often jeered and booed, but if they just sat and listened even this behaviour was regarded as aimed at promoting their feminist concerns. Their desire to play an active role in the movement and to use the power of the positions they held to fight for the common cause was seen to be incompatible with the overall aims of the movement.

This gathering also represented a significant turning point for SNOQ concerning a number of critical questions. These included its desire to be accessible 'across-the-board' and simultaneously be effective; whether it should cooperate with political parties (and if so, which ones) or challenge them from outside? Giulia Bongiorno's contribution exemplified these dilemmas. Bongiorno, a former representative of Berlusconi's coalition who had then moved to opposition with Gianfranco Fini's party, was harshly criticised when she took the floor to share with the audience her difficulties in being both a career woman and a mother, and the hard choices she had to make between investing in her job and having a baby. The underlying question was whether an inclusive process could be developed without the risk of simplifying important issues and while remaining loyal to the paths that Italian feminist movements had traced in history? One activist asked (perhaps ironically);

> What does 'across-the-board' mean? That women in Italy, unique in the whole universe, have the same problems, independent of their being left, right, centre [referring to parties]. Or better, they have problems whose solutions are universal…this is the problem, a gigantic problem, which has run through women's movements around the world, everywhere and all the time.

The implicit suggestion underlying her comment is that no solutions to women's problems can be found without taking a political perspective and that, by definition, progressive solutions will differ from conservative ones. There is no neutral territory; thus, the willingness to be inclusive cannot bypass the necessity of addressing controversial issues. Without this important work the movement will either become paralysed or will find itself behaving inconsistently.

The meeting in Siena also provided a channel for the rage and indignation that had brought so many women onto the streets in February and into action. It seemed as though a new, big and potentially powerful movement might be about to be created. Many young women, some of them barely adult and having grown up after the feminist activism of the 1960s and 1970s, others shocked to just discover that the rights their mothers and grandmothers had fought for could not be taken for granted, said they were ready to take action. Even some men came, not only to learn 'what women wanted', but also to find out what contribution this movement could make and maybe, what role they could play. Thus, the meeting could be regarded as a success, but also a challenge, since the need for a medium- to long-range perspective and battle plan, often lacking from feminist initiatives in the past, was well understood by the SNOQ activists.

An organised structure and an effective management system were also required. Therefore, a 'General Assembly' was called, during which the following issues emerged: the organisational structure adopted by the movement would be critical for its development and action; media relationships would be strategically important in supporting the movement's actions; the relationship with other feminist movements and associations would also be critically important as well as the question of how to build an effective relationship with institutions and political parties.

These themes are also the ones relevant to the present analysis, which intends to assess how and to what extent SNOQ can be said to have contributed to the emancipation of Italian women. Therefore, in the following sections each of these issues will be examined in turn.

Organisation and management structure of the SNOQ movement

All national initiatives promoted by SNOQ until 2013 (including 13 February mobilisation and the Siena meeting) had been launched with a strong national communication campaign and supported, both organisationally and financially, by the same group of intellectuals who had written the first appeal. This group had at first called itself *Comitato Se Non Ora Quando?* but subsequently, during one of the national meetings that followed Siena, changed its name to 'Promoting Committee'. Behind this name change was the desire to distinguish between those who had 'invented' SNOQ and the local committees in the territories, which had latterly joined the initiative. However, another intention was also to maintain the founding group's pre-eminence. Because of the celebrity of its members the centrality of the role played by the Promoting Committee was credited more by the media and the institutional system than by the other committees and local associations. The other committees and local associations were certainly thankful to the 'promoters' for the initiative they had taken and their strong focus and determination, but were much less willing to let them interfere with local committees' independence and actions. Many women acting within the local committees had a long history of participation within feminist movements or political action at different levels, and this, combined with the levels of awareness already present within the groups, or raised by the events of 13 February and the Siena convention made it impossible to stop the local committees from taking action autonomously.

The names the local committees chose for themselves are proof of this: while several named themselves *Comitato SNOQ*, followed by the name of their city or town, others only added the acronym SNOQ to the name they had before; names which either referred to a topical issue they were addressing, or gave recognition to an event that had brought them together. Some of them also created federations of territorial or regional entities in order to better coordinate interventions, strategically plan activities and use available resources as efficiently as possible. Among the newer groups that had emerged spontaneously, several realised the importance of acquiring an official status, and therefore constituted themselves as third sector organisations, primarily associations, in order to be able to interact officially with institutions as well as public and private entities. Others chose to wait for the movement to adopt an organisational structure that could incorporate local branches (the SNOQ Promoting Committee had by that stage established itself as a not-for-profit association able to create local branches), and until then were drawing on the support of existing constituted associations if need arose.

The relationship between the Promoting Committee and the local committees was somewhat peculiar from the very beginning. No central coordinating role was allocated within the overall structure, as this would have been impossible to do. However, the national role the Promoting Committee played influenced the identity and the actions of the local committees on several occasions. For example, when a public rally was launched by the Promoting Committee for 11 December 2011, without any prior discussion in a public assembly, local committees could only choose whether or not to join in.

In the beginning the Promoting Committee's influence was undoubtedly very important; it was successful in bringing together a large number of women in public squares and in providing them with issues to work on together. However, with the increase in the quantity and quality of locally implemented activities, the local committees became progressively more autonomous from the Promoting Committee, and this made the need for a national federation more necessary. Each day that passed without a clear redefinition of the balances of power inside the movement marked a deterioration in the relationship between the territories and the Promoting Committee. Some suggested that SNOQ might soon fall apart, and for the same reason that so many feminist movements had failed in the past: a lack of democracy or, conversely, an excess of it. Members were very free to talk and discuss, but they were unable to produce an effective political platform upon which to structure long-term actions.

Furthermore, the excessive reliance of the Promoting Committee on the internet as the main instrument of communication for linking the territories, responding quickly to diverse issues and planning rapid activities was also one of the risk factors that SNOQ faced during this phase. The internet proved to be insufficient for all these communication needs, thus requests from all over Italy to hold face-to-face meetings started to be pressing. Such meetings have now been held regularly since October 2011, mainly in Rome. However, until 2013 (the period under review in this chapter) neither a formal structure for the movement at national level had been established nor the relationship between the Promoting Committee and the Local Committees been defined. Nonetheless, many initiatives were carried out, both at local and national level, for example those aimed at combating 'femicide', a widespread phenomenon in Italy that caused the death of nearly one woman every two days between 2000 and 2012 (Eures Report, 2012).[9]

Media relations and agenda setting: fame, competence and strategy

Why did SNOQ attract both national and international attention? How did the movement manage to bring thousands of women out onto the squares of Italy twice in a 12-month period (on 13 February and 11 December 2011)? How was it able, without a central organisation, to spread through all of Italy and to create associations, groups and collectives which were able to continue working for over two years, producing structured and well-coordinated initiatives?

One immediate answer can be given by recognising how the SNOQ movement differs from preceding initiatives within the Italian feminist scenario. The context in which it began was certainly unique: attention from all over the world was focused on the behaviour inside and outside the government of the then Prime Minister, Silvio Berlusconi, his 'bunga bunga' parties and other scandals. Italian women were angry with being under-represented or – worse – merely being represented as bodies. Furthermore, they were overwhelmed with the struggle imposed by the economic crisis, and with their talents being unrecognised. The time was right for action and SNOQ was able to capitalise on these factors to make the initiative a success.

The strategic capability of SNOQ may also have been positively influenced by the profound knowledge of the mechanisms governing information and the media that many within the movement held, unlike previous Italian feminist initiatives. SNOQ seems to have always known that good ideas would be important to reach success, but also that the way those ideas would be communicated was crucial, as well as by whom. From the very beginning, the promoters worked on the movement as if they were building a 'brand'. They created it as such, and they communicated it accordingly.

This strategy can be primarily be attributed to the fact that the intellectuals who first created the appeal were all national figures, among them the filmmakers Cristina and Francesca Comencini, the actress Lunetta Savino, the writer Lidia Ravera, the economist Elisabetta

Addis (names and biographies of the promoters can be found at www.
senonoraquando.eu). The promoters also had good connections with
the national media – and they used them wisely; they knew how to
adopt an integrated communication strategy to reach different audiences
(utilising varied media such as written appeals, videos, the internet) and
always recognised that their ideas needed support, however good their
ideas were. Structure and content have, therefore, always gone together
in the communication strategy of SNOQ. This strategy included a
highly identifiable, original logo (this was a solid pink rectangle with
a small white figure in the centre, holding an enormous white flag
above her head with the question: *Se Non Ora Quando?* written on it,
in pink, capital letters) as a means of recognition, and around which to
build affinity, identity and, ultimately, a community. T-shirts, pins and
bags with the logo, at first made primarily for fundraising purposes,
soon also became means of recognition, something to wear to show
one's allegiance to the movement.

Se Non Ora Quando? met the media's criteria for being newsworthy,
and the media responded by following the movement's events and
providing structured coverage of its initiatives and actions. An indirect
example of the success and effectiveness of this approach is a letter
written by several female journalists of RAI (the main national public
TV channel) to the general Director of RAI in July 2011. In the
letter, the journalists complained about the silence that surrounded
the SNOQ event of 2011 in Siena. The letter read:

> We write to you, whom we saluted enthusiastically on your
> appointment as the first female General Director. We are
> a group of TG1 journalists [newscasters of RAI] who –
> with different roles and backgrounds – have been working
> for years to keep the citizens – all citizens – informed in
> the spirit of public service, pluralism and information. We
> also are citizens and viewers, and we need to express the
> dismay we felt regarding the silence of the first newscast
> about the big rally of women who gathered in Siena –
> they were over 2000 – an across-the-board event, with
> 200 committees, filmmakers, actresses, writers, workers,
> unions' representatives, members of Parliament from all
> parties, who claimed their right to build a fairer country,
> for women as well. Dignity of work, maternity, careers,
> temporary employment, public image: all these themes were
> aired and discussed by all the major newscasters except for
> the most important one, TG1. During the two days of the

rally in Siena, we saw no reports on the event, while on the Sunday edition of 10 August the 'Women on high heels race' was duly documented. This choice to remain silent on the part of the leading newscaster hinders the right of all women paying the Italian television tax to be informed about the events which concern them, and proves us right in our belief that a fundamental transformation in thinking is crucial in order for information to be made more available to the people, about the issues of women, the young, the weakest and the more disadvantaged people, and we hope that all this will happen soon.[10]

Meanwhile, some of the creators of SNOQ used their film-making abilities to produce videos, commercials and short films. Social networks profiles were created and the media strategy was followed effectively, thus ensuring that every significant deadline was met and every relevant issue covered. All of this mostly happened at the national level but also contributed to boosting the communications made by local committees, who could draw on the 'brand' as well as on the relevance of their issues and the reputation of their members.

The relationships with other feminist movements in Italy

'The women's revolution', writer Lidia Ravera wrote in the left-wing newspaper *L'Unità* in August 2009 'has not been won or lost. It has merely been interrupted' www.unita.it/donne/la-rivoluzione-interrotta-delle-donne-1.3506, author's translation). She highlighted the situation in which the feminist movement in Italy, although initially making a significant impact, had somehow become unheard; its voices drowned by powerful agencies from the media. It is not by chance that the last demonstration that had been organised by a feminist network prior to 13 February 2011, had called itself *Usciamo dal silenzio* (Let's break the silence). This event took place in January 2006 and encouraged women – who had never been silent at all, especially within the feminist movements – to tear down the barriers preventing their voices from being heard. The focus of that demonstration was the continuous threats to the law guaranteeing the right to undergo abortion, and it was a success in terms of mobilisation: over 200,000 women came to the demonstration in Milan (www.retedelledonne.org). In 2011, when SNOQ's appeal reached feminist movements and associations, various eyebrows were raised. Among the most authoritative voices was Luisa Muraro, who stated:

It must be clear, though, that there is no such thing as a collective thought: either one thinks in the first person or does not think at all. Massed crowds of people who do not think in the first person are either blind or are being manipulated…And thinking is not reacting to what others say with a 'yes' or a 'no', but locating oneself with one's own desire and interest in what is happening…In my opinion there's a risk that the mobilisation will be used by those who haven't done what they should. And what's that? The work that we demand from our leaders. (Muraro, 2011, www.corriere.it, author's translation)

Muraro's proposition was that when it comes to political action, movements can never replace personal responsibility, especially that of leaders. Many women also thought that the SNOQ appeal was excessively naïve, that it risked falling into a moralistic approach and that its focus on the necessity of raising women's voices was disrespectful to the action already being carried out by feminist collectives. Among them was Nadotti, who pointed out:

What makes me most sad [referring to the appeal], what unnerves and frightens me is the fact that behind your invitation to 'wake us up again' there could lie a veiled, maybe subconscious, form of racism steeped in sexism and class consciousness: sacrificial women (those who go to bed early and get up early) against call girls (those who sleep with their bosses), morality against apathy of feelings, souls against bodies. Us, both women and men, are made of all these things. (Nadotti, 2011, www.corriere.it, author's translation)

The risk was, then as now, that the feminist movement would be torn apart by an initiative which asked women to commit themselves to it individually, leaving aside previous memberships, a risk feminist initiatives in Italy had taken before, as well documented by Lussana (2012). It was a choice regarding the identity of the movement, which probably wanted to facilitate that 'special attention to young women' claimed in its ID card, but it was nonetheless seen by some feminist activists as a means of diminishing the role and historical relevance of prior movements.

This risk has been only partially averted over time. The movement's activists have made efforts to acknowledge the experience of other associations and movements, but at the same time they have signalled SNOQ's difference by promoting autonomous initiatives, and also by bringing so many 'new' women alongside, especially those young women who had enthusiastically joined the movement, never having experienced feminist activism before. Many of these young women had never thought that they would need to defend their alleged equality to men nor their right to express themselves fully, until they faced the difficulties in entering the labour market on account of their being female, or faced discrimination in public or in private life. They were sometimes not even sure exactly what 'feminism' meant. Feminism seemed to them to be something in the past, far removed from their daily life and experience. In order to include and not exclude them a new language had to be created, new ways had to be found through which they could publicly claim their rights. Words and actions had to be found that engaged them rather than repelling them, as could have easily happened with the use of more traditionally feminist language and forms of behaviour. The efforts made to identify this new 'code' helped SNOQ to distance itself from previous feminist experiences, while simultaneously acknowledging its debt to the earlier forms of activism.

However, although this may have been too much to expect, what was still missing from SNOQ was the capacity to fulfil its 'across-the-board attitude' towards other contemporary feminist groups and to facilitate a more inclusive and strategic perspective, not only when big rallies were organised, but also on a day-by-day basis. Arguably, this capacity might have produced more effective results.

The relationship with politics and political parties

Is SNOQ the first feminist lobby in Italy? Given the negative connotation 'lobby' has in the Italian language, nobody with a good understanding of the movement would be likely to agree. But if a lobby is taken as a 'group of persons attempting to influence legislators on behalf of a particular interest' (www.collinsdictionary.com), then looking more closely at the actions of the movement and of the Promoting Committee at the national level, enables us to identify some of the features typical of a lobby. They are: first, the movement's desired 'across-the-board attitude' which, while harshly criticised by some of the older feminists (and also by some members of SNOQ) was aimed at creating a common platform through emphasising terms such as 'openness' and 'pluralism' in the second version of the ID card.[11] The emphasis by SNOQ on being across-the-board reflected its desire to gather a wide consensus around its initiatives and causes, in spite of different political views and credos.

Second, SNOQ adopted a 'result orientation' strategy. It focused on achieving specific, practical goals rather than presenting a more diffuse, general critique of the status quo. This resulted in several critical comments addressed to the Promoting Committee which argued that SNOQ was a 'project which comes to an end when a single goal is met' rather than taking on board the view that 'the autonomy of women expresses a critical point of view on all forms of politics' (SNOQ website),[12] as had been more common in previous feminist experiences in Italy. Certainly, SNOQ still made use of more traditional activities (such as conferences, publications, studies, press releases and so on) focused on specific themes of relevance to women, where its aim was primarily to stimulate debate and raise awareness. However, SNOQ simultaneously put pressure on political parties and institutions in relation to more specific political decisions, such as designations and appointments, hoping, by exerting this pressure, to force them to acknowledge and respond directly to their requests. Examples include the meeting of a delegation of promoters of the appeal '188 women for the restoration of Law number 188' (the law against the 'blank resignation' phenomenon) with the Labour and Welfare Minister Elsa Fornero or the series of encounters of representatives from the SNOQ movement at national and local level with authorities such as the President of the House of Parliament,[13] leaders and Members of Parliament from left-wing parties, the General Secretary of the Italian General Confederation of Labour (CGIL) and the Minister of Territorial Cohesion. The main issues discussed in these meetings included women's representation in the media, violence against women and 'femicide', women's employment, electoral reform (in order to guarantee equal representation of men and women within institutions at all levels), the political representation of women and the presence of women's issues within public debate and the rights and needs of homosexual women, including the recognition of common-law marriage.[14]

That this strategy proved effective can be demonstrated by, for example, SNOQ's influence on the decision-making process concerning the renewal of the Board of Directors of State Broadcaster RAI, which took place in 2012. Such appointments are made by the government, but on that occasion the left-wing Democratic Party consulted with important civil society organisations, among them SNOQ, before deciding whom to appoint.

Another relevant effect was that on the movement itself, as political elections were approaching. Perhaps the strategy of the SNOQ strategy was too new within the feminist scenario not to raise doubts about its integrity, especially since the political engagement of many of its members reinforced the prejudice that they might have some hidden agendas, and they might be using SNOQ as a springboard to climb (or help someone else to climb) the 'real' ladder of politics. This accusation was made by some inside the media as early as July 2012, when the question was raised as to whether the feminist movement could play politics without being co-opted by political parties. Again, in January 2013, immediately before the political elections, the web magazine *Dagospia* re-published an article by Elena Bernini that had originally been written for *Gli altri, la Sinistra quotidiana* ('The others, the daily left'). The tone of the article was clear and is exemplified by this quote:

> "If not bimbo, when?" – that is what the Comencini sisters' feminist movement is so far: in a Mafia Commission made up of Roman snobbish bourgeoisie whose main business is to place friends in the Democratic Party to the detriment of true activists.[15]

Conclusions

By reviewing the brief but intense life of the SNOQ movement from its inception in 2011 to the political elections in 2013, this chapter has tried to answer the questions as to whether civil society can play a role in the emancipation of women in Italy, and if so, to what extent. In conclusion, a positive answer can be ventured. Italy may still lag behind many European countries regarding a number of women's issues – women's equality and recognition of numerous needs are still far from being achieved – but, thanks to the efforts of the SNOQ movement among others, many of these matters have been kept under close scrutiny, both at the national and the local level, and this not only by the women of the movement itself.

A significant element in the success of SNOQ lies in the social, economic and cultural situation in which Italy found itself when the movement began, and in the concomitant frustration that Italian women were experiencing. At the same time, SNOQ was able to build on the ongoing activism of those in the feminist movement, who had never been silent and who had struggled and won crucial issues such as those concerning divorce and abortion. The sometimes conflictual relationship between SNOQ and the pre-existing feminist associations testifies to the difficulty of maintaining the balance between recognition of their common inheritance and the compelling necessity to innovate.

These innovations have been significant and represent major achievements for the movement. The first one concerns the ability of SNOQ to offer Italian women – especially those who had been distant from the traditional feminist movement – a new version of 'feminism', one that they could understand, and around which they could mobilise. The second achievement is its sophisticated use of the media. The movement was able to use the media to realise its own agenda; it was able to market itself in such a way as to capture and maintain media interest, through timely and targeted media releases, the use of high profile public figures, and intriguing images.

The third achievement is its relationship with political parties. Through the interventions of SNOQ political parties were forced to review their position on feminism and to put feminist concerns at the top of their agendas, thus enhancing the participation and engagement of all their activists, but especially of women.

It is probably, however, too early to gauge whether the movement will produce effective and long-lasting change in Italian culture and politics. What can be concluded from this analysis is that SNOQ has made significant steps in promoting the emancipation of Italian women. It has offered Italy tangible proof that civil society is capable of effectively challenging the status quo and producing new forms of culture, in the sense of new ways of thinking, new knowledge and new language. To do so requires civil society to be structured into organisations that are able to coordinate, to balance centralised and de-centralised activism, to invest in democratic procedures, both as an aspiration and as a ruling principle, and to innovate while not forgetting history. And that is what all Italian women owe to those who fought so hard, no more than a few decades ago, for those rights that all can now enjoy.

Notes

[1] Smith, Z, 2009, Notes on Visconti's *Bellissima,* cited in http://thewip.net/contributors/2010/11/combating_berlusconis_vision_o.html.

[2] www.tempi.it/gli-omicidi-contro-le-donne-sono-uno-scandalo-ma-i-numeri-del-femminicidio-sono-gonfiati#.VgKc69_tmko.

[3] http://en.rsf.org/europe-ex-ussr-europe-ex-ussr-20-10-2010,38592.html.

[4] www.unita.it/italia/da-roma-a-new-york-tutte-le-piazze-del-13-febbraio-1.271247.

[5] www.senonoraquando.eu/?p=2948, published on 30/01/2011. Text in English.

6   www.lastampa.it/2011/02/13/esteri/lastampa-in-english/berlusconi-and-feminism-do-italian-woman-need-to-defend-their-dignity-Za7El6vxXtZF3JmWTZRVqK/pagina.html

7   Some references: www.dailymail.co.uk/news/article-1356600/If-A-million-furious-Italian-women-protesters-demand-head-Berlusconi-underage-sex-scandal.html; www.theguardian.com/world/2011/feb/13/silvio-berlusconi-protests-italian-women; www.spiegel.de/international/europe/women-rise-up-against-berlusconi-italy-is-not-a-brothel-a-745507.html.

8   This phrase is used by the movement.

9   Data from the Eures Report 2012, cited by the theatrical project 'Wounded to Death', www.feriteamorte.it/femminicido-per-litalia-non-e-piu-un-tabu/.

10   The full text of the letter can be found at: www.senonoraquando.eu/?p=2350. Author's translation.

11   The document 'Carta d'identità di SNOQ: un anno dopo' ('SNOQ ID card: a year after') can be found at www.senonoraquando.eu/?p=8976, author's translation.

12   www.senonoraquando.eu/?p=6139. Author's translation.

13   www.senonoraquando.eu/?p=7188.

14   www.senonoraquando.eu/?p=7679 and www.senonoraquando.eu/?p=8560.

15   www.dagospia.com/rubrica-3/politica/se-non-oca-quando-ecco-cosa-serve-movimento-femminista-49392.htm. Author's translation.

References

Banca d'Italia, 2012, *Relazione annuale,* Annual report of the Bank of Italy

Bernini, E, 2013, Se non oca, quando?, *Dasgospia,* www.dagospia.com/rubrica-3/politica/se-non-oca-quando-ecco-cosa-serve-movimento-femminista-49392.htm

Collins Dictionary, www.collinsdictionary.com/dictionary/english/lobby

Corbetta, P, 2003, *Social research: Theory, methods and techniques,* London: Sage

DeWalt, KM, DeWalt, BR, 2002, *Participant observation: A guide for fieldworkers,* Walnut Creek, CA: AltaMira Press

Lussana, F, 2012, *Il movimento femminista in Italia,* Rome: Carocci

Muraro, L, 2011, Il grande errore è andare in piazza per conto di altri, *Corriere della Sera,* www.corriere.it/cronache/11_febbraio_10/muraro-errore-scendere-in-piazza-per-conto-altri_3957321a-34e9-11e0-b824-00144f486ba6.shtml.

Nadotti, M, 2011, Le contraddizioni e il no alla crociata, *Corriere della Sera,* www.corriere.it/cronache/11_febbraio_07/le-contraddizioni-e-il-No-alla-crociata_6f033bca-329b-11e0-8ce8-00144f486ba6.shtml

Nicchiarelli, S, 2011, Perché le conquiste sono state smantellate?, *l'Unità,* www.unita.it/italia/nicchiarelli-perche-le-conquiste-sono-state-smantellate-1.270851

FOUR

Street harassment activism in the twenty-first century

Rochelle Keyhan[1]

Introduction to street harassment: 'Men always bother you, all the time'

In an early episode of the television series *Mad Men* (episode 2 of season 1), Joan, the voluptuous, self-assured office manager, approaches Peggy, the 'new girl', about a letter she had submitted that was filled with typographical errors. Peggy, clearly upset, begins to express her frustration over the constant sexual harassment she is experiencing from her male colleagues, asking Joan; 'Why is it that every time a man takes you out to lunch around here, you're the dessert? It's terrible. It's constant, from every corner.' Joan, who plays to her advantage the regular attention she receives from the men, responds; 'You're the new girl, and you're not much, so you might as well enjoy it while it lasts.' Joan's response suggests that the harassment is something for which Peggy should be grateful, diminishing her discontent. While Joan attempts to coach Peggy into the 'right' way of handling the harassment, she comments that 'Men always bother you, all the time. They follow you down the street', highlighting that some women (in this case, Joan herself) come to accept gender-based harassment as an inevitable part of public life. However, as evidenced by the number of mistakes Peggy made in the letter she wrote, the sexual harassment had an impact on her ability to function at work. Unable to brush the harassment aside, as Joan seemed to, the script suggests that Peggy's only choice is to grow a thicker skin: if she cannot learn to enjoy the harassment, she must at least learn to ignore it.

Mad Men presents a workplace environment in which women were forced to navigate sexual harassment on a daily basis, which from our current perspective clearly seems unacceptable. Within the office environment men asserted their power over, and ownership of, the public sphere by blatantly objectifying their female co-workers, reducing them to sex objects. While in many ways this situation persists, there is no denying that social norms around workplace sexual harassment have shifted dramatically since the 1960s. Recognising this form of harassment as an impediment to women's full access into the workplace, there is now established case law and legislation that officially condemns it in the United States. What has not changed, however, is the perception that at least some measure of male harassment is inevitable. This perception indicates that the problem is much wider, extending beyond the confined workplace and onto the unbounded public streets.

It is hard to address a problem when the widespread attitude towards it is one of inevitability. In this sense, street harassment today is regarded in much the same way that workplace sexual harassment was regarded in the 1960s. Both forms of harassment are manifestations of male power and control over the public sphere. There is now general public agreement that everyone should be treated respectfully and equally by colleagues in the workplace. Sexual harassment in public, however, is rarely recognised as a legitimate problem. Women and lesbian, gay, bisexual and transgender (LGBT) individuals learn from a young age to navigate their daily lives through sexual harassment not only in professional settings, but also in public. This second form of sexual harassment has come to be known as 'street harassment'. It is a separate but still harmful form of sexual harassment, one that is now in the early stages of recognition. While workplace harassment is bounded within the parameters of the office and the relationships in the workplace, street harassment has no boundaries. Strangers harass people on the streets, at the coffee stands in office buildings, in the hallways of apartment buildings, on public transportation, from cars driving past – in any and all public spaces. The unbounded nature of street harassment, being that it can happen at any moment in public, and happen without recognition or admonishment, does affect the recognition it receives as a form of harassment. Street harassment is considered to be fleeting, without consequence, just 'boys being boys', when in reality it carries many of the same consequences as workplace harassment, in which career and livelihood may be at risk, and is just as reprehensible.

Although it is still far from being a household term, street harassment has begun to garner appropriate levels of attention as a necessary element in the struggle for women's rights. The goal of anti-street harassment activists is that one day we will look back on the apprehension women experience in just walking down the street with the same mixture of awe and horror with which we now regard sexual harassment in the 1960s workplace. This chapter begins with the identification of the nature, context and roots of street harassment as a global problem in need of comprehensive solutions. The efforts by community-based organisations to remedy street harassment are described, informed primarily through document analysis, alongside newspaper articles and first-hand accounts of street harassment experiences, and empirical data is presented from a case study of Hollaback!, an international not-for-profit organisation dedicated to ending street harassment globally. The case study of Hollaback! focuses specifically on its use of the internet platform to match street harassment's unbounded parameters with a similarly unbounded organisational model for implementing those solutions on a global scale.

The development of the movement to end street harassment

In the nineteenth century, men in the United States and Canada who ogled women in public were referred to as 'mashers' (Johnston, 2011). Newspaper articles and studies done in the early nineteenth and twentieth centuries reveal stories of harassment similar to stories reported today, together with a range of responses including those from fierce opponents to the harassing behaviour to people who focused on what the women might have done to invite the harassment, alongside others that attempted to find the best way to deal with this widespread problem.

Today we still see a similar range of responses. Despite that early attention, street harassment persists. But today activists all over the world are speaking out against our modern day 'mashers' and placing the blame rightfully on their harassing behaviours. Thanks to modern technology, activists are also speaking out globally, both through local, grassroots action and also through online activism with sites like Hollaback!, Harassmap, Blank Noise, and Stop Street Harassment. The new technological capabilities have allowed people to connect and unite together through the internet to create a tremendous platform that highlights street harassment as a global issue and locates it firmly on the continuum of gender-based violence. The belief that the safe access of individuals to public space must be 'established as a political right' is an echo of Dolores Hayden's 1980s demand that such safe access is necessary in order to overcome what she termed the 'thereness' of women and LGBT individuals, meaning that they are present as part of the scenery but not permitted to play active roles (Presler and Scholz, 2000, 40). The international movement is taking activism to new levels, demanding a public policy-oriented response to street harassment and an end to the culture that regards gender-based violence as acceptable.

The international scope of activism against street harassment

Modern anti-street harassment activism is heavily internet-based, but does have large components of on-the-ground action. Whether called 'piropos' in Latin America, 'chikan' in Japan, 'eve-teasing' in India and neighbouring countries, or 'street harassment', the behaviour occurs on a global scale and it has similar impacts on women's mobility all over the world. People are starting conversations to raise awareness, many are actively intervening to interrupt instances of harassment. Some are even approaching their legislators and demanding formal responses. Each of these forms of activism is important to the end goal of challenging the culture of acceptability that surrounds gender-based violence more generally, and street harassment in particular. To change this culture, we have to change the mind-set that supports and enables it, and every conversation that occurs at a local level is a step in that direction.

Community groups and safe spaces

Many organisations have emerged across the world that provide safe spaces for women to talk about what they can do to both cope with and end street harassment. For example, women in a remote village in Bangladesh who were under virtual house arrest, subjected to public sexual harassment and even violence whenever they dared to leave the home, were empowered by a CARE programme called *Shouhardo* (a Bangladeshi word that means 'friendship') to confront the harassment. Through community-based groups of women and girls, they discussed decision-making power, violence against women, and other issues affecting the women of the village, as well as the Bangladeshi legislation available to ultimately confront the men of the village until it eventually ceased. Women and girls now walk more freely and are more informed of their rights (Gayle, 2012).

Art and public education

Art has been used by organisations to educate others about street harassment as well as by individuals as a means of working through their personal experiences. The Adventures of Salwa is a project based in Beirut, that campaigns against sexual harassment both in public and in the workplace. The centrepiece of the campaign is a cartoon character, Salwa, an ordinary Lebanese girl who combats sexual harassment by breaking cultural taboos and fighting back. This project works through public service announcements, cartoons and community engagement activism to share information and encourage local dialogue (www.youtube.com/user/adventuresofsalwa, online video channel, YouTube).

HollabackPHILLY similarly released a comic book dealing with the nuances of street harassment, which is used as part of their youth educational programme. The comic book follows three characters and their different experiences with street harassment, outlining diverse gender experiences, including the perspective of a male bystander. The comic book medium relies heavily on superb visuals with little text, so that the comic book becomes an accessible tool to engage audiences who might otherwise not be interested in reading literature on street harassment. In this way, the comic book is an engaging way to encourage people to think about the issue, allowing them to take it home and digest the information in their own time.

Public advertisements have also been used to address harassing behaviour. Public transport vehicles and stations are major sites of harassment incidents, making them the perfect platform for educational efforts. Strategically, the passengers are also a captive audience, so many organisations have taken to creating public service advertisements to run on their local transit systems. For example, in Sri Lanka the Chairman of the Legal Aid Commission, SS Wijeratne, spoke out against street harassment, most rampant in public transportation (Lanksari News, 2011). Wijeratne said that women were reluctant to report harassment to the bus conductors, drivers or the police, and the bus drivers are also reluctant to report harassment for fear of losing income (Lanksari News, 2011). The Chairman and the Road Passenger Transport Authority in Sri Lanka allocated a two-week public awareness campaign, to raise awareness and spread messages aimed at deterring men from harassing, and encouraging women and bystanders to report the harassment (Lanksari News, 2011). The Latin American Women and Habitat Network in Colombia created a no-groping campaign for the Bogota bus system (Valente, 2010). Similarly, in the United States, DC Metro in Washington DC and the Massachusetts Bay Transit Authority in Boston, each released a public service campaign focused on groping in public transit. HollabackPHILLY released a public transit ad campaign in spring 2013 that was the first to address the roots of street harassment at every level, from menacing stares to unwanted comments and more extreme forms of harassments such as following and even touching. In partnership with Feminist Public Works, HollabackPHILLY published a more expansive campaign across the entire Philadelphia transit system in the spring of 2014. This second campaign again defined street harassment, attempted to instil a sense of community accountability, and encourage people to intervene when they witness harassment occurring. Both campaigns received international attention, as well as local legislative attention, and were adapted for use by Hollaback! Boston in the Boston transit system in 2014.

Another powerful use of art to combat street harassment is also found in Tatyana Fazlalizadeh's wheat pasting project. Fazlalizadeh has travelled the world, drawing portraits of local women on posters in public spaces, with captions that speak directly to offenders (http://stoptellingwomentosmile.com). In 2014 she partnered with Fusion Digital to take her anti-street harassment wheat pasting project to Mexico City, where they interviewed 76 women. The project, portraits and stories were turned into an interactive website.

Academic research projects and community-based responses

The Blank Noise Project in India started as a college student's senior project in 2003, designed to combat 'eve-teasing' (as street harassment is called in India). This project has since blossomed into an organisation with a local presence through on-the-street activism and community engagement. The Blank Noise Project has reached out to legislators, created public art, engaged in performance-based activism, as well as developing an international presence through their blog and social media presence (http://blanknoise.org).

Harassmap, based in Egypt, encourages real-time reporting of harassment via mobile technology and social media. In partnership with the Egyptian Centre for Women's Rights, the United Nations Population Fund and the European Union, Harassmap conducted a sociological study of the reach and impact of street harassment across Egypt, releasing a ground-breaking report detailing the scope and nature of Egypt's street harassment problem (Hassan, 2010). In 2014, they partnered with a number of local organisations and officials to release a follow-up survey on the effectiveness of crowdsourcing data in the fight to end street harassment (Fahmy, 2014).

Stop Street Harassment was founded by Holly Kearl after she had completed her master's thesis, entitled *Stop street harassment: Making public spaces safe and welcoming for women*. Following the publication of her thesis as a book, Kearl (2010) founded the online resource website StopStreetHarassment.org, which is filled with international resources to support anti-street harassment activism. She is also the organiser of International Anti-Street Harassment Week, held the first week of each spring, which encourages international organisations to host local discussions and activism around street harassment, which are then documented on her site (www.stopstreetharassment.org).

Government responses

Numerous cities worldwide have launched segregated public transportation programmes, most recently in Delhi where one subway car or bus will be designated 'women only'. Although not an ideal solution, it is an official, citywide acknowledgment that the harassment is a problem (Times of India, 2012).

Women all over the world have demanded public and political responses to street harassment including formal legislation. In March 2012 the UK Prime Minister, David Cameron, committed the government to taking a harder stance against street harassment and stalking, supporting international initiatives and improved local laws (Hill and Jowit, 2012). In May 2012, France's parliament overturned the country's sexual harassment law on the grounds that it was too vague and thus did not adequately address the problem, and subsequently, in July 2012, unanimously approved clearer and more comprehensive legislation criminalising sexual harassment (De La Baume, 2012). An anti-sexual harassment bill was introduced in Chile specifically focused on groping in public space (Kearl, 2011). The Shoura Council in Saudi Arabia issued a new law punishing men who harass women in public with a fine and public defamation (Saudi Gazette, 2012). A bill against street harassment was introduced to Panama's national assembly in February 2015 (Asamblea Nacional, 2015). As reports of sexual harassment increased in Peru, the Peruvian government passed a law in March 2015 outlawing sexual harassment, while proscribing enforcement mechanisms at local and national levels, with a penalty of up to 12 years imprisonment. The new law defines sexual harassment as 'physical or verbal conduct of sexual nature or connotation by one or more persons against another or others who do not wish or reject such behaviour as affecting their dignity and their fundamental rights' (Ojeda, 2015).

These instances of activism in cities across the world, although sometimes powerful agents for change at the local level, don't often expand beyond the individual communities in which the organisations are based. For a global response to succeed in crafting sustainable, culturally nuanced, long-term solutions to street harassment, it requires international collaboration.

Global activism in a digital age

> I was wearing sunglasses, so no one could see me cry on my way home. I don't let anyone talk to me like that, but he was so much bigger and filled with so much anger. I felt so powerless and so small.[2]

Hollaback!, a community-based organisation dedicated to ending street harassment, began in 2005 with a group of friends who were discussing their discontent with the harassment women experienced while walking down the street. As an initial response they started a blog, HollabackNYC. Five years later, in 2010 Hollaback! was incorporated as an official not-for-profit organisation. By the close of that year Hollaback!'s initial goal of launching five branches had been exceeded nine-fold, with 45 branches, operating in nine languages spread out over 16 countries across the world. By the end of 2014 the organisation had established 84 branches spanning 25 countries in every continent except Antarctica.

Members of the Hollaback! network from 84 cities share a common experience of street harassment and the goal of emancipation from the fear of gender-based violence. They aspire to a world where safety on the streets has nothing to do with gender. Technological advances have created innovative options for today's CSOs to unite in unprecedented ways, and these have enabled Hollaback!'s rapid growth. The organisation utilises the internet to facilitate a prodigious platform for activism, uniting over 300 site leaders on an international stage. These leaders run activist branches in local communities all over the world, holding workshops and creating dialogue about street harassment. Through its international branches Hollaback! collects accounts of personal experiences of street harassment from community members via community meetings, online networking and mobile technology. Those stories are then shared on local Hollaback! websites, and are mapped globally. Mapping the stories illustrates the scope and tenor of the problem, while also allowing for direct comparison of the styles of street harassment that span the globe.

Unique to the Hollaback! model is its approach which recognises and highlights the intersections of oppression present in street harassment behaviour through regular collaboration and skill-sharing between its global site leaders. The diversity of its site leaders (as of 2014, 78 per cent of Hollaback! site leaders were under the age of 30, 36 per cent identified as LGBT, 29 per cent as people of colour, and 17 per cent as having disabilities) is magnified by the cultural variances in their experiences and perspectives, which informs the movement's activism at both local and global levels. Many Hollaback! site leaders have the opportunity to interact regularly via the internet, collaborating and transforming their activism to be culturally relative and sensitive. This model of global collaboration provides the potential for Hollaback! site leaders to learn from each other's strategies and to be inclusive of sub-cultures within their own cities while expanding access to perspectives and approaches through brainstorming within the network. The diversity of Hollaback!'s leadership also makes the movement more accessible to a diversity of constituents. As each new site launches the site leaders are trained in the movement's goals and objectives as well as ways of problematising street harassment and organising effectively so that the volunteer leaders are at least operating within the same messaging frameworks.

When a Hollaback! branch starts in a new city, its initial activity is to familiarise their community with what the term 'street harassment' actually means. Sexual harassment is normalised behaviour to some women; 'simply routine, a commonplace part of everyday life, and thus not something that can be challenged' (Riger, 2000, 93). Such normalisation prevents people from even recognising the harassment let alone acknowledging the negative emotions people experience in response to harassing behaviours. For example, many workshops done by HollabackPHILLY with high school- and college-aged students have begun with little response to the question, 'What is street harassment?' But when asked, 'How many of you have been sexually harassed by strange men on the street? How many of you have been followed by strange men on the street?', many more hands are raised (from an interview with Anna Kegler, 16 July 2013). People have an intimate knowledge of street harassment, but haven't, until recently, been given a name for the experience or been told it's an experience which they are entitled to consider as harassment.

Naming street harassment and labelling it a problem in need of a solution is the first step to validating the unique realities of women and LGBT individuals and placing them into mainstream consciousness. The collective consciousness-raising that occurs online through the Hollaback! platform provides a way to literally write the experiences of street harassment into a reality that is both qualitative and quantifiable, and on a global scale. Hollaback! provides hundreds of names and human reactions to street harassment from all over the world in a visible, accessible way. The blogs documenting these experiences humanise the issue and provide solidarity for the various people speaking out about being harassed. Additionally, they serve as a resource for those in need of a community who are still uncomfortable speaking out.

Street harassment often goes unreported, as many people are still uncomfortable reporting gender-based violence. Research into the experiences of rape survivors suggests that there are two preconditions for people to be comfortable reporting a rape: they must identify themselves as a victim of a crime, and they must be confident that they will be perceived as such by others in their lives (Williams, 1984). Being unable to get support from community, friends, and family 'causes harmful psychological effects that are more severe than effects of other crimes and engenders fear among women that leads them to restrict their behaviour to avoid sexual victimization' (Ullman, 1996, 505). If a survivor 'detects a scepticism and lack of support by those to whom the report is made, her feelings of guilt and lack of self-worth may be enhanced, and the psychological impacts may thereby be increased' (Norris and Feldman-Summers, 1982, 562). This logic also applies to the reporting of street harassment, even informally to friends or colleagues, which can have lasting benefits to the person harassed.

Hollaback! sites all over the world challenge the more mainstream, sceptical approach to survivor accounts by providing safe spaces for women and LGBT people to post their stories, creating a sense of community with people who have had similar negative experiences. Survivor narratives 'give voice to heretofore silent histories; help shape public consciousness about gender-based violence; and thus alter history's narrative' and can be essential to recovery (Hesford, 1999, 195). Collecting anecdotes of experiences illustrates the world which many inhabit, emboldening those with similar but silenced experiences, and enlightening those to whom the experience is foreign. Hollaback!'s global community names the problem of street harassment, validates the experience of those who are harassed, and allows them the freedom to identify themselves as having been victimised by harassers. Many site leaders also email individuals who have submitted stories, thanking them for sharing their experience, and reminding them that the Hollaback! community 'has their back': humanising the reporting experience, even when it happens anonymously online. Such responses emphasise acceptance, empathy and a sense of community outrage that street harassment is not okay, and allow 'members of stigmatized groups...[to] evaluate themselves in comparison with others who are like them rather than with members of the dominant culture. The in-group may provide a reappraisal of the stressful condition, yielding it less injurious to psychological well-being' (Meyer, 2003). Support and encouragement allows for healing, and helps survivors to resist the more common reaction of internalising the shame of the harassment.

The psychological benefits to people who feel able to respond to their harassers are numerous. Countless user submissions describe the relief and even uplifting feelings associated with talking back to their harassers. On the Hollaback! website, Asasia (2011) recounts:

> Now sure, it wasn't the most clever comment in the world. It wasn't the toughest either. It wasn't revolutionary or life changing, or anything. But it made me feel good. It felt good knowing that I stood up to those boys and put them in their place. It felt good to let them know that I meant business and I wasn't going to put up with their harassment. It felt good to be able to walk away with no regrets other than not saying something cooler.
>
> For the rest of the walk I felt great and I told my stepmom about it immediately when I got home, then popped right on here at Hollaback! to share my story with other girls. For the first time, at sixteen years old, I stood up to the boys who wanted to show their superiority over me and proved that hey, I might be a girl, and a hot one at that, but I won't let anyone try to make me feel like that's all I am. (Asasia, 2011).

For many, Hollaback!'s sense of community is what empowers them to speak out against street harassment. Kristin credits that sense of community for giving her the courage to stand up to her harasser:

> I told him his version of a compliment was fucked in all directions. I told him that this wouldn't go under the rug, like so many experiences like this I've had before.
>
> He started walking away, I was making a big scene. I started stopping women on University Ave, asking them if they have ever been harassed by this man? None were, and if they were they never told me. I yelled to sisters further up the street to watch out for that 45 year old in the orange shirt with the beer gut. 'He harasses women!' I screamed. He slinked around the corner and away, tail between his legs. I am livid, hurt, vulnerable and in desperate need of reassurance. This shouldn't have to happen...to anyone! If it wasn't for Hollaback! I would have never had the guts

> to stand up and say something. I hope this humiliation
> is something he carries with him everywhere he goes.
> (Kristen, 2011)

Letty shouted after her groper, calling out his behaviour and announcing the shame he should feel at having violated her.

> A stranger grabbed my crotch on the metro today. And
> then tried to deny it and get away from me when I started
> screaming at him. Eventually he mumbled 'sorry' and
> walked away and I didn't have the energy to keep following
> him. But I'm proud of myself for yelling: 'You can't treat
> women like that! You are disgusting! You should be ashamed
> of yourself! That is unacceptable!' Next time I'll be mentally
> prepared to take the next step and report it. (Letty, 2011)

Although she was unaware of his reaction, or whether he even heard her, Letty felt empowered at having said something, and encouraged to take her response further the next time she encounters street harassment or groping. Of course, she still mentions the inevitability of 'next time', but at least she is heartened enough by having spoken up to imagine that next time as one where she might act even more powerfully.

The testimonial, community-based approach also has value to those outside the community. The frequency and severity of the harassment catalogued by women of various ages and locations provides the basis for reshaping our conception of reality to include the marginalised voices of those who are harassed. The stories collected across sites are available on the same online map, providing a sense of global community around the experience. The Hollaback! smartphone applications available internationally, in multiple languages, provide geo-mapping capabilities which can transform the reporting of street harassment anecdotes beyond that of providing solidarity to providing a tool for organisations and legislators to monitor the pervasiveness and severity of street harassment in their regions. This information can be used to agitate for action and also to further academic discussion about long-term remedies for street harassment at the local level, while supporting the identification of the issue as a global problem.

Hollaback!'s global platform unites international activists to share diverse resources and ideas and educate one another about different cultures and their approaches. The model also has the ability to harness the wide-reaching capabilities of the internet, mobile technology and global partnerships to incorporate as many perspectives as possible and to create a more accurate appraisal of street harassment and solutions that correspond to those geographic and cultural variations. The local voices and actions are then magnified as those in the network support and are supported by one another, largely through social media and e-mail. The reporting and cataloguing of the reality of this experience from the perspectives of those harassed, coupled with the international scope of the anecdotes and activist efforts, encourages state actors to notice and take action. Once the state takes action it creates a cycle where, having expressed interest in the issue, the state's involvement encourages more reporting. Study results have showed that 'women who perceived that leaders made honest efforts to stop harassment felt significantly freer to report harassment, were more satisfied with the complaint process, and reported greater commitment than those viewing leaders as more harassment tolerant' (Offerman and Malamut, 2002, 885). The more women and LGBT individuals who are reached by Hollaback! and encouraged to give voice to their experiences, the more successful the movement will be in inspiring policy and long-term, systematic change.

In the spring of 2011, the site leader of the Buenos Aires branch of Hollaback! in Argentina was threatened by a prominent local journalist, Juan Terranova at the *El Guardian* newspaper, for her outspoken response to a Coca Cola advertisement that encouraged street harassment. He explicitly threatened to physically and sexually assault her for her activism. Hollaback! demanded the journalist be fired and an apology be issued, but *El Guardian* refused. So, the Hollaback! network rallied, created petitions, and lobbied advertisers to pull their contracts from the paper until it issued an appropriate response to the published rape threats. Hollaback! convinced Fiat and Lacoste to pull their ads from the paper, which finally pressured *El Guardian* to fire Terranova and to apologise publicly. The Hollaback! network's ability to rally around the site leader demonstrated a strong showing of public support against the media attempt to silence her voice and her efforts.

The future of anti-street harassment activism

> Social practices change when the conditions that support them change…They change when the costs of the behaviour begin to exceed the rewards. (Langelan, 1993, 73)

The Hollaback! model stresses the importance of widespread public education and legislative pressure in bringing about the cultural shift necessary to end street harassment, including incorporating street harassment into middle and secondary school curricula, and encouraging employers to educate their employees about street harassment as a public health issue. These are all important steps in bringing about the cultural shift away from one of acceptance of harassment and towards awareness of its multi-layered consequences. Hollaback!'s long-term goal is that we will look back on street harassment with reactions similar to those we feel when watching *Mad Men* at the beginning of the twenty-first century. We will ask ourselves how and why people endured such behaviour, and we will feel grateful for the shift in cultural and societal attitudes. To reach this objective, Hollaback! has many more short- and long-term goals.

In the short term, Hollaback! champions the development of training and comprehensive guides for those who most often come into contact with survivors and perpetrators of street harassment, including service providers, educators, law enforcement and healthcare providers. Next, Hollaback! emphasises learning about community needs through safety audits of local neighbourhoods which will provide concrete evidence to bring to local legislatures and law-making bodies. In training and encouraging local activists on a global platform, this data and information is being collected by and from locals in the network who can then learn from, and replicate the efforts to enhance the scope of data collection and distribution. Longer-term goals include continued educational efforts and legislative outreach, but as the data develops and the movement grows, Hollaback! is poised to have robust data sets from countries spanning six continents, which will allow for larger scale academic discussion and policy change. Seizing the opportunity provided by that data, the Hollaback! leadership, based in New York City in the United States, can also expand their goals to incorporate social change relevant to their international network of activists.

Ideally, the future will be one without street harassment. Women and LGBT individuals will feel safe walking down the street. Men will not feel entitled to constantly evaluate others' bodies. The explicit perception that women and LGBT individuals are less-than, or are valued only for their sexualities, will be distant memories. While this ideal is the solution to which we should all work, realistically, that is not a short-term goal. The extent and types of harassment are difficult to ascertain 'because of what is counted as sexual harassment and, secondarily, how data on the phenomenon are collected' (Gruber, 1992, 460). The community-building, narrative form of data collection produces rich data but is often perceived as less objective. An examination of street harassment at its various intersections and within its various cultural and geographic contexts is necessary before a holistic solution can be found.

While Hollaback! works to shift culture and to lay the groundwork for reform, it also recognises that deeper legal and legislative analysis will be necessary to reach the long-term goal of uprooting street harassment from our societal landscape. Long-term solutions require legislative and legal action, both of which are blunt instruments that require extensive research and society-wide reform in order to be effective. Even when that time and energy has been expended, they are also arguably imperfect tools, as evidenced by how far workplace harassment policy and legislation still need to go in ultimately ending gender-based harassment in workplaces.

Workplace harassment is the closest model from which street harassment activists would work in establishing laws and policies, but street harassment would not be able to follow quite the same form. Though street harassment is a form of sexual harassment, it's quite different from workplace harassment. Street harassment occurs between strangers in public spaces where no formalised power structures are in play, because the streets are unbounded and less defined than the workplace, for example. Laws and policies on workplace harassment have been over 50 years in the making and, while those laws have dramatically improved workplace culture, workplace sexual harassment is still rampant and far from resolved. While streets and sidewalks often provide a hostile environment for women and LGBT individuals, there's hardly a single actor that can be held accountable for the environment created. Instead, we have to collectively hold each other accountable, and value our communities enough to recreate them as nurturing and safe environments.

However, although the process of legislative changes is long and imperfect, this has not deterred Hollaback!. Site leaders collectively met with a total of 94 elected officials around the world in 2012 and an additional 68 in 2013 (Hollaback! website, 2012 and 2013). Even if no formal laws or policies are put into place, having the awareness of an issue plaguing our cities recognised in legislation goes a long way to validating and empowering the efforts toward ending street harassment. Additionally, relationships with those officials can significantly empower local activism. Governments are able to fund and assist with research, the conducting of safety audits, the release of public service advertisements to help educate the public, and to expand the reach of activists, helping them get into schools to host educational workshops. These are resources and opportunities which they would have great difficulty in accessing on their own.

Progress within western countries is, of course, necessary, but expanding its scope to include legislative and cultural shifts in other countries where the Hollaback! network operates is an essential step in progressing from an internet-based collaboration into a movement able to create large-scale, cross-cultural social change. Much more extensive research needs to be done at an international level, examining different aspects of street harassment behaviours in order for these goals to be achieved. Important details that need to be determined are the frequency with which men harass and women experience harassment; the tenor and scope of harassment experienced by members of LGBT communities; the frequency with which women and members of LGBT communities perpetrate harassment; the degrees to which race, gender, and LGBT identity factor in to both the harasser and harassee experiences; how, and how often, street harassment limits the mobility of women and LGBT individuals, and has an impact on their willingness to enjoy access to the streets; how, and how often, that harassment escalates to violent speech or physical action; and how often physical assaults, sexual assaults, rapes, and stalking, begin with harassment. All of these variables, and many more, need to be evaluated before lasting policy solutions can be found and implemented, as they vary by country and among cultures and subcultures within each country.

While Hollaback! has incredible potential for revolutionary work, it also perpetuates problematic social power constructs. As Hollaback! expands its programming efforts outside the United States, it is essential for the organisation's leadership to expand as well, from its current arrangements where the staff and board are based in the United States, to a more globally representative leadership. This diversification of the leadership is essential for challenging street harassment at the global level and incorporating the cultural variations and legal customs unique to each location in the movement's long-term strategic planning. Additionally, having a leadership centred in the United States diminishes the potential for truly international expansion and limits access to funding for international action. In order to fully utilise their robust network of activists, Hollaback!'s long-term goals must include a diversification of the leadership and its location, as well as an expansion of their created resources to include culturally relative school and employer curricula, and legislative pressure for the implementation of acts and treaties that are relevant outside the United States. Hollaback!'s funding structure is also problematic. The decentralised leadership inherent in an international, digital network empowers active citizenship, created out of a collective need to challenged gendered access to public space. However, although Hollaback! started as a member-led collective of activists, as fundraising became a primary focus in order to pay the staff in New York, the staff began asserting themselves as the face and voice of the movement, while capitalising on the unpaid labour of the international network to continue the income stream. While the earned funds pay salaries for staff in New York, the organisation does not provide financial support to the activists on the ground, while also charging a fee for use of the 'Hollaback!' name.

In addition to the internal impediments this system creates for the networked activists to fund their work, it also creates external competition. When the New York branch publicises the work of the international leaders as part of their fundraising campaigns, it implies that the money earned would assist in that on the ground. When Hollaback! then doesn't directly fund the international site leaders, this actually impairs those individual activists from using their own work to justify additional funding as the work has already been funded through grants won by the main New York branch. Given the dearth of funds available to fund gender-based activism these issues create a cycle where the transformational work the domestic and international site leaders do is not compensated, but is used as the basis of generating funds for the New York based paid staff.

Conclusion

People experience and understand street harassment in many different ways, therefore its remedies cannot presume one uniform definition or response. When we compare it to the legislative and legal frameworks surrounding response to sexual harassment we see that such a uniform response is limiting and imperfect. If someone alleging sexual harassment cannot meet the strict conditions required by the law, s/he has no remedy. Sexual harassment in public is even more unbounded and expansive than sexual harassment in the workplace, it occurs between strangers and it is more difficult to monitor or regulate. This unbounded nature of street harassment thus calls for a similarly unbounded response; one that can adapt and respond to the behaviour in a collaborative but expansive way. Organisations and individuals must work together as part of a global society, at the personal, organisational and governmental levels, to determine street harassment's behavioural roots and create effective solutions that are focused on eliminating the offensive behaviour while supporting the people who endure the harassment. Organisations such as Hollaback! have begun to seize the opportunity provided by the internet to collaborate across cultural and social borders to create inclusive, skill-sharing spaces where meaningful, culturally sensitive and relative change can be made at local and global levels. However, they must be careful to avoid the risk that they perpetuate abuses of their networks with an over-emphasis on centralised power and finances. The global platform which the internet provides is one that enables a truly global response, not only revolutionising activism, but transforming the ways in which we relate our struggles to one another, allowing for more comprehensive, inclusive solutions. As the organisations continue to grow, they have the power and duty to expand their leadership, legislative and cultural goals beyond their home countries by harnessing the collective power of these international networks.

Presler suggests that it is time to expand the phrase 'think globally, act locally' to 'think futuristically, act daily' (Presler and Scholz, 2000, 40). By focusing on the future we want to achieve and living our lives on a daily basis in ways that actively create that future we can bring about an end to street harassment and a cultural ethos that actively condemns gender-based violence.

Note

[1] Debra Gilbert and Anna Kegler's assistance with the research and organisation for this article is sincerely appreciated.

References

Asamblea Nacional, 2015, *Anteproyecto de Ley 177. Que previene, prohibe y sanciona el hostigamiento, acoso callejero, acoso sexual, acecho, favoritismo, sexismo y racismo en todos los ámbitos*, Asamblea Nacional Panama, www.asamblea.gob.pa/antproy/2015_a_177.pdf

Asasia, 2011, Not yours!, *hollaback!,* www.ihollaback.org/blog/2011/09/29/asasia-not-yours

De La Baume, M, 2012, France passes a tougher sexual harassment law, *The New York Times*, http://rendezvous.blogs.nytimes.com/2012/07/31/france-passes-a-tougher-sexual-harassment-law

Fahmy, A, 2014, Towards a safer city – Sexual harassment in greater Cairo: Effectiveness of crowd sourced data, *HarassMap*, http://harassmap.org/en/resource-center/research-studies

France 24, 2012, French parliament adopts sexual harassment law, www.france24.com/en/20120801-france-parliament-unanimously-adopts-new-law-sexual-harassment

Gayle, HD, 2012, Look to women for a better future, *Investing in women and girls: An Independent Supplement by Mediaplanet to USAToday*, http://doc.mediaplanet.com/all_projects/5706.pdf, which is the original source and is active

Gruber, JE, 1992, A typology of personal and environmental sexual harassment: Research and policy implications for the 1990s, *Sex Roles* 26, 11/12, 447–64

Hassan, RM, 2010, *Clouds in Egypt's sky. Sexual harassment: From verbal harassment to rape. A sociological study*, UNFPA, http://egypt.unfpa.org/Images/Publication/2010_03/6eeeb05a-3040-42d2-9e1c-2bd2e1ac8cac.pdf

Hesford, WS, 1999, Reading rape stories: Material rhetoric and the trauma of representation, *College English* 62, 2, 192–221

Hill, A, Jowit, J, 2012, Sexist remarks and wolf-whistles could become criminal offences, *Guardian*, www.guardian.co.uk/society/2012/mar/08/sexist-comments-to-become-criminal-offence

Johnston, T, 2011, 'Smashing the masher': The early women's movement against street harassment in America, *Gender News from the Clayman Institute for Gender Research*, http://docslide.us/documents/smashing-the-masher-the-early-womens-movement-against-street-harassment-in-america.html

Kearl, H, 2010, *Stop street harassment: Making public places safe and welcoming for women*, Westport, CT: Praeger Publishers

Kearl, H, 2011, New anti-sexual harassment bill proposed in Chile, *Stop Street Harassment*, www.stopstreetharassment.org/2011/05/new-anti-sexual-harassment-bill-proposed-in-chile

Kristin's Story, 2011, Taken off guard, *hollaback!*, www.ihollaback.org/blog/2011/09/14/kristins-story-taken-off-guard

Langelan, M, 1993, *Back off! How to confront and stop sexual harassment and harassers*, New York: Fireside/Simon and Schuster

Lankasri News, 2011, 70% sexual harassment in public transport, *Lankasri*, http://eng.lankasri.com/view.php?2eTm42c2CA342AYza00xOY3d4Alx22d5Kde3OMo3acABB2

Meyer, IH, 2003, Prejudice, social stress, and mental health in lesbian, gay, and bisexual populations: Conceptual issues and research evidence, *NIH Public Access*, www.ncbi.nlm.nih.gov/pmc/articles/PMC2072932/

Norris, J, Feldman-Summers, S, 1982, Factors related to the psychological impacts of rape on the victim, *Journal of Abnormal Psychology* 90, 6, 562–7

Offerman, LR, Malamut, AB, 2002, When leaders harass: The impact of target perceptions of organizational leadership and climate on harassment reporting and outcomes, *Journal of Applied Psychology* 87, 5, 885–93

Ojeda, H, 2015, Peruvian Gov't enacts sexual harassment prevention law, *Peru This Week*, www.peruthisweek.com/news-peruvian-govt-enacts-sexual-harassment-prevention-law-105671

Presler, J, Scholz, SJ, 2000, Peacemaking and procedural justice: A critique an article, in J Presler, SJ Scholz (eds) *Peacemaking: Lessons from the past, visions for the future*, pp 33–50, Leiden and Boston, MA: Brill Academic Publishers

Riger, S, 2000, *Tranforming psychology: Gender in theory and practice*, Oxford: Oxford University Press

Saudi Gazette, 2012, Shoura finalizes draft law on sexual harassment

Times of India, 2012, Women-only bus service launched in Delhi, http://timesofindia.indiatimes.com/city/delhi/Women-only-bus-service-launched-in-Delhi/articleshow/16577239.cms

Ullman, S, 1996, Social reactions, coping strategies, and self-blame attributions in adjustment to sexual assault, *Psychology of women quarterly* 20, 505–26

Valente, M, 2010, Making Latin America's cities women-friendly, *Inter Press Service*, www.ipsnews.net/2010/05/making-latin-americas-cities-women-friendly

Williams, LS, 1984, The classic rape: When do victims report?, *Social problems* 31, 4, 459–67

FIVE

New gender-political impulses from Eastern Europe: the case of Pussy Riot

Eva Maria Hinterhuber and Gesine Fuchs
(in collaboration with Anica Waldendorf) [1]

The phenomenon of Pussy Riot: an introduction

Some of the most intriguing and exciting impulses for gender-political protest in recent years have come from Eastern Europe, thereby contradicting the conventional (western) wisdom that feminism does not resonate well with Eastern values, norms and experiences. This is true for the provocative body-politics of the Ukrainian group Femen which were displayed in various contexts by diverse actors in order to protest against a wide array of patriarchal evils (for a critical account of Femen, see O'Keefe, 2014; for a comparison with Pussy Riot, see Channell, 2014). It equally applies to the oppositional Russian punk band Pussy Riot, the pictures of whose members – young Russian women in bright summer dresses and colourful balaclavas performing a 'punk prayer for freedom' (Pussy Riot, 2012a) who were subsequently convicted for 'hooliganism motivated by religious hatred' (Elder, 2012) – have gone around the world, procuring an unexpected reach for their agenda.

Anchored in Russian traditions of art activism, including certain characteristics of the Russian women's movement as well as incorporating specific western feminist thought and practices, Pussy Riot directs its protest against the increasingly authoritarian state and its interconnectedness with an autocratic church hierarchy, questions hierarchical gender relations and, additionally, claims to criticise the current economic order. Due to the specific forms of expression they adopt, their spectacular actions and their recent history of criminal prosecution, Pussy Riot has been able to spread its political, feminist and capitalism-critical message to a national and international public.

Its impact has been mixed, although it has probably been higher on the international level than in Russia itself.

The fascinating phenomenon of Pussy Riot takes centre stage in this chapter. We are not alone in choosing it as a research subject: Pussy Riot has sparked not only the interest of media, civil society and politics, but also that of academia. Sociology and contemporary history has placed Pussy Riot in the context of the (second) spring of Russia's civil society on the eve of Duma and the presidential elections in 2011/2012 (Gabowitsch, 2013). Political scientists have analysed the regime's repressive reaction against Pussy Riot as a successful attempt at stabilisation (Smyth and Soboleva, 2014), while others scrutinised strategies of media manipulation (for example, Smirnova, 2012). The Pussy Riot trial also serves as an example of the endemic problems of the rule of law in Russia (for instance Storch, 2013; Koenig, 2014). Attention has also been paid to Pussy Riot's 'Punk Prayer' in the context of state–church relations, the Russian Orthodox Church (ROC) and Russian religiosity (for instance Denysenko, 2013; Willems, 2013). Another body of mainly critical work has focused on western reactions and re-enforcements of old images of Russia in the aftermath of the Pussy Riot trial (Tochka, 2013; Steinholt, 2013; Yusupova, 2014). Equally important are texts that contextualise Pussy Riot in contemporary art movements and the post-Soviet gender order (Steinholt, 2013; Rüthers, 2012). Last but not least, recent work has analysed the feminism of Pussy Riot and its interconnections with Russian feminist traditions as well as with the development of informal feminism (Johnson, 2014; Sperling, 2014).

We consider the insights of many of the approaches named above but classify our contribution to this volume into the latter context. Our underlying hypotheses are the following: first, we argue that Pussy Riot implicitly takes an emancipatory standpoint in the sense that Nancy Fraser proposes: 'a standpoint from which domination can be identified and challenged from wherever it is manifested' (Fraser, 2013, 233). Within society *and* in the economy Pussy Riot identifies, criticises and challenges domination (not only patriarchal) as well as power relations in state and society in a comprehensive manner: in their context, the new state authoritarianism, the interconnection of the state and the Orthodox Church, renewed traditional gender regimes, and they also challenge the growing inequalities in the economic system. Second, Pussy Riot combines western impulses with Russian traditions of feminism and action art to produce new forms of protest. These methods have successfully generated domestic and international publicity for their claims and demands. Third, the success of Pussy

Riot's specific approach is that it confronts different threats in different settings, thus demonstrating that the challenges differ between the national and the international contexts.

In order to address the key problematic raised throughout this volume, namely the extent to which CSOs promote women's emancipation, we draw primarily upon source material created by Pussy Riot itself, including lyrics, publications, blog posts and statements made by the group and its members in interviews, press releases and during their trial. Altogether, this corpus includes approximately 40 texts. Due to space limits, only actually cited sources are included in the bibliography.

Our study relies on qualitative text analysis, which is well suited to exploring the intentions, ideological position and strategies of the civil society actor at stake. Structures and identification schemes provided in the texts are decisive; the authors' intention to produce these effects comes second. In our data analysis we followed the interpretation procedure suggested by Meuser and Nagel (1991), consisting of the following five steps: paraphrasing, thematic sequencing, topical comparison, sociological conceptualisation and theoretical generalisation (Meuser and Nagel, 1991, 457–64). The outcome of this approach, especially of the last two steps, is reflected in the following discussion.

The conditions for feminist activism: the state, religion and civil society in contemporary Russia

The 'Putin system' and civil society

There is a broad consensus that the level of democracy in Russia has fallen steadily since the turn of the millennium (Stykow, 2010, 74f). Under the 'Putin system' (Mommsen and Nußberger, 2008) '[t]he reforms of recent years [fortified] the autonomy of the presidential executive body, which has been consolidated as dominating not only the state apparatus and the administration, but also non-political actors' (Stykow, 2010, 89). As a result, democratic institutions are not functioning; the Russian parliament seems to be part of the executive. The rule of law has yet to be successfully implemented. Corruption is widespread. Due to the current legal situation the foundation of new political parties is hindered and political competition is not taking place. The media is state-controlled (Quiring, 2006). Economic policy under Putin is assessed ambivalently, especially concerning the prominent role of raw materials. However, the fact that social inequality has reached unprecedented levels is without controversy. For example, 'the difference between the incomes of the richest 10 per cent of Russians and poorest 10 per cent increased from 4 to almost 17 times' since the beginning of the market transition in 1991, and 'one per cent of the richest people in Russia now own 71 per cent of the country's wealth' (Oxfam, 2014, 3, citing the Russian Federal State Statistics Service).

Fundamental socio-political reform is still missing; instead, Fruchtmann (2012, 17) sees the real success of social policy under Putin as being able to avoid social protest such as industrial action and distribution conflicts.

The attitude of the Russian state towards civil society can be described as paternalist, if not authoritarian. Increasingly, civil society groups are marginalised and perceived as 'dissidents' (Evans, 2006, 155). A number of contradictory laws dealing with civil society severely hamper civic activities (Lang, 2004; Hinterhuber and Rindt, 2004; Bidder, 2012). Despite these circumstances, Russian civil society experienced a new spring in the wake of the allegedly forged presidential and Duma elections in 2011/2012. The following mass protests in the capital, as well as in dozens of other cities, were said to be the biggest demonstrations since the collapse of the Soviet Union and relied on new segments of the population (for instance the middle class) that had not been active before (Siegert, 2012). Additionally, new, unconventional forms of political participation developed (such as flash mobs or mobilisation via the Russian version of Facebook, *vkontakte*), using new social media. The state reacted with an iron fist, with high numbers of arrests and long prison sentences. Yet under increasing pressure, the organised and the informal parts of Russian civil society are still active. Nowadays it is civil society organisations rather than political parties that are the most independent actors in Russian politics; some even see them as substitutes for strong and autonomous parties (Siegert, 2010).

The leading democracy indices (EIU, 2014) now classify Russia as an authoritarian regime. However, Russian officials do not interpret this development as a backward step in terms of democracy. On the contrary, it is presented under the guiding principle of sovereign democracy as 'an attractive and viable alternative to the idea of the representative liberal democracy of the West' (Stykow, 2010, 90).

A close connection: the church and the state in Russia

Current relations between church and state are substantially influenced by two important developments in the twentieth century. After the Bolshevik revolution in 1917, the church was subjected to repression to such an extent that it was brought to the brink of its existence (Bremer, 2010). In Soviet times however, collaboration between church representatives and government agencies existed, including collaboration with the KGB (Bremer, 2010). A critical reappraisal of this history is still missing.

After the collapse of the Soviet Union, the percentage of those who call themselves believers rose steadily (Bremer, 2010). In 2010, three-quarters of the population committed themselves to Orthodoxy. The public discourse reflects a 'pro-orthodox consensus' (Willems, 2012, 180). The high degree of religiosity and appreciation of the church does not mean, however, that 'the people lead their lives according to rules of the Church' (Bremer, 2010, 450).

State and church representatives emphasise that Russia is a 'secular' state (Willems, 2012, 181) and both sides seek partnership, mutual aid and assistance (Willems, 2012). However, the preamble of the 1997 law on religion emphasises that Orthodoxy has played a central role in Russian history as well as in the development of Russian culture and spirituality (Willems, 2012). Accordingly, the Russian Orthodox Church 'has access to virtually all state institutions; partly relations between Russian Orthodox Church and the State are governed through formal agreements, in part, they simply exist in fact' (Bremer, 2010, 448). The Russian Orthodox Church emphasises 'the loyalty of the church and the believers to the State' (Bremer, 2010, 449). The Church leadership, namely the head, Patriarch Kirill, evaluated the authoritarian developments under Putin as the restoration of order after the chaotic 1990s. It is 'Russia's modernisation in accordance with "traditional Russian organisation principles of society" which distinguishes itself from "Western individualism"' (Willems, 2012, 185). Conversely, '[f] or the Russian State the Church represents an institution that gives it legitimacy' (Bremer, 2010, 448) and is a symbol for Russia's greatness.

Gender relations in Russia

Gender relations face a lot of challenges in today's Russia. In contrast to the Soviet era, women have basically disappeared from institutional politics (Kraatz and Zvinkliene, 2003; Cook and Nechemias, 2009). Horizontal and vertical gender segregation in the labour market is high and care work is unequally divided between men and women. Women suffer from both old and new forms of sexualised violence, such as domestic violence and trafficking in women (Khodyreva and Tsvetkova, 2000; Karbstein and Hinterhuber, 2003). Neo-traditional gender stereotypes dominate in public discourse. The Soviet model of emancipation – namely gainful employment for all and possibly the socialisation of household chores – has been discredited; this had already started in the last years of the Soviet Union (Zdravomyslova and Temkina, 2005) when the model was accused of responsibility for the 'feminisation' of the state, for emasculating men, suppressing birth rates and even ecological disaster (Bloemsma, 1993). The media spread contradictory westernised ideals of femininity and the Orthodox Church propagated restorative women's roles and family models (Cheauré, 2010).

Russia's women's movement, however, has a long and rich tradition, and during the last two decades women's organisations were founded all over the country (for a discussion of the spectrum, see Hinterhuber and Strasser-Camagni, 2011). In the 1990s and at the beginning of the millennium, the Russian women's movement achieved some notable successes in networking, but also in influencing legislation. However, given the lack of implementation, such political successes are primarily symbolic (Hinterhuber and Strasser-Camagni, 2011). But optimism evaporated in the Putin era and the small movement was partly demobilised (Cheauré, 2010). After Perestroika, Russian feminism has increasingly shifted towards an empirically fruitful, yet politically confined academic gender studies discourse (Gabowitsch, 2013). The women's movement is thus neither rooted in Russian society nor does it have a broad impact.

Pussy Riot: feminist 'anti-Putinism'

In contrast, the explicitly feminist punk band Pussy Riot was founded at the end of September 2011 by about a dozen women in their 20s (Windisch, 2012). In interviews (Tupikin, 2011; Khomenko, 2012) the group members named the Arab Spring, and especially the strong participation of women within it, as inspiration for the founding of the group, and described their political activism as motivated by 'anti-Putinism'. Pussy Riot focus their attention on developing critiques of the political structures and their entanglements with the Russian Orthodox Church, alongside the existing Russian gender regime, as well as criticism of the current (global) economic system.

Since October 2011 (before the aforementioned election period) the members of Pussy Riot have staged performances in public places without prior notice, thus reminiscent of flash mobs. The chosen 'stages' included metro stations, the roof of a bus and Red Square (Gabowitsch, 2013, 189). They are always masked and wear their typical outfits of brightly coloured leggings, shirts and balaclavas. After the performances videos are released on YouTube. Members of Pussy Riot would also regularly express their opinions in interviews, blogs and via Twitter.

With these actions, members of Pussy Riot broke the rules from the beginning. Nevertheless, reactions to their performances initially remained cautious, and neither civil nor criminal charges were brought against them. However, this changed with the so-called 'Punk Prayer', an illegal concert performed in the Christ the Saviour Cathedral in Moscow, the centre of the Russian Orthodox Church, on 21 February 2012, staged to protest against the imminent re-election of Putin as President of the Russian Federation. Given the patriarchal foundation of both the State and the Church, the gender political bias of the action gave the protest an additional explosive force. On the initiative of church representatives, the prosecutor's office initiated an investigation (Gabowitsch, 2013). Three members of the band, Nadezhda Tolokonnikova, Maria Aljochina and Ekaterina Samutsevich, were arrested in March 2012. In the same month, the head of the Russian Orthodox Church, Patriarch Kirill, sharply attacked Pussy Riot in a sermon. Surprisingly, he did not justify his reproach of blasphemy with religious arguments, but stressed 'Putin's important role and the role of the Church in Russia's military successes' (Gabowitsch, 2013, 209).

The indictment against the three women of Pussy Riot referred to the excitation of religious hatred according to Article 282 of the Russian Criminal Code and to severe 'hooliganism' according to Article 213 (von Gall, 2012). The charge itself was characterised by vague wording. In the course of the trial, all legal remedies were rejected, and remand was extended several times (Amnesty International, 2012). Legal scholars in Russia and abroad sharply criticised the judgement itself (Amnesty International, 2012). After nearly six months in custody, the three women were finally convicted and sentenced to two years in labour camps for 'hooliganism motivated by religious hatred' (Elder, 2012). Thus, the court focused on the alleged insulting of the religious feelings of believers. The criticism of the ruling regime that Pussy Riot had expressed in its performance was ignored. The group subsequently appealed against the judgement and filed a lawsuit against Russia at the European Court of Human Rights in Strasbourg. Because a security guard had overwhelmed Samutsevich at the start of the performance in the cathedral, her appeal was upheld. However, the applications for parole for Aljochina and Tolokonnikova, both mothers of small children, were rejected, and the two women were imprisoned in different labour camps. As far as possible, both continued to spread their political convictions within prison and to the outside world, for example through hunger strikes. Aljochina used a hunger strike to protest against not being allowed to participate in a hearing and Tolokonnikova used it to protest against the detention conditions in the labour camp. Moreover, Tolokonnikova also protested through her public correspondence with the prominent Marxist philosopher Slavoj Žižek (Tolokonnikova and Žižek, 2014). The other members of Pussy Riot were also not silenced, as they organised support and accompanied the whole process from trial to jail with critical publications.

In December 2013, after 21 months of detention, Aljochina and Tolokonnikova were released during an amnesty launched by the State Duma shortly before the beginning of Sochi Winter Olympics. Following their release (and in response to their experiences in prison) they founded Zona Prava (www.zonaprava.com), an NGO monitoring the rights of inmates, as well as MediaZona (www.zona.media), a news portal dealing with human rights, prisons and the judicial system. In an open letter written in February 2014, the other members of Pussy Riot stated that this new focus no longer conformed to the original aspirations of the group: feminism, separatist resistance, fighting against authoritarianism and a personality cult, and they stated that Tolokonnikova and Aljochina were no longer members of Pussy Riot. Nonetheless, both of them appeared together with the group in Sochi, where they found themselves attacked by Cossack security personnel and temporarily arrested by the local police. In quoting their attackers, Pussy Riot performed the song 'Putin will teach you to love the motherland' immediately afterwards on the site, again distributing the corresponding video clip via the internet (Williams, 2015).

These more recent activities suggest a shift in the focus and form of Tolokonnikova and Aljochina's activism; the artistic performances of the collective seem to be losing weight in comparison with their legal protection activism carried out by journalistic means. The most recent published video to date, 'I can't breathe', differs in many ways from the previous ones. This video is performed exclusively by Aljochina and Tolokonnikova without the typical balaclavas, but also differing from their previous performances in terms of the style of music, the language used (English instead of Russian) and the focus – racism in the American police force – on a subject outside of their home country (Williams, 2015).

Strong reactions have accompanied the group since its foundation: with their performance of the 'Punk Prayer', and the criminal charges brought against them, Pussy Riot caught the attention of the media both in Russia and beyond its borders. In Russia, the population seemed to be on the side of the political and religious authorities:

according to surveys nearly two-thirds of the population assessed their action as 'hooliganism' or even as a targeted attack on the Orthodox Church (Levada). For the general Russian public, Pussy Riot's protest was not easy to understand as a meaningful and feminist protest, mainly due to an 'informational vacuum' (Yusopova, 2014, 605). Even opposition actors, while denouncing the trial and imprisonment, judged the forms of protest as idiotic or as a failure (Yusopova, 2014, 606). However, many within the Russian civil society defended the group, including human rights organisations as well as anonymous supporters who appropriated the symbolism of the group in mass protests. Moreover, Russian lawyers described the trial as a 'judicial scandal' (Die Tageszeitung, 2012). Genri Reznik, president of the Moscow chamber of lawyers, publicly accused the court of contempt of law (www.novayagazeta.ru/politics/54157.html). Even within the Russian Orthodox Church there was criticism, ranging from the lower levels to prominent Orthodox officials (Willems, 2012).

In the international context, the repressive reaction of the state led to massive criticism from politicians, media and civil society. Transnational networks in support of the activists were formed (most prominently amongst them the freepussyriot.org website and twitter feed). Furthermore, Amnesty International acknowledged Tolokonnikova and Aljochina as political prisoners (Amnesty International, 2012).

The national and international attention on Pussy Riot is perhaps what is really special about the case, because from a legal perspective the trial is no exception but rather a typical example of the shortcomings of the Russian rule of law (von Gall, 2012), the majority of which rarely attract international or even national attention (Gabowitsch, 2013, 194). The different reception Pussy Riot received may also be connected to their specific form of activism, encompassing political, religiously motivated, and last, but not least, feminist protest.

Pussy Riot as political protest

First of all, Pussy Riot criticises political power, and thus, their work has to be interpreted in the context of civil society protests against Putin and in the tradition of artistic political protest rather than being seen as purely punk music. On the eve of the election, Pussy Riot positioned itself politically by supporting the claims raised during the mass demonstrations (for instance in the online interview with Khomenko, 2012) and also through their virally distributed performances. This specific form of expression is closely connected with Pussy Riot's roots in the art scene. Individual members of the group include the Moscow faction of the art group Voina (Russian for 'war'). Since 2007, Voina has attracted more and more attention with spectacular, extreme and increasingly political actions (Gabowitsch, 2013). 'Performance artists were among the first who protested after the parliamentary elections and gave a voice to the emerging movement' (Gabowitsch, 2013, 195). Activists expressed their political opposition through the media of fine arts, performances, street art, films, music and other forms. The liaison between arts and politics has a long tradition in Russia (thus beyond the mass protests against electoral fraud) and occurs throughout the country. Firmly placed in this context, Pussy Riot is thus, contrary to popular perception, not primarily a punk rock band, but a radical political performance collective (Willems, 2013).

This assessment is reinforced by a review of the lyrics of Pussy Riot's songs, which are dedicated to political topics and include significant criticism of the current political system, usually using rude and offending words as the titles demonstrate, for example, 'Putin is wetting himself', 'Kill the sexist', 'Death to prison, freedom to protest', 'Putin lights up the fires', or 'Putin will teach you to love the Motherland'.

Pussy Riot position themselves as 'non-authoritarian leftists' (Pussy Riot, 2011b) in relation to Soviet state socialism. Their political agenda comprises a critical assessment of Russia's political regime with reference to the given democratic deficits and an analysis of the role of the people in maintaining it. They advocate more 'self-governance... and rights' for the citizenry (Pussy Riot, 2011b). In their view the rise of activism and the concomitant development of civil society will act to fight authoritarian tendencies in the Russian state (Tolokonnikova, 2012a).

Pussy Riot as a religiously motivated protest

Pussy Riot's activities are also directed against the Russian Orthodox Church and its close connection with the political regime. Their protest is a synthesis of religious arguments and references showing a profound knowledge of and rootedness in Christianity. The 'Punk Prayer' illustrates this fusion: the song changes from 'shrill punk shouting' (Gabowitsch, 2013, 188) to a chant adapted from Rachmaninoff's 'Bogoroditse Devo, Raduisya' (Ave Maria); the accompanying dance also reflects religious practices (Bremer, 2012). Meanwhile the lyrics are directed against the political system, the interdependence of the Church and secular power and against traditional gender stereotypes. The coarse invective and severe insult is directed towards the interconnectedness between political and church leadership, namely at President Putin and Patriarch Kirill, but not at God or Mary Mother of God or other Christian beliefs. A crucial detail is that the performance took place during the 'butter week', which is the Orthodox carnival, and continued the tradition of the 'fools in Christ' ('jurodivye'); 'We were looking for real honesty and found these properties in the jurodstwo [holy stupidity] of Punk' (Tolokonnikova, 2012b,106). Representatives of the Russian Orthodox Church shared this interpretation. For example, Andrej Kurajev, an influential upper deacon and publicist, who is not known as a liberal, supported this perspective (Gabowitsch, 2013).

Although the activists chose the symbolic centre of the Russian Orthodox Church with the Christ the Saviour Cathedral as their venue, they deliberately did not perform during religious services, so as to not disturb any religious celebrations (Aljochina, 2012a). However, given the outstanding importance of the iconostasis, the wall decorated with icons that separates the sanctuary and the nave in Orthodox Churches, as well as the Ambo, the elevated place in front of the iconostasis, by choosing to stage the performance there, their performance was undoubtedly a severe violation of internal church regulations. The activists justified the entering of the sanctuary – especially by women – as a conscious challenge to the church's ban. In doing so, they wanted to criticise the Russian Orthodox Church's conservative worldview (Pussy Riot, 2012a, 2012b, 2012d). Elsewhere (in an online interview with Moiseev, 2012) they claim that '[t]he Orthodox Church must give up its sexist rhetoric'.

In fact, the argument in the 'Punk Prayer' has a Christian framework: Pussy Riot invoke the Virgin Mary, claim her as their patron saint and appeal for true faith, juxtaposing their prayer to the hypocrisy, the secularisation, the penchant for mundane luxury and finally the tendency towards corruption of the Orthodox Church leaders. In blog posts, the Orthodox Church is characterised as 'an instrument of political control' (Pussy Riot, 2012f) and is accused of manipulating religion for political purposes (Pussy Riot, 2012d, 2012f).

Religious references already existed in Pussy Riot's previous song texts, including a former invocation of Mary Mother of God (in 'Putin has pissed himself'; see Pussy Riot, 2012c, 40). Even in the wake of the performance, the three defendants remained consistent in this regard: they refer to themselves not only as believers, but locate themselves within the Russian Orthodox Church (Aljochina, 2012a). And in fact, Marija Aljochina was part of an Orthodox youth organisation (the *danilowzy*) and worked as a volunteer with disabled children in church institutions (Gabowitsch, 2013). In their letters from prison as well as in their opening statements and closing arguments in court all three defendants located themselves within a Christian frame of reference. They began their written statements with quotes from the Bible (Pussy Riot, 2012d), they regularly referred to Biblical passages (Aljochina, 2012b; Tolokonnikova, 2012b) and describe Jesus Christ as a role model who influences their thinking and behaviour, for example, in terms of dealing with marginalised groups (Tolokonnikova, 2012b). Their beliefs are also evident in a letter from the group as a whole, addressed to Patriarch Kirill (Pussy Riot, 2012d). Samutsevich (2012, 103) described their specific standpoint: 'In our performance we dared, without the Patriarch's blessing, to combine the visual image of Orthodox culture and protest culture, suggesting to smart people that Orthodox culture belongs not only to the Russian Orthodox Church, the Patriarch and Putin, that it might also take the side of civic rebellion and protest in Russia.'

Pussy Riot as feminist protest

Another important aspect of Pussy Riot's protest is its gender-political component. According to Gabowitsch, they have developed a 'unique aesthetic' and a correspondent gender-political 'action repertoire' which 'deliberately offended against social conventions' (Gabowitsch, 2013, 217). The members of Pussy Riot openly identify themselves as feminists and call upon others to do the same, even though in Russia, as elsewhere, 'feminism' has become a stigmatised word. However, Pussy Riot challenge the more common perception of feminism that defines it over-simplistically as the oppression of men by claiming (in an online interview with Tupikin, 2011) that feminism is about 'fighting with the image of the "real man"', which is cultivated in the Russian society. 'Feminism rejects instilling such images, relieving men and women from the detrimental pressure.'

Theoretically, Pussy Riot draw (in the same interview, Tupikin, 2011) on the whole range of feminist theory building in the last two centuries (from liberal to radical to postcolonial, as well as poststructuralist gender theories) referring to the works of Emily Pankhurst, Simone de Beauvoir, Kate Millett, Shulamith Firestone, Andrea Dworkin, Gayatri Spivak, bell hooks, Rosi Braidotti and Judith Butler. On a panel together with Judith Butler and Rosy Braidotti they also underline their inspiration to the historical roots and traditions of Russian feminism as embodied through examples such as Aleksandra Kollontai (www.youtube.com/watch?v=BXbx_P7UVtE, at minute 9'00). In the same panel (at minute 14'45), Pussy Riot argues that in Russia all these strands of feminism have been repressed, because they have never been openly debated. And because feminism has not developed in the last decades, women need to invoke classical feminist strategies such as consciousness raising.

Within this broad continuum of feminist theory, Pussy Riot places itself within the post-structuralist tradition. However, Russian feminist activists expressed ambivalence about Pussy Riot's stance; some criticised their agenda for being only superficially feminist; some suggested that Pussy Riot didn't really understand feminism. Their critique noted that some of the song texts invoked gender stereotypes rather than dismantling them. They also questioned whether Pussy Riot's adoption of 'adolescent shock value' resulted in media attention that reinforced these stereotypes while more grass-root initiatives to overturn stereotypes 'fly under the radar' (Sperling, 2014, 600).

Pussy Riot's response is that feminism has a wide range of tasks to fulfil and that different theoretical approaches exist. In a documented conversation (Volkova and Pussy Riot, 2011), they put it as follows: 'Poststructural feminism is what we base our actions on. This approach puts forward the issue of masquerade as a form of ridiculing and redefining classical gender norms and roles. There are feminists who do not share the ideas of the subversive revolution, but it is not a ground for rejecting the parody strategy' (Volkova and Pussy Riot, 2011).

Furthermore, Pussy Riot argue that 'feminism and freedom is not something you can inherit from your ancestors. Each generation must struggle for it' (www.youtube.com/watch?v=BXbx_P7UVtE, at minute 13'30).

The result of their own struggle is to combine theoretical approaches and feminist praxis, arising from western as well as specific Russian traditions. Their texts, music, appearance and forms of action follow in the tradition of the Riot Grrrls, the feminist subcultural movement that was founded in the 1990s and is rooted in the US punk scene (Pegelow and Engelmann, 2011; Gottlieb and Wald, 1995). Riot Grrls is still active today, and provides a suitable framework for gender-political engagement in contemporary Russia as well as in the US.

At the same time, the activists of Pussy Riot also build on traditions of the Russian women's movement. The worship of the Christian Mother of God is widespread in Russia, and female-dominated as well as feminist civil society organisations refer with some regularity to Mary (Hinterhuber, 2012). Thus, Pussy Riot's approach is surprisingly in harmony with that of Russian women's organisations in their appeal to the Blessed Mother as a strong female figure in the Russian Orthodox Church challenging women 'not to resign to the existing conditions, not humbly bow to the fate, but to rebel against injustice and oppression' (Schreiner, 1994, 18). The 'unholy intercession of the Mother of God' (Windisch, 2012) by Pussy Riot in the Moscow cathedral can thus be interpreted as a symbolic political quotation. Analogous to the work of the Riot Grrrl movement the members of Pussy Riot adopt traditional gendered stereotypes in order to subvert them to criticise the existing system.

The existing system gives them a lot of incentives to do so: first, Pussy Riot makes a connection between authoritarianism, traditional gender relations and sexism. Putin is perceived as a symbol of sexism and patriarchy, continually making sexist statements and disregarding gender-political achievements such as the UN Convention on the Elimination of all forms of Discrimination Against Women (CEDAW, www.un.org/womenwatch/daw/cedaw) (Pussy Riot in an online interview with Moiseev, 2012). In order to strengthen the protest against the Putin system gender issues should form an integral and important part of a comprehensive, and thus persuasive protest agenda.

Second, the lyrics in Pussy Riot's songs like 'Kill the sexist' target the sexism inherent in everyday life, as, for example, in the uneven workload between the genders – the 'triple working day for women' (Pussy Riot, 2011c).

Third, Pussy Riot also tackles issues of reproductive health, commenting on the lack of protest against the limiting of women's rights in the newly tightened abortion law that has resulted in women having to choose between paying for a costly abortion or to giving birth to an unwanted child (Pussy Riot, 2011a).

Finally, Pussy Riot's commitment to the rights of homosexuals is particularly noteworthy in the Russian context (Gabowitsch, 2013). Homosexuality was decriminalised in Russia in 1993 and for a short period following homosexuals felt able to appear openly in public. In larger cities, a small lesbian, gay, bisexual, transgender, queer and intersex (LGBTQI) 'scene' came into being alongside the development of single-issue civil society organisations. These groups articulated their interests and defended their rights. Such modest achievements, however, soon faced strong resistance. The Gay Pride parades held in Moscow since 2006 are regularly broken up with violence; mass demonstrations and assaults against homosexuals regularly accompany the parades. Now, through the legislation enacted in 2013 that rendered statements about same-sex lifestyles 'propaganda of homosexualism', homosexuality has again been criminalised. Pussy Riot argues that such legislation is not marginal, but is characteristic of the authoritarian nature of the regime. Pussy Riot's lyrics and their participation in Gay

Pride demonstrations have 'made the group for many in the LGBT scene an icon' (Gabowitsch, 2013, 223).

Pussy Riot and their critique of the economic system

Pussy Riot's lyrics only criticise economic domination and the newly developed capitalism in passing, for example in their suggestion that Patriarch Kirill is taking bribes from Putin in exchange for political support (Pussy Riot, 2012a). Here, they face a dilemma shared with many feminist grassroots organising in former state socialist societies: the old regimes derived much of their legitimacy from their provision of social security, egalitarianism and full employment, as well as their stated aims of emulating communist ideals. In order to distance themselves from these regimes and to frame themselves as progressive, democratic and emancipatory, they cannot easily resort to this old rhetoric. NGOs in the region, alongside western donor organisations have thus been harshly criticised for promoting neoliberalism as an emancipatory response to such regimes and through filling the gaps that emerged after social retrenchment (Fraser, 2009; Funk, 2006). Yet, the reality is more complex, and since the mid-2000s economic rights are entering feminist agendas in the region (Fuchs, 2013). In Russia especially, economic rights and practical gender interests are being reframed, such that violence against women is reframed to incorporate economic violence and domination (Hemment, 2004; Hinterhuber, 2012).

After their trial, however, Pussy Riot developed a more outspoken criticism of global capitalism, as an exchange of letters with the philosopher Slavoj Žižek illustrates. Tolokonnikova (Tolokonnikova and Žižek, 2014, 54) emphasises that Pussy Riot is part of the movement to bring 'criticism, creativity, co-creation, experimentation and constantly provocative events' into the newly constituted capitalist order in Russia (*The Guardian*, 2013). Tolokonnikova's critique is aimed at Russia and the 'west'. She attempts to reveal the lie of modern capitalism; 'modern capitalism has a deep interest in seeing that you and I believe the system runs completely on principles of free creativity, limitless growth, and diversity, and that the flip side – millions of people enslaved by all-powerful and (take it from me) fantastically stable standards of production – remains invisible' (Tolokonnikova and Žižek, 2014, 54).

Tolokonnikova condemns what she considers to be western hypocrisy, an 'exaggerated loyalty' towards oppressive governments such as Russia; she points out that Russia could have been massively weakened by a boycott of oil and gas. According to her, the continued trade in raw materials 'shows implicit support for, even approbation of, the Russian regime (not in words, of course, but rather in the flow of capital)' (Tolokonnikova and Žižek, 2014, 67). Yet, in Russia the political and economic practices are specific: 'here I sit, in a country where the ten people who run and profit from the most important spheres of the economy are quite simply Vladimir Putin's oldest friends – buddies from school, the people he plays sport with, cronies from his KGB days' (Tolokonnikova and Žižek, 2014, 68). Thus, as expressed by Tolokonnikova, Pussy Riot's political critique is of the 'from plan to clan' style of capitalism.

Conclusion

In this chapter we set out to assess the role of Pussy Riot as a civil society actor in the emancipation of women in a national as well as international setting. Pussy Riot is acting under very adverse conditions, taking high personal risks under the rule of an increasingly authoritarian state that seeks legitimation through cooperation with religious institutions, in a society deeply divided by economic inequality and in the context of a backlash against gender-political achievements. Within this context Pussy Riot cannot be regarded as merely a punk band, but clearly has to be located within the (second) spring of Russia's civil society that manifested itself in a new political movement from the eve of Duma and the presidential elections 2011/2112. Within this movement, the group expresses their political opinion via music and art. Some of their statements reflect their self-placement in the punk scene, as they are indeed insulting the head of state, alongside the head of the church and the ecclesiastical structures. They are anti-clerical, but they are not anti-religious; indeed they could even be regarded as presenting a religiously motivated protest. Against this background, Pussy Riot deserves credit for 'enrich[ing] the new protest culture with a religious dimension and – vice versa – [for] claim[ing] the area of religion for the open expression of oppositional Christian beliefs' (Gabowitsch, 2013, 213–14).

Pussy Riot also criticises the economic system, both on a global and a national level (although to a lesser extent and as a later development). Their criticism is reminiscent of Wallerstein's (2004) characterisation of the new world system as a capitalist world economy where exploitation is not limited to the borders of one's own country, but is widely exported to semi- and periphery states, resulting in whole countries being kept in poverty. The conditions in Russia's economic system are criticised for promoting corruption and nepotism, leading to a mixture of oligarchy and authoritarianism (Mommsen, 2012); and an oil-dependent west is accused for its ambivalent behaviour towards Russia.

Last but by no means least, with Pussy Riot a new generation of feminists has appeared within the Russian women's movement, bringing together western and Russian traditions and creating a new, successful, form of opposition. The members of Pussy Riot openly propagate and exemplify feminism within their own lives (Gabowitsch, 2013). It is not surprising that they have faced resistance, however, they have opened up new spaces for 'other creative feminists' such as the graphic artist Wiktorija Lomasko (Gabowitsch, 2013, 220). In a context where feminist voices had become barely audible Pussy Riot has added not only a religious, but also a gender-political dimension to the protest movements in Russia. The question, however, remains as to whether – and how – Pussy Riot's feminism can resonate sufficiently with Russian social practices and historical experiences to attract more women for the feminist cause.

Fraser (2009; 2013) defines emancipatory movements as those that protest against any actor who creates domination; they do so by identifying, criticising and challenging hierarchies wherever they appear – be it in politics, society and culture, or economy. In this sense, Pussy Riot can be interpreted as offering a comprehensive form of emancipatory activism as the group attacks authoritarian political, societal and economic developments in Russia. Pussy Riot campaigns for increased democracy and criticises the alliances between state institutions and the official church hierarchy. They consistently argue against the narrowing of social roles available to women.

One testimony for the effectiveness of their emancipatory activism is that state and church felt directly attacked by the protests as evidenced by the open and selective repression with which the state responded. Civil society remains the only political space, which is still not controlled by the Kremlin and may indeed be, at least to some extent, uncontrollable. Furthermore, the international publicity which Pussy Riot's trial received, the extent to which their appearance has become iconic, the spreading of their messages and their adaptations in diverse parts of the world demonstrates the value of their form of action.

There are challenges to Pussy Riot's approach, however, from both national and international perspectives. Whereas in Russia itself the main obstacle is that of authoritarian tendencies increasingly destroying an open public and a free civil society (and successfully avoiding an eventual support of the broader population by mobilising traditionalist feelings), in the international context co-optation, instrumentalisation and commercialisation may distort the original message of the group. An additional challenge is that of gender policy formation in an increasingly globalised world. Pussy Riot has to balance their visibility within a gender-sensitive international public, maintaining the connection with western gender activists and theorists, and not lose sight of what is going on in Russia. They must acknowledge the specific traditions as well as current difficulties of Russia's women's movement. Through their actions and their lines of argumentation, but also with their international interconnectedness they indeed created something new, sending a strong signal across the borders. The question is whether their emancipatory message will be taken into account, listened to and, above all, further developed by future gender activists both in an international and national setting.

Note

[1] The authors want to thank the editors Christina Schwabenland, Chris Lange, Sachiko Nakagawa and Jenny Onyx for their scientific inspiration, comprehensive support, and determined encouragement without which this contribution would not have come into being. Eva Maria Hinterhuber would like to dedicate this article to the memory of Martin Riesebrodt, who first motivated her to engage with the topic of Pussy Riot and, in a decisive moment, encouraged her to continue her academic career. Throughout the chapter, all translations from the original German or Russian texts into English are the authors' own.

References

Aljochina, M, 2012a, Opening courtroom statement by Masha, in The Feminist Press at the City University of New York (ed) *Pussy Riot! A punk prayer for freedom*, pp 38–40, New York and London: The Feminist Press

Aljochina, M, 2012b, Closing courtroom statement by Masha, in The Feminist Press at the City University of New York (ed) *Pussy Riot! A punk prayer for freedom*, pp 104–11, New York and London: The Feminist Press

Amnesty International, 2012, Urgent Action – Prozessbeginn, www.amnesty.de/urgent-action/ua-122-2012-3/prozessbeginn?

Bidder, B, 2012, Kreml brandmarkt Bürgerrechtler als 'ausländische Agenten', *SpiegelOnline*, www.spiegel.de/politik/ausland/ngo-in-russland-putin-brandmarkt-buergerrechtler-als-agenten-a-842259.html

Bloemsma, J, 1993, Neuzheli budushchee russkikh zhenshchin – tol'ko na kukhne? [Is the future of Russian women only in the kitchen?], *Regional'naja Politika* 3, 43–55

Bremer, T, 2010, Die orthodoxe Kirche als gesellschaftlicher Faktor in Russland, in H Pleines, H-H Schröder (eds) *Länderbericht Russland*, pp 441–56, Bonn: Bundeszentrale für Politische Bildung

Channell, E, 2014, Is sextremism the new feminism? Perspectives from Pussy Riot and Femen, *Nationalities Papers* 42, 4, 611–14

Cheauré, E, 2010, Frauen in Russland, in H Pleines, H-H Schröder (eds) *Länderbericht Russland*, pp 466–92, Bonn: Bundeszentrale für Politische Bildung

Cook, RJ, Nechemias, C, 2009, Women in the Russian State Duma, in M Rueschemeyer, SL Wolchik (eds) *Women in power in post-communist parliaments*, pp 25–59, Bloomington, IN: Indiana University Press

Denysenko, N, 2013, An appeal to Mary: An analysis of Pussy Riot's punk performance in Moscow, *Journal of the American Academy of Religion* 81, 4, 1061–92

die tageszeitung, 2012, Prozess gegen Pussy Riot: Putin macht den milden Mann, www.taz.de/!5087451/

EIU (Economist's Intelligence Unit), 2014, *The Economist's Intelligence Unit's Democracy Index 2014*, www.eiu.com/public/topical_report.aspx?campaignid=Democracy0115

Elder, M, 2012, Pussy Riot sentenced to two years in prison colony over anti-Putin protest, *Guardian*, www.theguardian.com/music/2012/aug/17/pussy-riot-sentenced-prison-putin

Evans, AB, 2006, Vladimir Putin's design for civil society, in A Evans, L Henry, L McIntosh Sundstrom (eds) *Russian civil society: A critical assessment*, pp 147–60, Armonk, NY and London: ME Sharpe

Fraser, N, 2009, Feminism, capitalism and the cunning of history, *New Left Review* 56, Mar–April, 97–117

Fraser, N, 2013, Between marketization and social protection: Resolving the feminist ambivalence, in N Fraser, *Fortunes of feminism: From state-managed capitalism to neoliberal crisis*, pp 227–41, Brooklyn, New York: Verso Books

Fruchtmann, J, 2012, Analyse: Sozialpolitik in der Krise, in Bundeszentrale für Politische Bildung (ed) *Dossier Russland,* Bonn, www.bpb.de/internationales/europa/russland/135733/analyse-sozialpolitik-in-der-krise

Fuchs, G, 2013, Using strategic litigation for women's rights: Political restrictions in Poland and achievements of the women's movement, *European Journal of Women's Studies* 20, 1, 21–43

Funk, N, 2006, Women's NGOs in Central and Eastern Europe and the former Soviet Union: The imperialist criticism, *femina politica* 15, 1, 68–83

Gabowitsch, M, 2013, *Putin kaputt?! Russlands neue Protestkultur*, Frankfurt am Main: Suhrkamp

Gottlieb, J, Wald, G, 1995, Smells like teen spirit: Riot Grrrls, Revolution und Frauen im Independent Rock, in C Eichhorn, S Grimm (eds) *Gender killer: Texte zu Feminismus und Politik*, pp 167–89, Berlin, Amsterdam: ID-Verlag

Guardian, The, 2013, Nadezhda Tolokonnikova of Pussy Riot's prison letters to Slavoj Žižek, www.theguardian.com/music/2013/nov/15/pussy-riot-nadezhda-tolokonnikova-slavoj-zizek

Hemment, J, 2004, Global civil society and the local costs of belonging: Defining violence against women in Russia, *Signs* 29, 3, 815–40

Hinterhuber, EM, 2012, *Zwischen Überlebenssicherung und Partizipation: Zivilgesellschaftliches Engagement von Frauen im Bereich Sozialwesen in Russland*, Baden-Baden: Nomos

Hinterhuber, EM, Rindt, S, 2004, *Bürgerstiftungen in Russland: Community foundations in Russia*, Berlin: Maecenata

Hinterhuber, EM, Strasser-Camagni, A, 2011, 'The new doesn't come from the new, but from reshaping the existing resources': Gender Studies und Frauenbewegung im postsozialistischen Russland, in B Binder, G Jähnert, I Kerner, E Kilian, HM Nicke (eds) *Travelling gender studies*, pp 147–68, Münster: Westfälisches Dampfboot

Johnson, JE, 2014, Pussy Riot as a feminist project: Russia's gendered informal politics, *Nationalities Papers* 42, 4, 583–90

Karbstein, I, Hinterhuber, EM, 2003, 'Ein Huhn ist kein Vogel und eine Frau kein Mensch': Der internationale Frauenhandel und Gegenstrategien von Frauenorganisationen in Russland, *Zweiwochendienst Frauen und Politik* 199, 9–10

Khodyreva, N, Tsvetkova, MG, 2000, *Rossijanki i javlenie treffika*, Moscow: Rossijskaja akademija nauk

Khomenko, S, 2012, 'Feministische Peitsche für Russland!' Die feministische Punk-Band 'Pussy Riot' über Wladimir Putin und Männerhass, http://mokant.at/1205-interview-pussy-riot-html/

Koenig, D, 2014, Pussy Riot and the first amendment: Consequences for the rule of law in Russia, *New York University Law Review* 89, 2, 666–99

Kraatz, S, Zvinkliene, A, 2003, Zwischen Superpräsidentialismus und Staatsfeminismus: Frauen in den Parlamenten Russlands und Litauens, *Osteuropa* 53, 5, 647–61

Lang, S, 2004, *Zivilgesellschaft und bürgerschaftliches Engagement in Russland*, Bonn: Friedricht-Ebert-Stiftung

Levada, www.levada.ru/print/02-10-2012/nakazanie-uchastnitsam-gruppy-pussy-riot-tret-rossiyan-sochla-adekvatnym

Meuser, M, Nagel, U, 1991, ExpertInneninterviews – vielfach erprobt, wenig bedacht, in D Garz, K Kraimer (eds) *Qualitativ-empirische Sozialforschung*, pp 441–71, Wiesbaden: Springer

Moiseev, V, 2012, Bunt feminizma [Feminism's revolt], *Russkij Reporter*, http://rusrep.ru/article/2012/02/24/pussy_riot

Mommsen, M, 2012, Einleitung, in Bundeszentrale für Politische Bildung (ed) *Dossier Russland*, Bonn, www.bpb.de/internationales/europa/russland/47932/politisches-system

Mommsen, M, Nußberger, A, 2008, *Das System Putin,* München: beck'sche reihe

O'Keefe, T, 2014, my body is my manifesto! SlutWalk, FEMEN and femmenist protest, *Feminist Review* 107, 1, 1–19

Oxfam, 2014, *After equality: Inequality trends and policy responses in contemporary Russia*, http://policy-practice.oxfam.org.uk/publications/after-equality-inequality-trends-and-policy-responses-in-contemporary-russia-319874

Pegelow, K, Engelmann, J (eds), 2011, *Riot Grrrls revisited: Geschichte und Gegenwart einer feministischen Bewegung*, Mainz: Ventil Verlag

Pussy Riot, 2011a, Pochemu feministskij khlyst polezhen Rossij? [Why is a feminist whip useful for Russia?], *Pussy Riot Live Journal*, http://pussy-riot.livejournal.com/2011/11/08/

Pussy Riot, 2011b, Interv'ju Pussy Riot v LiveJournal: 'My voobshche ne govorim ob intensivnosti seksual'noj zhizni' [Interview of Pussy Riot for LiveJournal: 'We do not talk about the intensity of sexual life at all], *Pussy Riot Live Journal*, http://pussy-riot.livejournal.com/2011/11/10/

Pussy Riot, 2011c, Agenstvo 'FederalPress' [sic] pishet o Pussy Riot: 'Besedy o radikal'nom feminizme' [Agency 'Federal Press' writes about Pussy Riot: 'Discussions about radical feminism'], *Pussy Riot Live Journal*, http://pussy-riot.livejournal.com/2011/11/08/

Pussy Riot, 2012a, Pank-moleben 'Bogoroditsa, Putina progoni' v khrame Khrista Spasitelia [Punk prayer 'Mother of God, chase away Putin' in the Cathedral of Christ the Savior], *Pussy Riot Live Journal*, http://pussy-riot.livejournal.com/2012/02/21/

Pussy Riot, 2012b, Vyn'prezhde brevno iz tvoego glaza i togda uvidish [First take a look from your eye and then you will see], *Pussy Riot Live Journal*, http://pussy-riot.livejournal.com/2012/02/23/

Pussy Riot, 2012c, Putin has pissed himself, in The Feminist Press at the City University of New York (ed) *Pussy Riot! A punk prayer for freedom*, pp 36–7, New York and London: The Feminist Press

Pussy Riot, 2012d, Letter to Patriarch Kirill, in The Feminist Press at the City University of New York (ed), *Pussy Riot! A punk prayer for freedom*, pp 26–9, New York and London: The Feminist Press

Pussy Riot, 2012e, Pussy Riot: Art or politics?, in The Feminist Press at the City University of New York (ed) *Pussy Riot! A punk prayer for freedom*, pp 15–17, New York and London: The Feminist Press

Pussy Riot, 2012f, Nash otvet zhestokoj mesti – Mezhdunarodnyj den' solidarnosti zhenshchin [Our answer to the tough revenge – International day of solidarity of women], *Pussy Riot Live Journal*, http://pussy-riot.livejournal.com/2012/03/08/

Quiring, M, 2006, Russlands Medien – gleichgeschaltet demokratisch, *Blätter für deutsche und internationale Politik,* 12, 1433–6

Rüthers, M, 2012, Mädchen schlägt man nicht: Militanter postsowjetischer Feminismus, *Neue Zürcher Zeitung,* www.nzz.ch/aktuell/feuilleton/uebersicht/maedchen-schlaegt-man-nicht-1.17530521

Samutsevich, Y, 2012, Closing courtroom statement by Katya, in The Feminist Press at the City University of New York (ed) *Pussy Riot! A Punk Prayer for Freedom*, pp 87–90, New York and London: The Feminist Press

Schreiner, K, 1994, *Maria*, Munich and Vienna: dtv

Siegert, J, 2010, Zivilgesellschaft in Russland, in H Pleines, H-H Schröder (eds) *Länderbericht Russland*, pp 172–90, Bonn: Bundeszentrale für Politische Bildung

Siegert, J, 2012, Politische Opposition in Russland, *Russlandanalysen* 232, 6–9

Smirnova, J, 2012, Der Kampf um die öffentliche Meinung, *Internationale Politik* 67, 6, 126–9

Smyth, R, Soboleva, I, 2014, Looking beyond the economy: Pussy Riot and the Kremlin's voting coalition, *Post-Soviet Affairs* 30, 4, 257–75

Sperling, V, 2014, Russian feminist perspectives on Pussy Riot, *Nationalities* Papers 42, 4, 591–603

Steinholt, YB, 2013, Kitten heresy: Lost contexts of Pussy Riot's punk prayer, *Popular Music and Society* 36, 1, 120–4

Storch, L, 2013, The Pussy Riot case: Anti-westernism in the paradigm of the Beilis trial, *Russian Politics and Law* 51, 6, 8–44

Stykow, P, 2010, Die autoritäre Konsolidierung des politischen Systems in der Ära Putin, in H Pleines, H-H Schröder (eds) *Länderbericht Russland*, pp 71–94, Bonn: Bundeszentrale für Politische Bildung

Tochka, N, 2013, Pussy Riot, freedom of expression, and popular music studies after the cold war, *Popular Music* 32, 2, 303–11

Tolokonnikova, N, 2012a, Opening courtroom statement by Nadya, in The Feminist Press at the City University of New York (ed) *Pussy Riot! A punk prayer for Freedom*, pp 41–7, New York and London: The Feminist Press

Tolokonnikova, N, 2012b, Closing courtroom statement by Nadya, in The Feminist Press at the City University of New York (ed) *Pussy Riot! A punk prayer for freedom*, pp 91–103, New York and London: The Feminist Press

Tolokonnikova, N, Žižek, S, 2014, *Comradely greetings: The prison letters of Nadya and Slavoj*, London: Verso

Tupikin, V, 2011, Pussy Riot protiv Putina I Filippa Kirkorova, za Tachrir v Moskve [Pussy Riot is against Putin and Phillip Kirkorov, for Tahrir Square in Moscow], *Pussy Riot Live Journal*, http://pussy-riot.livejournal.com/2011/11/12/

Volkova, T, Pussy Riot, 2011, Chat Tat'iany Volkovoj s gruppoj Pussy Riot [Tat'jana Volkova's chat with the group Pussy Riot], *Pussy Riot Live Journal*, http://pussy-riot.livejournal.com/2011/11/19/

von Gall, C, 2012, Vorerst gescheitert: 'Pussy Riot' und der Rechtsstaat in Russland, *Russlandanalysen* 246, 2–6

Wallerstein, I, 2004, *World-systems analysis: An introduction*, Durham, NC: Duke University Press

Willems, J, 2012, Die Russische Orthodoxe Kirche. Stütze der Macht und Spiegel der Gesellschaft, *Osteuropa* 6–8, 179–89

Willems, J, 2013, *Pussy Riots Punk-Gebet: Religion, Recht und Politik in Russland*, Berlin: Berlin University Press

Williams, G, 2015, Pussy Riot schlagen zurück, *Wired Germany* 5, 415, 102–5

Windisch, E, 2012, Pussy Riot – Frauenaufstand gegen Putin: Die russische Punkband Pussy Riot fordert die Obrigkeit heraus und muss dafür büßen, *Der Tagesspiegel*, www.tagesspiegel.de/weltspiegel/russland-pussy-riot-frauenaufstand-gegen-putin/6346712.html

Yusupova, M, 2014, Pussy Riot: A feminist band lost in history and translation, *Nationalities Papers* 42, 4, 604–10

Zdravomyslova, E, Temkina, A, 2005, Gendered citizenship in Soviet and Post-Soviet societies, in V Tolz, S Booth (eds) *Nation and gender in contemporary Europe*, pp 96–113, Manchester: Manchester University Press

SIX

How a feminist activist group builds its repertoire of actions: a case study

Fabien Hildwein

Introduction

In France feminist activism is currently thriving. This activity is accompanied by an evolution in the nature of feminist claims and ways of expressing them, due, in part, to closer connections between feminist movements and movements defending homosexuals, alongside the growing importance accorded to gender issues. Thus, feminism is rapidly changing, with the appearance of new groups and performances (Tilly, 2008), and claims now being made that were previously unrecognised, or difficult to express in contentious periods such as the 1970s.

Feminists are now more likely to focus their critique on management practices arising from their concern with the working conditions of women, their salary levels and their access to power (Acker, 2009). Feminist activist groups address new criticisms to institutions and organisations, specifically organisational practices regarding women's issues and status.

This chapter analyses the case of a feminist activist group denouncing the absence of women in positions of power. It describes the tactical repertoire (Taylor and Van Dyke, 2004; Fillieule, 2010) of this movement in order to understand how activists aspire to effect remedies for inequality in organisations (Acker, 2009). In this chapter I draw on a qualitative methodology to document how discourse, objects and the activists' demeanour interact and are used to induce change in an organisation. I also demonstrate how this transformation is constrained and shaped by the convictions and experience of the activists, within the context of current debates in contemporary French feminism.

Conceptual framework

The main concept employed here is that of the 'tactical repertoire' (Taylor and Van Dyke, 2004; Fillieule, 2010), which refers to the various actions and interactions gathered into performances, that a given activist group may use to express its claims, and which are constrained by its culture and the past experience of its members.

This concept stems from the well-known notion of 'repertoire' articulated by Charles Tilly (Tilly and Wood, 2004; Tilly, 2008). Repertoires are situated at the level of a whole nation and can be apprehended through historical and statistical analysis. The term 'repertoire' refers to the metaphor of a theatrical troupe having a limited number of performances to play in front of an audience. Repertoires, in this sense, refer to the performances that individuals are likely to use to express their claims. They are limited in number and change slowly. Tilly speaks of 'strong' repertoires to describe this slow evolution. Individuals may innovate, but only by within the confines of already existing performances. Radical new innovations are rare.

The importance of ideology and symbolism in a feminist movement's selection of tactics has been demonstrated (Taylor and Whittier, 1992; Taylor and Whittier, 1995; Whittier, 1995), as well as the impact on tactical repertoires generated by the prior participation of activists in other movements (Van Dyke, 1998). Activists may use their previous experiences in other movements to answer the perceived limitation of a movement's tactical repertoire. Thus, activists may innovate by using theoretical inspiration as a resource. This chapter shows how this is possible.

Empirical approach

This chapter is based upon the observations made during one year (July 2011–July 2012) during which I followed the activists of the French group *La Barbe* taking notes of observations at 12 of their actions and 25 meetings and researching their ideological inspirations through intensive readings of feminist theory. I was able to take photos during actions, but not to take part directly. I also conducted 16 semi-structured interviews.[1] The results were presented to members of the group and their reflections and criticisms taken into account. This approach draws on ethnographic methodology as applied to organisation studies, feminist analysis and analysis of social movements (Snow and Trom, 2002; Naples, 2003; Beaud and Weber, 2010; Cunliffe, 2010; Watson, 2011).

La Barbe, a feminist activist group

La Barbe is a French feminist activist group that aims to make visible the invisibility of women in positions of power, motivating women to take power, and establishing 'gender confusion'.[2]

La Barbe was founded in 2008. Its name is a play on words as it refers to the fake beards (*barbe* in French) used by the activists, while 'la barbe!' is also a French expression expressing irritation.

La Barbe was founded and organised as a 'horizontal' organisation, to use the activists' words, that is, an organisation without hierarchy. A 'coordinator' (*coordinatrice*) is in charge of organising the whole group by supporting the specific design of an action and by setting the order of the day during internal meetings. However, her powers are limited to this and she is replaced every six months. Activists also insist that newcomers have to be absorbed rapidly into the group and its performances, for instance by being able to answer journalists' questions or by playing important roles.

La Barbe is composed of approximately 30 active members, all female, aged between 25 and 65. They have on average a high level of education (Master's degree or higher). A high proportion of *La Barbe*'s members are openly lesbian, as is consonant with research that highlights the importance of lesbians in radical feminism (Taylor and Whittier, 1992), and take part in movements defending the rights of homosexuals, for example on the issue of gay marriage.

'La Barbe's main performance: 'congratulating organisations'

'*La Barbe*'s tactical repertoire (Taylor and Van Dyke, 2004; Tilly, 2008) focuses primarily on one particular performance called 'congratulating an organisation'. Other performances exist, but they remain rare. The activists of *La Barbe* 'congratulate' an organisation by disrupting a public meeting (conference, general assembly, round table) of an organisation lacking women in positions of power and with few or no women among the invited experts or speakers. They stand on, or in front of the podium, facing the audience. They adopt a 'dignified demeanour' by remaining still and silent. They all wear false beards. Some of them hold A4 placards (similar to the subtitles in silent films) on which are written on one side '*La Barbe*' and on the other 'Bravo', 'Marvellous', 'How bold!' or 'Thanks!' They may also bear a banner inscribed '*La Barbe*'. One or two activists remain in the audience to take photos or to shoot film footage (a role that I often played). An activist reads aloud a text prepared before the action and distributed afterwards to the audience in which the activists ironically congratulate the organisation for having been able to keep women in subordinate positions. The activists then leave the meeting (see Image 6.1).

La Barbe performed approximately 120 actions (either by the original Parisian group or an offshoot group) between February 2008 and June 2012.

Image 6.1: An activist reads the tract on the podium while the others face the audience, wearing false beards and holding boards

Interpreting *La Barbe* tactical repertoire

Through its tactical repertoire, *La Barbe* highlights the unfairness of the absence of women in positions of power, which the performance suggests is attributed to powerful men preventing women from reaching such positions. To do so, *La Barbe*'s members create an aesthetic shock, decomposed into four 'interactions' in the sense that Tilly (2008) proposes: the scripted actions relating those expressing their claims to their targets. I name these interactions 'congratulation', the 'mirror', the 'hybridisation' and the 'repetition'. Each of these interactions creates a transgression and highlights male domination in a particular way. This is an explicit goal of the founders:

> I was looking for a visual system of inversion that would speak for itself, that would show alone, I wanted people to see how serious this is, to see how men are holding the strings and to see it immediately... So deconstructing and making ridiculous those roles. I wanted to do all of these, I was looking for this inversion mechanism, I knew that we would have to look for places of power, to show the absence of women and men's supremacy and I wanted that one would see very quickly, at one glimpse, what a scandal it is. (Interview with Manon, a founding member, 26 September 2011)

La Barbe explicitly 'congratulates' the organisation for having been able to restrict women's access to power. This irony creates a shock by expressing an implicit sexist discourse, which is accepted in a given situation but unacceptable when expressed aloud. Thus, *La Barbe*'s irony focuses attention on male domination and on the responsibility of men in positions of power.

The term 'mirror' is used by activists themselves to designate an interaction, in which they position themselves behind men in power positions on the podium – if possible by locating one activist behind each man. The activists therefore are 'reflecting' men in power positions (see Image 6.2). The transgression is inherent in the actions of stepping onto the podium without being authorised and imitating men in power positions, thus revealing the overwhelming presence of men:

> You see, what I imagined was exactly the action we did in the Sénat, the first action in the Sénat, where we're all standing in line...we're all standing in line, as a mirror for these men, and where our simple speechless presence, states the hegemony, the male domination. (Interview with Manon, 26 September 2011)

'Hybridisation' is the interaction in which members of *La Barbe* put on false beards. The term 'hybrid' is used here in the sense that these women become hybrid by blurring their gender, and it is this blurring that constitutes the transgression of this interaction. This is another way of imitating the masculinity of the men in power positions, and thus questioning their legitimacy.

Image 6.2: Example of a mirror, with an activist reading a tract aloud on the left

The repetition consists in the fact that *La Barbe* repeats the same performances again and again, sometimes with exactly the same target in the same place, and at the same time of day or night. By doing so, they 'reflect' their position that male domination is omnipresent and men in power positions are (almost) all white and likely to come from similar social and educational backgrounds.

> And so, seeing the places where indeed there are only men, they're all white, they have all the same mug, the same suit and tie, they come out of the same schools, they're all made from the same mould. It freaks you out, you don't laugh anymore and you say to yourself: 'Huh, yeah, there is a real problem.' (Interview with Caroline, 21 September 2011)

This repetition also aims to highlight the ways in which individuals holding powerful positions often chose to work primarily with people whom they see as similar to themselves, and reward and praise each other for their contributions; thus making this self-replicating system ever stronger.

> This is really nice stuff at *La Barbe*. We love redundancies, co-optation, repetition, self-congratulation, uniformity, suits, suits, suits, plurality of offices, well, we do the same

thing, we always do the same thing. We are boring. We always come back to the same places, we always do the same things, we are always with you boys, until you get tired. (Interview with Manon, 26 September 2011)

These interactions are reinforced by films[3] and by the speeches being read aloud during the performance.

Relevance of *La Barbe* tactical repertoire for organisation studies

The analysis of *La Barbe* and its tactical repertoire helps to understand how a civil society organisation can advocate for changes in management. *La Barbe* represents a particularly relevant case for this research field for three main reasons. First, a notable feature of *La Barbe* is that it never targets individuals, but only organisations. To quote Manon: 'We don't target individuals, we target the structure' (interview with Manon, 26 September 2011); meaning that *La Barbe* is not interested in criticising men as individuals, but rather as members of a social group, holding privileged positions within specific networks and places such as the targeted organisations. Second, *La Barbe* challenges management by illuminating the invisibility of discrimination in organisations (Acker, 2009), and focuses on the injustice rather than on the lack of performance discrimination produces (a common trope in management, see Béréni, 2009). Third, *La Barbe*'s critique represents a new form of feminist activism. Former movements seeking to address issues concerning women and power in organisations and firms have existed, in particular those advocating for parity between men and women (Riot-Sarcey, 2002; Béréni and Lépinard, 2004; Béréni and Revillard, 2007; Sénac-Slawinski, 2008; Béréni, 2009), but never with such an innovative repertoire as that of *La Barbe*.

La Barbe influences and inspirations

The tactical repertoire of *La Barbe* is both built upon, and constrained by the feminist convictions and the experiences of its members, particularly its founding members, thus supporting Taylor and Van Dyke (2004) and Tilly (2008) in their conclusions on 'strong repertoires'. It has changed very little over time; the main performance has remained almost the same during the five years after *La Barbe*'s founding.

Three sources of ideological or cultural inspiration may be distinguished within *La Barbe*'s tactical repertoire: the criticism of

French feminism; the theoretical inspiration for materialist feminism; and the theoretical inspiration of queer feminism.

Criticism of French feminism

Efficiency through action

The most important limitation expressed by founders of *La Barbe* with regard to French feminism as a social movement is its lack of efficiency. *La Barbe*'s focus on effectiveness is perceptible before and after each performance as well as during the group's meeting and is shared by all members of *La Barbe*. Their critique is supported by their observation that debates tend to divide feminist groups along ideological lines (as, for example, the debates concerning such sensitive issues as the Muslim hijab or prostitution) and therefore hinder action and change. Action and performances are seen as more efficient than debates.

> This is the kiss of death. The more we discuss ideology, the less efficient we will be. (Interview with Henriett, 27 September 2011)

> There are lots of debated topics within *La Barbe* that, I think, are not our main issue and there is no interest in addressing them. Our image is blurred and it is not efficient at all. (Interview with Manon, 26 September 2011)

French feminism is seen as being well theorised but lacking in activism.

> I thought that reflection was very developed in France on feminist issues, but that it lacked activism. I wanted a group doing simple actions, spectacular, about which the media would quickly speak, so I wanted to grab attention, something sensational. (Interview with Manon, 26 September 2011)

Therefore, performances are seen as the essential purpose of *La Barbe*. Debates are not ignored, but rather limited to dinner gatherings during which members meet and discuss a given issue.

Second, French feminism is also seen as inefficient because it avoids the structural issues of the condition of women. Feminists are too focused upon the *consequences* of patriarchy and male domination and they do not address the *cause* of the problem (the issue of power): 'What are the other risks?…We lose our identity, we lose our strength, we are blurred and we end up with the same inefficiency that affects a lot of other feminist groups which did not take enough care of the structural issues' (interview with Manon, 26 September 2011).

The image of feminism

Another difficulty that *La Barbe* sought to overcome was the negative image that feminism has for many people alongside the sexism and homophobia towards feminist lesbians. *La Barbe*'s tactical repertoire seeks to challenge and destroy this negative image through their use of irony and by overtly addressing issues of power. At the same time, the activists insist upon maintaining the legacy of the 1970s feminists.

La Barbe's irony can also be understood as a response to the accusation that feminists have no humour. However, their use of humour is not done to please an audience and the media, but represents a critical position with numerous other dimensions, as will be shown.

> During the first year, the media said of *La Barbe* 'well, finally some feminists who do not have hairy legs, who are not lesbians, and so on'…So, of course, we sent them reports saying that we are indeed lesbians, yes, we have hairy legs… It's funny because we didn't even need to have a say about whether or not we are lesbians, or whether we have hairy legs, and so on. No matter what, they decided that we are different, that we are not like the others. And slowly we could accept our identity and to say 'no, no, no, we are not different, we are the same, we claim the same ancestors'. The MLF [Mouvement de Libération des Femmes, the most prominent French feminist group of the 1970s] was funny too and now the media is changing its attitude to the MLF. We start speaking of their humour and so on, really emphasising that this is the same tradition, we recognise ourselves in them, they are with us, they address the same issues, this is the same family. But at first, it is not easy to break this taboo which says 'feminists are ridiculous, they need to get laid' and, in fact, by exaggerating, by caricaturing men, we manage to undergo this change, which made the media want to speak of *La Barbe*, and therefore to speak about feminism. (Interview with Manon, 26 September 2011)

The limitation of feminist discourse

La Barbe criticises activists who limit their concerns to just those topics defined as 'feminist' and thereby moving away from the topics that matter the most and that interest the dominant social groups. In particular, there is the idea that feminism speaks too much of women and women's issues and not enough of the responsibility of men for male domination. One could say that *La Barbe*'s repertoire is an attempt to confront this aspect of feminist discourse in order to broaden the range of subjects addressed and gain legitimacy for them:

> [T]he idea of *La Barbe* is to stop speaking about women, and to starting speaking about men, this is the great shift of paradigm, to say that feminism has locked itself in feminist subjects, which are extremely limited, which are those in which we are gently allowed to speak and which are 'go take care of female circumcision', 'look at those nasty sexist strangers', 'go take care of the misery and the suffering of female bodies' and so on. Go take care of the symptoms but, above all, do not take care of us, do not look where all this comes from…But there was, there is this difficulty of looking at what oppresses us, which is particular to feminism by the way, it is very difficult to name the enemy. It's not the done thing, because there is this idea that men and women love each other and that therefore the sex war will not take place. So we stay between ourselves, we deplore our condition of women but we do not go, we hesitate to attack the subjects, which interest dominant people. (Interview with Manon, 26 September 2011)

> There was this idea at *La Barbe* that actions would allow you to show your indignation and your impatience and where no one would ask you to conform to the position of a victim, which often happens in feminist movements, but I think it often happens in movements that fight discrimination, oppression, people. Dominant discourses often put oppressed people in the position of a victim, whereas what I see in *La Barbe* is that we start with individuals who are allergic to any discrimination, who are proud. (Interview with Michèle, 11 January 2012)

Finally, attacking causes and structures rather than consequences and symptoms seems to be the most effective way to act. Indeed, some subjects such as the monopoly of men within power positions do not need to be debated.

> The idea was to change paradigm, to say that we're going to stop speaking about women, to stop speaking about the bodies of women, to stop speaking about victims, to stop speaking about rape, to stop speaking about the Muslim headscarf, to stop speaking about prostitution, we are going to speak about money, about power, about status, about high politics, we are going to speak about important things, about which the media speak every day. And like this, we will all agree, we won't even need to discuss, because all feminists will agree, because it is not normal that men have all the power, this is not debated among feminists. (Interview with Manon, 26 September 2011)

Feminism and power

La Barbe's founding members also seek to address the absence of women in positions of power, which, they perceive, has been neglected by French feminists. The aspiration of female–male parity is certainly the most prominent within this issue and was first supported by female politicians and individuals from both political sides. After 1981 it was gradually implemented in governmental institutions with a major development taking place with the foundation of the *Observatoire de la parité entre femmes et hommes,* an organisation dedicated to the production of information and research (Béréni and Revillard, 2007). This cause has also been supported and legitimised since the 1950s by international organisations and particularly the Council of Europe with a clear acceleration in the late 1970s (Béréni and Lépinard, 2004; Sénac-Slawinski, 2008). The two laws on male–female parity (in political parties in 2000 and in companies in 2011[4]) are the most important outcome of this process. Thus, the issue of female–male parity has not been regarded as an important area for activist engagement.

La Barbe's members, however do include male–female parity among their goals, although it is also important to note that they refuse to be limited to this cause, particularly when journalists attribute this label to them:

> I wasn't into parity, I wasn't for parity, and at *La Barbe* there is a lot of discussion, particularly Céliane who reminds us often to 'watch out! Our goal is not parity' and she is perfectly right, one should not think that *La Barbe* aims for parity. It is absolutely not its goal, particularly if we speak of gender trouble. It is a way to unlock doors. It is not a goal per se for us. We don't aim for parity, we aim at making it possible that women may reach power positions just as men do…And we have no other means actually, outside of the laws on parity, because obstacles are huge. (Interview with Babette, 12 October 2011)

In the same way that *La Barbe* criticises feminists for not addressing the issue of men's power and responsibility, they also say that the absence of women in powerful positions was only marginally included in feminist activist discourses. One possible explanation for the reluctance of activists on this issue might be attributed to their left-wing political orientation. Béréni and Revillard (2007) observe: 'This cause was indeed perceived as an elitist claim, far from the socialist point of view, according to which women's emancipation comes first from work' (Béréni and Revillard, 2007, 7).[5] Christine Delphy, who provides one of the main theoretical inspirations for *La Barbe*, shows how socialist and Marxist ideology can ignore the fact that women exist as a dominated social class distinct from their husbands' class, and that even women in positions of power are dominated as women (Delphy, 1998).

The issue of women and power is central to *La Barbe* for several reasons. The foundational indignation of *La Barbe* comes from France's 2007 presidential campaign in which the right-wing candidate, Nicolas Sarkozy campaigned against Ségolène Royal, the left-wing, and female candidate. Shocked by the sexist comments Ségolène Royal received, even from people within her own political party, the group was created to protest against the omnipresence of men in positions of power.

La Barbe perceives this monopoly of men over positions of power as the primary cause of patriarchy, upon which all other feminist issues depend. As previously quoted, Manon comments, 'Go take care of the symptoms but above all do not take care of us, do not look where this all comes from' (interview with Manon, 26 September 2011). This point of view is consistent with the materialist feminism of Christine Delphy (1998), since it highlights the interests of one social group over another (as will be developed further on).

Finally, talking overtly about the relative imbalance of women in positions of power helps feminists to challenge depictions of themselves as victims, showing instead the core issue of sexism.

> We really wanted to tackle the issue of power and the fact that we are excluded, without saying 'we're excluded, we're excluded, we're victims, it's horrible, help us!' This is not what we wanted, we wanted to challenge this power and why this power has the right to decide who's in, who's out, so it was really that, we wanted to criticise power and this is what motivated us, this was really important, whereas the right to abortion or things like this, are really, really narrow. (Interview with Henriett, 27 September 2011)

The trap of essentialism

Another lesson taught by feminist experience is the trap of essentialism. 'Getting free of the trap that everyone execrates, "essentialism" in brackets, according to which women should have rights because they have specific qualities' (interview with Manon, 26 September 2011).

Essentialism designates the idea that women are *naturally* different from men, that because of their essence, they have different characteristics and qualities (Béréni et al, 2008). Essentialism tends to promote a vision of society in which women have predetermined social positions – at home, as social workers, as assistants of men; arguably rather a conservative point of view on society and the female condition. Essentialism is embedded in discussions and thinking about the issue of male–female parity, as Manon suggests:

> I found by chance a book, at a friend's, the book by Gisèle Halimi [one of the most important promoters of male–female parity in France] about the contention on parity, and I said to myself 'Wow! They got so trapped by the Conseil Constitutionnel, fuck!' So I saw the traps they fall into and which we would have to avoid. So reading this book, I really admired those women who got us male–female parity but at the same time I thought that they were really trapped, they let themselves become locked up in things. And it helped me to define strategies in order to avoid such traps in order not to fall victim to essentialism. (Interview with Manon, 26 September 2011)

Manon is referring here to a particular event. In 1982, following the campaign promises of the recently elected French President François Mitterand, Gisèle Halimi, a socialist member of Parliament, wrote a bill forcing political parties to ensure that lists of possible candidates for local elections would contain at least 30 per cent of candidates of each gender. The bill was voted for, albeit with a reduction from 30 per cent to 25 per cent. However, the Conseil Constitutionnel, which has the responsibility to ensure that voted laws comply with the French constitution, censored this bill (Béréni and Revillard, 2007).

The viewpoint of the Conseil Constitutionnel is particularly informative, especially as it reflects the main argument of the adversaries of male–female parity. Male–female parity is said to be unconstitutional since it creates a division among citizens (Sénac-Slawinski, 2008), which is not acceptable to a French Republic built upon the principle of universalism (all citizens being equal in law, regardless of gender, race, religious beliefs and so forth). This argument fails to recognise the extent to which men and women can be seen as belonging to *socially constructed groups* that have a concrete existence from an economic point of view (women being paid less for the same job, regardless of qualifications), and from a political point of view (the relative absence of women in power positions) (Béréni and Lépinard, 2004). Therefore, male–female parity would be a legitimate aim as long as such economic and political differences exist. What Manon means here is that essentialism brought confusion by focusing the attention on *natural* differences (which are off topic) rather than economic and political ones (Béréni et al, 2008). Thus the achievement of the institutionalisation of male–female parity was prevented. The influence of essentialist thinking is not limited to politics, but is also problematic in organisations. For instance, Béréni (2009) shows how managerial rhetoric gave rise to the issue of gendered discrimination in firms by placing emphasis upon the competences and qualities that women can bring to a firm and how performance can thus be increased. The problem of essentialism is more subtle here. Women are accepted into powerful positions not to erase patriarchy, but rather because they are supposed to bring gender-specific qualities and competences to organisations. The main argument becomes that of efficiency rather than social justice.

La Barbe dialectical continuity with former feminisms

To have a complete understanding of *La Barbe* and its relation to feminism, it is important to note that *La Barbe*'s activists insist upon their indebtedness to the legacy of former feminist movements, particularly the emblematic Mouvement pour la Libération des Femmes (MLF) of the 1970s. For instance, in January 2013 a journalist came to a meeting of *La Barbe* and asked if he could interview them about the differences between older and newer forms of feminism. An activist answered rapidly that they do not accept the notion of a split between those two forms of feminism,[6] a conviction that was found many times in my own interviews. Despite that, there does exist a strong critique of feminism among the activists of *La Barbe*, but this is not expressed outside of the group, particularly not to the media. I suggest that there is a particularly *dialectical* relation between *La Barbe* and feminism in general, in the sense of integrating previous forms while going beyond them. *La Barbe* benefits from the efforts and achievements of earlier feminists, from a symbolic as well as from a theoretical point of view; and *La Barbe* activists recognise this legacy. But they also recognise the importance of acknowledging the limitations of these earlier forms of feminism in order to go beyond them. In this sense, *La Barbe* can be regarded as representing a significant breakthrough for social movements in general: the possibility that it can evolve through tackling its own limitations.

The theoretical inspirations of *La Barbe*

Understanding the theoretical inspirations of *La Barbe* illuminates its particular vision of feminism and helps us to better understand its tactical repertoire. Although these theories are many and complex, the following section focuses upon the aspects that are the most closely related to *La Barbe*.

Materialist feminism

As continually stressed, *La Barbe*'s main theoretical inspiration is Christine Delphy's materialist feminism (Delphy 1998), which she has been developing since 1970. The inspiration of Delphy's work for *La Barbe* including her use of the concept of 'materialist feminism', is claimed by both founding members and newer members, who invited Delphy to participate in the symbolic one hundredth action of *La Barbe* (Delphy accepted the invitation).

Delphy's work draws on Marx but focuses specifically on the economic exploitation of patriarchy, and its workings in the domestic sphere and through housework. A huge amount of goods and services are produced in this sphere. Because they do not appear on the market, they are not taken into account by most economic analysis and are not considered worthy of payment or even analysis. Those who work in the domestic sphere are predominantly women. Women work for other members of the family, particularly their husbands, for no salary. Their husbands do not pay them a salary, but rather 'support' them,[7] which means that they receive goods and services from their husbands (including gifts) that allow them to live, but they are not free to choose their consumption. For this reason the husband's support can be seen as qualitatively inferior to that of receiving a normal salary. Furthermore, such support may be apportioned differently among the different members of the family. Furthermore, when it comes to the labour market, women are likely to be underpaid compared to men for similar jobs, and subject to the 'glass ceiling' effect that prevents them from reaching higher positions. This represents a strong material incentive for women to get married and, for a heterosexual couple, to have the housework done by the wife.

Delphy's work is closely related to *La Barbe*. Delphy criticises social sciences for excluding the issue of the exploitation of women from its analyses by refusing to consider men, women and the relationships between them as social objects:

> One of the axioms, if not the fundamental axiom, of my reasoning, is that women and men are social groups. I start from the undeniable fact that they are socially named, socially distinguished, socially relevant, and I ask myself about that social practice: how is it realized? How is it used? (Delphy, 1998, 24)

Delphy argues that sociology should explain social facts *with* social facts. 'Women' and 'men' are social groups in the sense that they are defined by social structures and representations (rather than by biological or *natural* factors, as essentialism states it). This also means that these groups have different material interests and that they are in a particular relationship to each other. Male domination is embodied by the monopoly of men in power positions. This domination has an economic dimension (the exploitation of women by men), and an ideological support, that of sexism and anti-feminism. It is in this Marxist sense that Delphy calls her approach 'materialist'. The (domestic) process of production creates a relationship of domination between two socially constructed groups. That is also how *La Barbe* responds to such social critique: their work is deeply rooted in the indignation they feel when confronted with men's egoism.

From this point of view, ideology and values are not sufficient to explain male domination.[8] In a Marxist sense, ideologies support domination based upon economic exploitation; they depend on this domination while simultaneously masking and justifying it. Therefore, male domination cannot be reduced to the representation, values and beliefs that assign hierarchical gender roles to men and women. Delphy rejects such idealism as a position that would entirely explain social facts by values or ideas seen as external to society and that reduce male domination to an ideological issue. 'Nature does not know, and cannot create values. Values are made by societies, and human societies, like any phenomenon involving consciousness. The idea that values of society could find their source outside of it…is simply a comeback to the Platonic ideas' (Delphy, 1998, 229).

And she says with humour:

> The ideas of this school are simple: the domination from women over men is a bad thing, and it has to stop. But the issue is not something mundane like the economic dependency of women, like their materialistic oppression. No. Everything happens at the level of the values. What is bemoaned is the lack of consideration they suffer. (Delphy, 1998, 239)

In the same way, Delphy rejects naturalism as an attempt to search for biological explanations for social facts, whereas society hides how many constraints (emotions, roles, representations) are socially constructed and add to the ways in which physical phenomena are experienced: 'Society does everything to make us believe that the material conditions of periods or of maternity follow from the physical event: that those socially constructed conditions are natural conditions' (Delphy, 1998, 224).

For Delphy, patriarchy and capitalism support each other. Patriarchy supports capitalism because it allows firms to maintain lower wages on the basis that one part of the population works for no salary for another part of the population. In this way capitalism also supports patriarchy because it is economically more rational for women to work at home and for their husbands, who can earn higher wages for the same quantity of work, to be employed outside the home.

This has two main implications for *La Barbe*'s position. First, *La Barbe* targets the most obvious manifestations of men's material interests, their monopoly of positions of power, and its direct consequence, the absence of women in those positions. It addresses these issues rather than other feminist claims, which are more clearly directed at the material interests at stake in male domination. Second, *La Barbe* targets men not as individuals, but as members of a social group. They perceive that the problems of male patriarchy do not arise from an individual, but rather from general behaviours and representations, particularly among men, who maintain their domination by protecting the homogeneity of the group.

This position provides us with a means for interpreting the tactical repertoire of *La Barbe*. The 'mirror' focuses the audience's attention on the huge predominance of men in positions of power positions (the use of false beards also help to focus attention on the masculinity of those men). Whereas the 'repetition' suggests that this is not a random, or isolated occurrence, but rather one, which it tends to repeat itself in every assembly of powerful people. This also means that the targets of *La Barbe* will be organisations rather than individuals, in contrast to many other activist groups.

Queer feminist theory

Queer feminism (Butler, 1990) focuses on the idea that gendered identity is mainly built upon performativity and rejects the notion of a *natural* or *essential* differentiation between women and men. This performativity means that gender is both enacted by individuals (they 'perform' the role of a woman or a man) and is imposed, or inscribed on them by others (through being recognised, or addressed as woman or man in every interaction). Gender is, therefore, a linguistic and social construct; gender is artificial. Referring to Foucauldian philosophy, Butler insists that gendered classification is based upon biological criteria that do exist, but are given an excessive and artificial importance, as any other physical feature could be used to classify individuals.

Queer feminism inspires *La Barbe*'s tactical repertoire in the means it adopts to highlight the artificiality of gender, particularly the masculinity of men in positions of power. It is an additional resource to denounce patriarchy and the lack of legitimacy of men in power positions in the targeted organisation. If 'man' is an artificial construct, there is no reason to confer particular positions on this category of individuals. The hybridisation process, in particular, the wearing of false beards, aims to make this artificiality visible.

Queer feminism has also managed to reunite feminism and the defence of the rights of homosexuals under the same banner through representing the fight against gender as a system of oppression. This interpretation has had both a direct and an indirect impact on *La Barbe*'s work and also demonstrates that social movements can learn from each other's theorising and strategy formation.

In contrast to strategies that emphasise differences between men and women (Taylor and Whittier, 1992; Whittier, 1995), the tactical repertoire of *La Barbe* highlights the illegitimacy of men in positions of power rather than focusing on the supposed specificities of women. This is another lesson from queer theory, a warning to avoid essentialism.

Thus, *La Barbe* is at the junction of both types of feminism, appropriating some aspects of each in building its tactical repertoire.

Conclusion

This chapter has documented how an activist group attempts to trigger change in organisations and how its tactical repertoire is structured by the particular context of contemporary feminism and its theoretical inspirations. It describes a strategy to affect targeted organisations and pays attention to the fact that activists may actively use theoretical resources as well as previous experience in social movements to innovate and create new tactical repertoires. As demonstrated, *La Barbe*'s choice of tactical repertoire is also the result of its reflection on French feminism, leading it to develop innovations in its approach. These innovations are not only the outcome of new ideas and claims (such as different ways of understanding gender issues, queer theory, the importance of making men aware of their responsibilities), but also of new forms of action and expressions of those claims (their use of irony, of activists' bodies, and symbolic work on the representation of men and power).

La Barbe's position has significant implications for management. Their critique cannot be answered with short-term negotiations or small innovations. Its ideological strength requires solid arguments in response and deep changes in management practices. Managers need to be able to recognise and understand such arguments in order to be able to answer them properly and efficiently.

Notes

[1] The names of the activists have been changed; quotations were translated from French to English.

[2] 'rendre visible l'invisibilité des femmes dans les lieux de pouvoir, donner envie aux femmes de prendre le pouvoir et instaurer la confusion des genres'

[3] A typical example can be found here: www.youtube.com/watch?v=XYAuRcRqcHY

[4] See www.vie-publique.fr/actualite/panorama/texte-vote/loi-relative-representation-equilibree-femmes-hommes-au-sein-conseils-administration-surveillance-egalite-professionnelle.html

[5] All translations by the author.
[6] 'on ne croit pas à la rupture'
[7] 'entretenues'
[8] See in particular, '"Paroles d'homme" ou l'idéalisme à l'œuvre' in the chapter 'Nos amis et nous' (Delphy, 1998, 169–73).

References

Acker, J, 2009, From glass ceiling to inequality regimes, *Sociologie du travail* 51, 2, 199–217

Beaud, S, Weber, F, 2010, *Guide de l'enquête de terrain*, Paris: La Découverte

Béréni, L, 2009, 'Faire de la diversité une richesse pour l'entreprise': La transformation d'une contrainte juridique en catégorie managériale, *Raisons politiques* 35, 3, 87–105

Béréni, L, Lépinard, E, 2004, 'Les femmes ne sont pas une catégorie': Les stratégies de légitimation de la parité en France, *Revue française de science politique* 54, 1, 71–98

Béréni, L, Revillard, A, 2007, Des quotas à la parité: 'Féminisme d'État' et représentation politique (1974–2007), *Genèses* 67, 2, 5–23

Béréni, L, Chauvin, S, Jaunait, A, Revillard, A (eds), 2008, *Introduction aux gender studies: Manuel des études sur le genre*, Bruxelles: De Boeck

Butler, J, 1990, *Gender Trouble: Feminism and the subversion of identity*, New York: Routledge

Cunliffe, AL, 2010, Retelling tales of the field, *Organizational research methods* 13, 2, 224–39

Delphy, C, 1998, *L'ennemi principal. L'économie politique du patriarcat*, Paris: Editions Syllepse

Dobbin, F, 2009, *Inventing equal opportunity*, Princeton, NJ: Princeton University Press

Fillieule, O, 2010, Tombeau pour Charles Tilly. Répertoires, performances et stratégies d'action: Penser les mouvements sociaux, in O Fillieule, E Agrikoliansky, I Sommier (eds) *Penser les mouvements sociaux*, pp 77–100, Paris: La Découverte

Naples, NA, 2003, *Feminism and method: Ethnography, discourse analysis and activist research*, London: Routledge

Patouillard, V, 1998, Une colère politique. L'usage du corps dans une situation exceptionnelle: le ZAP d'Act-Up Paris, *Sociétés contemporaines* 3, 31, 15–36

Riot-Sarcey, M, 2002, *Histoire du féminisme*, Paris: La Découverte

Sénac-Slawinski, R, 2008, *La parité*, Paris: Presses Universitaires de France

Snow, DA, Trom, D, 2002, The case study and the study of social movements, in B Klandermans, S Staggenborg (eds) *Methods of social movement research*, pp 146–72, Minneapolis, MN: University of Minnesota Press

Taylor, V, van Dyke, N, 2004, 'Get up, stand up': Tactical repertoires of social movements, in DA Snow, SA Soule, H Kriesi (eds) *The Blackwell companion to social movements*, pp 262–93, Malden, MA: Blackwell Publishing

Taylor, V, Whittier, N, 1992, Collective identity in social movement communities: Lesbian feminist mobilization, in AD Morrism, CM Mueller (eds) *Frontiers in social movement theory*, pp 104–29, London: Yale University Press

Taylor, V, Whittier, N, 1995, Analytical approaches to social movement culture: The culture of the women's movement, in H Johnston, B Klandermans (eds) *Social movements and culture*, pp 163–87, Minneapolis, MN: University of Minnesota Press

Tilly, C, 2008, *Contentious performances*, New York: Cambridge University Press

Tilly, C, Wood, LJ, 2004, *Social movements 1768–2004*, London: Paradigm Publisher

Van Dyke, N, 1998, Hotbeds of activism: Locations of student protest, *Social Problems* 45, 2, 205–20

Watson, TJ, 2011, Ethnography, reality, and truth: The vital need for studies of 'How Things Work', in organizations and management, *Journal of Management Studies* 48, 1, 202–14

Whittier, N, 1995, *Feminist generations: The persistence of the radical women's movement*, Philadelphia, PA: Temple

From feminist extravagance to citizen demand: the movement for abortion legalisation in Uruguay

Inés M Pousadela

Introduction

The legalisation of abortion has been under debate in Uruguay since the mid-1980s. Discussions have been especially intense since 2002, when a legalisation bill was debated and passed by the House of Representatives. Several attempts later, a legalisation bill received full congressional approval in late 2008, only to be partially vetoed by the country's first left-wing president. A similar bill was reintroduced two years later; however, congressional negotiations turned it into a watered-down decriminalisation proposal that was eventually passed in late 2012. This bill satisfied neither proponents nor opponents; right after its approval, pro-life groups started campaigning for the bill's revocation, while the women's movement found itself defending a minimalist law that it had not wanted in the first place. The attempt to revoke the bill eventually failed due to low turnout in a popular consultation calling for a plebiscite on the issue.

Focused on the evolving struggle for women's rights in Uruguay, this chapter is based on data from primary and secondary sources. The initial 20 years of the abortion debate (1985–2005) are covered using information contained in academic publications and reports produced by governmental entities and social organisations. The more recent process was reconstructed with data obtained from the websites of newspapers, magazines and radio stations, and organisations' and campaigns' websites and Facebook profiles.[1] Publications, brochures, declarations, videos and photos were also compiled. In addition, the discourse of the protagonists was reconstructed through press sources and in-depth interviews and informal conversations with qualified informants, leaders and activists.[2]

The Uruguayan process is analysed within the framework of social movement theory. To express their demands, social movements work within available repertoires of contention. According to Charles Tilly (1995, 42), a repertoire is 'a limited set of routines that are learned, shared and acted out through a relatively deliberate process of choice'. The concept of contention, in turn, is defined as 'the discontinuous making of claims that bear on other people's interests' (Tilly, 1995, 16); it is therefore distinguished from continuous claim-making activities such as parliamentary representation and trade unions' routine tasks. The existence of repertoires of contention explains why certain forms of organisation and protest are used instead of others; repertoires, however, are not fixed, as actors repeat them as much as they innovate within their scripts. Innovation can be the product of marginal, accumulative change or may occur, more abruptly, in contexts of crisis (Tarrow, 1998; Tilly, 2006; 2008).

While the ways in which contentious repertoires are used and innovated upon is still a matter of controversy, social movements around the world have actually widened their repertoires and exhibited increasing ability to appropriate various forms of artistic self-expression, putting them to political use. As they have succeeded in enhancing the visibility of the movements' demands and thereby increasing their chances of being heard, new staged forms of protest have become a part of contentious repertoires. Preliminary studies support the idea of a 'carnivalesque reinterpretation of protest' (Teune, 2005, 12). Combining old and new, contemporary protests have encompassed traditional forms such as demonstrations and rallies, alongside a wide variety of colourful, innovative cultural expressions that have helped sustain mobilisation over time, catch the public's attention, creatively frame issues and introduce ideological debate – a debate that, in the case of the Uruguayan women's movement, has ably sown together the emancipatory feminist discourse with the emancipatory discourse of the left.

This account begins with the efforts of the women's movement[3] to build itself as a political subject and forge lasting alliances with other social movements and civil society organisations (CSOs). As legalisation of abortion requires legislative action, much of the story involved strategies – not just by the women's movement but also by its 'pro-life' counter-movement – to introduce or oppose new legislation and influence the legislative process. Given the links between political representatives and public opinion, also relevant to the process were the contenders' efforts to shape the opinions of the citizenry.

What this story ultimately shows is the crucial the role played by the women's movement in the promotion of women's emancipation in Uruguay. Its unfinished character, in turn, demonstrates that emancipation is truly a never-ending process involving setbacks, upgrades and challenges. The pages that follow explore the factors contributing to or hindering such emancipation, as well as the political actions and initiatives that brought about these women's notable achievements.

The Uruguayan women's movement

Since the beginning of the twentieth century, Uruguay stood out for its early legislation in the field of civil and social rights and its rapid processes of urban development, secularisation and decrease in fertility rates, which had equalising effects on the situation of women. Uruguayan women entered the labour market relatively early and soon caught up with their male counterparts in the field of education. The first women's organisations were founded in the early 1900s and comprised female workers' mobilised by the demand for equal compensation for equal work, alongside feminist organisations demanding the right to vote (Lissidini, 1996). In 1905 a law regulating labour safety and work schedules for women and children was passed; two years later the first Divorce Law was approved. After almost two decades of organised action, women were allowed to vote in 1932; the first female legislators entered Congress in 1942. In 1946, an initiative presented by those legislators resulted in legal recognition of equal legal capacities of men and women.

As the use of the birth-control pill became widespread in the 1960s, sexuality became dissociated from reproduction and women's autonomy increased. At the same time a process began of the feminisation of university ranks: these very women who gained educational spaces would very soon protagonise a true cultural revolution by entering leftist parties and movements, and even guerrilla organisations (Sapriza, 2009). The 1970s, in turn, saw the massive entrance of women into the labour market, which entailed new discussions regarding the roles that had been traditionally assigned to women and the division of labour within the home.

Under the dictatorship (1973–85) two markedly different periods can be distinguished. During its early, more repressive years, women's organisations remained sheltered in their traditional formats, were scarcely visible, and focused mostly on the development of cultural, sports, recreative and welfare spaces. After 1978 – and especially since the beginning of a very gradual political liberalisation process in 1980 – new social movements began to arise which focused, on the one hand, on the satisfaction of subsistence needs; on the other, on the defence of human rights against state terrorism (Barreiro and Cruz, 1988). In sum, women's responses to state terrorism and socioeconomic deterioration propelled the emergence of an important social movement that Sapriza (2009, 65) describes as 'structured by feminism'.

The restoration of democracy brought a brief interval of inaction, during which the illusion prevailed that democracy by itself would solve the problems that had given rise to women's organisations in the first place. Nevertheless, the women's movement soon gathered new momentum. In 1987 the Plenary of Mothers and Relatives of Defendants under Military Jurisdiction led a campaign to force a referendum on the Law of Expiration (*Ley de Caducidad*) that had granted immunity to those who had committed human rights violations under the dictatorship. At the time, 24 women's organisations, most of them very young, were surveyed across the country. They formed an increasingly diversified movement that also included research institutes, professional associations, and women's groups within unions and political parties (Barreiro and Cruz, 1988).

In the following years more organisations were created and new networks formed, among them the Network of Women's Health of Uruguay (1988) and the Uruguayan Network Against Domestic Violence (1990). A survey in 1991 identified almost a hundred organisations, from grassroots groups to umbrella organisations (Mujeres Latinoamericanas en Cifras, no date).

Democracy, however, did not bring about instantaneous or dramatic changes in the institutional inclusion of women within the political system. Although a special parliamentary commission was created in the 1985 legislature regarding the situation of women, and women's commissions were subsequently established within all main political parties, no female legislator was elected to the National Congress during the period 1985–89, and the few who ended up there as alternatives did so for extremely brief periods (but some did play relevant roles). On the other hand, a Network of Women Politicians was formed in 1992; and in that same year the First National Meeting of Women in Political Positions was convened and the Feminist Space also started meeting. Finally, early in the 2000–05 legislative period the Women's Bicameral Caucus was formed within Congress.

Surprisingly, in 2005, the percentage of women in the House of Representatives was still only 12 per cent (IDEA, 2005). The situation varied widely across parties: in fact, only the left-leaning Frente

Amplio had experienced a continuously upward trend in female representation (Johnson, 2005). However, according to a 2007 national survey, a majority of Uruguayans favoured a more balanced political representation. Eventually a Law of Political Participation was passed in 2009, forcing parties to include in their electoral lists at least one female candidate for every three. A study on that year's primaries showed the prevalence of a minimalist application of the law; nevertheless, there was a significant increase in women's representation in party conventions, averaging almost one third. This effect was more noticeable within the traditional parties, which had the lowest female participation rates (Mujeres Convencionales, 2009).

Within the executive branch, the first woman to (very briefly) head a ministry – not surprisingly, that of education – did so in 1968. In the 1980s and 1990s state institutions were created to work for the advancement of women. These government units, however, endured the same fate of most of their Latin American counterparts, as a result of their insufficient budgets and resources and their marginal position within the administrative structure of the state. By 2005 Uruguay had no female minister (IDEA, 2005). As for the judiciary, in the early 1990s there were still no women in the Supreme Court, and only 16 per cent of the judges in the Courts of Appeals were female.

At the time of writing, sexual and reproductive rights and gender equality are the main themes of the Uruguayan women's movement. The latter, in turn, has become a dense network of political, union, feminist and social development organisations, plus academic units and highly specialised research institutes. These have have been joined by LGBT (lesbian, gay, bisexual and transsexual) groups, their natural allies in the struggle for the inclusion of sexual rights within the framework of human rights. These organisations are located within national, regional and global networks and working groups. Among them stands out the National Monitoring Commision: Women for Democracy, Equality and Citizenship (CNS Women), a network – the widest in the country – that brings together some 60 feminist and women's organisations, founded in 1996 with the aim of promoting in Uruguay the fulfillment of the Action Plan drafted at the United Nations' Fourth World Conference on Women in Beijing, 1995. It connects grassroots groups with more institutionalised organisations, both of the capital city and the interior provinces; and it has, according to its leaders, an 'armoured position' regarding the legalisation of abortion (Anabel Cruz, personal communication).

Among CNS members are the Association of Prostitutes (AMEPU), the Association of Transvestites of Uruguay (ATRU), the Group Black

Sheep (an LGBT organisation founded in 2004), the Institute Woman and Society, the Gender and Family Network, and the organisation Woman and Health in Uruguay (MYSU). The latter, a feminist NGO founded in 1996 and devoted to the promotion and defence of health and sexual and reproductive rights from a gender perspective, has been among the most active ones along the process analysed here.

Since the 1990s, when the left was elected to the government of Montevideo – and even more since 2005, when the candidate from the Frente Amplio, a leftist coalition, was elected as the president of Uruguay – new spaces of participation emerged, while a number of services formerly (or newly) provided by the state were outsourced by means of agreements with CSOs. These became an important source of income for CSOs, including women's rights organisations, as international cooperation funds declined (ICD et al, 2011).

The process towards legalisation, 1985–2012

Starting in 1938, the Uruguayan law imposed three- to nine-year prison sentences on women obtaining abortions, and sentences running from 6 to 24 months to those helping a woman get an abortion (except in cases of rape, when necessary to save the woman's life, or for reason of extreme poverty). These exceptions, however, were rarely invoked because the article spelling them out was never regulated, which meant that there were no actual mechanisms that could be used to obtain a legal abortion. In practice, punishments were rarely applied, and anti-abortion organisations have long campaigned for a more punitive approach. During the past decade prosecutions for unlawful termination of pregnancies averaged one per month, a number exceeding that of many other crimes. In addition, the penal system is highly selective, involving mostly women who lack the means to get safe abortions.

According to Sanseviero et al (2003), 55,000 live births and 33,000 abortions take place every year in this country of little more than three million. According to NGO sources, the actual number of abortions might be twice as high. It is no surprise that Uruguay has discussed alternatives to clandestine abortions for over 25 years: starting in 1985, when the dictatorship came to an end, about a dozen decriminalisation projects were drafted. However, only a few were even discussed in congressional committees, and even fewer were eventually debated in the House or the Senate.

Until the late 1980s the decriminalisation of abortion was demanded almost exclusively by feminist organisations, which were not yet recognised as legitimate stakeholders nor able to set the public debate agenda (Johnson, 2011). The public relevance of the issue increased since the early 1990s, just as the Fifth Feminist Meeting of Latin America and the Caribbean declared 28 September as the International Day for the Decriminalisation of Abortion. In the following years the date was turned into the focus of a campaign led by women's organisations of more than 20 countries and by seven regional networks, grouped under the motto 'Women decide, society respects, the state guarantees' (MYSU, 2007). As a result, the topic of sexual and reproductive rights became part of public debate, capturing the attention of other actors beyond the feminist movement – such as the Medical Union of Uruguay (SMU) – and eventually widening the concept of human rights.

Indeed, as early as 1992 the SMU convened an international seminar on bioethics and legislation; and in 1993 a Bioethics Committee was created in the House of Representatives. Around the same time three influential UN conferences took place: the World Conference on Human Rights (Vienna, 1993), the International Conference on Population and Development (Cairo, 1994), and the Fourth World Conference on Women (Beijing, 1995). These events caused repurcussions in Uruguay, such that in 1996 it began implementing sexual and reproductive health programmes from a gender perspective and with a focus on the expansion of rights (López Gómez and Abracinskas, 2009).

Public debate increased in the 2000s, within the context of an economic crisis that provoked a steep increase in the number of abortions performed in high-risk conditions, which became the major cause of maternal mortality. Health professionals reacted strongly which resulted in the foundation of a group, Sanitary Initiatives, speaking out against abortions in high-risk conditions, and in favour of decriminalisation. Their message, delivered by people with respected medical knowledge, gave legitimacy to the discourse of the feminist and women's movement.

As a result of the initiatives of feminist organisations, the National Coordination of Organisations for the Defence of Reproductive Health was formed in 2002, comprised of a variety of women's organisations, trade unions, neighbourhood, professional, human rights, youth and sexual diversity organisations, advocacy groups for people of African descent and even religious associations. In September 2002, an initiative was drafted for a Law of Defence of Sexual and Reproductive Health, which would make it compulsory for the state to provide sexual education, as well as services of reproductive health, family planning and contraception. It also declared the right of every woman to 'make a decision regarding the interruption of her pregnancy during its first twelve weeks'. Under the administration of Jorge Batlle (Partido Colorado), who had already announced to the Pope that he would veto it if it were to be passed by Congress, the initiative received half congressional sanction in December 2002. In April 2004, while the bill was being discussed in the Senate, the SMU publicly supported it. The National Coordination developed a strong campaign to 'give a hand' to legislators; the ensuing social debate ended up yielding a 63 per cent citizen support for decriminalisation. In turn, those opposed to the initiative, led by the hierarchy of the Catholic Church, conducted an intense campaign including appeals to the senators' 'Christian morals'. Eventually, in the midst of the presidential campaign the initiative was defeated in the Senate.

After this setback, pro-legalisation activists expected that the imminent Frente Amplio presidential victory would improve the situation. But that optimism did not last: even before taking office, president elect Tabaré Vázquez announced that, due to his personal convictions, he would veto any law decriminalising abortion. In spite of the president's opposition, in mid-2006 some Frente Amplio senators introduced a new decriminalisation initiative, which was passed by the Senate in late 2007 and by the House of Representatives a year later. However, the intense activism deployed in the hope of averting the anticipated presidential veto was fruitless; the president's partial veto remained firm.

The bill could only be reintroduced during the following legislature, that is, in or after 2010. Subsequently, the movement's goal was to force the issue onto the centre stage of the 2009 electoral campaign. This time the Frente Amplio included the issue in its programme, and both members of its presidential ticket, José Mujica and Danilo Astori, had as senators voted in favour of the bill.

The Frente Amplio won the presidency in a runoff election and obtained majorities in both houses of Congress. Soon after, two bills were introduced; one advocating legalisation, one favouring decriminalisation. Throughout 2010, however, debate focused on the preparation of the five-year budget, and the issue was only tackled again in mid-2011. The joint project that was eventually drafted – entitled Voluntary Interruption of Pregnancy Bill and advocated by two female *frenteamplista* senators – finally passed on 27 December. However, after the summer recess the bill entered the House of Representatives in February 2012, where it was subject to intricate negotiations and substantial modifications. Due to the reluctance of some of its own representatives, the Frente Amplio did not have enough votes to get it passed. It was eventually decided to work on an alternative decriminalisation proposal put forward by an Independent legislator. This resulting new bill still defined abortion as a crime, albeit one whose legal consequences were suppressed under certain circumstances, and imposed a number of conditions on women who wanted to have an abortion within the first 12 weeks of pregnancy. Among them was the obligation of attending a consultation with an interdisciplinary team of specialists, followed by a compulsory five day 'reflection period'. It also included a conscientious objection clause for health professionals and an exemption from performing the procedure for those institutions whose values were opposed to it (who should instead provide referrals to other institutions). This stipulation of what was deemed an 'inquisitory tribunal' was rejected as humiliating, condescending and disrespectful of women's autonomy (*La República*, 05/02/12). Following tough negotiations, the conscientious objection clause was eliminated; however, the consultation and the waiting period remained mandatory, and definitions stayed in place that removed abortion from the field of rights. Legalisation, that is, the recognition of abortion as an enforceable right, gave way to decriminalisation, that is, the elimination of the criminal consequences derived from committing an act that was still treated as evil.

In September, the initiative was approved first by a special congressional committee and then, after a close vote, by the House. Following a favourable vote in its Health Committee, the Senate soon turned it into law. Just hours later, even before the president had signed it, at least two initiatives were launched to have it revoked.

Throughout this process all parties (including the Frente Amplio) experienced divisions or at least some disagreement. Bills were always presented as individual rather than institutional initiatives even when, as occurred in some cases, all signatories belonged to the same party. Rather than reflecting a conflict between the executive and legislative branches of government, Vázquez's veto revealed a division within a ruling party that had a congressional majority. Similar divisions existed in the other parties.

Movement and countermovement: the two faces of civil society

Civil society is far from homogeneous; it typically contains diverse and even antagonistic expressions – such as, in this case, conglomerates of organisations in favour and against the legalisation of abortion. On one side there is a network headed by feminist and women's rights organisations that cuts across Uruguayan society; on the other, a movement led by high ranking Catholic Church officials and some evangelical pastors in addition to religious groups within academic, political and labour union settings.[4]

Uruguayan society has long been highly secularised, and it is probably the country with the lowest proportion of baptised Catholics in Latin America. The prevalence of Catholicism is also threatened by the growth of other Christian, mostly evangelical, churches in the country. Still, the Catholic Church remains a powerful institutional, transnational force with considerable influence over public policy – or, rather, over the limits of progressive public policy as sought by women's and LGBT movements, among others.

The two major positions on the abortion issue are not symmetrical. While the pro-legalisation movement is proactive in pushing for the transformation of a negatively assessed situation, the countermovement is typically reactive and focuses on preserving the status quo. Whereas the former is internally diverse and focused on sexual and reproductive rights and gender equality, the latter is more homogeneous, predominantly religious, and has an agenda encompassing a much wider range of issues. The legalisation movement includes autonomous organisations and consolidated networks with a long history of work related to health and women's rights issues; the countermovement contains both weak, ad-hoc organisations as well as well-known and high-ranking personalities backed by the Catholic Church.

While women are the main protagonists of the pro-legalisation movement, the leadership of the countermovement is overwhelmingly male. The revision of campaign materials and the analysis of the main actors' media discourse reveal that strategies also differ significantly: while both groups have resorted to lobbying, public campaigns, street demonstrations and protests, it has not been uncommon for prominent individuals from the countermovement to resort to metaphysical terror and threats as well (such as that of excommunication, aimed at Catholic legislators) (*El País*, 08/11/08; 27/12/11). On the other hand, the legalisation movement relied more heavily on an information-giving strategy through the prolific production of research and publications, while these materials were more rare on other side (a few texts were produced by Catholic institutions, typically focused on the bioethical dimension and controversially presented as 'scientific', and some seminar-like events – such as the one entitled 'Let's save both' – did take place) (Johnson et al, 2011). Consequently, the emphasis by the legalisation movement on public debate strongly contrasts with the countermovement's use of weapons aimed at reaffirming and/or disciplining the faithful rather than convincing the wider citizenry through rational argumentation.

The public debate advocated and staged by the women's movement was articulated in the language of rights, which allowed for the productive convergence of two perspectives. One of them was the classic feminist discourse that foregrounded the right of women to make decisions regarding their own bodies, thus placing the abortion issue within the realm of civil rights. The other one was the discourse of the left that underscored social inequalities regarding access to safe abortions and, therefore, placed the right to abortion (along with its delivery by the public healthcare system) within the framework of the widening of social rights. The main leaders of the pro-legalisation movement synthesised both perspectives by asserting the autonomy of *all* women, including the poorest ones, to make decisions regarding their own bodies, their lives and the composition of their families. This synthesis was the foundation for the movement's alliances with other social movements that shared their quest for a more radical democracy (see the interview with Lilián Celiberti in www.feminismo.org.br/).

Organisations, leaders and alliances

From 2002 onwards, the newly established National Coordination of Organisations for the Defence of Reproductive Health led the legalisation movement. Its spokespersons included the leaders of various organisations and networks such as Lilián Abracinskas, Lilián Celiberti and Milka Sorribas. All of them, as well as others with less public exposure, had been activists for many years. Many had brought into the movement a variety of experiences: typically, activism in leftist movements that had included jail time, torture and exile under the dictatorship.

Within the political system, one of the main allies of the women's movement was socialist senator Mónica Xavier, a physician, elected to lead the Frente Amplio in 2012. Other women, also Frente Amplio party members, were active in the House and the Senate at various stages in the process. Although they gathered the support of numerous male colleagues, the bills under discussion were most often authored by women and women were over-represented both in the signatures and the affirmative votes of the bills compared to their rates of participation in Congress and in their own party factions (Jones, 2007). Hence the insistence of the women's movement on the relevance of female political representation, which, they pointed out, would have resulted in the earlier legalisation of abortion, had it reached a higher threshold.

In the absence of a critical mass of female legislative representation, the leadership – the 'critical acts', as conceptualised by Dahlerup (1988) and Childs and Krook (2008, 2009) – of a few female legislators was key in the process. These women, who were in close contact with the social movement, wrote and introduced parliamentary initiatives, argued vehemently, and patiently built alliances. The significance of the presence of women with a gender agenda in key places was apparent beyond the legislative branch: for example, when the newly appointed female president of the Supreme Court (the first woman in 17 years) declared herself to be in favour of legalising abortion (*El Espectador*, 25/01/07).

Although the pro-legalisation movement included many men, its main leaders and activists were women. In contrast, while the marches and protests by the Pro-Life National Coordinating Council did include women, its leaders (as well as those of its member organisations) were mostly men. Among them were the archbishop of Montevideo and the bishops that made up the Episcopal Conference, as well as a tele-evangelist pastor and a few Partido Nacional legislators.

The number of players involved in the legalisation movement increased as public opinion began leaning towards legalisation. The first perceptible change took place among medical practitioners when a group of renowned professors, researchers and medical doctors founded the already mentioned Sanitary Initiatives group as a reaction to the increase in mortality due to unsafe abortions. Three years later, this led to the implementation of a set of guidelines by the Ministry of Public Health stating that, although abortion was not legal, to prevent an unsafe abortion a woman who wished to end her pregnancy would receive advice and support, as well as immediate post-abortion care. From then on, the physicians' organisations monitored the guidelines' implementation and insisted their opinion be taken into account regarding the technical component of any proposed bill regulating abortion.

A milestone was reached in 2004, when the first explicit pronouncement by the Workers' Confederation (PIT-CNT) favouring legislation took place on Labour Day. This position was repeatedly voiced in the following years; later on, labour leaders also testified in parliamentary commissions and attended events organised by the women's movement. Also in 2004 support for legalisation was expressed by the main public university and by national student organisations. From then on, the Universidad de la República produced copious research (presented in widely publicised public events) backing the movement's arguments and was the site for numerous information-providing events and public debates. In turn, the Federation of University Students of Uruguay (FEUU) repeatedly demonstrated their support for legalisation.

Repertoire of actions and campaigns

Since 2002, the pro-legalisation movement used an orange-coloured hand as a symbol of its campaign, initially with the slogan 'I vote for reproductive health'. Its repertoire encompassed a large variety of actions of mobilisation, denunciation, creation and dissemination of information, awareness and advocacy. These included producing and distributing books, sexual and reproductive health booklets and brochures contributing to the debate (in print and electronically); publishing open letters to the citizenry; organising and participating in seminars, forums and workshops with human rights specialists, representatives of political parties and unions, international experts and local academics; developing campaigns on websites and in the social networks; and participating in media debates, particularly on television and promoting street debates. 'Urban interventions', public performances and various 'creative protests' took place alongside more traditional actions such as collecting signatures and distributing flyers. Actions specifically targeted at legislators were also designed and implemented, including lobbying, releasing public declarations, meeting with likeminded legislators, providing input for parliamentary debate, and attending and participating in parliamentary committees. The presence of acivists during sessions both in the vicinity of the Legislative Palace and in the chambers' balconies was an important component of this strategy.

A variety of campaigns were held, all with two clear targets: the citizenry and parliamentary representatives. The slogan used in 2006, 'Citizen campaign for legal change', captured these two aspects well. Change had to come about through Congress; however, according to polls legislators were less liberal than their voters (although more so than their religious leaders). At the same time, legislators were cautious about risking their constituencies' votes. Therefore, the pro-legalisation movement worked on two fronts: first, it informed the citizenry, presenting them with arguments aimed at creating support for the issue, while simultaneously documenting advances in public opinion by administering and disseminating the results of opinion polls, with the aim of forcing legislators to 'respect the majoritarian will of the citizenry'. On the second front, intense one-on-one work was done with legislators in an attempt to obtain their votes.

Not all campaigns were launched by the National Coordination itself; some were promoted by autonomous groups of activists linked through social networks. For example, in June 2007, an internet campaign was organised to protest the arrest of a young woman who had gone to a public hospital to seek care for complications resulting from a clandestine abortion. A statement signed by thousands of people including both well-known individuals and anonymous citizens read: 'the undersigned have broken Law 9763 of 1938...by having had or paid for an abortion, by accompanying a woman to have an abortion or by knowing the identity of many such women and keeping silent. Either we are all criminals or the law is unfair' (*Página/12*, 17/06/07). In turn, the Facebook campaign 'No one else stays silent' asked participants to post a personal photo expressing their support for the bill (*La República*, 20/05/12).

Major institutional campaigns included the 'I vote for' logo featuring an orange-coloured hand raised to vote for the Sexual and Reproductive Health Law and, since 2009, the words 'These are your rights, assert them (the decisions regarding your body, your health and your life are yours)' and 'Your sexual and reproductive rights count'. After the newly elected President, *frenteamplista* José Mujica, was inaugurated, a new campaign was launched entitled 'Yes to the law – legal abortion 2010' that continued throughout the following years with the slogan 'Legal abortion – Uruguay. These are your rights, assert them'. Lastly, when the bill remained stalled due to the reluctance of two Frente Amplio representatives, the movement responded with the slogan 'The time is now'.

The latest campaign radically altered the framing of the movement's demand. Since 2009, the portion of the bill that former president Tabaré Vázquez had not vetoed established a set of sexual and reproductive rights. Thus the original campaign, centred on the recognition of such rights, gave way to the new Campaign for Legal Abortion. This was the first time that the movement directly mentioned abortion (and demanded that it be made legal, no less). Interviewed leaders and activists alike refer to this change as a monumental success: after intense internal debate, euphemisms had finally been left aside (Anabel Cruz, personal communication). However, this development also caused a rift with those organisations that preferred the broader, and less offensive, reproductive rights slogan. The composition of the movement's coordination, renamed Coordination for Legal Abortion, therefore changed.

The Coordination's members – social, trade union, student, feminist, women's, human rights and LGBT organisations – performed a large number of urban interventions revolving around the campaign's main themes: for instance, in October 2009, some 20 women walked through downtown Montevideo with their torsos exposed and painted to claim rights over their own bodies. Similarly, with the slogan 'While they set the conditions, we put our bodies on the line', a naked 'photographic performance' was staged next to the Congress building in September 2012 so as to express dissatisfaction with the decriminalisation initiative that was being debated in the House, underscoring the idea of a mostly male political body legislating on (and against) the rights of women (http://aldabe.org/gallery/v/performance+mysu/).

In August 2011, an intervention entitled 'What else is there to see?' was launched. Signs were placed on giant glasses with arguments supporting legalisation that read: 'Let's look at the reality'; 'More than 60 per cent of the population is in favour of legalising abortion'; '30,000 clandestine abortions per year, no one sees them but they exist' (*La Diaria*, 29/08/11). As a result of so-called 'orange dusk' interventions, various areas surrounding the National Congress and other landmarks woke up decorated with the movement's colour. Numerous spots supplemented these street actions and were widely viewed on the internet.

Throughout the campaign, actions intensified on select dates belonging to either the electoral or legislative calendars (or in reaction to decisive events, such as the signing of the presidential veto), and on iconic dates such as International Women's Day (8 March), International Workers' Day (1 May), the International Day of Action for Women's Health (28 May), and the International Day of Struggle for the Decriminalisation of Abortion in Latin America and the Caribbean (28 September). The countermovement also commemorated its own anniversaries, such as the Day of the Unborn Child (25 March). However, its main political expressions emerged from the Christmas and Easter messages delivered by the Episcopal Conference as well as from Sunday sermons and other public interventions of bishops and priests.

Regional and international linkages and networks

The international context is an inescapable point of reference for the women's movement, whose leaders frequently emphasise that abortion is legal in the 'developed world' and refer to statistics from those countries to demonstrate that the consequences of legal change are nothing like as apocalyptic as their adversaries sugggest. The pro-legalisation movement also has a regional dimension. First and foremost, there is the conviction that change on these issues cannot be sustained in one country alone. Therefore, progress in neighbouring countries is viewed as a sign of hope for one's own. Regular exchanges of experiences and cross-participation of civil society and parliamentary leaders of other countries in the region are considered to be of the utmost importance. Grassroots expressions of transnational support, such as demonstrations at Uruguayan embassies abroad, have indeed regularly taken place.

Similar links can be observed for the countermovement. These links are not restricted to the transnational actions of its main engine, the Catholic Church, or of the successive Republican administrations that sought to prevent US cooperation funds being used for policies promoting contraception, the prevention of sexually transmitted diseases, or abortion care (Abracinskas and López Gómez, 2007). The alliance of the Uruguayan movement with conservative pro-life sectors in the United States even included an attempt by the latter to directly influence the Uruguayan legislative process (Johnson, 2011, 208). Integration within a regional movement also brought about frequent visits of other Latin American pro-life activists; notably, however, their discourse emphasised the denounciation of the 'foreign' character of the pro-legalisation movement and its subordination to international foundations and organisations that view 'world population growth as a security problem' (*El País*, 01/12/11; 16/12/11).

Culture wars and the political battle for public opinion

In Uruguay, as in the rest of the world, abortion is at the centre of an authentic 'culture war' (Hunter, 1994). The debate that arose from it was highly asymmetrical, as it appealed for legitimacy to sources as disparate as science, religion and human rights. In addition, the contenders rarely appeared to be truly speaking to one another but rather addressing a specific, separate audience of their own.

Nevertheless, during the process, a more substantial debate was increasingly heard, promoted in great measure by the women's movement. Discussion took place not only in the media but also in everyday interactions, both face-to-face and virtual, and within social and labour organisations and academic institutions – and eventually within the political system as well. Building on each individual controversy the women's movement successfully informed and involved the citizenry, which slowly moved towards supporting decriminalisation.

Abortion is a divisive issue: every citizen seems to have a clear-cut opinion about it, and changes of mind are not likely to occur (Bottinelli and Buquet, 2010). Based on data from the 2007 Latinobarómetro poll, Rossi and Triunfo (2010) conclude that Uruguay is the Latin American country where abortion is most widely accepted. In most socio-demographic segments, decriminalisation was embraced by a majority of Uruguayans ever since the issue was inserted in opinion polls. The preferences expressed by those against, however, seem to have been more intense, which has had a strong impact on political and partisan dynamics.

Acccording to the Uruguayan public opinion research firm Factum, support for legalisation/decriminalisation has ranged between 55 and 63 per cent, with its highest point in 2003–04 and its lowest in 1993 (when the first poll was taken); while opposition to it has ranged from 27 per cent (2006, 2007) to 38 per cent (1993, 1997, 2000) (Bottinelli and Buquet, 2010). Favourable positions began to increase around 2002 (Selios, 2007). Other studies indicate that approval is higher among those with greater information, and that it is positively correlated with education and socio-economic levels and negatively correlated with religiosity. They also register a broad pro-legalisation majority among Frente Amplio and Partido Colorado voters and a relative parity of opinions among supporters of the Partido Nacional (Rossi and Triunfo, 2010; also *La Diaria*, 26/04/12). At least since 2004, when a majority in favour of legalisation seemed to consolidate, survey results were systematically used as a political weapon, as the social movement invoked the will of the citizenry as expressed in opinion polls to urge legislators and even the president to do their jobs as representatives.

Conclusion

This chapter provides an example of civil society as a stage on which struggles for the redefinition and expansion of rights take place, and on which women's organisations with a feminist perspective function as a source of women's emancipation. Distinct from the concept of empowerment, emancipation is here defined as the scrutinisation of all forms of domination from the standpoint of justice, aimed at achieving freedom from restraints of any kind – that is, stemming from tradition, religion, the market or the state. In Uruguay, women's organisations successfully challenged the imposition of a religious worldview as the law of the land, while also rejecting the hypocritical market logic that had for many decades allowed wealthier citizens to buy themselves safe abortions (as well as discretion) while forcing poorer women to undergo serious risks to their autonomy, health and lives.

As a result of the women's movement's struggle, the legalisation of abortion has long ceased to be a demand posed by a handful of extravagant feminists to become a policy change demanded by a substantial proportion of Uruguayan citizens. Initially promoted by a few isolated groups, it was eventually embraced by a broad coalition of social, trade union, youth, student, African-descendent and sexual diversity organisations. Far from its origins as a 'women's thing' belonging in the domestic sphere, abortion has become a social issue, a concern for both men and women and a legitimate object of public policy.

This change must be understood in the post-transitional Uruguayan context as well as within the broader international context marked by the emergence of new sets of rights – in particular, those of reproductive rights since the early 1990s and sexual rights since the 2000s. Five components of this process are especially noteworthy. The first is the centrality of the cooperation between feminist organisations and popular women's organisations, and later with other social movements. These linkages produced a synthesis between the classic feminist discourse of women's autonomy and their right to decide regarding their own bodies, and the discourse of the left, focused on social inequality and the resulting discrimination regarding access to resources – safe abortions in this case.

Second, a slow but decisive evolution became apparent from the concept of reproductive rights to the broader notion of sexual rights – both of them components of the so-called 'sexual citizenship' (Di Marco, 2010, 2). This demand for full sexual citizenship is as much a demand for civil rights (to the extent that it involves the recognition and provision of guarantees for the exercise of individual autonomy) as it is for social rights, since it assumes that these rights should be provided through the public health system. It was under this umbrella that the women's and sexual diversity movements converged. This natural alliance was only strengthened by the attacks received from their common Christian fundamentalist enemy.

Third, the movement under study was not a mass movement (nor is the countermovement, for that matter). Rather, it was a movement of activists that was able to summon mobilisations of a few hundred people at most. Therefore, the reasons for its effectiveness are not located in the numbers mobilised, but rather in the depth of the transformations in the prevailing common sense of Uruguayan citizens and, as a result, in the expressions of the so-called 'public opinion'. These changes can be credited in large measure to the intense information-giving campaigns and the efforts at promoting public debate that were carried out by the women's movement for decades, and were enhanced through tactics involving a wide array of artistic performances in public spaces.

Fourth, the asymmetry of the public arguments displayed for and against the legalisation of abortion is striking and effectively meets all requirements for it to be considered a cultural war: a dispute over the authority to name, interpret and regulate social life. The reason why these arguments rarely meet each other and result in true debate is that they are formulated at different levels. On the one hand, the question is raised as a 'moral problem'; therefore, what needs to be decided upon is whether abortion is 'good' or 'bad'. Once defined as bad, there is no question that the power of the state should be used to enforce its prohibition. Accompanied by a virulent aesthetic including the waving of crucifixes and the sensationalist exhibition of (not necessarily authentic) images of aborted foetuses, the pro-life discourse is not short on scientific fallacies, questionable analogies and even false information. On the other side of the divide, the question is raised as a political issue. Within the framework of the Weberian 'polytheism of values' that is the hallmark of modern society, no serious attempt is made to present a compelling argument against the religious convictions of evangelicals and Catholics; instead, arguments are advanced in favour of positioning these convictions (as well as their own) within the plurality of social life, while setting up the state as the protector of the right of every person to lead a life in accordance with their own values.

Finally, the complex links between the social movement and the political system highlight the problem of political representation. Abortion seems to be a unique issue in its capacity to open gaps between representatives and citizens, inasmuch as it allows the former to invoke reasons of conscience so as not to fulfill their promises to the latter – the very promises that elevated them as representatives in the first place. It is also an issue regarding which the implementation of gender representation quotas could produce huge differences in outcomes.

In a context of very limited female representation and major disconnection between the preferences of a majority of citizens and the positions of their elected representatives, the law passed in late 2012 left nobody happy. While pro-lifers readily mobilised to restore prohibition, the women's movement struggled to guarantee the implementation of a law that it deemed insufficient inasmuch as it withheld recognition of women as equal beings able to make up their own minds. In the end, activism and mobilisation remain the staple of democratic politics because, as lucidly observed by Mónica Xavier, 'rights are never secured once and for all' (*La República*, 13/05/12).

Notes

[1] Consulted online news sources include *Argenpress* (www.argenpress.info/), *BBC Mundo* (www.bbc.co.uk/mundo/), *Bioética Web* (www.bioeticaweb.com), *Clarín* (www.clarin.com/), *Diario Libre* (www.diariolibre.com), *El Espectador* (www. espectador.com), *El Observador* (www.elobservador.com.uy), *El País* (www.elpais. com.uy/), *IPS Noticias* (http://ipsnoticias.net), *La Diaria* (http://ladiaria.com.uy/), *La Nación* (www.lanacion.com.ar), *La Red 21* (www.lr21.com.uy/), *La República* (www.diariolarepublica.net), *Página/12* (www.pagina12.com.ar), *Radio 180* (www.180.com/uy), *Reuters* (http://lta.reuters.com) and Últimas noticias (www. unoticias.com.uy/). The main consulted organisations' and campaign websites are the following: Campaña por los Derechos Sexuales y Reproductivos (www. facebook.com/abortolegal), CNS Mujeres (www.cnsmujeres.org.uy/), Colectivo Ovejas Negras (www.ovejasnegras.org/), Hacelos Valer (www.hacelosvaler.org) and Mujer y Salud en Uruguay (www.mysu.org.uy/).

[2] Anabel Cruz conducted the interviews and provided me with invaluable insight on the issues and people involved, for which I am gratefully indebted.

[3] Women's rights CSOs are indeed integrated into a social movement, which for the purposes of this chapter is defined as 'a network of informal interactions between a plurality of individuals, groups and/or organisations, engaged in a political or cultural conflict, on the basis of a shared collective identity' (Diani, 1992, 13).

[4] Although the highest ranks of most (but not all) churches opposed the legalisation of abortion, there were dissident voices within all of them.

References

Abracinskas, L, López Gómez, A, 2007, Desde la arena feminista hacia la escena política, in L Abracinskas, A López Gómez (eds) *Aborto en debate. Dilemas y desafíos del Uruguay democrático. Proceso político y social 2001–2004*, pp 11–30, Montevideo: MYSU (Mujer y Salud en Uruguay)

Barreiro, F, Cruz, A, 1988, *La dificultad de ser. Organizaciones no gubernamentales en el Uruguay de hoy: el desafío de la democracia*, Montevideo: Fundación de Cultura Universitaria/Instituto Latinoamericano de Estudios Transnacionales/Instituto de Comunicación y Desarrollo

Bottinelli, OA, Buquet, D, 2010, *El aborto en la opinión pública uruguaya*, Montevideo: MYSU (Mujer y Salud en Uruguay)

Childs, S, Krook, ML, 2008, Critical mass theory and women's political representation, *Political Studies* 56, 10, 725–36

Childs, S, Krook, ML, 2009, Analysing women's substantive representation: From critical mass to critical actors, *Government and Opposition* 44, 2, 125–45

Dahlerup, D, 1988, From a small to a large minority. Women in Scandinavian politics', *Scandinavian Political Studies* 11, 2, 275–97

Diani, M, 1992, The concept of social movement, *The Sociological Review* 40, 1, 1–25

Di Marco, G, 2010, Luchas contrahegemónicas en Argentina: el 'pueblo feminista' vs. la nación católica, paper presented at the XXIXth LASA (Latin American Studies Association), International Congress, Toronto: Canada, October 6–9

Hunter, JD, 1994, *Before the shooting begins: Searching for democracy in America's culture war*, New York: The Free Press

ICD (Instituto de Comunicación y Desarrollo), Red Uruguaya de ONGs Ambientalistas (ANONG Uruguay/CNS Mujeres), 2011, *Vamos Andando…Las organizaciones de la sociedad civil rendimos cuentas*, Montevideo: Informe Colectivo Uruguay

IDEA (International Institute for Democracy and Electoral Assistance), 2005, *Women in parliament: Beyond numbers. A revised edition*, Stockholm: International Institute for Democracy and Electoral Assistance

Johnson, N, 2005, *La política de la ausencia: las elecciones uruguayas 2005–2005, las mujeres y la equidad de género*, Montevideo: CNS Mujeres

Johnson, N, López Gómez, A, Sapriza, G, 2011, *(Des)penalización del aborto en Uruguay: Prácticas, actores y discursos. Abordaje interdisciplinario sobre una realidad compleja*, Montevideo: Universidad de la República/CSIC

Johnson, N, 2011, El tratamiento de la despenalización del aborto en el ámbito político-parlamentario, in N Johnson, A López Gómez, G Sapriza (eds) *(Des)penalización del aborto en Uruguay: Prácticas, actores y discursos. Abordaje interdisciplinario sobre una realidad compleja*, pp 185–228, Montevideo: Universidad de la República/CSIC

Jones, D, 2007, El debate parlamentario sobre la 'Ley de Defensa de la Salud Reproductiva' en Uruguay (2002–2004), L Abracinskas, A López Gómez (eds) *Aborto en debate: Dilemas y desafíos del Uruguay democrático. Proceso político y social 2001–2004*, pp 53–98, Montevideo: MYSU (Mujer y Salud en Uruguay)

Lissidini, A, 1996, La 'modernización' de las mujeres: Una mirada al Uruguay del novecientos, *Revista de Ciencias Sociales*, 12, Montevideo: Universidad de la República

López Gómez, A, Abracinskas, L, 2009, *El debate social y político sobre la Ley de defensa del derecho a la salud sexual y reproductiva*, Cuadernos del UNFPA (Fondo de Población de las Naciones Unidas) 3, 3, Montevideo: Trilce

Mujeres Convencionales, 2009, Representación política de las mujeres y la cuota en Uruguay, Primer Encuentro Nacional de Mujeres Convencionales, Montevideo, www0.parlamento.gub.uy/ parlamenta/descargas/rep_pol_mujeres.pdf

Mujeres Latinoamericanas en Cifras, no date, Organizaciones sociales de mujeres, www.eurosur.org/FLACSO/mujeres/

MYSU (Mujer y Salud en Uruguay), 2007, Aborto en Uruguay: Las mujeres deciden, la sociedad respeta, y el Estado garantiza, *Cuaderno de Divulgación sobre Derechos y Salud Sexual y Reproductiva* 1, 5, Montevideo: MYSU

Rossi, M, Triunfo, P, 2010, Opinión ciudadana sobre el aborto: Uruguay y América Latina, *Working Paper* 15, Montevideo: Department of Economics, School of Social Sciences, Universidad de la República

Sanseviero, R, Rostagnol, S, Guchin M, Migliónico, A, 2003, *Condena, tolerancia y negación: El aborto en Uruguay*, Montevideo: Centro Internacional de Investigación e Información para la Paz

Sapriza, G, 2009, Memorias de mujeres en el relato de la dictadura (Uruguay, 1973–1985), Violencia/cárcel/exilio, *DEP (Deportate, esuli, profughe), Revista telemática di studi sulla memoria femminile* 11, 64–80

Selios, L, 2007, La opinión pública, la democracia representativa y el aborto, in L Abracinskas, A López Gómez (eds) *Aborto en debate. Dilemas y desafíos del Uruguay democrático: Proceso político y social 2001– 2004*, pp 151–66, Montevideo: MYSU (Mujer y Salud en Uruguay)

Tarrow, S, 1998, *Power in movement*, New York: Cambridge University Press

Teune, S, 2005, Art and the re-invention of political protest, paper presented at the 3rd ECPR (European Consortium Conference), Budapest, 8–10 September

Tilly, C, 1995, *Popular contention in Great Britain, 1758–1834*, Cambridge: Harvard University Press

Tilly, C, 2006, *Regimes and repertoires*, Chicago, IL and London: University of Chicago Press

Tilly, C, 2008, *Contentious performances*, New York: Cambridge University Press.

EIGHT

Sustainability from the bottom up: women as change agents in the Niger Delta

Charisma Acey

Introduction

The environmental destruction brought on by the irresponsible practices of multinational oil companies (MNOCs) in Nigeria has opened up social space for women's political mobilisation. The nine oil producing states comprising the Niger Delta (see Map 8.1) are among the least developed in Nigeria, despite the fact that the country is a top producer of oil globally and oil revenues account for the majority of Nigeria's GDP. Political unrest in the Niger Delta is tied to state corruption, neglect and oil company malfeasance (Jike, 2004; Ikelegbe, 2005). Women's traditional livelihoods in fishing, agriculture and trade have been lost due to the pollution of waterways, soils and vegetation. The impact on women's roles in society is acute in Niger Delta communities where women bear the responsibility of household survival of female-headed families or of their household unit within a polygamous household configuration (Omorodion, 2004).

Historically, in the Niger Delta, when women's economic livelihoods have been disrupted by changes in government policy, they have taken on the forces of their economic oppression. This in turn has had the effect of loosening the binds of other forms of oppression as well. However, does participation in local environmental and social struggles fit into a broadly transformational agenda of social, political and economic equality such as that first articulated by feminists in the 1970s, or into the more narrow conception of empowerment espoused in international development policy (Mosedale, 2005)? Using newly assembled data from Nigeria on women's participation in social protest and activism, women's household decision-making and attitudes towards women's empowerment, this chapter attempts to answer this question.

In measuring the freedom and power of women relative to men, most of the international development literature focuses on economic empowerment and the related choices women can and do make (Kabeer, 1999; Mosedale, 2005; Anderson and Eswaran, 2009). In Nigeria, such power can be measured by the choices women are able to make about whether to work, participate in politics, what to purchase for the household, the number of children to have, whether to buy and sell land and other critical life decisions (Kritz and Makinwa-Adebusove, 1999). However, Kabeer (1999) writes that women's empowerment is also 'about the process by which those who have been denied the ability to make strategic life choices acquire such ability' (Kabeer, 1999, 435).

Map 8.1: Niger Delta, Nigeria

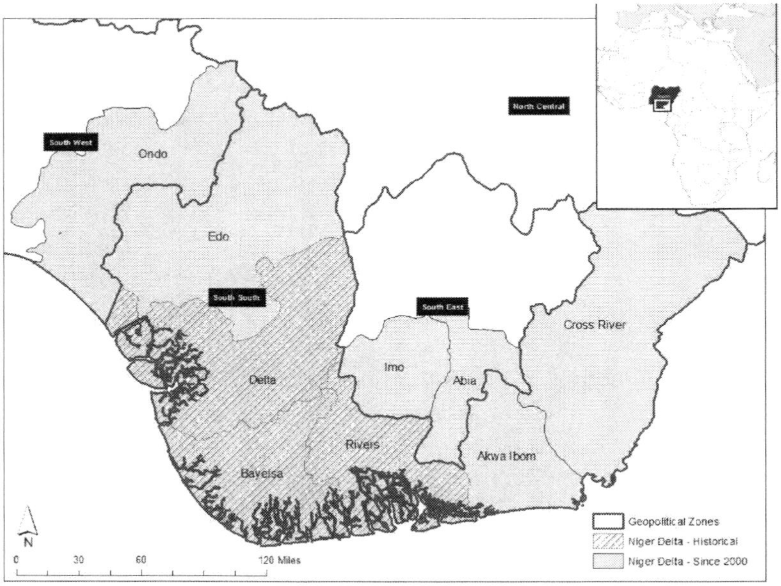

Source: Map by author

In order to assess the impact on women of civil society organisations in the Niger Delta, the working definition of empowerment employed in this chapter is two-fold: it is the ability of women to make autonomous, strategic life choices on the one hand, and, on the other, the ability to work strategically with others to advance their own interests. The latter part of this definition comes from observations made by Bina Agarwal, Srilatha Batliwala and others that true empowerment is a process of transformation that requires women to recognise and analyse the institutions and sources of their subjugation and to be able to act individually and collectively in ways that challenge and change those structures, such as increased political voice, bargaining power inside and outside of the household, and alteration of their roles in the labour market (Batliwala, 1994; Agarwal 1997; 2001; Mosedale, 2005).

These choices and actions involve certain preconditions, including political freedom, human capital, agency in actions taken (real choice, not only a lack of alternatives, but choice based on the equality of access to material and environmental resources) and expectations that the outcome of empowerment should be positive (Kabeer, 1999; 2005; Narayan, 2005; Grabe, 2012). This approach to empowerment goes beyond a single dimension, such as economic empowerment, and recognises that social and structural inequalities can limit empowerment as both process and outcome, even if women seemingly have more freedom to choose and to act.

This chapter explores how the environmental and social crises produced by decades of exploitation of natural resources and neglect of the people, have shaped opportunities for women to make choices they could not make before and to transform oppressive institutions. This analysis builds data from several established sources, including nationally representative household surveys conducted by ICF Macro/ MEASURE Demographic and Health Surveys (DHS), survey data from the Afrobarometer project, and the Social Conflict in Africa Database (SCAD) hosted by the Center for Climate Change and African Political Stability (CCAPS). Although the datasets were not originally collected to answer questions about women's empowerment, indicators relevant to women's empowerment and participation were selected from each source. Chosen indicators were then either geocoded or tallied by region, allowing for a regional, geographic comparison of various measures of women's empowerment between the Niger Delta and the rest of the country.

There are a number of challenges in attempting to analyse the data in this way. First, the lack of time series data makes it difficult to make an explicit causal link between environmental activism and the evidence for increased women's empowerment in the Niger Delta as compared to other regions. In addition, compiling diverse data sources by region that use slightly different geographic definitions makes for an imperfect comparison between datasets. The nine-state region that officially makes up the Niger Delta today actually crosses three of Nigeria's current geopolitical zones (see 8.2), although most of the area lies in the South-South zone.[1] While the ICF Measure DHS survey disaggregates data to geopolitical zone, Afrobarometer reports data at the state level. Accordingly, the Afrobarometer data had to be divided into two groupings, one comprising states making up the Niger Delta region and the other including all remaining states. The Social Conflict in Africa Database was used for mapping, and contains data geocoded to various levels of spatial accuracy (town/village, city and state). The data is mainly used here to provide a visual analysis of where social conflict has taken place in Nigeria, the nature of that conflict and the extent of women's roles as leaders of such conflict events. Additional insight concerning the impact on women of their involvement in and with civil society organisations comes from interviews and other secondary sources. This chapter now turns to describing women and civil society in the region, then assessing the impact of their civil society participation on two dimensions central to women's empowerment; their life choices and their ability to transform social structures that produce adversity.

Women, social movements and civil society in the Niger Delta

This section brings together a discussion of women's political activism in the Niger Delta with the notion of political ecology. A political ecology approach is one that views environmental hazards as resulting directly from power relations and social institutions at multiple scales that govern land use, property rights and the distribution of wealth (Blaikie and Brookfield, 1987; Robbins, 2004). Building on the experiences of women involved in the struggle for environmental and social justice and transparency in the oil sector in Nigeria, alongside prior studies of the movement, this section explores how the processes that produce environmental degradation in the Niger Delta have a direct impact on women's livelihoods, subsequently instigating their social mobilisation and, indirectly, their empowerment.

Civil society in the West African context does not only include formal non-governmental organisations (Ekiyor, 2008). There is a strong tradition of associational life in Africa that includes the plethora of institutions that establish and regulate the social order, and provide assistance and services to citizens outside or in parallel to the state (Bratton, 1989; Osaghae, 1999; Simone, 2001). These include organisations based on ethnic, kinship, trade, religious and traditional affiliations. The emergence of civil society groups concerned with environmental and economic justice in the Niger Delta reflects a broader trend of women and men across the country seeking to have

Map 8.2: States and geopolitical zones in Nigeria

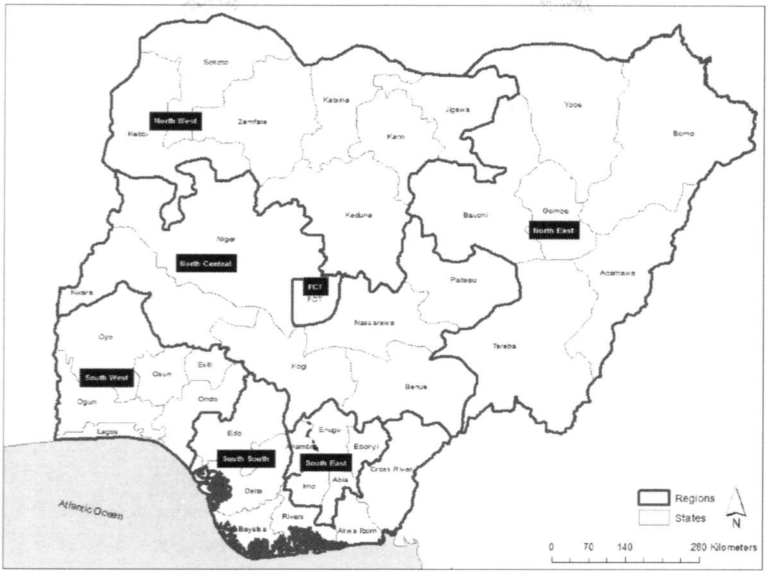

Source: Map by author

a direct voice in public affairs, conflict management and decision making following Nigeria's return to electoral democracy in 1999 (Olufemi and Adewale, 2012). The return of democracy has unleashed long repressed demands by various ethnic, religious and communal factions. Democratic transition is still a work in progress, as Freedom House indicators of the quality of democracy showed declines in the first two post-military elections (Ukiwo, 2003; Kuenzi, 2008).[2] The fierce struggle for power and the use of armed thugs to intimidate opponents in electoral contests have directly led to increased violent conflicts, insurgency and kidnappings in the Niger Delta carried out by the Movement for the Emancipation of the Niger Delta (MEND), and terrorism and kidnapping carried out by newer terrorist groups such as Boko Haram in the North.

Civil society groups have sought to speak out against environmental destruction by MNOCs, seek reparations for past damage since oil was first discovered in the late 1950s, demand increased allocation of state resources, argue for self-determination and full participation in development projects, press for employment of local indigenous people by oil companies and condemn publicly both state and militant violence. The types of actions undertaken by civil society groups include nonviolent protests at MNOC offices and facilities, government houses and embassies. Additional activities include production stoppages, rallies, use of print, radio and television media, direct communication to MNOCs about their destructive actions as well as alternative development proposals, structured meetings with state officials and MNOC representatives and lawsuits. The rise of civil society has brought a more collective voice to the grievances and demands of the peoples of the Niger Delta, and women are slowly emerging as leaders in this movement.

Faith Nwadishi is the Executive Director of the Koyenum Immalah Foundation (KIF). Founded in 2000, KIF seeks to improve the welfare and rights of women and children, and is also active in broad environmental coalitions such as the 'Keep the Oil in the Soil' campaign started in 2009. Currently, she is the national Publish What You Pay (PWYP)[3] coordinator in Nigeria, and was recently elected to the Nigerian Extractive Industries Transparency Initiative of Nigeria (EITI) Multi-Stakeholder Group (MSG).[4] Nwadishi's work has a strong focus on the gender impact of extractive industries with respect to pollution, loss of land and livelihoods and the resulting social conflict. The PWYP e-newsletter for International Women's Day on the effects of mining on women quotes Nwadishi: 'The pressure is on the women – they are the ones who have to take care of their homes and their children, in the hope that their children will live better lives than they have lived' (PWYP, 2013). Despite this, attempts to force the mining companies to provide more opportunity at the local level in Nigeria, through Community Development Agreements to create local jobs, typically exclude employment opportunities for women.

Similar concerns have been expressed by other women involved in the struggle for justice in the wake of environmental devastation and increasing violence in the Niger Delta. Emem Okon, founder of Kebetkache Women's Development and Resource Centre, who is featured in the film documentary by Schermerhorn (2010) *The Naked Option: A Last Resort* says, 'Education does not reduce the risks but it provides women with the skill and knowledge to confront that risk. It makes them bolder.' The film depicts the profoundly frustrated women residents of Ugborodo and Amukpe of Delta State as they directly confront the oil companies. Okon works to promote the advancement of women's education and leadership development and she plays a pivotal role in the widespread 2002 protests, helping the rural women to negotiate their demands with Chevron. In the process of holding workshops with the women throughout the Delta, many interviewed in the documentary acknowledge their own political transformation, realising that there are other avenues of personal and self-development and pathways to become involved in government and NGOs to address constructively the needs of their families, themselves and their communities in the long term.

Where does social activism by Niger Delta women fit into the spectrum of women's historical roles in civil society? This activism is not a new phenomenon. Women were mobilised as early as the colonial period, participating in popular protests against British taxation (Mba, 1982; Ukeje, 2004). One of the most notorious uprisings was that led by women of the Niger Delta; the Women's War of 1929 (which the British dubbed the Aba Riots.) Thousands of Ibibio and Igbo women protested against British administration of Southeastern Nigeria, demanding female representation in the system of warrant chiefs the British had established to govern the area (Van Allen, 1975; Falola and Paddock, 2011). In the conflict, the British opened fire, killing 50 women while suffering no casualties themselves. The protests, which led to the British revising their policies, were developed and led by women and continued in the 1930s leading up to the negotiations for Nigeria's independence.

Women were again at the forefront of protest actions in the 1980s when military rulers asserted further government control over oil resources, ignoring the ethnic revenue and power sharing that had been established under the regional governments (Patch, 2008). This control meant seizure of indigenous lands for use by oil corporations. The resulting pollution destroyed the local fishing industry, in which women were directly employed, along with subsistence farming. Such direct disturbance of the local economy meant that women could no longer perform their traditional roles. Many, as a result, became engaged in the full spectrum of resistance and struggle for environmental and social justice in the Niger Delta. The next section addresses two questions: do women in the Niger Delta have higher levels of civil society participation? Do attitudes about participation differ from other parts of the country?

Measuring attitudes towards participation and women's emancipation

In an earlier study using Afrobarometer data that compared interpersonal trust, political trust and democracy in Ghana and Nigeria, both countries were selected for having characteristics not conducive to social cooperation and trust necessary for the common good. Both countries feature ethnic heterogeneity, perceived and actual corruption in public institutions, widespread poverty and high levels of income inequality. The study found additional evidence that membership and participation in voluntary associations are higher where trust between citizens and between citizens and their government (due to corruption or autocracy) is low (Anderson and Paskeviciute, 2006; Kuenzi, 2008). This mirrors past work on association membership in Nigeria that has sought to explain the dramatic rise of voluntary organisations that provide services to the public in lieu of an indifferent and ineffective state, operating as a kind of shadow government (Osaghae, 1999).

The findings here are based on surveys administered by the Afrobarometer project in Nigeria, using data from Round 5 of the surveys, conducted between 2010 and 2012. The survey sample size is 2,400, selected with stratified random sampling to ensure national representation from all major demographic segments of the population; 579 of the responses came from residents of the nine Niger Delta states (out of Nigeria's total of 36 states plus the federal capital territory housing the national capital in Abuja).

The first thing to stand out is the profile of respondents from Niger Delta states, where men and women tend to have higher secondary school completion rates than the nation as a whole. The Afrobarometer asks a number of questions related to civil society participation and civic engagement, and attitudes about women's equality. Grouping them by type and topic, there are three questions around civic participation (attendance at community meetings, participation in protests or demonstrations, and joining with others to raise issues). Additional questions include respondent membership in voluntary associations and community groups, as well as attitudes about women having equal rights, being effective leaders, receiving equal treatment and the freedom to speak freely. In Table 8.1, results are summarised by gender and divided into responses from Niger Delta residents versus national responses. When it comes to civic participation, more respondents from the Niger Delta report willingness to engage in protest, organise around important issues, or attend a community meeting. There is also a dramatic difference between women in the Niger Delta and women nationally on these issues. For example, nationally, 33 per cent of women respondents say they would never attend a community meeting. Only 17 per cent of women in the Niger Delta said the same thing. In fact, higher percentages of women from the region report having attended community meetings. Similar patterns hold when asking about participation in demonstrations or protest marches and joining with others to raise issues of concern. Women in the Niger Delta are more likely to respond favourably to these questions than women across Nigeria.

When asked about actual membership in voluntary associations or community groups, nearly half of Niger Delta women report belonging to such an organisation, compared to a national average of 29 per cent for women. Active membership is about double the rate in the Niger Delta compared to the national membership.

Only 2 per cent of women respondents, however, identified themselves as official leaders of community organisations. This was the same percentage of women nationally who reported being community group leaders. For all of the questions in this category, men tend to participate or indicate a willingness to participate at higher rates than women. This is true in the region and nationally. However, men in the Niger Delta are also engaged more so than their counterparts nationally. Overall, there appears to be a relationship between the higher levels of activism in the Niger Delta and higher percentage of women participating in civil society.

The question remains whether this increased civic engagement also corresponds to improved status for women in the region or to local attitudes about women's role in society. An additional set of questions in the Afrobarometer survey asks how women are treated by courts and police, employers and traditional leaders. The survey goes on to ask whether women have equal rights under the law or should be subject to traditional laws, and whether women should take on leadership roles in society. Higher percentages of women and men in the Niger Delta than in the other regions report that women are treated unequally by traditional leaders 'often' or 'always'. Unfair treatment by employers and courts is common and similarly high in the region and nationally.

Where there is real difference between the Niger Delta and all of Nigeria is on questions of freedom and equality, where 46 per cent of women in the Niger Delta survey report being 'completely free' to say what they think versus 33 per cent of women nationally. Additionally, 50 per cent of women in the region say that women should have equal rights versus being subject to traditional laws. This is compared to 38 per cent of women nationally, and 38 per cent of Niger Delta men. However, the percentage of men responding favourably is higher than for Nigeria as a whole, where only 30 per cent of men agree strongly with the statement that women should have equal rights; 69 per cent of women from the Delta agree or agree strongly that women can be leaders (versus 59 per cent nationally). Women seem to feel more empowered, despite the fact their male counterparts do not (only 50 per cent of men in the Niger Delta agree and only 46 per cent nationally).

Table 8.1: Selected questions from Afrobarometer Round 5 (2010–12) with national and Niger Delta percentages

Attend a community meeting by gender of respondent				Niger Delta		
Total N=2,400; Weighted results	**Total**	**Male**	**Female**	**Total**	Male	Female
No, would never do this	26%	18%	33%	15%	14%	17%
No, but would do if had the chance	30%	29%	31%	20%	14%	27%
Yes, once or twice	11%	13%	10%	13%	11%	15%
Yes, several times	22%	27%	18%	32%	38%	25%
Yes, often	11%	14%	7%	20%	23%	17%
Don't know	0%	0%	0%	0%	0%	0%
Total	2,400	1,200	1,200	579	289	290
Attend a demonstration or protest march by gender of respondent				Niger Delta		
Total N=2,400; Weighted results	**Total**	**Male**	**Female**	**Total**	**Male**	Female
Would never do this	74%	67%	82%	63%	58%	68%
Would if had the chance	16%	20%	13%	24%	28%	21%
Once or twice	5%	8%	3%	6%	7%	6%
Several times	2%	4%	1%	3%	5%	2%
Often	1%	1%	0%	1%	1%	2%
Don't know	1%	1%	1%	2%	1%	2%
Total	2,400	1,200	1,200	578	289	289
Join others to raise an issue by gender of respondent				Niger Delta		
Total N=2,400; Weighted results	Total	Male	Female	Total	Male	Female
No, would never do this	30%	21%	39%	15%	13%	18%
No, but would do if had the chance	26%	28%	25%	20%	14%	25%
Yes, once or twice	17%	18%	16%	20%	21%	18%
Yes, several times	19%	24%	15%	30%	33%	27%
Yes, often	7%	9%	4%	15%	20%	11%
Don't know	0%	0%	0%	0%	0%	0%
Total	2,400	1,200	1,200	580	289	291

Member of voluntary association or community group by gender of respondent				Niger Delta		
Total N=2,400; Weighted results	**Total**	**Male**	**Female**	**Total**	**Male**	Female
Not a member	64%	56%	71%	44%	38%	51%
Inactive member	10%	11%	10%	12%	10%	15%
Active member	22%	27%	16%	38%	45%	31%
Official leader	4%	6%	2%	5%	7%	2%
Don't know	0%	0%	0%	1%	1%	1%
Total	2,400	1,200	1,200	577	288	289

Freedom to say what you think by gender of respondent				Niger Delta		
Total N=2,400; Weighted results	**Total**	**Male**	**Female**	**Total**	**Male**	Female
Not at all free	10%	11%	9%	10%	11%	9%
Not very free	21%	20%	21%	19%	16%	23%
Somewhat free	35%	34%	37%	20%	20%	21%
Completely free	34%	35%	33%	49%	53%	46%
Don't know	0%	0%	0%	1%	1%	1%
Total	2,400	1,200	1,200	578	290	288

Women have equal rights vs. subject to traditional laws by gender of respondent				Niger Delta		
Total N=2,400; Weighted results	**Total**	**Male**	**Female**	Total	Male	Female
Agree very strongly with 1	34%	30%	38%	44%	38%	50%
Agree with 1	34%	37%	31%	31%	31%	30%
Agree with 2	18%	20%	16%	12%	15%	10%
Agree very strongly with 2	14%	13%	15%	13%	15%	10%
Agree with neither	0%	0%	0%	1%	1%	1%
Don't know	0%	0%	0%	0%	0%	0%
Total	2,400	1,200	1,200	578	289	289

Men only as leaders vs. women leaders ok by gender of respondent				Niger Delta		
Total N=2,400; Weighted results	**Total**	**Male**	**Female**	**Total**	**Male**	Female
Agree very strongly with 1	22%	25%	19%	22%	29%	16%
Agree with 1	24%	27%	21%	17%	19%	14%
Agree with 2	26%	25%	27%	26%	24%	27%
Agree very strongly with 2	27%	21%	32%	34%	26%	42%
Agree with neither	0%	0%	0%	1%	1%	0%
Don't know	0%	0%	0%	1%	1%	0%
Total	2,400	1,200	1,200	577	288	289

Women's empowerment as strategic decision-making

The data in this section provide some insight on women's control over strategic life and household decisions and bargaining power in the household – part of the empowerment definition explored here. In an EU-sponsored study of 120 Niger Delta communities in Bayelsa and Delta states conducted by the Niger Delta based-NGO, Leadership Initiative for Transformation and Empowerment (LITE), only 8 per cent of communities were found to have women who said they were included in any way in decision making. Moreover, whether or not the women participate was reported to be completely up to men. The willingness of men to allow for women's participation in governance was strongly correlated with the number of generations of exposure to formal education (LITE, 2013).

The data to measure women's decision-making agency are tabulated from the Women's Questionnaire from the 2008, 2003 and 1999 Nigeria Demographic and Health Survey (NDHS). The survey investigates a comprehensive set of factors affecting maternal healthcare, such as household expenditures, postpartum family planning (birth spacing and prevention of unplanned, high risk and unwanted pregnancy, leading to increased risk of maternal death). These data are used to track progress towards improving maternal health, Millennium Development Goal 5. The ability to manage one's own reproductive health is fundamental, yet, according to the 2008 DHS, only 10 per cent of Nigerian women use modern methods of birth control, 11 per cent of pregnancies are unplanned, resulting in higher fertility rates, and only 29 per cent of married women had ever used any form of family planning (NPC and ICF International, 2009). Some questions focus directly on women's healthcare, while other questions delve into the context of household decision-making, such as women's earnings, who controls how those earnings are spent. Additional questions directly relating to women's empowerment status are asked, such as the ability of a woman to refuse sex and women's attitudes towards wife beating. Selected variables on literacy and contraceptive use are presented in Table 8.2. All of these measures represent measures of the choices women are able to make and a precondition of empowerment – awareness of the conditions of oppression around which women might organise with others to change.

When asked about their own earnings over the previous 12 months, and who decides how those earnings are spent, women from the South-South region are more likely to indicate that others are in control of those earnings. A higher percentage of women in the South-South region are literate (78 per cent versus 53 per cent of women nationally).

In addition, married women in the region do report higher rates of modern contraceptive use (15.5 per cent versus 9.7 per cent nationally) and having an unmet need for family planning (26.4 per cent versus 20 per cent nationally). When it comes to women's attitudes towards wife beating, and whether such abuse is justified for a variety of reasons (for example, arguing, going out without telling him, burning food, refusing sex, or neglecting the children), women in the southern part of the country (South-South, South-East and South-West zones) are less likely to respond that such beatings are acceptable, compared to their northern counterparts. The number of women finding beatings to be justified fell between the 2003 and 2008 surveys. This is likely to be attributable to education levels, higher rates of participation and awareness of rights, and the declining prevalence of polygamous marriage.

Activism as a strategic life choice

Using a broad definition of civil society, which encompasses 'uncivil' behaviour and contentious politics (Kopecký and Mudde, 2003), female members of civil society organisations in the Niger Delta adopt multiple tactics, such as engaging in civil disobedience, for instance occupying oil platforms, flow stations, shutting down crude oil production, and denying oil companies such as Shell and Chevron access to oil facilities. In 2002 and 2003, women mobilised to shut down 40 per cent of crude oil production, in some instances using the threat of stripping naked in public (a traditional tactic long employed by women of the area to shame leaders to act) to force the oil companies to account for the environmental destruction, loss of jobs and their complicit involvement in state-sponsored violence and attacks on their villages (Turner and Brownhill, 2004). This was accomplished through international and regional solidarity networks that connected the efforts of small, village based operations.

In forging a multi-ethnic (also referred to as Pan-Delta) non-violent resistance movement, women have also been effective agents in realising economic empowerment goals for the region (Patch, 2008). This activity, along with the civil disobedience described above, is not as visible, and stands in stark contrast to the cycle of violence engaged in by the region's male youth and the deadly response by the state that receives constant attention in media reports. While militant actions forced oil companies and government officials to acknowledge that severe problems exist in the region, the side effects of incessant violence have also motivated women in the region to find alternative ways forward. Another contributing factor to the increase in women's social activism has been the relatively little compensation directed towards women by oil corporations or the state despite the direct and specific effects on women of the devastation wrought by the oil economy (Ikelegbe, 2001; 2005).

Women have also participated in the insurgent movement and violence in the Niger Delta. Few studies have examined women's role in direct violence and conflict, but at least one has found that women perform fundamental roles, including reconnaissance, cover

Table 8.2: Women's literacy and family planning

	Women's literacy (%)	Modern contraceptive use: married women	Unmet need for family planning among married women
Nigeria: 2008 DHS			
Total	53.7	**9.7**	**20.2**
Region: North Central	47.6	10.5	19.2
Region: North East	22.8	3.5	17.7
Region: North West	21.1	2.5	20.2
Region: South East	81.3	11.8	18.5
Region: South West	79.8	21	19.8
Region: South South	77.8	15.5	26.4
2003 DHS			
Total	48.2	**8.2**	**17.5**
Region: North Central	43.4	10.3	22.3
Region: North East	25.6	3	18.8
Region: North West	20.9	3.3	11.7
Region: South East	85.6	13	18.8
Region: South West	79.1	23.1	18.3
Region: South South	75	13.8	24.9
1999 DHS			
Total		**8.6**	**20**
Region: North Central		13	17.5
Region: North East		2.6	22
Region: North West		2.1	21.3
Region: South East		8	17.9
Region: South West		16.6	16.8
Region: South South		10.9	24.2

Source: ICF International, 2012, MEASURE DHS STATcompiler, www.statcompiler.com.

and spiritual fortification (Oriola, 2012). Between 2006 and 2009, tens of thousands of young women and men in various groups under the loose umbrella of MEND engaged in violent rebellion against oil company employees and facilities (Ugor, 2015). If empowerment means freedom to make fundamental life choices, then it also includes the extent to which women, as active subjects, freely decide to engage in militancy. In fact, the more women participate in civil society, engage in civil disobedience, move up the ranks within organisations, they may increasingly find themselves deciding whether or not to engage in or lead insurgent activities, such as oil worker kidnappings, as pressure tactics. Oriola (2012; 2013) describes the various ways that women are involved in both violent and nonviolent resistance in the region.

Women and social conflict in Nigeria

Although social conflict occurs throughout the country, there are clusters of conflict activity in the Niger Delta, Lagos and in the North. Lagos is the most populous state in Nigeria, is the commercial capital and former capital, with many government ministries and headquarters located there, making it an obvious target of protest activity. In the north, the capital of the country is in Abuja, in the Federal Capital Territory located in the geographic centre of the country. There have been a number of high profile incidents there, as well as in Kano (the most populated state in Northern Nigeria). The SCAD database does not contain conflict events that are classified as national, widespread protests throughout the country, as such events are not tied to specific geographic locations in media reports. However, outside of these populated or government areas, the third significant cluster is in the Niger Delta, where the oil economy is based.

When classified by environment and oil as the issues at stake, the overwhelming majority of those actions take place in the Niger Delta. While women may have been involved in many of the protests, several actions in the database were identified as being led by, and comprised of women. While few in number, the largest cluster of women–led social protest actions are in the Niger Delta. In Table 8.3, the environmental focus of protests in the region can be seen more clearly along with the general location of social conflict incidents led by women. For the incidents led by women, Table 8.3 breaks down the types of social conflicts and issues at stake. As classified in the SCAD 3.0 database, these are overwhelmingly environment and livelihood, and more volatile compared to protests in other regions of the country.

Women's participation, power and agency

Table 8.3: Women-led social conflict incidents: Nigeria, 1990–2011

	Type of event	Count
	Spontaneous demonstration	3
	Spontaneous violent riot	2
Niger Delta	Issues	Count
	Economic resources	1
	Food, water, subsistence	3
	Jobs	3

Tallied by author from CS Hendrix and I Salehyan (2013) Social conflict in Africa database (SCAD), www.scaddata.org

Empowerment has become an important concept in international development, seen as a critical component necessary to improve human well-being (Hill, 2003; Mosedale, 2005; Campbell and Teghtsoonian, 2010). Women's empowerment and equality made up one of the eight Millennium Development Goals (MDG 3) and is now part of the Sustainable Development Goals (SDG 5), and major multilateral and bilateral donor institutions all have programmes and policies designed to support the attainment of this goal. The challenge for researchers seeking to measure and assess the idea of empowerment is the lack of consensus about what empowerment means. In part, this stems from the interdisciplinary nature of inquiry into gender empowerment. Much of the social sciences research focuses on how social structures and context affect empowerment, while psychological studies focus on the individual locus of control (Grabe, 2012).

This chapter has attempted to assemble evidence of women's involvement in civil society organisations in the Niger Delta and the associated impact, if any, on women's empowerment. Establishing that connection is difficult, as the data used for this chapter comes from several sources featuring different levels of geographic aggregation collected in different years. In the DHS data containing indicators of household decision-making and attitudes about women's household status, the South-South zone was used to approximate the Niger Delta region. The Afrobraometer data had to be grouped from individual states into the Niger Delta region. However, both data sources do not capture differences within the Niger Delta region between communities that live in close proximity to oil extraction activity where environmental impacts are more acute.

Ideally, there would be a single, longitudinal dataset with indicators on women's participation and leadership, along with attitudes about women's roles in society, household decision-making and empowerment status. This data would be sampled at a level that could allow direct comparison between women in the Niger Delta and other parts of the country. Future ethnographic studies could follow the small but emerging group of women in leadership positions within civil society organisations to tease out the causal linkages between civil society participation and empowerment, and the strength of those linkages between women in the Niger Delta and elsewhere. In the absence of a longitudinal survey with all the indicators or ethnographies, the data for this chapter does suggest that in the Niger Delta there is both more participation in civil society and more empowerment, as measured by changes in attitudes about women's roles in society.

In the Niger Delta, history has shown that women have a direct incentive to become involved in public affairs. The terrible history of the petroleum extraction industry in the region has had specific, devastating effects on women's livelihoods, health and social standing. Not only is there incentive, but the direct loss of livelihood and ability of women to provide food and water for their families, roles they are traditionally prescribed, has actually opened the space for women to take on roles as activists, protestors and active community members (Acey, 2010). The rise of newer environmental justice-focused civil society has increased opportunities for women to participate in decision-making. However, the effects of this increased activism on women's control, household decision-making and strategic life choices are mixed.

While participation is on the rise, the opportunity for leadership is still rare. As a result, concerns and issues specific to women's justice as well as their advancement and development are not on the agenda. As the head of her own non-profit organisation, and serving at the national level on organisations directly involved in energy and mining, Faith Nwadishi is one of the few women leaders operating at such a high level, or even at the local level. Along with a number of other women leading or involved in the civil society sector in the Niger Delta, Nwadishi is seeking to create spaces for women to participate. She has written about the lack of women at the highest levels of EITI and on mining company boards.[5] Within Nigeria, she spread awareness about the lack of *any* mention of gender in the recent petroleum industry bill in Nigeria in a communiqué to national PWYP supporters and in other public forums. PWYP itself has formed a partnership with UN Women to begin the work of examining and documenting the gender implications of the extractive industry, and promoting leadership by women in the field.

Map 8.3: Social conflicts 1990–2011 in the Niger Delta, including environmental and women-led conflicts

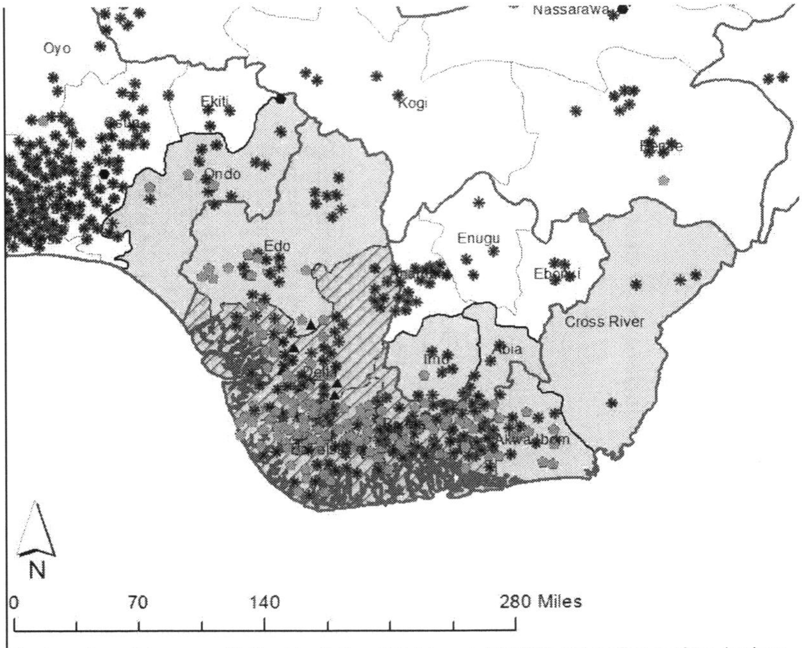

Map by author;, data source: CS Hendrix , C. S. and I Salehyan I. (2013) 'Social conflict in Africa database (SCAD)', www.scaddata.orgwww.scaddata.org.

Using a more holistic concept of women's empowerment as the guiding conceptual framework for this chapter, there is an indication that the struggle for environmental justice in the Niger Delta, the negative impact of the oil economy on women's livelihoods and their families, along with the rise of formal civil society organisations in the region, has created the space and opportunity for enhanced political and civic engagement among women. By measures of process and activity, and the ability to act in concert to advance their own interests, women in the Niger Delta are more empowered. The SCAD data highlights the involvement of women in environmental protests in the region. This not only reflects the long history of women in the region directly confronting authorities when facing threats to their livelihoods, but the specific roles that environmental justice organisations have placed in establishing a Pan Delta movement for social justice.

Overall, the evidence presented indicates there is some increased empowerment, in terms of women's ability to recognise and assess their situation, and act collectively to address their issues. The rise of newer civil society organisations around environmental justice in the region have provided increased outlets for women to participate beyond informal protest and traditional structures. This can be seen in the Afrobarometer results, where women in the Niger Delta report higher rates of participation or willingness to participate in protests and community actions. However, this has not translated into increased leadership roles for women, at least as captured in the national datasets. Much more difficult to ascertain, is to what extent this increased space for civic action has affected women's standing in society, attitudes towards women, and their own ability to control household decisions and make strategic life choices (such as family planning, career goals, education and so forth).

Women in the Niger Delta have higher rates of education and literacy, and higher rates of family planning practices, and they also report facing unequal treatment in social institutions. In fact, women and men in the Delta are more likely to report women facing more discrimination from traditional authorities, likely because they are more aware of their rights. While fewer women in the Niger Delta find wife beating to be justifiable, the numbers are high. For example, a quarter of women in the South–South zone think a beating is justified if a woman argues with her husband, and 31 per cent think a beating is justified if a woman leaves the house without telling her husband. Also, the data show, somewhat surprisingly, that women in the Niger Delta are less likely to indicate that they are in control of their own income. The same factors which create the space for women to become mobilised also serve to disempower them, in terms of limiting their ability to control their own bodies and make strategic life choices. As Omorodion writes, 'The unavailability of jobs for women in oil multinationals confines women to the home, promotes female sexuality for men's good, promotes early onset of sexual intercourse, marriage and childbearing, and fosters dependency of women on men' (Omorodion, 2004, 11).

Towards a gendered justice agenda in the Niger Delta

Women have made fundamental contributions to advancing the cause of the Niger Delta people. Tens of millions of people, forming thousands of rural, riverine, and urban communities in the Niger Delta, are fighting to reverse decades of exploitation, neglect and violent repression with social and economic development, full representation and environmental justice. Women have placed their lives at risk to engage in protest, occupations and confrontations with multinational oil companies and government authorities. Increasingly, through civil society organisations, women are taking part in larger Pan Delta, national and international networks, engaging in policy and advocacy work, and finding a way to insert their voices at decision-making tables. However, the transformation of the Niger Delta cannot be achieved until the gendered impacts of the crisis are fully understood and those issues that are specific to women become explicitly integrated into any solutions. Women's involvement in the larger struggle is not a proxy for women's empowerment.

Given their roles as breadwinners, homemakers, caregivers and the cornerstones of their communities, attempts to solve the Niger Delta crisis that do not explicitly and fundamentally address the impact of the crisis on women are not real solutions. Sustainable, long-term initiatives and solutions to the problem should be structured to address the specific ways that women are affected by the oil economy. As described in this chapter, these effects include their shifting economic positions, the impact on their specific livelihoods, the increased burden for women to earn in the face of increased school dropout rates and seasonal employment for men and the compromises this imposes, the direct health effects on women related to their specific roles in society (having to fetch polluted water, fishing in unfamiliar deep water, exposure to chemicals, the inability to harvest non-timber forest products, among other impacts). Key examples of poor solutions are the negotiated settlements and set-asides between oil companies and male-dominated Community Development Associations, which ignore women, and only serve to increase the burden on women to earn for their households while their opportunities to earn are increasingly limited. Even the emergent model of oil company and community relations in Nigeria, the Global Memorandum of Understanding (GMOU), continues to exclude women from leadership roles (Acey, 2016; Aaron 2012).

In order for a gendered justice agenda to emerge, the emancipation and empowerment of women must be a reality. One cannot occur without the other. The issues of women's choices in the home, their ability to participate in decision-making in the communities, and how these choices and their participation are shaped by the larger international oil economy and the economies of violence created by the on-going conflict, mirror the issues facing the few women in leadership positions who are attempting to operate at broader scales. In the past, the lack of significant women's involvement in high level negotiations and discussion, deal making and monitoring meant that women's issues would continue to be left out of major organising and activism and calls for reform put forth by local, national and international civil society organisations, much less government agencies or the private extractive sector. The government's current Affirmative Action plan to increase women's representation at the highest levels of government may change this. In spring of 2015, the former president, Goodluck Jonathan, appointed 31 per cent of his cabinet positions to women (following a campaign promise in which he and the First Lady had pushed promoting at least 35 per cent) (www.naij.com/16522.html). It is the highest number of women in federal cabinet positions in Nigeria's history and includes such powerful and high profile positions as Minister of Petroleum Resources (Diezeani Alison-Madueke) and Minister of Finance (Dr Ngozi Okonjo Iweala),[6] the latter position overseeing all other government ministries.

The question at the heart of this chapter is whether women's involvement in civil society organisations in the Niger Delta contributes to their empowerment. It does, to the extent that women are increasingly choosing to participate in the activities of voluntary associations, engaging in protest, organising with others (within the community and through broader pan Delta coalitions) to raise issues of importance to them, and becoming aware of the importance of participating in governance. The measure of women's empowerment is not only one of their participation, but of the discourse of the Niger Delta justice movement itself becoming transformed into a political, ecological and gendered discourse, that addresses the root of the problem. In the long term, this will be measured by the extent to which participation becomes transformative, by women taking on leadership and governance at every level, and by the agenda itself and associated policy initiatives and solutions recognising gendered impacts, and, ultimately, in outcomes. As gender becomes an explicit part of the solution space, the economic and social position of women themselves will be transformed, transforming their resources, agency and improving their life possibilities and outcomes.

Notes

[1] Nigeria has six geopolitical zones recognised by the government, which divide the country into geographic areas with common ethnicity, linguistic groupings and ancestry.

[2] The 2015 election of former military ruler Muhammadu Buhari as President may signify a new shift towards authentic electoral democracy in Nigeria. It marks the first time that power has transitioned to an opposition party.

[3] Founded in 2002, the Publish What You Pay initiative is a global network of civil society organisations campaigning for transparency in the energy and mining sectors.

[4] At the World Summit for Sustainable Development in Johannesburg in 2002, the Extractive Industry Transparency Initiative (EITI) was founded to establish a global system for reconciling what companies pay and what governments receive from oil, gas and mining. The Multi-Stakeholder Group (MSG) in each country is comprised of selected representatives from civil society, the private sector and government, who oversee implementation of EITI in country and the publishing of the annual report providing financial, physical and process audits of the oil, gas and mineral sectors.

[5] See PWYP International Women's Day Update, at http://publishwhatyoupay.org/about/newsletter.

[6] Dr Okonjo Iweala's appointment ended in May 2015.

Acknowledgments

The author wishes to thank Faith Nwadishi of Koyenum Immalah Foundation and Emeka Bertram of Persons with Disabilities Action Network (PEDANET) for sharing their insights on the Niger Delta. The author is also grateful to Karen Frick, Carolina Reid and Karen Tani for their helpful comments on an earlier version of this chapter.

References

Acey, C, 2010, Gender and community mobilisation for urban water infrastructure investment in southern Nigeria, *Gender and Development* 18, 1, 11–26

Agarwal, B, 1997, Bargaining and gender relations within and beyond the household, *Feminist Economics* 3, 1, 1–51

Agarwal, B, 2001, *UN expert group meeting on gender and poverty: Some issues*, United Nations, Division for the Advancement of Women, www.un.org/womenwatch/daw/csw/empower/documents/Agarwal-EP2.pdf

Anderson, CJ, Paskeviciute, A, 2006, How ethnic and linguistic heterogeneity influence the prospects for civil society: A comparative study of citizenship behaviour, *Journal of Politics* 68, 4, 783–802

Anderson, S, Eswaran, M, 2009, What determines female autonomy? Evidence from Bangladesh, *Journal of Development Economics* 90, 2, 179–91

Batliwala, S, 1994, The meaning of women's empowerment: New concepts from action, in G Sen, A Germaine, LC Chen (eds) *Population policies reconsidered: Health, empowerment and rights*, pp 127–38, Cambridge, MA: Harvard Center for Population and Development Studies

Blaikie, PM, Brookfield, HC, 1987, *Land degradation and society*, London and New York: Methuen

Bratton, M, 1989, Beyond the state: Civil society and associational life in Africa, *World Politics*, 41, 3, 407–30

Campbell, ML, Teghtsoonian, K, 2010, Aid effectiveness and women's empowerment: Practices of governance in the funding of international development, *Signs* 36, 1, 177–202

Ekiyor, T, 2008, The role of civil society in conflict prevention: West African experiences, in K Vignard (ed) *The complex dynamics of small arms in West Africa* (pp 27–34), Geneva: United Nations Institute for Disarmament Research (UNIDIR)

Falola, T, Paddock, A, 2011, *The women's war of 1929: A history of anti-colonial resistance in Eastern Nigeria*, Durham, NC: Carolina Academic Press

Grabe, S, 2012, An empirical examination of women's empowerment and transformative change in the context of international development, *American Journal of Community Psychology* 49, 1–2, 233–45

Hill, MT, 2003, Development as empowerment, *Feminist Economics* 9, 2–3, 117–35

Ikelegbe, A, 2001, Civil society, oil and conflict in the Niger Delta region of Nigeria: Ramifications of civil society for a regional resource struggle, *Journal of Modern African Studies* 39, 3, 437–70

Ikelegbe, A, 2005, The economy of conflict in the oil rich Niger Delta region of Nigeria, *Nordic Journal of African Studies* 14, 2, 208–34

Jike, VT, 2004, Environmental degradation, social disequilibrium, and the dilemma of sustainable development in the Niger-Delta of Nigeria, *Journal of Black Studies* 34, 5, 686–701

Kabeer, N, 1999, Resources, agency, achievements: Reflections on the measurement of women's empowerment, *Development and Change* 30, 3, 435–64

Kabeer, N, 2005, Is microfinance a 'magic bullet' for women's empowerment? Analysis of findings from South Asia, *Economic and Political Weekly* 40 , 44–5, 4709–18

Kopecký, P, Mudde, C, 2003, Rethinking civil society, *Democratization* 10, 3, 1–14

Kritz, MM, Makinwa-Adebusoye, P, 1999, Determinants of women's decision-making authority in Nigeria: The ethnic dimension, *Sociological Forum*, 14, 3, 399–424

Kuenzi, MT, 2008, Social capital and political trust in West Africa, *Afrobarometer, Working Paper* 96, Centre for Democratic Development (CDD, Ghana), the Institute for Democracy in South Africa (IDASA), and the Institute for Empirical Research in Political Economy (IREEP), http://afrobarometer.org/publications/wp96-social-capital-and-political-trust-west-africa

LITE (Leadership Initiative for Transformation and Empowerment), 2013, Rural women's development strategies when excluded from community decision making, *LITE Leadership Initiative for Transformation and Empowerment*, www.nidprodev.org/index.php/community-reports/good-governance/rural-womens-development-strategies-when-excluded-from-community-decision-making

Mba, NE, 1982, *Nigerian women mobilized: Women's political activity in Southern Nigeria, 1900–1965*, Berkeley, CA: Institute of International Studies, University of California

Mosedale, S, 2005, Assessing women's empowerment: Towards a conceptual framework, *Journal of International Development* 17, 243–57

Narayan, D, 2005, Conceptual framework and methodological challenges, in D Narayan (ed *Measuring empowerment: Cross-disciplinary perspectives*, pp 3–38, Washington, DC: World Bank Publications

Olufemi, FJ, Adewale, AA, 2012, The role of civil society organizations in conflict management in Nigeria, *International Journal of Asian Social Science* 2, 5, 720–9

Omorodion, FI, 2004, The impact of petroleum refinery on the economic livelihoods of women in the Niger Delta region of Nigeria, *JENDA: A Journal of Culture and African Women Studies* 6, 1–15

Oriola, T, 2012, The delta creeks, women's engagement and Nigeria's oil insurgency, *British Journal of Criminology* 52, 3, 534–55

Oriola, T, 2013, *Criminal resistance: The politics of kidnapping oil workers*, Farnham: Ashgate

Osaghae, EE, 1999, Exiting from the state in Nigeria, *Journal of African Political Science* 4, 1, 83–98

Patch, J, 2008, Women and non-violent forms of activism in the Niger delta oil resource conflict, *Undercurrent: The Canadian Undergraduate Journal of Development Studies* 5, 3, 39–44

PWYP (Publish What You Pay), 2013, Special Issue for International Women's Day, http://pwyp.createsend1.com/t/ViewEmail/r/0E5 4D14A4681EBB42540EF23F30FEDED/62599669E76A0BA80F8 C96E86323F7F9

Robbins, P, 2004, *Political ecology: A critical introduction*, Malden, MA: Blackwell Publishers

Schermerhorn, C (writer, producer and director), 2010, *The naked option: A last resort*, [Film], Santa Barbara, CA: Candace Schermerhorn Productions, LLC

Simone, A, 2001, Straddling the divides: Remaking associational life in the informal African city, *International Journal of Urban and Regional Research* 25, 1, 102–17

Turner, TE, Brownhill, LS, 2004, Why women are at war with Chevron: Nigerian subsistence struggles against the international oil industry, *Journal of Asian and African Studies* 39, 1–2, 63–93

Ugor, P, 2015, Armed Insurgency, young women and the feminization of resistance in the Niger Delta, in SR Poyntz and J Kennelly (eds) *Phenomenology of youth cultures and globalization: Lifeworlds and surplus meaning in changing times* (pp 132–53), New York: Routledge

Ukeje, C, 2004, From Aba to Ugborodo: Gender identity and alternative discourse of social protest among women in the Oil Delta of Nigeria, *Oxford Development Studies* 32, 4, 605–17

Ukiwo, U, 2003, Politics, ethno-religious conflicts and democratic consolidation in Nigeria, *The Journal of Modern African Studies* 41, 1, 115–38

Van Allen, J, 1975, Aba Riots or the Igbo Women's War? Ideology, Stratification and the Invisibility of Women, *Ufahamu: A Journal of African Studies* 6, 1, 11–39

Section Two:

Emancipating organisation(s)

NINE

A women's NGO as an incubator: promoting identity-based associations in Nepalese civil society

Masako Tanaka

Introduction

Over the last two decades, civil society organisations (CSOs) have played significant and increasingly visible roles in advocacy campaigns, particularly at the global level. CSOs have undeniable bearing in the world today, as do their partnerships with CSO and non-CSO counterparts. The World Bank, which itself interacts with many CSOs, defines civil society as 'the wide array of non-governmental and not-for-profit organisations that have a presence in public life, expressing the interests and values of their members or others, based on ethical, cultural, political, scientific, religious or philanthropic considerations' (The World Bank, 2013). CSOs include NGOs, community-based organisations (CBOs), community groups and trade unions, among other bodies. Some groups advocate issues relating to their own lives while others act as proxies lobbying on behalf of particular sets of people (Hudock, 1999). In either case, representation of marginalised groups through CSOs is critical for understanding their diversity and perspectives.

In this study, identity-based associations (IBAs) are defined as membership-based organisations formed exclusively by marginalised groups that: a) suffer social stigma, social exclusion and rights violations, and b) struggle to regain a sense of dignity in their identity through empowerment. Today, IBAs broadly contribute to integrating human rights into the development sector through the promotion of rights-based approaches. IBAs can be distinguished from NGOs as, although both work in the interest of a specified group, NGOs may be formed by persons outside of that target population. They are also discernible from peoples' organisations and CBOs, which, due to their limited geographical scope, are more susceptible to the influence of social bonding. Socially bound groups are often complicit in the oppression of sub-groups, such as women, certain labour classes and persons without land tenure.

IBAs are an important platform for marginalised groups to raise their voices and address oppression. However, without external backing and/or access to empowerment, marginalised individuals face difficulty in forming IBAs since they are frequently isolated from each other and not well organised. Thus, NGOs may play an important role in facilitating IBA formation and organisational development.

In Nepal, where the rights-based approach is widely applied in the development sector, CSOs regularly contribute to transforming Nepali society through the on-going state restructuring process. Oppressed populations too have become active via the formation of several IBAs (Gellner, 2009). Women's NGOs have assisted in the formation of IBAs, not only those for ethnic minorities, but also IBAs for and by human trafficking survivors and women working in the entertainment sector, for instance dance bars, duet restaurants and massage parlours. IBAs aim to assert both their voices and their rights. In many cases, ethnicity and caste-based organisations gain popular visibility through their affiliations with political parties. However, civil society and government do not yet generally recognise IBAs formed around other (non-caste, non-ethnicity based) identities. To further complicate matters, the importance of promoting and supporting IBAs is not yet understood fully within international development. As a result, IBAs usually struggle to obtain adequate recognition and/or resources, even relative to NGOs. This is a cause for concern for many reasons, including the fact that NGOs and IBAs should not be framed as competitors.

This chapter highlights the unique roles played by one women's NGO, the Women's Rehabilitation Centre (WOREC) in Nepal, which promoted the formation of two women-led IBAs based on a strong belief in the importance of self-representation, namely *Shakti Samuha* formed by trafficking survivors and *Mahilako Nimti Mahila Manch* (Women's Forum for Women in Nepal (WOFOWON)). WOREC began by defending women's rights while providing essential support to IBAs during their formative stages. Next, it developed leadership among IBA members in addition to offering continual back-up support until each IBA became fully independent. WOREC facilitated the formation of a new IBA, uniting women working in the informal and entertainment sectors.

The term 'partnership' is commonly used in the development sector to describe relationships between organisations based on a long-term vision, shared responsibility, reciprocal obligations, equality, mutuality and a balance of power (Fowler, 2000).

Relationships between WOREC and IBAs could be considered as such partnerships today, but were not reducible to the same form of partnership in the early days of each IBA's establishment. In this chapter, the role played by WOREC in fostering IBAs is analysed, using the UK Business Incubation Ltd's Development Framework (BIDF). The term 'incubator' originally surfaced in the field of medical science to describe life-saving equipment that sustains premature babies. Here, it suggests the delivery of 'hands-on' support for nurturing newly emergent small businesses to help them survive and grow through the difficult and highly vulnerable early stages of development while simultaneously determining the limits to such support (UKBI, 2012). Though the environment surrounding civil society is not necessarily the same as that surrounding business, the concept of an incubator can aptly describe the 'hands on' approach to capacity building offered by CSOs to IBAs.

This chapter will highlight WOREC's distinctive role as an incubator in promoting IBAs. Analysis in this chapter is based on documentary review, as well as extensive field visits and interviews, conducted between 1996 and 2013, with members, staff, leaders, supporters and donors linked to WOREC and IBAs both inside and outside of Kathmandu. The author, once employed by an international NGO, did not initially have direct working relations with WOREC and related IBAs until later returning as a feminist activist from 1995 to 1999 and 2004 to 2009.

CSOs, NGOs and IBAs in Nepal

CSOs in Nepal are structurally, functionally and contextually diverse due to variations in working areas, organisational scale, operational patterns, memberships and positions relative to other actors in society. The term CSO is understood as generic and inclusive of 'all forms of people's associations within civil society' (Dahal and Timsina, 2007, 18). As such, a large segment of society uses the word CSO interchangeably with NGO (Singh and Ingdal, 2007, 4). Though there is no standard definition, CSOs in Nepal include 'NGOs, religious organisations, trade unions, social and cultural groups, identity-based associations, professional associations, networks, federations and trusts' (Uprety, 2011, 53).

In the past, NGOs in Nepal – as in other countries – were led almost exclusively by elites who provided their expertise to short-term projects for others, whereas IBAs commit to their own constituencies in self-instigated, self-directed long-term movements. Some NGOs support so-called 'beneficiaries', generally comprising socially excluded populations who have been denied their rights. The formation of IBAs became possible after Nepal's 1990 constitution ensured the rights of citizens. IBAs can be based on a variety of identifiers, such as ethnicity, caste, gender and religion. Most groups form through their own initiative, while some come into being as a consequence of development projects. Though statistical records are unavailable, the number of IBAs seems to be steadily rising as social inclusion has become an integral part of the national agenda.

According to the Social Welfare Council (SWC) under the Ministry of Women, Children and Social Welfare, as of July, 2010, 284 organisations were registered under the Social Welfare Act 1992 – a legal framework for regulating both foreign and national organisations (SWC, 2012). The SWC categorises registered organisations into ten sectors: AIDs and abuse control, child welfare, community and rural development, educational development, environmental development, handicapped [sic] and disabled, health services, moral development, women services and youth services. The women services sector has the third highest number of registered organisations at 2,305, which trails only the community and rural development and youth service sectors. These figures include NGOs, IBAs and grassroots-level CBOs.

IBAs in Nepal have played a number of different roles, not only in service delivery for their own constituency but also in lobbying for drafting of a new constitution. However, not all IBAs are the same. Well-organised IBAs are largely led by activist male leaders, who inherited the assets of their fathers or grandfathers (Karki, 2006, 41). Some already had high levels of education or achieved positions of leadership before forming their IBAs. On the other hand, a number of male-led IBAs were not formed by elites, as seen in people's organisations for highly marginalised, indigenous groups.

However, even these latter organisations have at least a few members who were trained as political activists or religious leaders (Tanaka, 2011; 2013). Gender disparity rooted in Nepal's patriarchal systems means that patterns underlying the establishment of IBAs for women within marginalised groups differ from those formed by male peers. Even when women belong to groups that are otherwise relatively unified, such as people living with HIV/AIDS or as part of one of the sexual minorities, they tend to be marginalised or excluded relative to men and, therefore, face difficulties in organising. When it comes to any given issue, men's groups typically take shape first, followed later by women's. Women's IBAs are relatively small and tend to not have sufficient resources for mobilising and fulfilling members' needs, or extending advocacy.

Resource mobilisation and leadership development are challenges for a majority of women's IBAs. They must mobilise external resources owing to members' overall poverty and lack of access to government support. At the same time, however, it is not easy for many women in IBAs to write English proposals and reports since women have, overall, less access to education than men, as demonstrated by Nepal's gender gap in school enrolment and literacy rates, among other indicators. Capacity and leadership development within women's IBAs takes time because of the need for psychosocial counselling and basic livelihood support for members.

Little attention has been paid to contributions by women's NGOs in supporting women's empowerment and the establishment of IBAs. Some NGOs try to support IBAs while others prefer to act as proxies or intermediaries that link, yet add layers between, IBAs and donors. Apart from a few exceptions, IBAs were often overshadowed in the 1990s by both Nepali NGOs and international NGOs supporting their work. However, the political turmoil and social conflict that erupted following Nepal's 2005 royal coup created a space for IBAs to represent their own people. During the conflict, IBAs discovered that they had an inherent advantage: first, NGOs face difficulty in reaching conflict-affected areas and second, IBAs were not directly targeted by the warring parties. In 2006, IBAs actively joined the second People's Movement and proceeded to assert their right to democratic inclusion.

A women's NGO working towards transformation of the society

There are more than 2,000 organisations working for women in Nepal. They are diverse in terms of size, scope and presence. Only a few strive to transform their roles in line with national changes. To illustrate, this section looks at the achievements of one women's NGO, WOREC, as an IBA incubator and facilitator of IBA alliances.

As one of Nepal's most progressive women's organisations, WOREC has transcended its initial scope, namely, the 'rehabilitation of women', and broadened its activities from grassroots-level community development to global-level lobbying with a goal of 'ensur[ing] economic, social and cultural rights and minimis[ing] violence against women through women's empowerment' (WOREC, 2012, 7). WOREC is a pioneering NGO engaged in issues of trafficking and the promotion of women's rights through eliminating unequal power relations based on gender, age, class, ethnicity, caste and religion, among other things. WOREC became involved in numerous campaigns positively affirming women's rights, and this has led to a number of successes in Nepal including amended property rights, approval of an abortion bill, a new national policy on women's health (with particular emphasis on uterine prolapse) and the lifting of a ban on women's migration to the Gulf countries.[1] Today, WOREC directs various programmes for women's empowerment, women's health rights and safe migration among other issues, under the umbrella of three principal campaigns on violence against women; economic, social and cultural rights; and sustainable peace (WOREC, 2012, 11). In 2013, the organisation was active in 11 districts: Morang, Sunsari, Udaypur, Siraha, Dhanusha, Rupandehi, Kathmandu, Lalitpur, Dang, Salyan and Kailali as well as maintaining extended nationwide networks via the Women Human Rights Defenders (WHRD).

WOREC was established in 1991 with a target of 'contribut[ing] in nation building by motivating, empowering and mobilising the local women' (WOREC, 1994, 2). Although it aimed 'to motivate and mobilise the Nepalese women', it did not have a clear strategy in its early days as to how it would promote the 'exercise of women's rights'. Therefore, it defined itself as 'a service oriented' NGO (WOREC, 1994, 1). In the early 1990s, WOREC conducted numerous activities in rural areas, such as rehabilitation programmes for HIV-positive individuals and 'resourcing poor rural women', as well as programmes for community-based STD and AIDS education, entrepreneurship development, informal education and rural community services such as drinking water. In addition, WOREC also engaged in outreach work with Nepalese sex workers in India by collaborating with Indian organisations to conduct surveys and provide AIDS education.

Most WOREC activities were designed under a 'community-based' concept. The NGO encouraged rural women to form groups with special attention to marginalised populations. It supported self-help groups including, for instance, women from the most marginalised Dalit group, the Musahars, traditionally regarded as untouchable in the low-lying Terai region along Nepal's southern border with India. After three years of work in rural communities, WOREC leaders realised that as outsiders they could not stay in the community forever. Consequently, WOREC established a training centre in Udaypur – the working area where it had been involved the longest – to develop human resources based in rural communities for the sake of programme sustainability.

Promoting self-representation among trafficking survivors

Human trafficking is pervasive in Nepal. It is estimated that 7,000 to 12,000 Nepali women and children are trafficked each year; although reliable figures are hard to obtain (Terre des hommes, 2010, 18). While some work as domestic labourers or in factories, circuses and sweatshops, many trafficked women and girls also end up in brothels. It was an event in 1996, involving the repatriation of trafficked women from Mumbai brothels that added momentum to the women's movement in Nepal.

Also in 1996 NGOs went to great lengths to support the re-integration and rehabilitation of 168 young women and girls below 17 years old. In 1997, WOREC, under the initiative of the then chair, brought together numerous anti-trafficking NGOs to form a network (including 26 affiliated organisations) leading to the formation of the Alliance Against Trafficking of Women in Nepal (AATWIN) (WOREC, 1998, 11). This leadership put WOREC in a key position among multiple agencies in the women's movement in Nepal.

Together with other NGOs, WOREC supported the formation of *Shakti Samuha* (literally 'Power Group' in Nepali) in 1996, the first organisation established in South Asia by survivors of trafficking. The formation of *Shakti Samuha* was one product of the social reintegration and rehabilitation programme implemented by WOREC and other women's NGOs (WOREC, 1999, 25).[2] One major contribution of *Shakti Samuha* was the positive change in the public image of the 'Bombay-returned girls'. Initially stigmatised, the girls were soon seen as survivors and agents of change responsible for pro-actively addressing trafficking and the best interests of their peers. Based on its strong belief in the importance of trafficking survivors' self-representation, WOREC played a substantial role in promoting *Shakti Samuha*, as did other NGOs including the child rights organisation Child Workers in Nepal Concerned Centre (CWIN)[3] (Ploumen, 2001, 58).

WOREC introduced *Shakti Samuha* to feminist organisations abroad and facilitated international communications. In 1998, *Shakti Samuha* obtained seed money from Mama Cash, a Netherlands-based feminist organisation providing financial and moral support to women's groups. The funds were channelled towards the establishing of an office and salary for two staff members. This initial financial support enhanced *Shakti Samuha*'s activities, such as their counselling services for trafficked girls and women, peer education classes, street drama for awareness-raising and networking with other actors.

WOREC acted as an incubator in the literal sense from 1998 to 2000, when *Shakti Samuha* had a room in the building where WOREC was located. *Shakti Samuha* members had access to advice and support from WOREC whenever they needed it (WOREC, 2001, 29). Getting legal entity status was a hurdle for *Shakti Samuha* since its founding members (trafficked before they reached the age of eligibility for citizenship certificates) lacked identification papers and could not get them without returning to their families. However, with WOREC's assistance, a few trafficking survivors succeeded in getting citizenship certificates. In due time, *Shakti Samuha* registered successfully after some of WOREC's own staff listed themselves as founding members and submitted their own certificates for documentation (interview with Renu Rajbhandari, 2008). After its formal registration in 2000, *Shakti Samuha* gradually became an independent organisation.

Shakti Samuha received additional funding from the Global Fund for Women (GFW), a US-based women's organisation serving 'the rights of women and girls worldwide by increasing the resources for and investing in women-led organisations and women's collective leadership for change' (GFW, 2012). Between 2000 and 2010, the Fund directed financial support towards education programmes for survivors, such as those fostering re-enrolment in schools, for the sake of human resource development – and six leaders moved on to formal education institutions as a result.

Oxfam GB was the first international NGO based in Nepal to act as a donor to *Shakti Samuha* ((email communication with Meena Poudel in 2013). In 1999, Oxfam GB's then Country Representative took a risk by providing funding to *Shakti Samuha* prior to the latter's legal registration with the SWC. Save the Children International, known at the time as Save the Children Norway (SCN),[4] also began aiding *Shakti Samuha* soon after its legal registration. SCN shared programme costs with Oxfam GB for mobilisation of adolescent groups, survivor support and capacity building for human resources.[5] Owing to SCN and Oxfam GB's assistance, *Shakti Samuha* members benefited from numerous capacity development training courses in leadership, management, counselling, lobbying, advocacy, computers and the English language, as well as employable skills trainings designed to improve opportunities for work at beauty parlours, stationery shops or in offices as secretaries. Once *Shakti Samuha* started to receive support for capacity building through these organisations, WOREC gradually changed its role from an advisory agency to that of a partner in an alliance with AATWIN and WHRD.

Advantages and challenges faced by IBAs

Shakti Samuha's aspirations are that trafficking survivors will be empowered to lead dignified lives in society. Its goal is to establish a progressive society devoid of trafficking and other kinds of violence against women through seven programme themes: 1) repatriation, rehabilitation and reintegration, 2) training and employment support, 3) income generation and skill development, 4) awareness raising, 5) organisational development, 6) education, and 7) legal support and advocacy (*Shakti Samuha*, 2013). *Shakti Samuha* works directly with communities in Kathmandu, Makwanpur, Bara, Rautahat, Nuwakot, Sindhupalchok, Kaski, Jhapa, Kailali and Bardiya districts as well as in eastern and mid-western Nepal through its two regional networks. As of August 2013, *Shakti Samuha* had 50 staff – 70 per cent of whom are trafficking survivors – as well as 135 members[6] and more than 500 trafficking survivors with whom they maintain contact.

Shakti Samuha, as an IBA, has three principal tenets: 1) trafficking survivors should have the same rights as any other members of society; 2) trafficking survivors should lead the movement against trafficking to ensure their own rights and those of others; and 3) no member of *Shakti Samuha* shall be discriminated against in their service to the organisation. Moreover, the organisation states that the following is crucial to carrying out their mission: 'trafficking survivors and women and children at risk of trafficking will be organised, empowered and made aware, which will enable them to contribute to campaign against human trafficking, as well as protect women and girls living in vulnerable conditions' (*Shakti Samuha*, 2013).

Self-representation by trafficking survivors makes a difference for three reasons. First, it means that *Shakti Samuha* can better reach their target population since members, through their own experiences with trafficking, more closely understand issues affecting their constituency. Second, it helps *Shakti Samuha* bridge ideological gaps among some of the women's NGOs that are divided by party politics, despite their intent to act in survivors' best interests. Third, it bolsters *Shakti Samuha*'s ability to address the issue of trafficking explicitly as their highest priority, unlike other non–IBA organisations engaged in simultaneously tackling multiple issues.

Shakti Samuha has a significant advantage over other groups reaching out to and engaging with trafficking survivors and girls vulnerable to trafficking. According to Poudel, a long-time researcher of human trafficking with experience in investigating social rejection of repatriated trafficking survivors, *Shakti Samuha* was 'the most important source of help' for trafficked women.[7] Poudel noted that some trafficking survivors expressed 'resentments towards Nepalese NGOs' that forced them to take HIV blood tests and insisted on 'making their trafficked identity/ies known to the media, government authorities and their families' (Poudel, 2011, 22). *Shakti Samuha*, on the other hand, served as a home, a source of power, a living world and almost everything, as one member recalls (Poudel, 2011, 233). Not only do trafficking survivors view *Shakti Samuha*'s members and leaders as respected role models, but so do trafficking-prone adolescent girls living in vulnerable areas like squatter settlements; women and girls working with *Shakti Samuha* are proud of their affiliation with the organisation (interview with a youth group girl leader, Tanaka, 2006). *Shakti Samuha* also conducted a study on women and girls working at massage parlours and dance bars with the assistance of a US-based NGO called Free the Slaves. These activities demonstrate their strength, and relative advantage, in reaching out to unorganised segments of the target population.

Shakti Samuha has been trying to position itself as a neutral party – one not swayed by ideology and party politics. The women's movement in Nepal is often criticised for being split into parallel networks that work for the same objectives through different channels, primarily owing to divergent ideological convictions led by party politics (Lama, 1997; Sherchan, 1997; Tamang, 2009). In the 1990s, organisations belonging to Nepal's women's movement almost always occupied different platforms because of affiliations to either of Nepal's two major political parties, the Nepali Congress or the Communist Party of Nepal–United Marxist Leninist (CPN–UML).

There are two networks actively engaging in trafficking issues in Nepal: the Alliance Against Trafficking of Women in Nepal (AATWIN) and the National Network against Trafficking of Women and Girls (NNTWG). AATWIN, which comprises organisations close to CPN–UML and part of a global movement called the Global Alliance Against Trafficking in Women (GAATW), recognises the rights of sex workers and distinguishes between forced and voluntary prostitution, the latter of which it does not oppose. NNTWG, on the other hand, is closer to the Nepali Congress and backs the abolishment of all prostitution in line with its ties to the Coalition Against Trafficking in Women (CATW). *Shakti Samuha* leaders realise that networks are an effective tool for combating trafficking, so they spend significant time mobilising key network actors and organisations regardless of their political affiliation. In this way, *Shakti Samuha* aims, as an IBA, to lead the movement beyond party politics. To some extent, *Shakti Samuha* has succeeded in gaining the support of multiple organisations from each of NNTWG and AATWIN, both networks to which *Shakti Samuha* belongs.

With growing recognition of *Shakti Samuha* by government, NGOs and donors, *Shakti Samuha*'s members are increasingly invited to participate in various programmes on human trafficking. They also contributed to formulating Nepal's National Plan of Action Against Trafficking in Children and Women for Sexual and Labour Exploitation finalised by the Ministry of Women, Children and Social Welfare, in 2001 (Poudel, 2011, 233) as well as the 2007 Human Trafficking and Transportation Act. Moreover, they prepared guidelines on rescue, reunion, rehabilitation and reintegration programmes from a survivor's point of view for a manual entitled *Procedures for safety and personal protection* (Terre des hommes Foundation and *Shakti Samuha*, 2012).

Shakti Samuha did not find it easy to maintain its distance from other organisations working on trafficking. Often, its members felt that they ought to have their own representatives presenting demands at the national level. During the 2008 Constituent Assembly election, *Shakti Samuha*'s then chair ran as a candidate for the Communist Party of Nepal (Samayukuta) but could not become the assembly member due to shortage of votes in the proportional representation system.

In September 2012, *Shakti Samuha*'s present chair (at the time of writing) was elected as a central executive committee member to the NGO Federation of Nepal (NFN),[8] an umbrella organisation established in 1991 and comprised of 5,370 NGOs from all over the country (NFN, 2013). She has been attempting to conduct a diversity survey of member NGOs in order to promote one of NFN's core values, the 'empowerment and inclusion of poor, marginalised and excluded communities' (NFN, 2012, 7). She believes that her presence within the central executive committee will encourage other NGOs to implement inclusive employment policies as well (interview with Sunita Danuwar, 2013). Self-representation by marginalised persons within NGOs acting on their behalf is low despite promotion of workforce diversity by NFN. Promoting IBAs representing marginalised groups is an essential step for creating an inclusive civil society. The initiative taken by *Shakti Samuha*'s chair is expected to bring changes to NFN.

The founders and members of *Shakti Samuha* are widely recognised in Nepal. On 31 August 2013, the organisation received the 2013 Ramon Magsaysay Award – a prize often referred to as Asia's Nobel Prize – for their dedicated service to human trafficking survivors and for presenting to the world a shining example of an IBA working to reassert human dignity. The board of trustees of the Ramon Magsaysay Award selected *Shakti Samuha* for their contributions to the formation of the 2007 Human Trafficking and Transportation Act and other measures taken in Nepal against human trafficking. *Shakti Samuha* tries to share their experiences with other parts of the world.

Incubating another women's IBA

In the mid-2000s, WOREC facilitated the formation of a new IBA, *Mahilako Nimti Mahila Manch* (Women's Forum for Women in Nepal (WOFOWON)), uniting women working in the informal and entertainment sectors. Underlying this development was Nepal's prolonged domestic conflict from 1996 to 2006 which, compounded by a stagnant peace process, triggered a rise in rural to urban migration rates and forced more women into working under vulnerable conditions. As instability undermined the wellbeing of large numbers of people including migrant workers, internally displaced persons and trafficked persons, WOREC decided to respond in 2005 by establishing a drop-in-centre and health clinic for young women and girls working in Kathmandu's dance restaurants, bars, clubs and massage parlours. Their initial objective was to provide health and counselling services for women susceptible to violence and harassment from employers, co-workers and clients in the informal and entertainment sectors (WOREC, 2006, 18). Ultimately, WOFOWON was born from WOREC's women's health counselling programme, known as *Chhahari*, which literally means 'cool shade' in Nepali.

WOFOWON is the first organisation in Nepal established by women in the informal and entertainment sectors with the aim of protecting and promoting their rights and interests. Before WOFOWON's registration in March 2008, WOREC conducted informal education classes and offered various services such as legal advice, health education, reproductive and sexual health care, and development training – all designed to improve their constituency's professional lives (WOREC, 2008, 24–5). Programme participants started to form unions in the informal and entertainment sectors, and raise their voices against violence. They came to see violence as rooted in patriarchal systems within both society and the state as evidenced by, for example, the arbitrary unwarranted arrests which they often endure (WOREC, 2009, 48). Through leadership development and advocacy training, members of WOFOWON have been empowered to a higher level. Today, they coordinate meetings with police, central government ministries and agencies, restaurant associations, business owners, human rights activists and women's rights networks to provide education on issues relevant to women in the informal and entertainment sectors, while advocating for their labour rights and need for security (WOREC, 2009, 49).

WOFOWON's most notable achievement was the 2008 Supreme Court directive against the sexual harassment of workers in dance bars and restaurants. WOFOWON also initiated a partnership with the National Women's Commission (NWC) in order to create pressure for the legalisation of entertainment work and the effective implementation and monitoring of the directive. The organisation's work has helped cultivate sensitivity, in human rights organisations and multiple other stakeholders, with regard to issues surrounding women in the informal and entertainment sectors.

As of July 2013, WOFOWON employed three staff and had more than 500 members. Sixty members were also affiliated with the Nepal Independent Hotel Casino and Restaurant Workers' Union, one of 27 trade unions under the General Federation of Nepalese Trade Unions (GEFONT). The fact that WOFOWON members joined the trade union as a means of self-advocacy is of significant importance, particularly for the realisation of rights. WOFOWON staff have undertaken research using feminist participatory action methodologies on the lives of women working in the informal and entertainment sectors, including internal migrants, so as to identify and document the conditions they face. Such knowledge will enhance the capacity of female workers as well as WOFOWON's own outreach and organisational capacity.

Solidarity across sectors for an inclusive women's movement

WOREC has fostered an alliance, spanning both groups formed through its work and outside organisations, in an effort to link all segments of society and facilitate inter-sectoral coordination among women defending human rights. This alliance, founded in 2005, is called the National Alliance of Women Human Rights' Defenders (NAWHRD). NAWHRD is itself part of the International Campaign on Women Human Rights Defenders.

By May 2013, 2,500 defenders of women's rights across all of Nepal's 75 districts were affiliated with NAWHRD. They represent different movements, such as those against violence against women and those for women's health rights, the rights of sexual minorities, the rights of women living with HIV/AIDS, women's rights to natural resources, land rights, housing rights, the rights of women working in informal sectors, the rights of women in bonded labour, the rights of minority and marginalised women, the rights of Dalit women, the rights of women with disabilities and the rights of widows. *Shakti Samuha* and WOFOFON are active members in the alliance, a unique platform for addressing different types of human rights violations and providing opportunities for women to take leadership roles at the national level.

NAWHRD organises meetings in an 'inclusive' style, with sign language interpreters and the use of multiple languages from across Nepal. Such arrangements are found not only at key events, but also within WOREC's organisational culture. From its earliest days, WOREC regularly brought trafficking survivors and HIV positive women into the organisation as staff and provided internship opportunities to youth from excluded groups. Today, in WOREC staff with disabilities work together alongside women and men from different ethnicities, castes, regions and age groups.

From an incubator to a partner

This section draws on the previous analysis to highlight key factors of relevance to NGOs that wish to serve as incubators for IBAs, focusing on the three development phases as defined in UKBI's (2012) Business Incubation Development Framework (BIDF): the foundation phase, the development phase and the leading edge phase.

Foundation phase

During *Shakti Samuha's* and WOFOWON's foundation phase, WOREC was a facility that shared space with them and physically protected trafficking survivors and vulnerable IBA members. An outsider observed that over the course of this phase, 'WOREC treated *Shakti Samuha* as a younger sister' (interview with Sita Ghimire, 2008). Early on, *Shakti Samuha* members were often besieged by curious outsiders trying to take photographs by aiming their cameras through WOREC's office balcony. WOREC actively protected survivors, but refrained from treated them or portraying them as 'victims' since its aim was to help them develop into change agents. One *Shakti Samuha* member refers to WOREC as *maita*, or 'family home' in Nepali, which shows her sense of comfort. *Shakti Samuha's* present chair and programme director recalls that immediately after her return from India in 1996, WOREC's chair asked her; 'Why you should be ashamed of yourself? You should not feel guilty. You were trafficked by others. Your rights should be assured, just as any other citizen's' (interview with Sunita Danuwar, 2008). This message instilled confidence and assertiveness in survivors like herself.

For WOFOWON, WOREC's women's health counselling centre *Chhahari* has also served as a nurturing space. *Chhahari* provides a safe shelter for women who have reproductive health problems and a day care facility for the children of working mothers in the entertainment sector (WOREC, 2010, 23). Between 2005 and 2013, *Chhahari* referred more than 8,000 women and girls to essential services and inspired many to establish a relationship with WOFOWON. This shows the importance of providing safe spaces as soon as possible.

Development phase

Capacity building is essential for fostering IBAs, not as subordinate to NGOs but as partner organisations. Support provided during the development phase is comprised of three core elements: training, joint advocacy and facilitating access to funding. Incidentally, WOREC was not the sole organisation responsible for capacity building at *Shakti Samuha*: organisations belonging to the AATWIN alliance against trafficking also provided continuous support. However, the relationship that IBAs form with WOREC is different from their partnerships with other groups, mainly because WOREC invests significant time and energy into providing IBAs with hands-on involvement and back-up support.

WOREC's trainings are not limited to the field of capacity building, such as leadership development and management, but also extend to strengthening knowledge on human rights, labour rights, (anti) trafficking matters, safe migration, and sexual and reproductive health, which instils IBA leaders with the confidence they need to work with specialists and counsel their own members. NGOs often cite IBAs' poor skills in management or reporting as an impediment to NGO efforts to strengthen IBA work, and a reason for NGOs to not partner with IBAs. The examples presented here demonstrate that IBAs can be empowered to run their own organisations and address their own issues as long as NGOs and other supportive parties provide adequate input.

IBAs are typically involved in joint advocacy through alliances. During development stages, however, it is not easy for NGOs and IBAs to maintain equal relations. Instead, IBAs often rely heavily on NGOs and are not sufficiently empowered. As long as NGOs and IBAs maintain purely bilateral relations, unequal footing is difficult to remedy. Thus, alliance building by IBAs serves as a useful strategy for empowering single IBAs while encouraging solidarity among the group. NAWHRD, the alliance founded by WOREC in 2005, became a platform for IBAs to enhance their solidarity across different sectors. Primarily the alliance helped IBAs address their common concerns with greater vigour and strength. In addition, IBA members engage in individual exchanges to learn from each other and improve their understanding of the root causes to their problems, such as patriarchy and globalisation. Participation in such a large forum bolsters the leadership skills of women's IBAs. *Shakti Samuha* and WOFOWON are each actively involved in NAWHRD and play a role in addressing gender-based violence within the women's movement. NAWHRD's secretariat office was based at WOFOWON between 2012 and 2013. One female leader working on housing rights shared her experience with NAWHRD:

> Now it is clear to me why housing rights are so important for people in squatter settlements. There are no women's rights without housing rights. Women's testimonies at NAWHRD's public forums were eye opening for me. I learnt about different types and forms of violence against women. I already knew how to raise money to run the project before joining NAWHRD. However, WOREC provided me with guidance as I directed the movement on the streets. It supplied me with very pragmatic skills for negotiating and locating persons to talk to. (Interview with Bimala Lama, 2013)

Communicating with donors in English can be a hurdle for women's IBAs. A majority of female leaders never had the opportunity to develop a command of English while, on the other hand, numerous male leaders at other IBAs have had the advantage of a good academic foundation. IBAs face language barriers when organising, particularly when it comes to writing proposals and reports for donors in English. As such, IBAs often need external support early on for the preparation of English documents. However, over time IBA core leaders do develop proficiency in managing work in English. WOREC facilitated the procurement of seed money for the early stages of *Shakti Samuha's* and WOFOWON's organisational set-up. Some leaders and members at *Shakti Samuha* and WOFOWON studied English in order to build more effectual communication skills. Overcoming language barriers effectively extends the horizons of IBAs, enabling not only contact with foreign donors but also participation in international conferences and networking with NGOs and IBAs abroad, where, *Shakti Samuha*, for instance, has been trying to assemble a global network of human trafficking survivors.

Leading-edge phase

Shakti Samuha has been at the leading edge of the anti-trafficking movement while WOFOWON raises issues relating to women's labour rights in the informal and entertainment sectors. *Shakti Samuha's* former chair explains how the establishment of *Shakti Samuha* influenced a re-think in WOREC's emphasis: 'In the mid-1990s, WOREC and multiple other women's organisations were working to fight trafficking, but today WOREC's thematic focus has shifted to safe migration. However, we will always work for our own interests regardless of trends in development financing' (interview with Januka Bhattarai, 2008). Again, we see here that the primary difference between NGOs and IBAs is that the latter directly represent the needs and rights of their own members and are not easily captured by other agencies.

Why is an incubator necessary for IBAs?

Renu Rajbandari, WOREC's former chair, made the following observation with regard to the process of empowering groups such as *Shakti Samuha* and WOFOWON: 'a same model will not work for every organisation. Different groups need different approaches' (interview with the author, 2008). The 'different approaches' are possible thanks to her 'open-ended' working style in which she tailors her support and/or training to each group's circumstances. As these two IBAs have developed, WOREC has changed its role from an incubator to a partner in the alliance, NAWHRD. *Shakti Samuha's* leaders and staff still visit WOREC intermittently for meetings and trainings and WOFOWON's core members still maintain close contacts with WOREC. WOREC, however, is no longer directly responsible for the day-to-day operation of *Shakti Samuha*. WOFOWON also is progressing its own path without being guided by WOREC. On 22 July 2013, WOREC officially handed over the *Chhahari* programme, along with its health clinic and drop-in centre, to WOFOWON who now manages the programme independently.

IBA's involvement is essential for building a sustainable social movement. However, the formation of IBA by outside projects is sometimes criticised as 'paid-activism' because the salaries of IBA members are often subsidised by such projects. Moreover, the differences between the roles and the functions of IBAs and those of

NGOs are not well understood. In fact, the movements advanced by IBAs are more effective for social change and more sustainable relative to those promoted by NGOs as we saw in the movements of slum dwellers in India (Patel and Mitlin, 2009) and those of sex workers in Bangladesh (Drinkwater, 2009).

People struggling for survival often encounter greater obstacles to engage themselves in field-based action research or in organising communities, compared with paid NGO workers. In order for IBAs to overcome such obstacles, NGOs ought to think of investing their resources in the capacity building of IBA activists rather than promoting their own 'outsider' movements.

As an experienced trainer, Renu Rajbandari often discusses the merits and the demerits of 'paid activism'. She admits that some IBA activists could be regarded as the 'employees' of donors, noting that only 30 per cent of IBA trainees commit to their movement for longer term. At the same time, she stresses the importance of involving survivors as paid workers in IBA projects, especially considering their limited access to job opportunities. Therefore, she provides the survivors with the best quality training to motivate them to become real activists. Thus far, her trainings have facilitated participants' active involvement in NAWHRD, where newly trained activists keep learning advocacy together.

Capacity building of IBAs takes time and requires human resources. Numerous actors must be mobilised, including international donors and INGOs, to highlight the importance of promoting IBAs. Thus, its success requires a paradigm shift on the side of the donors. Donors often encounter difficulties in developing IBAs' capacity because of the geographical distance to reach them and of their different languages, outlooks, cultures and environment, among other things. Locally-based NGOs, on the other hand, are much closer to IBAs, and can contribute to the capacity development of IBAs more effectively and efficiently. Donors need to include IBA capacity building as an essential component of their funding schemes. Donors can monitor NGOs' performance by recording the growth of IBAs in the women's movement, for example. Under such an arrangement, IBAs can better recognise and select effective NGOs as their partners.

Donors once regarded NGOs as effective and efficient conduits of service delivery. However, by doing so, donors run the risk of crowding out similar services offered by government channels and of leaving target groups with no alternative behind when their projects are finished. Because of this, many donors today have shifted their focus to their partnerships with the state as primary service providers.

NGOs and IBAs, on the other hand, ought to fulfil their roles as civil society actors by holding the state accountable.

Conclusion

This chapter has analysed the unique role of a women's NGO, WOREC, as an incubator of IBAs representing women from marginalised groups. IBAs supported by WOREC include *Shakti Samuha*, an organisation founded by trafficking survivors, and WOFOWON, an organisation formed by women in the informal and entertainment sectors. The formation of *Shakti Samuha* and WOFOWON came about as a result of WOREC's programmes as well as, and just as important, the rights movements initiated by human trafficking survivors to assert their interests through self-representation and overcome stigma, social exclusion and rights violations.

IBAs have three advantages, as demonstrated by *Shakti Samuha*: the capacity for reaching out to target populations, for bridging ideological gaps and for astutely addressing relevant issues. WOREC, acting as an incubator, provided various types of support throughout different phases. During the foundation phase, it acted as a literal 'incubator' by protecting IBAs and providing backup whenever necessary. WOREC's various trainings contributed significantly to the empowerment of IBAs. Moreover, joint advocacy and alliance building initiated by IBAs re-set the IBA–WOREC relationship to one of equal partners.

The role of 'incubator' is unique to this milieu and cannot be found in male-led IBAs in Nepal. Self-representation as practised by *Shakti Samuha* and WOFOWON members has gradually transformed the conception of civil society in Nepal. Members of both organisations have joined other networks, such as AATWIN and GEFONT, including in leadership roles. One notable achievement is the entry of *Shakti Samuha*'s chair to NFN's Central Executive Committee.

The cases presented above stand as evidence that IBAs can be empowered to address their own issues if NGOs and other supporters provide adequate input for capacity building. WOREC's experience and the achievements of *Shakti Samuha* and WOFOWON are perhaps too limited for generalisation but can be replicated by women's organisations in other parts of the world. In addition, donors can also channel aid to NGOs supporting IBAs so as to better contribute to the promotion of self-representation in the women's movement.

Acknowledgements

I am indebted to the members, staff and supporters of WOREC, *Shakti Samuha,* WOFOWON, NAWHRD and other activists in Nepal for their suggestions and encouragement during my fieldwork. I would like to specifically thank Dr Renu Rajbhandari of WOREC, Ms Sunita Danuwar and Ms Laxmi Puri of *Shakti Samuha,* Ms Srijana Pun Magar of WOFOWON, Ms Sita Ghimire of Save the Children International Nepal Country Office and Dr Meena Poudel, former Country Representative of Oxfam GB in Nepal. I am thankful for their generosity in providing time for interviews and proof reading for early versions of this article. Thanks also to Ms Rayna Rusenko for her professional support in English copy-editing. Any acknowledgement would be incomplete without also thanking the members of the Affinity Group for Gender of the International Society for Third Sector Research, who so kindly provided me with the opportunity to write this article.

Notes

[1] The Government of Nepal lifted a 12-year ban on women working in Gulf countries in 2010 but reinstated a ban once more in August 2012 preventing women under the age of 30 from working there after several publicised cases of abuse of Nepali domestic workers (Human Rights Watch, 2012).

[2] The programme by WOREC was funded by MISEREOR, an overseas development agency of the Catholic Church in Germany established in 1958.

[3] CWIN, established in 1987, was Nepal's first child rights organisation. It was formally registered in 1991 as a child rights activist and advocate organisation.

[4] During the repatriation of rescued girls from India in 1996, Save the Children Norway supported joint efforts led by seven local NGOs in Nepal, namely: ABC-Nepal, CWIN, *Maiti-*Nepal, *Navajyoti Kendra, Shanti Punasthapana Kendra, Shree Shakti* and WOREC. This resulted in the formation of *Shakti Samuha.*

[5] Oxfam GB continued funding to *Shakti Samuha* until 2005, Save the Children until 2012.

[6] Originally, *Shakti Samuha* accepted as members any women or girls with the experience of trafficking. In 2010, the criteria were modified such that central committee members also had to be trafficked and sexually abused women and girls.

[7] Poudel's doctoral thesis was based on in-depth interviews with members of *Shakti Samuha* after their return from trafficking. This is the first academic research in Nepal on individuals' lived experiences after trafficking.

[8] She was placed third among 24 candidates for 11 seats (*Shakti Samuha,* 2013)

References

AATWIN (Alliance Against Trafficking in Women and Children in Nepal), 2013, www.aatwin.org.np

Dahal, DR, Timsina, TP, 2007, *Civil society in Nepal: Searching for a viable role*, Kathmandu: Institute of Cultural Affairs Nepal

Drinkwater, M, 2009, 'We are also human': Identity and power in gender relations, in S Hickey, D Mitlin (eds) *Rights-based approaches to development: Exploring the potential and pitfalls*, pp 145–62, Sterling: Kumarian Press

Fowler, A, 2000, Beyond partnership: Getting real about NGO relationships in the aid system, *IDS Bulletin* 31, 3, 1–13

Gellner, DN (ed), 2009, *Ethnic activism and civil society in South Asia*, New Delhi: SAGE

GFW (Global Fund for Women), 2012, Mission and history, www.globalfundforwomen.org/who-we-are/our-mission

Hudock, AC, 1999, *NGOs and civil society: Democracy by proxy?*, Cambridge: Polity Press

Human Rights Watch, 2012, Nepal: Protect, don't ban young women migrating to Gulf, *Human Rights Watch*, www.hrw.org/news/2012/08/14/nepal-protect-don-t-ban-young-women-migrating-gulf

Karki, MB, 2006, Social networking and the recruitment process among activists in Nepal, *Contributions to Nepalese Studies* 33, 1, 33–72

Lama, ST, 1997, Remarks on the political within the Nepali women's movement, *Studies in Nepali History and Society* 2, 2, 327–35

NFN (NGO Federation of Nepal), 2012, *Three-year strategic plan October 2012–September 2015*, Kathmandu: NGO Federation of Nepal Central Executive Committee

NFN (NGO Federation of Nepal), 2013, Introduction, www.ngofederation.org

Patel, S, Mitlin, D, 2009, Reinterpreting the rights-based approach: A grassroots perspective on rights and development, in S Hickey, D Mitlin (eds) *Rights-based approaches to development: Exploring the potential and pitfalls*, pp 107–26, Sterling: Kumarian Press

Ploumen, L, 2001, Mama Cash: Investing in the future of women, *Gender and Development* 9, 1, 53–9

Poudel, M, 2011, *Dealing with hidden issues: Social rejection experienced by trafficked women in Nepal*, Saarbrücken: LAP LAMBERT Academic Publishing

Sherchan, K, 1997, Political divisions among women's groups, *Studies in Nepali History and Society* 2, 2, 335–9

Singh, A, Ingdal, N, 2007, A discussion paper on donor best practices towards NGOs in Nepal, *Norad Collected Reviews* 10/2007, www. norad.no/no/resultater/publikasjoner/norads-samlede-rapporter/ publikasjon?key=109656

Shakti Samuha, 2005, 2010, 2011, 2012, *Annual Reports 2004*, Kathmandu: *Shakti Samuha*

Shakti Samuha, 2013, About us, *Shakti Samuha*, www.shaktisamuha. org.np

SWC (Social Welfare Council), 2012, *NGOs affiliated with Social Welfare Council*, www.swc.org.np/SWC_NGOs_Total.pdf

Tamang, S, 2009, The politics of conflict and difference or the difference of conflict in politics: The women's movement in Nepal, *Feminist Review* 91, 61–80

Tanaka, M, 2006, 'Bundan to renkei to: Kodomotachi ga tsunagaru chi'iki katsudo' [Segmentation and collaboration: Children work together for community development], *Alta* 369, 18–21

Tanaka, M, 2011, The changing roles of NGOs in Nepal: Promoting emerging rights-holder organizations for inclusive aid, *Voluntas* 22, 3, 497–517

Tanaka, M, 2013, Balancing between politics and development: The multiple roles played by indigenous people's organizations in Nepal, *History and Sociology of South Asia* 7, 1, 61–78

Terre des hommes, 2010, *Trafficking and exploitation in the entertainment and sex industries in Nepal: A handbook for decision-makers*, Kathmandu: Terre des hommes

Terre des hommes Foundation and *Shakti Samuha*, 2012, *Procedures for safety and personal protection: Transportation during repatriation or between in-country venues*, Kathmandu: *Shakti Samuha* and Terre des hommes Foundation

UKBI (UK Business Incubation Limited), 2012, Business incubation development framework, www.ukbi.co.uk/resources/the-framework. aspx

Uprety, U, 2011, A reflection on the legal framework for civil society in Nepal, *International Journal of Not-for-Profit Law* 13, 3, 50–89

WOREC (Women's Rehabilitation Centre), 1994, *Annual Report 1992/03*, Kathmandu: WOREC

WOREC (Women's Rehabilitation Centre), 1998, *Annual Report 1997*, Kathmandu: WOREC

WOREC (Women's Rehabilitation Centre), 1999, *Annual Report 1998*, Kathmandu: WOREC

WOREC (Women's Rehabilitation Centre), 2001, *Annual Report 2000: Social Mobilization and Dimensions of Change*, Kathmandu: WOREC

WOREC (Women's Rehabilitation Centre), 2006, *Annual Report 2005: Putting grassroots efforts together*, Kathmandu: WOREC

WOREC (Women's Rehabilitation Centre), 2008, *Annual Report 2007*, Kathmandu: WOREC

WOREC (Women's Rehabilitation Centre), 2009, *Annual Report 2008*, Kathmandu: WOREC

WOREC (Women's Rehabilitation Centre), 2010, *Annual Report 2009*, Kathmandu: WOREC

WOREC (Women's Rehabilitation Centre), 2012, *Annual Report 2011*, Kathmandu: WOREC

World Bank, The, 2013, 'Defining civil society', *The World Bank*, http://web.worldbank.org/WBSITE/EXTERNAL/TOPICS/CSO/0,contentMDK:20101499~menuPK:244752~pagePK:220503~piPK:220476~theSitePK:228717,00.html.

TEN

Gender democracy and women's self-empowerment: a case of Somali diaspora civil society

Marco Tavanti, Cawo Abdi and Blaire MacHarg

Introduction

Somalia is currently reengaging with the international community after the 1988 civil war followed by a devastating complete collapse of the state. After decades of war and living without a government, many Somali families were forced to take their language, culture and skills and move to other parts of the world in search of a better way of life. In effect, they are a living example of the African diaspora. A diaspora is the dispersion of a people, language or culture that was formerly concentrated in one place, that is then scattered and displaced, to live in separated communities (DePaul University Center for Black Diaspora, 2015).

Somalia faces challenges in the establishment of a democratic, peaceful and just human development process. Somali authorities have identified the empowerment of women as a priority in the reconstruction and reengagement of the country. International development agencies support this priority through women's empowerment projects advocating for greater asset ownership and participation in decision-making processes. Similar to other developing, post–conflict and post-emergency countries, Somalia faces both challenges and opportunities related to mainstreaming gender equity into its agenda for poverty reduction, democratic governance, human security and sustainable development (Visvanathan, 2011). By providing support to relevant Somali stakeholders, the gender empowerment agenda in Somalia is recognised nationally and internationally as a priority for peace and development.

The necessary steps required for achieving women's empowerment in Somalia range from strengthening women's leadership capacities to developing women's political participation. This process also requires collaboration with community-based organisations and civil society to engage with communities on sensitive issues such as sexual and gender based violence (SGBV) and female genital mutilation/circumcision (FGM/C). Building gender mainstreaming capacity and promoting gender equality in Somalia requires cross-sector initiatives, which transcend national and cultural boundaries (Howell and Mulligan, 2005). This capacity development requires processes directed toward the promotion of gender equality and women's rights through advocacy campaigns, community dialogue and leadership development.

This study explores the empowerment and capacity development processes for Somali women through the examination of Somali diaspora civil society organisations. Within the analysis of the crucial role that the Somalia diaspora has in the reconstruction process of Somalia, we put forward an integrated, 'meso-level' model of women's empowerment connected to the assets and missions of selected SD-CSOs. Linking the macro- (from above) and micro- (from below) approaches are essential to bringing about sustainable changes and a comprehensive approach to women empowerment (Sahay, 1998; Demos and Segal, 2009). Women empowerment studies, however, generally fail to examine the strategic power of a mid-level (meso-) approach which links the macro- with the micro- while also providing organisational development opportunities. Through an examination of 'social remittances' (Levitt, 1998) we argue that such partnerships at the organisational level are critical in supporting the women's empowerment process in Somalia. Based on the examination of development literature and selected organisations, we also argue that gender empowerment through such a meso-level must be integrated with macro-level policies for gender mainstreaming and social inclusion as well as micro-level empowerment approaches to interpersonal gender dynamics within the household.

Gender mainstreaming and women's empowerment are key priorities for the establishment of a peaceful, just, prosperous and inclusive society in Somalia. The 2012 election of President Hassan Sheikh Mohamud, a civil society activist and education campaigner, led to the appointment of Fauzia Yusuf Haji Adan, the first female foreign minister and deputy prime minister. This was a historical first for Somalia. However, the many barriers challenging gender democracy initiatives are complex. Developing gender inclusivity within Somali society requires active engagement from both civil society and the Somali diaspora. Somalia is a nation spread worldwide with approximately one million Somalis living in the diaspora, concentrated in areas of the Horn of Africa and Yemen, the Gulf States, Western Europe and North America

(UNDP, 2009, 4). Achieving the third UN Millennium Development Goal (MDG 3) to promote gender equality and empower women in Somalia, requires national commitment, international support and diaspora cooperation.

Empowerment in the Somali context

Studies of women's empowerment in challenging contexts such as the Horn of Africa (HOA) and the Middle East and North Africa (MENA) state that it is vital to the region's progress that women play a larger role in the economy and society (Moghadam, 2008). In order to be relevant to Somalia's reconstruction process, women's empowerment must also be relevant to Somali cultural and development challenges. The Republic of Somalia, located in the Horn of Africa has an estimated population of ten million. The majority of the population are Sunni Muslim. In spite of the many important roles Somali women play in their society, they remain greatly disadvantaged in a context where their familial resources are limited. Discrimination against women is deeply rooted and evident in many aspects of Somali women's lives. The patriarchal norms that associate men with power and leadership in both the private and public spheres are evident in both family and social relations. Therefore, women's empowerment in Somalia cannot be effectively implemented without a full and realistic consideration of local and customary norms.

Women's 'empowerment' has different meanings at the local and international levels. To the international community, empowerment means the achievement of specific goals, while Somali society and activists may have different priorities and understandings of empowerment. It is in this gap between local worldviews and international worldviews about the rights of women where SD-CSOs emerge as important agents linking the macro- and micro-actors. At the meso-level, the Somali diaspora becomes an important bridge connecting the local perspective with the international perspective, and helping UN agencies and small domestic NGOs, who share a common agenda, to improve the status of women in society. Operating at the meso-level of empowerment requires contextual knowledge and the capacity to mediate between international expectations and local interpretations (Parpart et al, 2002). SD-CSOs uniquely possess this combination of knowledge and capacity, existing in an optimal position linking the macro- and micro-levels. Implementing women's empowerment programmes through the meso-level also requires new frameworks for dialogue allowing diverse interpretations, including interpretations within the Muslim framework. While there are no monolithic interpretations of Islam, many agree that challenges to women's rights in the Islamic world primarily utilise religious prescriptions and readings that place women in subordinate positions (Mernissi, 1987; Ahmed, 1992). But these religious documents, often the Koran and the Hadiths, or the practices of the Prophet Mohamed, also serve to strongly promote and support women's empowerment in all spheres of society (Mernissi, 1987; Ahmed, 1992) and can thus be used to counter gender oppression.

The report *Women empowering themselves* (WEMC, 2008) presents extensive research on the issues of gender, poverty and democratisation in achieving MDG 3 and is pertinent for the study of Somalia. This research confirms that gender equality is a precondition for reducing poverty and that women's empowerment needs a new narrative that is aligned with the international community's perspective on gender issues while still remaining contextually relevant. The report states:

> There is a broad consensus on what the priorities are for achieving women's empowerment...Yet we are far from achieving these in practice and there is little understanding of how to achieve them. Current research relating to these issues is relatively ad hoc and anecdotal. What works in one context does not appear to work in others and there is a lack of analysis and synthesis across different empirical contexts drawing together lessons learned. Organisations and decision makers working to empower women therefore need to know more about what strategies work, which ones don't and why this is the case in different situations. There is a strong need for a new 'narrative' that can reshape practical strategies and approaches at both country and international levels, build on current successes and bridge the gaps between the 'lived realities' of the poor and the actions of decision makers at all levels. (WEMC, 2008, 4)

Cultural and religious contexts that deny rights to women and actively disempower them are prevalent in patriarchal societies throughout the world. Gender norms in these contexts can be oppressive to women, even if they are presented as culturally endorsed forms of gender relations and norms (WEMC, 2008, 18, 39). Still, new narratives for women's empowerment have gained momentum over the course of the last few decades, and local narratives on the position of women in society have now become difficult to distinguish from international gender discourses and expectations. This shift can be said to be the result of increasing global awareness of the prevalence of gender-based violence and gender discrimination in education and employment (UNDP, 2012a; UN Women, 2011). However, this bridging of local and global attitudes is also linked to women's awareness of the conflicting discourses on the place of women, which are often justified based on cultural and religious norms. This awareness and increasing access to secular and religious education permits women of all regions, including women within the Muslim world, to question many taken-for-granted prescriptions of the role of women and their rights, both within their nation states as well as within the Islamic jurisprudence (Shukrallah, 1994).

Other empirical studies on women's empowerment in Muslim contexts confirm how religion is often confused with local patriarchal cultures (Chaudhary et al, 2012). The complex interconnections between cultural norms and religious beliefs require those involved in the process of empowering women to become aware and competent in these value systems. It is therefore empirically evident that the empowerment of women through consciousness raising, economic security and integrated development occurs even in less developed Islamic societies (Chaudhary et al, 2012). Beyond cultural and religious diversity, women's empowerment strategies still need to incorporate a holistic model which integrates consciousness raising (women's rights, self-esteem and education) with economic empowerment (strengthened economic security) and integrated human development (enhanced access to education, health and resources). These globally accepted strategies in women's empowerment need a culturally appropriate approach in an Islamic and Arab society. For instance, the 2005 Arab Human Development Report stated that the term 'women's empowerment' is not a culturally appropriate term in Arab societies.

> The first *Arab human development report* (2002) used the terminology 'women's empowerment' clearly an Arabisation of an English term. Perhaps a better term in the Arabic language is 'the rise of woman' in contrast to 'the empowerment of woman' to connote woman's struggle for her rights through the building of her capacity and its effective use in a conducive societal framework. (UNDP and AFESD, 2006, 55)

Effective women's empowerment programmes in Somalia need to take into account many contextual factors. Besides cultural and religious diversity, they need to consider the level of gender inequality and gender-based marginalisation in post-conflict and post-emergency fragile contexts. The United Nations Development Programme (UNDP) evaluates women's empowerment as a factor in the Gender Inequality Index (GII) based on two indicators: educational attainment (secondary level and above), and parliamentary representation. Somalia's strikingly low Human Development Index rating is among the lowest in the world (UNDP, 2014). Gender inequality in Somalia is alarmingly high as the fourth highest in the world with a GII value of 0.776 (where 1 is complete inequality). Illustrating the range of scores, the Netherlands GII value is 0.045; between these two extremes fall the United Kingdom at 0.205, China at 0.213, Brazil at 0.447, and Kenya at 0.608 (UNDP, 2012a, xviii).

Women in Somalia provide basic needs to family members, depending on natural resources such as water and vegetation. But displaced women have little access to property, education or healthcare. These women bear the brunt of hardships intensified by poverty, conflict and natural disaster (UNDP Somalia, 2011).

Gender mainstreaming through capacity-empowerment

Gender mainstreaming requires that both men and women become fully and equally included in all aspects of policy planning and implementation (UNDP, 2012a, 96; UN Women, 2012). It also requires a comprehensive strategy for empowerment that articulates economic, political and socially specific agendas. In the delicate Somali process for human security, political reconstruction, community development and poverty reduction, gender mainstreaming needs to be integrated and included in strategic national priorities and objectives of international cooperation initiatives. It is also necessary to include relevant Somali stakeholders in the implementation of gender-specific interventions. Gender mainstreaming needs to align local, national and international efforts for gender equality, female empowerment and gender integration. The United States Agency for International Development (USAID) and the United States Department of State (USDOS) recognise gender equality (same rights and opportunities) and female empowerment (women and girls) to be core objectives for diplomacy and development (USAID, 2012). In Somalia, as in other countries affected by poverty and violence, the focus on women's rights and empowerment as a means of achieving gender mainstreaming and integration are the conditions to attain poverty alleviation (development) and human security (peace). Hillary Clinton, during her tenure as Secretary of State, emphasised just this need for increasing efforts to achieve gender equality and women's empowerment, if peace and prosperity are not to have their own glass ceiling (USAID, 2012).

Due to a combination of systemic violence, institutional failures, social norms and coping strategies, Somalia remains one of the worst places in the world to be a woman. The UNDP study on the state of gender in Somalia describes this in detail: 'Somalia has extremely high maternal mortality, rape, female genital mutilation and child marriage rates, and violence against women and girls is common, though statistics are difficult to find. The participation and role of women in politics and decision-making spheres is extremely limited, perpetuating narrow gender based roles and inequalities' (UNDP, 2012a, 2).

Like other international development agencies, the UNDP aims to respond directly to the many acute challenges faced by Somali women, including the high rate of maternal mortality, which is among the highest in the world at approximately 1,400 per 100,000 live births (UNDP Somalia, 2011, 4). Contributing to this issue is the limited access to health services. Gender inequities are also demonstrated in literacy rates; the adult literacy rate for Somali women is 26 per cent compared to 36 per cent for men (UNDP Somalia, 2012b, 2). As a consequence, women experience lower rates of formal employment compared to men (UNDP Somalia, 2012b, 51).

Further challenges contributing to gender-based marginalisation include limited participation in decision-making and high child marriage rates; 45 per cent of Somali women aged 20 to 24 were married before the age of 18. Gender-based violence mainly goes unreported and unpunished. This is partly because customary or traditional law is more often followed than laws imposed by the state judiciary, and because women lack access to formal justice mechanisms (UNDP Somalia, 2011). The World Health Organization estimates that 98 per cent of women in Somalia undergo some type of female circumcision, which in the Somali context often involves the most severe form of cutting, removing the clitoris as well as the inner and outer labia. Female genital mutilation or circumcision (FGM/C) occurs most often between four and eleven years old. Community support for FGM/C is high, which perpetuates challenges associated with its eradication (UNDP Somalia, 2012b, 2). Sadly, many women experience lifelong medical problems as a result of undergoing FGM/C (UNDP Somalia, 2012b).

In Somalia's transition from post conflict to recovery, empowering women will contribute to building resilience in crisis prevention. Yet, the many challenges represented by Somalia's currently weak capacity for building international relations, national cultural identities and integration, require the women's empowerment process to be integrated into the peace process. Gender-specific challenges in Somalia require strategic agendas such as those illustrated by the UNDP Eight Point Agenda. The Agenda promotes practical, positive outcomes for girls and women in crisis through (1) an end to violence against women, (2) provision of justice and security, (3) advancing women as decision-makers, (4) involving women in all peace processes, (5) supporting women and men in disaster risk reduction, (6) promoting women as leaders of recovery, (7) including women's issues on the national agenda, and (8) working together to transform society (UNDP, 2015).

These points address gender empowerment in relation to human security and humanitarian emergencies. Working toward this Eight Point Agenda will facilitate Somalia's re-engagement with the international community, and allow support at the macro-level for the country to achieve these goals. However, such an agenda must be closely associated with other general development and capacity-building frameworks for women's empowerment. The United Nations has been at the forefront for the promotion of an integrative model for capacity development and women's empowerment (UN-ECOSOC, 2010; UN Women, 2012). Such a comprehensive and inclusive model considers empowerment at the political (governance), economic (sustainability) and socio–interpersonal (well-being) levels. These elements of women's empowerment are critical for gender mainstreaming and effective integration of women into the decision-making processes of their families and communities. The IFAD, the UN specialised agency for agriculture and development, utilises a similar model for achieving gender equality and women's empowerment (UN–IFAD, 2012). Specifically, IFAD recognises their work for gender equality and women's empowerment to be based around three priorities:

1. economic empowerment: improving women's access to income-earning opportunities and productive assets;
2. decision-making: increasing women's say in community affairs and strengthening women producers' organisations;
3. well-being: improving access of rural people, in particular women, to basic services and infrastructure.

These three areas are also central to a capacity development approach. Figure 10.1 represents a relational model between these general and integrated capacity frameworks with the more specific goals that are a priority in the context of Somalia.

Figure 10.1: Capacity and empowerment connected model

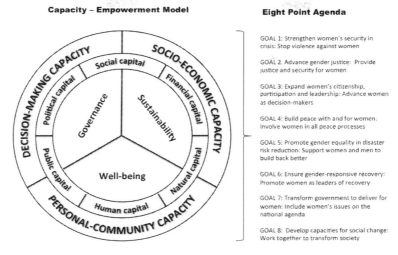

Source: Elaborated by Tavanti from various sources

The capacity–empowerment model in Figure 10.1 illustrates the frameworks through which Somali society can advance the empowerment of women and identifies outcomes related to these three frameworks. These frameworks, wellbeing, governance and sustainability, indicate the importance of women's empowerment in increasing economic opportunities (access to capital) while promoting human rights and development capacity (evidence of capabilities). Improved wellbeing can increase personal-community capacity; addressing empowerment through governance improves decision-making capacity; sustainability of empowerment can be achieved through improved socio-economic capacity. The inner ring of the model indicates the six types of capital to be affected by the achievement of empowerment in each framework. Various studies have shown the relationship between women's empowerment and capacity development relative to human rights, property rights, financial capital and capacity development (Christabell, 2009; Hallward-Driemeier and Hasan, 2013; Nussbaum, 2013).

This comprehensive model indicates that having an impact on gender inequality requires efforts coming from each of the three frameworks. Although the goals outlined in the UNDP Eight Point Agenda fall within the frameworks listed in the Empowerment Model, the points can be supplemented and strengthened with sustainable solutions to the challenges facing women's empowerment processes. Achievement of the Eight Points alone may not ensure lasting empowerment in Somalia. Addressing the Eight Points in conjunction with the Empowerment Model allows for a multifaceted, comprehensive approach to empowerment. Furthermore, we argue that applying the knowledge and resources of the diaspora and SD-CSOs will further improve the sustainability of empowerment initiatives.

Social remittances and transnational identities

The last 20 years of political and economic turmoil in Somalia have led to a complete collapse of the state and the displacement of millions of the population, either as refugees in neighbouring countries or as internally displaced peoples within Somalia. Throughout the many years of war, systemic violence, extreme poverty and recurring famine most of the talented and educated Somali men and women were forced to seek protection and opportunities in other parts of the globe. This situation illustrates the definition of diaspora as 'the dispersion of a people, language, or culture that was formerly concentrated in one place, to scatter, to displace, to live in separated communities' (DePaul University Center for Black Diaspora, 2015).

The study of growing diaspora communities around the world has recognised how these global kinship communities play a vital role in their homeland domestic affairs (Lum et al, 2013). The transnational ethnic linkages of diaspora Somali affect political, social and therefore empowerment dynamics for community development. This Somali diaspora community, settled throughout the Horn of Africa, the Middle East, Europe, Australia and the United States, has been vital to the survival of the country through remittances, family support, solidarity projects and advocacy.

Remittances are financial transactions between family members living abroad and their families back home. Somali migrants around the world send approximately $1.3 billion to Somalia, of which $215 million comes from Somali Americans. This makes up a significant share of Somalia's economy and provides an alternative to foreign aid dependency (Lindley, 2010; Orozco and Yansura, 2013). These remittances help Somali women achieve greater financial stability, increase savings and improve their family's quality of life (Orozco and Yansura, 2013). Studies show that when women receive and control remittances they are more likely to improve the overall well-being of their households through increased expenditure on health, education and nutrition (UN-IFAD, 2009).

Forced and voluntary migration has helped the Somali diaspora to access educational, social and cultural capital (Kleist, 2008; Langellier,

2010). The dynamic and transnational connections of Somali society make it possible for the transformations in gender dynamics that occur in the diaspora to also affect gender relations and debates in the home country. Diaspora women in particular represent agents of positive cultural change in Somalia. They have the ability to benefit local women who have never had the chance to migrate. Collaboration between civil society organisations, the diaspora and local women helps address problems such as gender-based violence, as well as social, political and economic marginalisation.

Research confirms that diaspora communities transmit new practices, ideas and norms to their families and communities of origin. In *Somalia's missing million*, a report for UNDP by Hassan Sheikh and Sally Healy on the role of the diaspora in Somali development, the notion of 'social' remittances was extensively discussed (UNDP, 2009). The term social remittances refers to those identities, practices and norms as well as social capital that migrants transmit and transfer to their homelands through letters, travel, phone and internet communication (Levitt, 1998; Levitt and Lamba-Nieves, 2011).

During this transitional period, the role of the Somalia diaspora has clearly emerged as very important for both economic and social capital development. Following the end of the interim mandate of the Transitional Federal Government (TFG), the flow of social remittances intensified after the Federal Government of Somalia was established on 20 August 2012. In addition to the value added by economic remittances, social remittances represented the skills, capacity and renewed identities that Somali people successfully established overseas, and then shared with their compatriots at home. These social remittances were key to changing attitudes and the roles of women in society through which women in the diaspora became transnational agents of renewed identities (Falah and Nagel, 2005).

The 'meso' level of capacity development

The meso-level of capacity development provides a vital link between international development efforts and the local population who are striving to improve their daily lives. The Somali diaspora, with their understanding of local culture and mores, in addition to their experiences of living abroad, provide a link to both cultures. Empowerment and capacity development efforts include both macro-level national and international institutions and micro-level individuals and families. But, empowerment initiatives that focus only at these two extremes risk being culturally incompetent and unsustainable.

The Somali diaspora community non-profit/non-governmental organisations are best placed to bridge these macro–micro gaps by providing culturally competent programmes and internationally aligned priorities. This recognition of the positive contributions of SD-CSOs suggests that international development policies and project criteria should prioritise this investment in diaspora communities. Surprisingly, the meso-level contribution is still missing in many programmes. This happens in spite of the international development challenges associated with bridging the gap between macro-level policies and micro-level local community organisations (Fowler, 1997; Malhotra et al, 2002; Easterly, 2006). While linking up, networking, building connections and strengthening interactions are still vital components in international development programmes, capacity development directed specifically to organisations located between macro-level institutions and local communities remains crucial to the empowerment process (Malhotra et al, 2002). Empowerment processes, capacity development approaches and social inclusion policies need to be clearly linked to this crucially important meso-level (Fukuda-Parr and Lopes, 2012).

Figure 10.2 demonstrates how SD-CSOs can work at this meso-level of intervention and outlines the programmatic priorities between the individual and the policy levels of capacity development for women's empowerment and gender mainstreaming.

Figure 10.2: The meso-level model for organisations

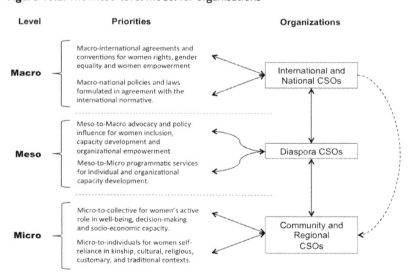

Source: Elaborated by Tavanti from various sources

Supported by empowerment findings in development literature, and also by promising examples of meso-level organisational partnerships, we argue that meso-level organisational development can provide such a bridge between international and local civil society organisations, and are vital for successful, socially integrated empowerment and capacity building. This is particularly urgent in the context of Somalia today, where numerous internationally funded official development assistance programmes are present, operating under low levels of accountability and little evaluation regarding the achievement of initial objectives. The SD-CSOs in the few cases shown below offer a strategic advantage in developing internationally aligned, culturally competent and sustainable empowerment solutions in Somalia's reconstruction process.

Somali civil society in diaspora

The Somali diaspora, although scattered across the globe, keeps in touch via telephone, internet and travel. These activities, which strengthen the diaspora network, are both political and economic (UNDP, 2009). Financial remittances constitute 24 per cent of household income and about 80 per cent of start-up capital for small and medium enterprises (UNDP, 2009, 19). The diaspora remains a bridge between the adopted countries around the globe and Somalia's economic, social and political stability and future development. Somali diaspora communities are valuable assets that could be the subject of investment for peace, empowerment, development and country reconstruction. The consequences of not involving them may be that the changes that are promoted are not culturally intelligent changes or leave a vacuum that radical recruitment and transnational repercussions of conflict might then fill (Hoffman et al, 2007).

Studies have shown that in spite of the human suffering due to separation and adaptation, the Somali diaspora has also provided opportunities for social integration, changing social values and the creation of a borderless Somali identity (Abdi, 2015; Kusow and Bjork, 2007; Farah, 2000; Kapteijns, 1993). The diaspora's established CSOs, along with its existing and potential relationships with Somalia-based CSOs, provide an opportunity for increased organisational capacity and the establishment of a link between macro-policies and local cultures. The SD-CSOs can fill a gap by implementing much needed meso-level programmes for women's empowerment that are both locally viable and internationally acceptable. When supported by larger partnership mechanisms, SD-CSOs are well positioned to implement culturally competent programmes. SD-CSOs are contextually knowledgeable and internationally poised, and therefore possess valuable dexterity required to expertly navigate international expectations, domestic agendas and Somali contexts.

We propose that the Somali diaspora also represents a positive force for governance leadership development that has been barely used thus far. Diaspora Somali women, often through education abroad and transformations in their gender relationships, have developed leadership capacity for public service administrative positions (Abdi, 2014). The international community could profitably recognise and invest in the pioneering leadership role of these Somali women in the post-colonial and post-conflict reconstructions (Ingiriis, 2015).

With an increasing returnee population coming from Europe and America, Somali diaspora members now occupy key positions in the new government. For example, the last three governments had prime ministers who returned from North America and several current ministerial positions are occupied by citizens who returned from England, the United States and Canada. These returnees are playing key roles in the reconstitution of governance in Somalia. The diaspora's remittances, both social and financial, also continue to be a lifeline for millions of Somalis aiding both in day-to-day survival and in developmental projects in the country.

Somali diaspora CSOs and their contribution to women's empowerment: some examples

Somali CSOs working in the United States, United Kingdom, Kenya and the Horn of Africa have played an important role in the empowerment of Somali women. These civil society organisations are based in large Somali communities such as Minnesota, Ohio and Nairobi, Kenya. These organisations work at the meso-level and strive to empower diaspora women's education, employment, financial literacy, political representation and health.

The Center for Somali Women's Advancement, the Somali Women's Study Center, and the Somali Women Education Network demonstrate how meso-level SD-CSOs can have an impact on Somali women's empowerment both in the diaspora and in Somalia. These examples of Somali diaspora organisations engaged in women's empowerment strategies exemplify diverse levels of engagement and priorities ranging from education, health and wellness to policy, leadership and political participation. They represent diverse but interconnected levels of women's empowerment, working at the micro-, meso- and macro-levels of the interpersonal, community, societal and political decision making. Each of these organisations has leaders based in North America who maintain linkages to developmental initiatives in Somalia. The leaders' transnational connections demonstrate their potential as models for other initiatives that might emerge from the diaspora community.

The Center for Somali Women's Advancement (CSWA)

CSWA is a non-profit organisation based in Columbus, Ohio, serving the needs of girls and women in the United States and the Horn of Africa. Their activities are focused on organising policy forums and community conversations on topics related to women. Its mission is 'to provide hope for Somali women and girls everywhere by offering women the tools they need to build secure and positive living environments and healthy relationships at all levels of society' (www. centerforsomaliwomen.org). Ms Khadra Mohamed, President of CSWA, explains that 'Somali women are the matriarchs of our families. When our husbands are away from home, we keep the family together and ensure that our children learn the Koran. We want to guarantee that our Somali culture be preserved. At the same time, we want to join with our husbands, fathers and decision makers to define our future in the United States and Somalia' (www.centerforsomaliwomen. org). CSWA asserts the demand for space for women in public fora, and acknowledgment of women's important contributions to society. Ms Mohamed's promotion of Somali women as actors within the public sphere led to CSWA developing crucial links and collaborations with Ohio state officials in Columbus County. This advocacy for the recognition of Somali women's many contributions to society, challenges the division of private and public space that are used by many gendered discourses to justify the marginalisation of women. Consequently, this advocacy and activism has the possibility to evolve into an instrument for social change, building on the support and resources available to these organisations through their established links and networks both within the diaspora and also within civic organisations in Somalia (CSWA, 2013). In discussions between Ms Mohamed and author, Cawo Abdi, Ms Mohamed stated that the goal of this advocacy work was to help the organisation become active both in the United States and Somalia and to utilise the know-how and organisational skills gained in the US to contribute to the advancement of Somali women's issues in Somalia.

The Somali Women's Study Center (SWSC)

The Nairobi-based SWSC is consciously striving to bridge the micro–macro gap in the realisation of women's empowerment. As of January 2015, there were 462,970 Somali refugees in Kenya that received assistance from the United Nations High Commissioner for Refugees (UNHCR, 2015). SWSC acts as a catalyst for positive change by focusing on advocacy, education, training, research development and increasing women's leadership and political representation. SWSC addresses the struggle for gender equity in governance. SWSC's leader earned a PhD in Women's Studies from a Canadian university and hopes to develop the organisation's research capacity so that they can help with both the micro- and macro-levels of support. They want to help with the efforts of local organisations that are often hampered by a lack of resources and networks at the micro-level, and help international workers at the macro-level who are supportive of women's empowerment but who lack the cultural understanding and local networks necessary to support educational and advocacy projects (www.somaliwomenstudies.org). Thus, the organisation can be instrumental in bridging the cultural, linguistic and religious barriers that might arise between macro-level international funders and actors and micro-level local activists and organisations.

Somali Women's Education Network (SWEN)

SWEN is based in Minneapolis, Minnesota, and provides educational services to young Somali women. Founded by Fardowsa Yousuf in 2009, SWEN's mission is to empower and build strong families through education. SWEN's approach is based on self-help and communal self-reliance for capacity development. They recognise the interdependence between their work with women in the diaspora and women in Somalia. Ms Yousuf is now based in Kenya but often travels between the United States and Somalia. Her experience of Somali community development and women's empowerment work in Minnesota is helpful in transferring leadership skills to benefit women in Somalia. The organisation's successful mentoring programme would need to be adapted for the Somalian context. For example, programmes for women's empowerment in career development and community engagement are rare in Somalia, especially in Southern areas where the presence of extremist militants limits young women's physical movements, access to schools and participation in sports activities. Therefore, Somali returnee women such as Ms Yousuf, who are advocating for young women's involvement in all spheres of society, can gain support from both local and international actors, with lessons learned from the macro- and micro-practices merging to produce programmes that are effective and sustainable. Ms Yousuf has already taken initial steps to get Somali women in Mogadishu interested in her projects.

Discussion

The organisations briefly described above represent culturally intelligent models for women's empowerment. While advocating changes and promoting women's capacity, SD-CSOs are also considerate of Muslim values and cultural norms in the diverse groups of Somalia. What is more important is that their 'insiderness' facilitates trust and connection with the local communities. Such communities may view non-Somali interventions with suspicion, concerned that they are imposing foreign ways on African and Muslim cultures. Their proximity to local culture along with their cultural transformations due to exposure to Western and non-Muslim values, make them well suited to bypass local suspicions about changing cultural practices such as FGM/C (Berg and Denison, 2013). In other words, the Somali diaspora, if well integrated in Somalia's sustainable development and transitional justice process, can be an agent for consciousness raising and cultural transformation (Haji-Abdi, 2014).

The experiences of the diaspora, especially those in democratic European and American societies provide Somali women with the leadership capacity to create organisations and programmes which respond to the needs of Somali communities both at home and abroad. CSWA, SWSC and SWEN are examples of organisations and programmes at the meso-level which have the ability to provide empowerment support for Somalia's political, social, economic and cultural development and reconstruction (IIED, 2005). These SD-CSOs, and other organisations like them, demonstrate the strategic opportunities available to invest in the local community and diaspora at the meso-level of empowerment. These women and their organisations developed the cultural competence to work effectively between two distinct cultures. They have the ability to collaborate with international development organisations at the macro-level and collaborate with local women's cultural groups at the micro-level. These SD-CSOs are uniquely qualified to help bridge the discussions about women's engagement in decision-making, socio-economic and personal community capacities. With proper support and a diverse spectrum of partnering organisations, SD-CSOs can implement meso-level programming for gender equality and women's empowerment in Somalia. Projects implemented without such SD-CSO involvement risk a lack of local legitimacy or misalignment with international norms such as the Convention on the Elimination of Discrimination Against Women (CEDAW).

One key challenge that needs careful monitoring is the potential for conflict and competition between Somalia-based civil society organisations and diaspora activists and their initiatives in Somali. Somali civil society organisations may perceive diaspora and returnee initiatives as a threat to their own existence. For example, Somali diaspora leaders may be perceived as having more cultural capital for accessing resources from international developmental institutions. In consequence, we argue for what Alan Fowler (2000) describes as a 'fourth position' for non-governmental development organisations: not a position of neutrality but rather a responsibility for creating effective cross-partnerships and collaboration at the meso-level, representing the rights of civil society (grassroots local CSOs) and articulating programmes aligned with the priorities of public and private actors. Such a carefully designed system of partnerships, alongside participation in decision-making processes, and effective monitoring and evaluation could provide capacity, accountability and communication. Concerns about Somali diaspora people and organisations could be countered by this fourth position strategy. This would require diaspora based civil society groups, as well as returnee gender activists, to be more inclusive as well as cognisant of the power this potentially harmful dynamic has to hamper their contributions to the women's empowerment in Somalia and elsewhere.

Alongside the role played by the diaspora in Somalia's reconstruction, both civil society organisations and the international community can do more to advocate for the empowerment of women. First, in the reconstruction process, the international community must provide political, economic and social aid at the macro-level. International agencies recognise the many challenges facing the gender equity process in Somalia. Somali leaders and the Somali state require constant reminders of the rights of women and girls, and support in striving for gender equality.

Second, initiatives by SD-CSOs at the meso-level can have an impact on, and supplement the successes of social aid provided by the international community. Representation of women in development and peace-building programmes is critical, as even well intended policies can be gender blind. Failure to include women in policy design and implementation at the macro-level may lead women to be further marginalised, albeit unintentionally.

Finally, Somalia should affirm the Convention on the Elimination of all Forms of Discrimination against Women (CEDAW) (UNDP, 2012a).

Conclusions

Throughout this chapter we have argued that SD-CSOs have a critical role to play in establishing culturally relevant and transformative women's empowerment programmes in Somalia. We have presented a meso-level approach that is inter-organisational, centred on civil society and its organisations. This model links macro-level policies and micro-level empowerment programmes. Developing such a model should be a strategic priority for the achievement of women's empowerment projects and for international development and capacity development programmes in Somalia.

International development agencies operate from the position that gender equality and women's empowerment permeates every aspect of capacity development. Somalia is no exception. Yet, its past history as a failed state, the on-going conflicts, humanitarian crises and chronic poverty require policies that promote women's empowerment initiatives, planning and operations within this context. To be effective and to achieve a sustainable impact, Somali women's empowerment programmes must be both culturally viable and internationally congruent, while also integrating issues of governance, the rule of law, human rights, development and human security.

The Eight Point Agenda for Somali women's empowerment provides a comprehensive approach, integrating notions of well-being, governance and sustainability with security, participation and capacity development. The points reflect the agenda of MDG 3 and the need to implement programmes for the achievement of women's empowerment, targeting health, education and decision-making. Through the mediation of multi-stakeholder groups, the implementation of such programmes will be more culturally acceptable when integrating Somali civil society organisations in the country and abroad. Gender equality and women's empowerment programmes in Somalia must be contextually competent, yet able to achieve standardised targets for assessing women's empowerment. These include: ensuring universal access to health services, accessing education opportunities and eliminating gender inequalities in accessing assets, employment and social mobility opportunities.

Our suggestion is that meso-level organisational engagement and programming strategies should be integrated with the macro- and micro-levels; and planned, managed and evaluated through partnerships and associations with multiple stakeholders. SD-CSOs can play a role in the establishment of legitimate and representative fora with local women leaders and government representatives for the purpose of evaluating the feasibility and impact of international development programmes. Such fora promote more legitimate and competent levels of self-governance.

Our study suggests that the Somali diaspora, working at the meso-level can be more locally competent while maintaining internationally agreed covenants of gender empowerment. SD-CSOs present an opportunity for partnership in the creation of a competent international capacity development sector that could be instrumental in creating sustainable, inclusive and human development in Somalia. Although not all SD-CSOs have the organisational capacity to engage in this level of cooperation, they are inter-culturally competent, contextually knowledgeable and internationally exposed entities that can effectively mediate women's empowerment process in Somalia. They can do so while understanding cultural contexts, cooperating with authorities and integrating international expectations. The priorities for SD-CSOs and diaspora-contextual intervention need to be operationally viable (culturally intelligent, politically grounded and socially acceptable) as well internationally aligned (for economic sustainability, international relations and intercultural dialogue).

Gender equality and promotion of Somali women's empowerment has a positive impact on Somalia's human, social, economic and political development. The inclusion of women in the political process positively contributes to Somalia's conflict management and peace-building in the long term. These changes will take many years and at this point potential for change is all that exists. However, these models are based on the assumption that the diaspora is instrumental in this transformation because it relates to all levels of local empowerment actors with a cultivated awareness of international standards. The meso-level approach channelled through SD-CSOs' engagement in Somalia can be expanded in relation to other international mainstreaming initiatives. Replication efforts elsewhere similarly require the consideration of culturally specific nuances prior to implementation. Although informal social remittances in the micro-level allow for some communication, international partnerships provide established, formal channels through which expertise can be transmitted. The engagement and closer collaboration of diaspora programmes for gender empowerment and gender democracy with organisations in the homeland could be instrumental in establishing, expanding and advancing Somali women's political representation and engagement in socio-economic development and peace-building.

References

Abdi, CM, 2014, Threatened identities and gendered opportunities: Somali migration to America, *Signs: Journal of Women in Culture and Society* 39, 2, 459–83

Abdi, CM, 2015, *Elusive Jannah: The Somali diaspora and a borderless Muslim identity*, Minneapolis, MN: University of Minnesota Press

Ahmed, L, 1992, *Women and gender in Islam: Historical roots of a modern debate*, New Haven, CT: Yale University Press

Berg, RC, Denison, E, 2013, A tradition in transition: Factors perpetuating and hindering the continuance of female genital mutilation/cutting (FGM/C) summarized in a systematic review, *Health Care For Women International* 34, 10, 837–59

Center for Somali Women's Advancement, 2013, www.centerforsomaliwomen.org/

Chaudhary, AR, Chani, MI, Pervaiz, Z, 2012, An analysis of different approaches to women empowerment: A case study of Pakistan, *World Applied Sciences Journal* 16, 7, 971–80

Christabell, PJ, 2009, *Women empowerment through capacity building: The role of microfinance*, New Delhi: Concept Publishing Company

Demos, VP, Segal, MT, 2009, *Perceiving gender locally, globally, and intersectionally*, Bingley: Emerald Jai

DePaul University Center for Black Diaspora, 2015, *Defining Diaspora*, http://las.depaul.edu/centers-and-institutes/center-for-black-diaspora/about/Pages/defining-diaspora.aspx

Easterly, W, 2006, *The white man's burden: Why the West's efforts to aid the rest have done so much ill and so little good*, New York: Penguin Press

Falah, GW, Nagel, CR, 2005, *Geographies of Muslim women: Gender, religion, and space*, New York: Guilford Publication

Farah, N, 2000, *Yesterday, tomorrow: Voices from the Somali diaspora*, London: Cassell

Fowler, A, 1997, *Striking a balance: A guide to enhancing the effectiveness of non-governmental organisations in international development*, London: Earthscan

Fowler, A, 2000, NGO futures: Beyond aid: NGDO values and the fourth position, *Third World Quarterly* 21, 4, 589–603

Fukuda-Parr, S, Lopes, C (eds), 2012, *Capacity for development: New solutions to old problems*, London: Routledge

Haji-Abdi, A, 2014, *Critical realism; Somalia, and the diaspora community*, London: Routledge

Hallward-Driemeier, M, Hasan, T, 2013, *Empowering women: Legal rights and economic opportunities in Africa*, Washington, DC: World Bank

Hoffman, B, Eidgenössische Technische Hochschule, Zürich, Rand, C, 2007, *The radicalization of diasporas and terrorism: A joint conference by the RAND Corporation and the Center for Security Studies, ETH Zürich*, Santa Monica, CA: RAND National Security Research Division

Howell, J, Mulligan, D, 2005, *Gender and civil society: Transcending boundaries*, London: Routledge

IIED (International Institute for Environment and Development), 2005, *Civil society and poverty reduction*, Participatory learning and action 51, April, London: IIED, http://pubs.iied.org/pdfs/9532IIED.pdf

Ingiriis, MH, 2015, 'Sisters: was this what we struggled for?': The gendered rivalry in power and politics, *Journal of International Women's Studies* 16, 2, 376–94

Kapteijns, L, 1993, *Women and the crisis of communal identity: The cultural construction of gender in Somali history*, Boston, MA: African Studies Center, Boston University

Kleist, N, 2008, In the name of diaspora: Between struggles for recognition and political aspirations, *Journal of Ethnic and Migration Studies* 34, 7, 1127–43

Kusow, A, Bjork, SR, 2007, *From Mogadishu to Dixon: The Somali diaspora in a global context*, Trenton, NJ: Red Sea Press

Langellier, KM, 2010, Performing Somali identity in the diaspora: 'Wherever I go I know who I am', *Cultural Studies* 24, 1, 66–94

Levitt, P, 1998, Social remittances: Migration driven local-level forms of cultural diffusion, *International Migration Review* 32, 4, 926–48

Levitt, P, Lamba-Nieves, D, 2011, Social remittances revisited, *Journal of Ethnic and Migration Studies* 37, 1, 1–22

Lindley, A, 2010, *The early morning phonecall: Somali refugees' remittances*, New York: Berghahn Books

Lum, B, Nikolko, M, Samy, Y, Carment, D, 2013, Diasporas, remittances and state fragility: Assessing the linkages, *Ethnopolitics* 12, 2, 201–19

Malhotra, A, Schuler, S, Boender, C, 2002, Measuring women's empowerment as a variable in international development, Background paper prepared for the World Bank Workshop on Poverty and Gender, Washington, DC: New Perspectives

Mernissi, F, 1987, *Beyond the veil: Male–female dynamics in modern Muslim society*, Bloomington and Indianapolis, IN: Indiana University Press

Moghadam, VM, 2008, Feminism, legal reform and women's empowerment in Middle East and North Africa, *International Social Science Journal* 59, 191, 9–16

Nussbaum, MC, 2013, *Creating capabilities: The human development approach*, Cambridge, MA: Belknap Press of Harvard University Press

Orozco, M, Yansura, J, 2013, *Keeping the lifeline open: Remittances and markets in Somalia*, Oxfam America, Adeso and Inter-American Dialogue, www.oxfamamerica.org/static/oa4/somalia-remittance-report-web.pdf

Parpart, JL, Rai, SM, Staudt, KA, 2002, *Rethinking empowerment: Gender and development in a global/local world*, London: Routledge

Pitkänen, P, Takala, T, 2012, Using transnational lenses to analyze interconnections between migration, education and development, *Migration and Development* 1, 2, 229–43

Sahay, S, 1998, *Women and empowerment: Approaches and strategies*, New Delhi: Discovery Publishing House

Shukrallah, H, 1994, The impact of the Islamic movement in Egypt, *Feminist Review* 47, 15–32

SWSC (Somali Women's Study Center), 2013, *Somali Women Studies*, www.somaliwomenstudies.org.

UN (United Nations) Women, 2011, *Annual Report 2010–2011*, New York: United Nations Entity for Gender Equality and the Empowerment of Women

UN (United Nations) Women, 2012, *Advancing gender equality and women's empowerment: An assessment of gender mainstreaming in UN operational activities for development*, www.un.org/esa/coordination/pdf/qcpr_final_report_6-15.pdf

UNDP (United Nations Development Programme), 2009, *Somalia's missing million: The Somali diaspora and its role in development*, Nairobi, Kenya: UNDP-Somalia

UNDP (United Nations Development Programme), 2012a, *Human Development Report, Somalia 2012*, Nairobi: UNDP, Somalia Country Office

UNDP (United Nations Development Programme), 2012b, *Somalia Human Development Report 2012: Empowering youth for peace and development*, http://hdr.undp.org/sites/default/files/reports/242/somalia_report_2012.pdf

UNDP (United Nations Development Programme), 2014, *International Human Development Indicator, Human Development Reports*, http://hdr.undp.org/en/countries/SOM

UNDP (United Nations Development Programme), 2015, *Eight Point Agenda for Women's Empowerment and Gender Equality*, www.undp. org/content/undp/en/home/ourwork/crisispreventionandrecovery/ focus_areas/gender_equality_andwomensempowerment/eight_ point_agendaforwomensempowermentandgenderequality/

UNDP (United Nations Development Programme) and AFESD (Arab Fund for Economic and Social Development), 2006, *The Arab human development report 2005: Towards the rise of women in the Arab world*, New York: United Nations Development Programme, Regional Bureau for Arab States

UNDP (United Nations Development Programme) Somalia, 2011, *Gender equality and women's empowerment strategy 2011–2015*, www.undp.org/content/dam/somalia/docs/Project_Documents/ Womens_Empowerment/Somalia%20Gender%20Progress%20 Rpt.%202013.pdf

UNDP (United Nations Development Programme) Somalia, 2012a, *Gender in Somalia Brief*, www.undp.org/content/dam/rbas/doc/ Women%27s%20Empowerment/Gender_Somalia.pdf

UNDP (United Nations Development Programme) Somalia, 2012b, *Gender in Somalia Brief II*, www.so.undp.org/content/dam/somalia/ docs/Project_Documents/Womens_Empowerment/Gender%20 in%20Somalia%20Brief%202.pdf

UN-ECOSOC (United Nations Economic and Social Council), 2010, *Achieving gender equality, women's empowerment and strengthening development cooperation*, Department of Economic and Social Affairs, Office for ECOSOC Support and Coordination, www.un.org/en/ ecosoc/docs/pdfs/10-50143_(e)_(desa)dialogues_ecosoc_achieving_ gender_equality_women_empowerment.pdf

UNHCR (United Nations High Commissioner for Refugees), 2015, *2015 UNHCR country/operations profile – Kenya*, www.unhcr.org/ pages/49e483a16.html

UN-IFAD (United Nations, International Fund for Agricultural Development), 2012, *Gender equality and women's empowerment*, www. ifad.org/gender/policy/gender_e.pdf

UN-IFAD (United Nations, International Fund for Agricultural Development), 2009, Sending money home to Africa, *IFAD*, www. ifad.org/remittances/pub/money_africa.pdf

USAID (United States Agency for International Development), 2012, *Gender equality and female empowerment policy*, www.usaid.gov/sites/ default/files/documents/1865/GenderEqualityPolicy_0.pdf

Visvanathan, N, 2011, *The women, gender and development reader*, Halifax: Fernwood

WEMC (Women's Empowerment in Muslim Contexts), 2008, *Women empowering themselves: A framework that interrogates and transforms*, Hong Kong: Southeast Asia Research Centre, City University of Hong Kong, http://r4d.dfid.gov.uk/PDF/Outputs/WomenEmpMus/3_ WEMC_Research_Framework.pdf

ELEVEN

The role of civil society organisations in emancipating Portuguese Roma women

Raquel Rego[1]

Introduction

Portugal belongs to the low social participation pattern, characterised by a low rate of associative engagement among national citizens, which we also find in other southern European countries alongside some of the new member states. Our chapter explores associative engagement specifically among the Roma community.

Roma people are approached here as an ethnic group, thus, a group without a state but who share the same cultural heritage, sometimes the same language, among other aspects. In Portugal there is no legal definition of ethnic group and sometimes it appears associated with minority groups from other countries. Roma is the only ethnic group self-designated as such.

The word 'Roma' is not much used, even by Roma themselves. Our respondents, as some quotations in this chapter will show, tend to use the terms *cigano* and *não cigano*. Other studies show that this is a generalised use between Portuguese Roma. We do, however, see the use of the Roma label in scientific and political contexts. A good example of this usage is found in the book collection *Olhares* (or 'viewpoints') which presents scientific studies and is promoted by a governmental agency (www.acm.gov.pt).

As in other European countries, Roma people suffer from social exclusion (European Commission, 2010). However, although there cannot be official discrimination of ethnic minorities in Portugal, even positive discrimination, political measures have been taken that addressed Roma in particular, as we will see later in this chapter.

Roma women are more disadvantaged than Roma men in many ways including access to the labour market, education, healthcare and such. Many social transitions occur earlier for Roma women than for women from the majority society. For example, they usually marry while teenagers, they drop out of school before reaching the official school-leaving age, they have many children, all of which contribute to their exclusion from active social participation.

In fact, gender issues are particularly relevant to Roma people, given the traditional deep-rooted submission of Roma women. Although in Portugal there are no reliable data available on school dropout rates, for instance, due to the anti-discriminatory policy being applied to the official collection of statistical data, several studies do make reference to them highlighting the early school drop-out of girls in particular (Reis, 1996; 1999; Silva, 2005; Bastos, 2007; Casa-Nova, 2009). We therefore assume that it is important to take gender relations into consideration when investigating participation in voluntary associations more specifically. This chapter presents the results of a sociological research project that sought to characterise Portuguese Roma associations and to analyse how they contribute to the group's social inclusion with particular consideration of gender inequality. Our aim is to contribute to the understanding of diversity in civil society organisations, not only by demonstrating the fragilities of top-down movements but also their capacities for facilitating empowerment. We have considered empowerment in economic and educational terms as well as in the civic sense. The concept of empowerment is indeed multidimensional (Thomas, 2003).

Our contribution provides some new insights on the role of civil society organisations in women's emancipation, usually referred to only secondarily in the scientific literature and with sparse empirical data. It also enriches Roma studies with a sociological perspective as the subject is mostly analysed from an anthropological perspective, as the *Olhares* collection demonstrates.

The chapter has six main sections: we first present the concept of social participation, noting that there are significant differences between southern European countries; second, we illustrate these differences by reference to the Portuguese and Spanish Roma cases; third, we introduce the emergence of Roma social participation and the current institutional framework in Portugal; fourth, we identify the main characteristics of Roma associations in Portugal; fifth, we describe the methodology used in our fieldwork; finally, we analyse our data on the Roma women's associations from the perspective of empowerment.

Social participation in southern European countries

Participation may be analysed from a political point of view, traditionally through voting percentages in elections; and from a social, or civic point of view, which is more frequently analysed by levels of engagement in voluntary associations. Obviously, this is an analytical distinction because in practice participation may take on a political dimension whenever, for instance, voluntary associations interact with the political powers. Participation is usually determined by engagement in formal legal associations, and does not include potentially important informal networks.

In any case, the data seem to reveal a positive correlation between the vitality of civil society and economic growth, as well as a negative correlation between participation and income inequality (Eurostat, 2004) and low education (Cabral et al, 2000). Such analyses tend to encompass measures of citizen trust in institutions but here the results are more inconclusive as trust may be both a cause and an effect of participation.

Therefore, considering participation in associations (in charitable, religious, cultural, trade union and sporting associations, among others), Portugal returns results broadly in line with other southern European countries such as Spain. Various research findings point in this direction with *The social situation in the European Union* (Eurostat, 2004) concluding that a clear majority of the population of these countries makes no such types of engagement.

However, despite the fact that quantitative data enable easy comparisons between countries, they do not provide any immediate evidence on the reasons for similarities and differences. The apparent convergence between countries such as Portugal and Spain, for instance, is revised when we take into account the requirements for founding associations. In Portugal, one needs about nine founding members in contrast to the three required in Spain.[2] One cannot ignore how this difference in practice may also indicate more significant differences beyond the numbers.

In Portugal, about six months after the democratic regime was established in 1974, the right to free association was legislated for by a general law.[3] Subsequently, other specific legal frameworks came into effect, in particular for trade unions, women, student, youth, immigrant, consumer, family, disabled people, sporting and professional associations, in addition to those associations composed of collective members.

Today, launching an association is neither simple nor cheap,[4] even though the state has, for several years now, provided much easier procedures under the 'association in an hour' (*associação na hora*) programme that resulted from Simplex, the last government's bureaucracy simplification programme.[5] In spite of this, we also have little information on how many associations actually exist in Portugal. The official statistics institution (Instituto Nacional de Estatística) does not collect this data systematically and provides only limited data based on census and employee statistics. Therefore, the findings of international studies such as the International Social Survey Programme or the Johns Hopkins Nonprofit Sector Project (Franco et al, 2005) are important as they have striven to overcome these difficulties even though they have been limited by the dearth of regular survey implementation.

In sum, Portugal has been included in the southern European pattern when considering its citizen social participation even though in-depth approaches reveal several significant differences between these countries, including the aforementioned disparate requirements for participation.

The hidden heterogeneity of the southern European pattern

The Roma originated in the Indian subcontinent, departing in around AD1000, according to linguistic data. Their diaspora continued to disperse throughout the Middle Ages and arrived in Portugal at the beginning of the sixteenth century (Fraser, 1995). Today, between 35,000 and 50,000 Portuguese citizens are considered to be of Roma origin, which is less than 0.5 per cent of the total population (Liégeois, 2007).[6]

Although Portuguese Roma share with the Spanish Roma their Iberian Peninsula sub-culture, for instance they share a language called Kalo, there are today many differences in customs between Portuguese and Spanish Roma. In fact, the Portuguese Roma are considered to be much more faithful in their following of supposed traditions than are the Spanish Roma (Lopes, 2008).

However, there are important similarities between both countries particularly those derived from their shared experience of the same Roma policies, handed down by Vatican II in the mid-1960s (Giménez Adelantado, 2004). These policies resulted in Roma being supported by Catholic volunteers. However, in Spain, some of the Roma who were involved in these policies did go on to attain greater levels of empowerment.

Today, unlike in Portugal, hundreds of Roma associations exist throughout Spain, in more than 20 Spanish cities, under the name of *mujeres gitanas*, whether with mixed gender or women only participants (Giménez Adelantado, 2004).

In summary, when we look at two neighbouring countries that fall within the same pattern of social participation, and we analyse the case of the Roma community, we observe that the variables seeming to explain patterns of convergence fail to make sense anymore.

The emergence of Roma associational participation

Roma associational participation dates from the end of the nineteenth century in Romania, and the first attempts to unite the representative bodies of one country were identified in Russia in 1925. However, in Western Europe these activities became known only after the Second World War, spurred by the need to help the survivors of Nazi persecution (Council of Europe, 2008). All these organisations had difficulties in overcoming internal rivalries and competing leadership claims and hence the first attempt to establish an international association, the Communauté Mondiale Gitane only came about in 1960, in France. The first World Congress was organised by the Comité International Rom bringing together organisations from 21 countries in 1971. This congress is considered to be the breakthrough in the development of a new political movement (Liégeois, 1976). Today, there are now important Roma civil society organisations active in lobbying in Brussels (Acton and Ryder, 2013).

Due in part to the comparatively small number of Roma in most western European countries when compared to the majority populations, the promotion of their social participation by European political institutions was not a priority. This has left a space for the development of NGOs led by non-Roma citizens concerned with the human rights or education of Roma.

In late 2006, in Portugal, for the first time a political step was taken with the objective of encouraging Roma social participation. A new institutional structure was set up by the governmental agency for the inclusion of migrants and ethnic minorities, the Alto Comissariado para a Imigração e Diálogo Intercultural (ACIDI) (High Commission for Immigration and Intercultural Dialogue). The Gabinete de Apoio às Comunidades Ciganas (GACI) (Roma Communities Support Office) was founded to promote Roma inclusion, by publishing research on the Roma and especially through running special training programmes for Roma people – both men and women – in order to prepare them for work as social and cultural mediators in municipalities.

One of GACI's roles was also to identify and support Roma representative associations. However, first of all, Roma associations had to be capable of such administrative tasks as sending letters, creating identification cards, compiling election minutes and activities reports as well as maintaining details about their respective membership. Taking into account the low education levels of some Roma (Reis, 1996; 1999; Silva, 2005; Bastos, 2007; Casa-Nova, 2009), it was expected that Roma associational actors might encounter special difficulties in providing all these documents without assistance. GACI is only based in Lisbon and is currently staffed by two officials, reflecting the scarcity of the resources available, and the little support likely to be given to such associations.

In sum, the empowerment of Roma people is centred mainly on the so-called Roma 'industry' organisations and projects designed to stimulate social empowerment are lacking, although there have been attempts to promote associational activity. Despite the political intent to contribute to Roma inclusion, support resources are few.

Portuguese Roma civil society organisations

Charitable activities targeting the Portuguese Roma community are closely associated with the Catholic Church. Although not numerous, ethnic minorities, immigrants and poor people have been supported by the Catholic movement since the period of authoritarian dictatorship in Portugal. The Catholic movement, to this end, founded a specific organisation to work with Roma, in 1972, the Obra Nacional da Pastoral dos Ciganos (National Pastoral Work with Gypsies).

Only after 1974 and the consolidation of the democratic regime did other civil society organisations enter the field. However, none of these organisations adopted an exclusive focus on the Roma; instead they tended to include this population alongside other groups. This is the case not only with the anti-racist association, SOS Racismo,[7] founded in 1990, but also with many others offering social services. This period also saw a series of special public initiatives aiming to foster the integration of immigrants and ethnic minorities.

Despite the first association of Roma which dated back to the 1970s and were located in the North of the country, only much more recently have Roma civil society organisations gained in profile. These organisations do not seem to have empowerment measures of either the Roma community as a whole, or of women in particular as a political priority. Nevertheless, following de Tocqueville's ([1835] 2010) proposition that voluntary associations are one of the most important ways of including and representing citizens, acquiring democratic values and mediating the implementation of public policies. Building knowledge and understanding about these Roma associations is an important objective.

Methodology

The aim of our research was to learn more about this initiative to promote greater Roma associational activity, to chart all Portuguese Roma associations and to ascertain whether and how their actions might be contributing to the inclusion and empowerment of Roma people, and women in particular.

One specific objective was to identify the impact of these associations from a gender perspective on the grounds that women represent a group particularly discriminated against in this community. In order to do this we first needed to identify just how these associations were founded and by whom, their respective stage of development, the scope and type of their activities, their leaders' profiles and the actual impact of these associations on change in the lives of their Roma members.

We immediately encountered major limitations in our empirical research, as there is no generally available data on Portuguese Roma participation in social participation. Due to a general European political position, which has opted against collecting ethnically based statistical indicators it becomes hard to ascertain just how many of these citizens participate in associations, for example.

First, we have no reliable sources for identifying all the existing associations nor obtaining their contacts. The registration of Roma associations was not updated on the GACI website but did at least provide a starting point from which to launch our research project. The snowball technique was crucial to being able to advance, although this ran the risk of our getting involved in tensions within the Roma community (for example, by asking for contacts from a Roma organisation that might be in conflict with the one for which we were searching).

Second, as our only main information sources stemmed from our interviewees, the data provided was not easily compared and contrasted with other sources and also risked being overly subjective. Most of the associations with whom they have been involved are, in essence, either inactive or undertake very low levels of activity, thus there is an important lack of data on them.

Finally, the tendency towards a more hierarchical culture, in which the leader is seen as playing the role of a patriarch, makes it inherently difficult to obtain information related to the extent of the association's democratic functioning.

We carried out the fieldwork between mid-2010 and 2011. The fieldwork incorporated two main phases. In the first stage, besides bibliographic and online research, we undertook exploratory interviews with the main social actors related to the Roma issues. We correspondingly engaged in discussions with:

• government representatives (GACI and ACIDI);
• representatives of the Catholic Church for Roma issues (Obra Nacional da Pastoral dos Ciganos);
• NGOs (SOS Racismo; Rede Europeia Anti-Pobreza);
• academic specialists (researchers in the social sciences and humanities).

These exploratory interviews helped us in several ways: identifying different positions vis-à-vis association roles and activities, collecting data on current Roma inclusion and related issues, especially through associations, and gathering some missing contacts.

We identified 14 Portuguese Roma civil society organisations, two of which were national umbrella organisations. These civic Roma organisations are located in the main cities of the country and their surroundings: from Oporto to Lisbon and taking in Coimbra and Leiria. However, we were not able to reach all of these Roma associations, because either they were not contactable by phone or we had insufficient or incorrect information.

The second fieldwork phase focused on interviews with the presidents of Roma associations. Based on a short questionnaire, we carried out nine face-to-face interviews, seven with men and two with women leaders.

Despite the aforementioned limitations, this is the first time that Portuguese Roma associations have been subject to academic study in an attempt to identify sociological regularities, considering in particular similarities and differences between associations led by men and by women.

Some findings

The youth stage of Roma association life cycles

Five of the nine presidents of the Roma organisations interviewed declared them to be active, and although it was difficult to confirm the truth of this, in all cases, they have been far more active in the past. As already mentioned, the first Portuguese Roma association traces its roots back to the 1970s in the North of the country, before the implementation of democracy, to the period when the dictatorship became known as the *Primavera Marcelista* (Marcelo's Spring), since the historical leader, Oliveira Salazar, had been replaced by Marcelo Caetano, and the new leader had begun by showing some signs of change and greater openness.

Nevertheless, the most important period for Roma associations was around the turn of the millennium when three associations were founded, generally led by social and cultural mediators – people prepared to help in solving local conflicts. The mediator training undertaken by people who, in the future, were to become the presidents of these new associations, mostly coincided with the opportunity to initiate the association project.

The main activity of all associations is practically the same and involves helping younger community members integrate into schools or activities such as sports and dancing. The main organisational difficulties focus on the lack of economic resources, not, of course, an issue specific to these associations only as it arises most frequently as the leading complaint among all voluntary associations in Portugal (Rego, 2010).

In sum, Portuguese Roma associations still remain at an embryonic stage of development and education

The top-down creation and the movement fragmentation

NGOs and other organisations working with the Roma community have sometimes encouraged the foundation of Roma-led associations in circumstances when partnership with a Roma association was a requirement for applying for designated funding. Such funding regimes have certainly reinforced the need to set up Roma associations. Furthermore, this situation also seems common in countries where Roma civic organisations are more developed (Pinnock, 2002). However, the Roma associations that were the focus of our study were created out of the support of other institutions that are not composed of Roma citizens nor are from Roma civil society, but rather work for Roma and belong to the public sector. We term these 'satellite' organisations.

These satellite organisations differ between the north, the centre and the south of the country. In fact, we identified a clear association between the Catholic Church and the government ACIDI and Roma associations from the Lisbon area, whereas in the north, Roma associations from Oporto especially, received support from the state social protection agency, and, in the centre, we identify greater closeness with municipality level entities. In all cases, we found evidence of strong and previous ties existing between members of Roma associations and members of public institutions. Since Roma cultural and social traditions, sometimes termed the 'gypsy law', gives especial power to men, these contacts are also primarily established and maintained with them.

Despite the scarce number of associations, the Roma movement has two parallel umbrella organisations, as mentioned earlier. The first is the União Romani Portuguesa, a member of the International Romani Union and located in Oporto. This organisation came to prominence in 2010 in street demonstrations following an international call to protest against the xenophobic positions of some European member states. Portuguese Romani Union activities are mainly visible through press releases and the organisation, according to our data, does not interact effectively with other Roma associations.

The second umbrella organisation, the Federação Calhim Portuguesa (FECALP) (Portuguese Gypsy Federation), is led by an evangelical priest, who is also the president of one of the Roma associations in our sample. Nevertheless, according to press reports, this federation encountered various difficulties around the time of its foundation and is now apparently inactive. The fragility of the two umbrella organisations is not surprising when taking into account the limited number of effective members.

In sum, founding a Roma umbrella association seems difficult in practice. As even the specific Portuguese Roma associations seem to be essentially 'top-down' in their inception, rather than emerging from grass roots activism, this may feasibly be related to the fragility of the attempts made to found those umbrella associations.

'Unipersonal' associations and the public sphere

Most Roma associations would appear to be family based, although this information is difficult to obtain because our interviewees did not mention it spontaneously. Some associations also accept non-Roma as members, such as the priest Francisco Monteiro from the National Pastoral Work for Gypsies organisation, who was one of the Roma association founders although he is not a Roma. In practice, these CSOs appear to be mainly 'unipersonal' associations in the sense that it is primarily run by its president. We were only able to obtain access to these organisations through their presidents, and thus, were unable to reach other participants, who were likely to be family members directly. This trait is not unique to these associations. Despite low levels of activity and representativeness, these associations have helped their leaders and the Roma community in a broader sense, to launch Roma empowerment, namely providing opportunities for accessing information and training, networking, communication skills, and so forth. Thus, these associations sometimes serve as more legitimate frameworks for public interventions.

For example, all interviewees maintained that they are sporadically invited to meetings, or deliberately choose to enter into the public sphere to represent their membership. In fact, as mentioned before, leaders may well get invited specifically as a Roma person, a local mediator, a Roma patriarch/woman's representative, or as an association leader. These differing social roles are blurred but would seem to mutually nourish each other and foster the formation of small elite. In sum, we may identify public visibility as one of the particular traits of Roma associations' leaders.

Emergence and dynamism of associations led by Roma women

Of the nine associations contacted, women ran only two of them. The other seven were run by men, and in their interviews they made little mention of women. Some did refer to the inferior status attributed to women. For example, the President of a Roma association in the North of the country stated that 'We also have some young women who support us. But most are men because they have more availability, versatility. Men are longer available for certain things and have more access to certain things because, you know, there are restrictions on women.'

The first (and only) Portuguese association of Roma women was founded at the turn of the century. The Associação para o Desenvolvimento das Mulheres Ciganas Portuguesas (AMUCIP) (Association for the Development of Portuguese Gypsy Women) was legalised in 2000 to provide support to school-age children and care for them while their families were out working. As the AMUCIP president explains:

> And, during this year of course, we began thinking – these five [Roma] women – it would be useful to open up a space to give support to our children, where we could get them to do school work, because no one was a teacher, but we supported these children, as their fathers and mothers do not know how to read or write. And on their days off, they spend them on the street – because their parents go off to markets, their parents will be off trading and they are practically on their own in the neighbourhood. And it was important that these children got a space that belonged to them, run by people like them. One of our trainers heard us talking about this and asked 'Why don't you form an association?' We did not even know what an association was.

The second association led by a Roma woman (although representing both men and women) was created more recently, in 2008. The Nossa Associação de Kalons Íntegros (NAKI) (Our Association of Full Roma) was also launched by trainees of a vocational training course in that year. As the president declares:

> NAKI was born in an institution that [runs]…training courses. In late 2008…there was interest in formalising a training course of three and a half weeks for Roma who were interested in doing a rehabilitation course…At the time, there were…around 200 people interested…I was one of the trainees…In the second week of training, there was [the news of a] large training programme…Nothing could be done without an association…there had to be a bridge to the community, since at the time [the city's other association] was not active. So, we all felt that we could move forward…we wanted to continue to study and realise some of our dreams…Then, before the end of the year, we made it known to the entire Roma population…it would be this association – at the time we still had no name – and it was a pleasant surprise that people were not opposed… that I was the president.

AMUCIP is the more active of these two associations today. This association is frequently interviewed by researchers and journalists and is invited to participate in policy discussions by public entities, including European institutions. AMUCIP also has its own headquarters in the Lisbon area. At AMUCIP House, which we had the opportunity to visit, we clearly see the signs of the organisation having gone through more dynamic periods, in particular via the evidence of equipment and documents on bookshelves. However, today this facility is usually empty, because funding tends to be time-limited, attached to specific projects, which have now come to an end.

Almost all association leaders (not just the two headed by women) stress that they have already had the opportunity to meet Roma people from other European countries through their association's activities. However, according to our interviewees and documental collection, this activity seems less systematic and with a lower impact than that of AMUCIP.

Contact between these Roma associations and more generalist associations seems to border on the negligible, although AMUCIP is a member of a platform of women associations represented on a government agency for gender equality. We would also note that more recently some associations, including those run by women, have succeeded in becoming social partners to local government councils, such as in the Rede Social, a public programme that involves different institutions in tackling poverty and social exclusion and promoting social local development.[8]

Nevertheless, no Roma association has to date maintained sufficient resources to retain full-time employees, which would be a sign of their emerging formalisation and professionalisation.

The associative engagement as part of a personal turning point

The two women leaders are from different generations but they share some profile similarities. The leader of NAKI, aged 37, is divorced, and does not present herself as a traditional Roma woman, while the leader of AMUCIP is older, a widow who partially follows tradition by wearing black clothes and long skirts, and concealing her hair. Nonetheless, our discussions with her demonstrated that she does not assume the resigned attitude to life, normally expected of a Roma widow following the 'gypsy law'.

The public visibility of leaders is so important that most of them have been contacted by representatives from political parties either to obtain their electoral support or even to join up to an electoral list, as our interviews show. However, these women leaders apparently prefer to maintain their distance.

We observed that the AMUCIP leader seems to hold the greatest prestige, as evidenced by her having visited the European Parliament through the European Women's Lobby as well as participating in several television programmes, alongside many other national and international meetings.

We noted several references to the inequality between Roma men and women in our interviews. The two women leaders, for instance, recalled the impact of the launch of their associations in the Roma community, noting that the reaction was 'surprisingly' positive, given the negative attitude towards the prominence of women in the Roma communities.

From our data, in fact, of all the Roma associations surveyed, those led by women seem to be the most successful in terms of the Roma representation function as well being the most successful in empowering their members, and leaders in particular.

The representation function these associations fulfil may not be effectively representative of Portuguese Roma women in their entirety, but it accomplishes a *voice* function, which has resulted from their increasing awareness about the importance of social participation. And the increasing empowerment of women through their associations has been facilitated by opportunities for increased participation in projects and European Union co-funded initiatives, such as Equal, which brought about the creation of women's own businesses.

Furthermore, the AMUCIP association won an award in the 2007 European Year of Equal Opportunities for All in recognition of its performance. This European award recognises the importance of the AMUCIP's contribution to helping Roma women and men reconcile their working, personal and family lives, and to the improvement of the educational perspective for Roma children. AMUCIP played an important role providing social-educational support outside school hours and also help in transporting children to and from school. Moreover, it provided an open forum in which women can discuss problems or issues that affect their lives (Equal, 2013).

The two women leaders interviewed have both had the opportunity to continue their education and vocational training and are now economically independent. This independence was facilitated by their involvement in their association's activities since they were obliged to attend training courses, contact people, manage activities and develop projects. For example, the president of NAKI told us:

> I live in Leiria, I am 34 years old. I started with my studies
> with the opportunity that happened [in 2008], the training
> course. And from then on, I never stopped. Courses upon
> courses…my desire is to be able to become a trainer, to
> train within our own area, presenting our own culture…
> The IEFP [the public employment and vocational training
> agency] is very interested in this project. Hence, I'm now
> completing secondary school…I was a marketer for 12
> years. After 12 years the opportunity arose, NAKI. As
> soon as I came across the opportunity of NAKI, everything
> came suddenly. There were many doors opening up many
> opportunities. I became a mediator in the Municipality
> of Marinha Grande. As the project ended there, today I
> am currently working in a shop…Also, I am working in a
> ceramics factory and I'm studying. So, as I was telling you,
> I do not have much time!

We also observed the existence of brochures in English at AMUCIP
House, which were intended for distribution at meetings abroad. As
AMUCIP's president stated during our visit: 'we did this [pamphlet]
very succinct in English, because as we sometimes find, it is interesting
to take something for people to know who we are'; thus demonstrating
her own facility with the language.

The younger leader of NAKI has a shorter personal history of
engagement with the association, although similar in kind to her elder
peer. Both leaders have met up with each other in training courses
but we are not aware of any special cooperation between the two
associations.

However, both women described their engagement with the
association as a turning point in their lives that began with the
opportunity to take a training course in mediation. As the AMUCIP
president says:

> And then dozens of women were called Roma and non-
> Roma to provide a first test to be able to apply for this
> course [of women mediators]. I, who had been widowed
> four years ago, I was upset! I never needed the guaranteed
> minimum income, lived very well up until then. There were
> three years of disease, huge, my children were teenagers,
> and then I had to support my husband for three years, with
> times at Santa Maria Hospital. And then…I was selling
> everything!…Then I was called for this interview and it

was one of the best things that happened to me after all that evil. All these women who were being interviewed, only five Roma were chosen and eleven African; we were sixteen women…I said, 'My God, this is too much! Roma and African!'…I made friendships that still last after eleven years!

In sum, while Giménez Adelantado (2004) has identified the existence of highly dynamic and quickly expanding Roma associations in Spain, calling it a 'silent revolution', in Portugal, we are still far from any such revolution.

Concluding remarks

In Western Europe and the United States the women's civil society organisations that emerged in the 1960s were mainly composed of white, educated and middle-class women (Castells, 2001; Nash, 2005). The feminist movement only adapted their perspective to respond to the differing experiences of minority groups, such as the ethnic groups belonging to their own society, in the following decades (Nash, 2005). These 'other' women have their own trajectories and for some of them gender equality may not necessarily be a priority, or may be interpreted differently (Nash, 2005).

In the 1960s, Portugal was still under a dictatorship, which lasted almost five decades. Therefore, we cannot say that there was a women's social movement. As Tavares (2011, 536) suggests, 'feminism diluted in anti-fascism'. Portuguese women's organisations began to emerge later, in the 1980s, with the consolidation of the democratic regime. At that time, their main concerns were focused on the decriminalisation of abortion. Indeed, only in the 1990s did they broaden their debates and consider the international dimension to their actions (Tavares, 2011).

We propose that, despite the neighbouring country also experiencing a long dictatorship, there is a lag of about one decade between the emergence of the Portuguese and the Spanish Roma women associations. In fact, Spain seems to have already attained a different stage of Roma inclusion, namely having had a Roma member of the national and the European Parliament, Juan de Dios Ramírez-Heredia (Giménez Adelantado, 2004).

Furthermore, Roma cultural norms are still very strong in Portugal, even where they conflict with the national regulatory framework. According to Roma law, women are subservient to men, dropping school early to be married during the teenage years and take care of their family. A Roma woman does not go out alone, unless she is a widow, and in that case she must wear black clothes. Women are not expected to go beyond tradition in the Roma community, to study or to be economically independent.

Therefore, it is hardly surprising that Portuguese Roma women associations are few in number and recent in origin. On the one hand, the women's movement is relatively recent in Portugal, and furthermore, the Roma community in this country is quite small.

Nevertheless, these civil society organisations have contributed in some part to the emancipation of Roma women, providing not only for greater economic and social independence of the few women represented but also endowing their leaders with opportunities to express their voice in public fora.

While Roma men have conceptualised the leadership of voluntary associations as a kind of duplication of their roles as a patriarch and/ or a religious leader; for Roma women voluntary associations have provided them with a possibly unique opportunity to take up such a leadership role.

The Portuguese case seems to confirm that 'the grassroots start-up of autonomous organisations, involving Roma women, is likely to be a promising channel to foster their empowerment, their appropriate interaction with welfare institutions and their skill-building' (European Commission, 2010, 14).

Although neither extensive nor very representative, these women have enabled the broader society to become more directly aware of the respectively different, prevailing realities of the Roma. And in that sense, Roma associations led by women seem to be more successful than those led by men. Considering that Roma women are especially responsible for the education of children, we may expect that through their participation in associational activity, these women leaders are giving a precious contribution to Roma empowerment in general, as well as to the women's movement.

Notes

[1]   This chapter benefited from the paper by R Rego and C Auzias, 2011, 'The institutionalisation of Roma social participation in southern European societies – preliminary data from ongoing research', *Sociologia Online*, 221–35.

[2]   Article 5, from chapter II, of *Lei Orgánica* 1/2002, from 22 March.

[3]   Decreto-lei 594/74, from 7 November 1974.

[4]   About €170 is needed which represents over a third of the national minimum wage, to found an association in Portugal.

[5]   www.associacaonahora.pt/index.htm

[6]   Our own calculations based on Liégeois (2007).

7   SOS Racismo has included a young and active Roma, Bruno Gonçalves, in its membership. Therefore, one cannot deny that this organisation tries to overcome the usual separation between Roma and non-Roma members.

8   Established by ministerial decree *Resolução de Conselho de Ministros* no. 197/97, 18 November, only subject to regulation in 2006.

References

Acton, T, Ryder, A, 2013, Roma civil society: Deliberative democracy for change in Europe, *Third Sector Research Centre (TSRC) discussion paper*, Birmingham: TSRC

Bastos, JP, 2007, *Sintrenses ciganos – uma abordagem estrutural-dinâmica*, Sintra: Câmara Municipal de Sintra

Blanes, RL, 2008, *Os aleluias – ciganos evangélicos e música*, Lisbon: Instituto de Ciencias Saude

Cabral, MV, Vala, J, Freire, J (orgs), 2000, *Trabalho e cidadania: atitudes sociais dos portugueses*, Lisbon: International Social Survey Programme-Instituto de Ciências Sociais (ISSP-ICS), http://issp.ics.ul.pt/

Casa-Nova, MJ, 2009, *Etnografia e produção de conhecimento – reflexões críticas a partir de uma investigação com ciganos portugueses, Colecção Olhares*, Lisbon: Alto Comissariado para a Imagracao e Minorias Etnicas (ACIME)

Castells, M, 2001, *The power of identity*, Oxford: Blackwell Publishing

Council of Europe, 2008, *Institutionalization and emancipation: Information fact sheets on Roma history*, www.coe.int/t/dg4/education/roma/Source/FS/6.2_emancipation.pdf

de Tocqueville, A, 1835, *De la démocratie en Amérique*, Paris: Flammarion-Poche, 2010

European Commission, 2010, *Ethnic minority and Roma women in Europe: A case for gender equality?*, Luxembourg: Publications Office of the European Union, http://ec.europa.eu/social/main.jsp?catId=738&langId=en&pubId=492&furtherPubs=yes

Equal, 2013, *Gypsy women becoming autonomous*, http://ec.europa.eu/employment_social/equal/data/document/etg1-exa2-plosonho.pdf, accessed on 4 March 2014

Eurostat, 2004, *The social situation in the European Union*, http://ec.europa.eu/employment_social/social_situation/docs/ssr2004_brief_en.pdf

Franco, RC, Sokolowshi, SW, Hairel, EM, Salamon, LM, 2005, *O sector não lucrativo português numa perspectiva comparada*, Lisbon: Faculdade de Economia e Gestão, Universidade Católica Portuguesa and Baltimore, MD: Johns Hopkins University.

Fraser, A, 1995, *The gypsies*, Oxford: Wiley-Blackwell Publishing

Giménez (Jimenez) Adelantado, A, 2004, Metamorfosis – reflexiones sobre el asociacionismo de las mujeres gitanas en la década de los 90, *Festa da Palabra Silenciada* 19, 16–23, http://dialnet.unirioka.es/ejemplar/300798, accessed on 4 March 2014

Liégeois, J-P, 1976, *Mutation tsigane*, Bruxelles: Édition Complexe

Liégeois, J-P, 2007, *Roms en Europe*, Strasbourg: Council of Europe Publishing

Lopes, DS, 2008, *Deriva cigana – um estudo etnográfico sobre os ciganos de Lisboa*, Lisbon: ICS

Nash, M, 2005, *As mulheres no mundo – história, desafios e movimentos*, Vila Nova de Gaia: Editora Ausência

Pinnock, K, 2002, The impact of the NGO sector and Roma/Gypsy organizations on Bulgarian social policy-making 1989–1997, *Journal of Social Policy* 31, 2, 229–50

Rego, R, 2010, *Dirigeants associatifs: engagement et professionnalisation*, Paris: L'Harmattan

Reis, FE (ed), 1996, *Comunidade cigana na diocese de Lisboa*, Lisbon: Secretariado Diocesano da Obra Nacional da Pastoral dos Ciganos

Reis, FE (ed), 1999, *O jovem cigano e a formação – atitudes e perspectivas frente ao mundo do trabalho*, Lisbon: Secretariado Diocesano da Obra Nacional da Pastoral dos Ciganos

Silva, LF da, 2005, Saúde doença é questão de cultura – atitudes e comportamentos de saúde materna nas mulheres ciganas em Portugal, *Colecção Olhares*, Lisbon: Alto Comissariado para a Imagracao e Minorias Etnicas (ACIME)

Tavares, M, 2011, *Feminismos – percursos e desafios (1947–2007)*, Alfragide: Texto

Thomas, K, 2003, *The role of voluntary associations on women empowerment in Kerala with special reference to Ernakulam district*, PhD dissertation in Economics, Kottayam: Mahatma Gandhi University

TWELVE

Breaking down dichotomies in the narratives of women's activism in Morocco

Aura Lounasmaa

Introduction

The situation of Moroccan women has gone through rapid changes in the last 20 years. Although the women of Mernissi's (1988) biographies from the 1980s still live and work in the cities of Morocco, the political changes, most notably the change of the king in 2000 and the reform of the family law in 2003 have given Moroccan women an unprecedented access to public life. The new family law – or *moudawana*, as it is commonly known – gives women the right to marry without a male guardian and to ask for a divorce in the court, abolishes repudiation, puts limits to polygamy and child marriage and extends women's right to custody of their children. The new constitution, which came to force in 2011 after the so-called Arab Spring, gives full equality between men and women as is stipulated in the human rights treaties to which Morocco is a signatory. However, in practice equality is still an aspiration in many areas of life. When it comes to family law, judges have full discretion regarding marriage of minors, divorce, polygamy and alimonies. Sexual harassment is rife and domestic violence and rape remains difficult to prosecute due to an outdated penal code. As Mernissi (1991) noted, Moroccan women have always worked and contributed to the family income, yet levels of illiteracy among rural women remain at 60 per cent and knowledge of the newly gained rights is taking a long time to reach the majority of Moroccan women.

This chapter discusses the development of women's civil society in Morocco. Of particular interest is the deep division that exists between women's groups with different political and ideological affiliations. I use the terms 'rights-based' and 'faith-based' organisations to refer to the ways in which different women's organisations prioritise available discourses in defining their goals. The terms do not define the organisations but are used descriptively in order to recognise and discuss differences between actors. As is further explored in this chapter, the ways in which available discourses are used by different organisations are complex and often issue-driven rather than for the formation and maintenance of fixed identities. I have opted to use the word 'referential', a word borrowed from activists' own vocabulary, to describe the way in which multiple discourses are evoked in activism in Morocco.

History of women's activism

When King Mohammed VI announced the reform of the constitution in March 2011 Morocco's major civil society groups were to be consulted. Perhaps the most powerful among these were women's groups, including both faith-based and rights-based organisations. Women's organisations were first founded in the 1980s, and since the success of the advocacy campaign of the rights-based groups to reform the family law in 2003 women's movements have been among the most important political lobby groups in Morocco.

As in many other postcolonial Muslim countries, women were first engaged in political activism in the nation's struggle for independence. Due to the high levels of education given to daughters of elite families, middle-class women were an important asset to the independence movement. Some women's organisations, linked to political parties, were born in this period concentrating on independence struggles and social work (Lopez Plaza, 1999). After independence, King Mohammed V initiated a women's group, the Union Nationale des Femmes Marocaines (UNFM), which was presided over by women of the royal family. This group organised meetings and gave statements about women's role in Islam and in the family and ran educational programmes to educate women in household management and some traditional forms of income generation (Brand, 1998; Lopez Plaza, 1999). The 1960s and 1970s saw the rise of human rights groups, who were protesting over the treatment of political prisoners, and leftist and Islamist political opposition who were both calling for major economic and political reforms. Registration of civil society and political organisations was strictly limited to those approved by the king, and thus, most of these groups were at the time considered illegal. Indeed, it has been noted, that the history of Morocco's civil society was written from prisons (Slyomovics, 2005). By the late 1980s the king, Hassan II, began legalising civil society groups and planning moderate political reforms. Political plurality and freedom of association are still contested, even after the extensive political reforms of Mohammed VI since 2000 (Cavatorta and Dalmasso, 2009; Pruzan-Jorgensen, 2010).

The first women's political organisations were non-structured protest movements by the mothers, sisters and wives of political prisoners who met at the prison gates and started protesting over the disappearance and maltreatment of their loved ones. Although the protest of mothers was tolerated more than the political action of young women, the authorities doubted the authenticity of the movement, suspecting the mothers would have been unable to get organised without help from the political activists (men) (Slyomovics, 2005, 162). Women's organisations also emerged from the women's sections of the political parties, Islamist organisations and human rights organisations, where largely middle-class women from political families were invited to take part in politics, but were unable to voice any of the woman specific concerns they felt needed to be raised. While many of the organisations have now officially severed links to political parties and are claiming total autonomy in their work, outsiders often consider them to be political party actors and are frequently looking to expose the compromising political liaisons of the organisations or their individual members.

The first issue over which rights-based women's CSOs were united was the reform of the family law. The Moroccan constitution of 1956 granted equal political rights to men and women. In reality however, women's ability to enjoy their political rights was severely limited by the family law, in which women were defined as minors. In practice, this meant that the consent of a husband, father or another male relative was required for most activities or bureaucratic transactions taking place outside the house. The family law reform concerned all women's NGOs in Morocco; most rights-based organisations were campaigning for reform and most faith-based organisations protesting against it. These often aggressive campaigns widened the gap between faith-based and rights-based women's CSOs. Women's organisations that have been founded after the *moudawana* reform are often less implicated in the division between rights-based and faith-based women's movements.

Methodology

This study is based on a social constructionist epistemology. People construct themselves and their surroundings through interaction with others and through narrativising their experiences and understandings of these interactions. This narratability cannot be reduced to the content of the story told (Cavarero, 2000), but reflects the structure and process of the narration (Tamboukou, 2008) and the internal consistency of the story (Tullis Owen et al, 2009). Therefore, the social constructionist theory of narrative concerns the actual creating of the story as well as analysis of its content.

Although none of us understand the world in exactly the same way as others, and none of us share the same ideas about how the world should be, shared goals become possible through acting on what Spivak (1987) terms 'strategic essentialism'. As Spivak explains, alliances can be built with others on certain subjects in order to achieve a common goal, although other goals may not be shared. Important to Spivak's strategic essentialism is the need for critical engagement with the differences and similarities in our positions (Danius et al, 1993). It is not enough to put those differences aside for the sake of one shared goal; actors must reflect on how these differences are present in the shared activities.

Furthermore, applying an intersectional lens to the study allows us to understand the participants as inhabiting several identities simultaneously, rather than applying the additive view on the different categories of oppression they meet (Nash, 2008). Thus, civil society organisations are not merely defined as faith-based or rights-based, rural or urban, small or large, but all of these categories are seen as fluid, constructed in relation to other actors and each other. An intersectional approach to applying strategic essentialism may be able to suggest possible links across divisions in women's activism. The term 'referential', adopted in this chapter to describe the political and ideological affiliations of participating organisations, also highlights this dynamic relationship between organisational structures, discourses and campaigned issues.

This study takes the form of a qualitative case study of politically active women's CSOs in Morocco. Data for the study consists of 24 in-depth interviews conducted over one month in January 2011, and again from September until December 2011, with women's CSO leaders or advocacy campaign managers and a qualitative content analysis of documents produced by women's organisations. Hitchings (2012) has found that asking participants to question their taken-for-granted practices has the potential to provide critical insights to both the researcher and the participants into how practices are performed and how they come about.

Rights-based women's activism

Many of the rights-based organisations were either founded from within leftist political parties and human rights organisations or at least by women activists whose history of activism began in those groups. Therefore, when first defining their referential as women's groups, they were already politically affiliated to certain ideologies. The question of which discourses they could draw from for inspiration, still needed to be debated. Some rights-based organisations opted for the exclusive use of international human rights discourses, some for a mixed referential using human rights and religion, and others for a referential based on cultural references emphasising the values of equality and dignity that can be found in cultural traditions. Although the referential used in each campaign varied greatly between organisations, the organisations defined here as rights-based highlight the primacy of human rights as the inspiration for their work.

> We organised seminars on women's personal status, I mean we had a reading of even the Koran and there was the problem of referential: as in what do we base ourselves on? So we based ourselves on the referential of human rights, as in the conventions of CEDAW and human rights in general and on the spirit of Islam. We concluded that the spirit of Islam is egalitarian; egalitarian; and the personal status of women was only one interpretation among others of Islam: and a patriarchal interpretation of Islam. And so with this referential we were able to assemble the committee and do a lobbying, a lobbying, and do an advocacy towards the political decision makers. (Interview with FM, rights-based activist)

This organisation has adopted a 'double stance' on Islam and human rights, which means that FM believes that human rights and women's rights can be compatible with Islam, if the Koran is approached hermeneutically. FM's view resonates with Othman (1999) who asserts that Muslims can respect the universal notion of human rights as they search for the equivalent values within their own traditions, and to refuse to engage with Islam and its potential for women's emancipation would allow the Islamists to monopolise the religion and to impose their own view of it.

However, in contrast to Othman's (1999) theory and the approach of FM, many of the rights-based organisations adopted human rights as their sole source of referential, refusing to engage with religious ideology within their activism. This approach is consistent with an interpretation, which suggests that the Koran can only ever be an interim solution to the inequalities created by the Islamic patriarchy; equality can only be created on the basis of internationally recognised women's rights (Einhorn and Sever, 2003; Barlas, 2005). Rejection of Islam can partly be understood to result from the marginalisation women activists faced after Moroccan independence, where Moroccan traditions, religion and nationhood became conflated and overshadowed all women-specific concerns (Hélie-Lucas, 1987; Mernissi, 1988). Partly it reflects the battles women activists faced in the 1990s, when their most ardent opposition came from the Islamist movements. Sadiqi (2003) traces the roots of this rejection to the encounter of the Moroccan civilisation with the west under French colonisation. The first developments of feminism in Morocco from the 1960s onwards Sadiqi defines as liberal, or secular feminism, but from the 1980s onwards she identifies a more religious, or conservative feminism co-existing alongside (Sadiqi, 2003, 21). Both have their roots in the wider political organisations of the country, the liberal feminism stemming from the leftist political rights movement and the religious feminism from conservative political parties and associations.

Moghadam (2002) considers the social and historical location of feminist praxis to be part of a wider, ever evolving feminist philosophy that should not be divided into oppositional binaries, but rather seen as a fragmented movement that reflects social realities in different regions in diverse ways. Thus, there cannot be one good or correct way to do feminism; 'women, and not religion, should be at the centre of that theory and practice' (Moghadam, 2002, 45). The main criticism Moghadam has for the Islamic referential in feminist activism is the possibility of it reinforcing the legitimacy of a patriarchal system supported by religious arguments and reproducing it. This fear is reflected in many of the rights-based activists' comments, such as that of AM:

> But it's very risky to search, as feminists, our arguments inside a religious system, because at that moment it's…even if we could find the elements of response, but that would mean at that moment that if Islam was in our favour, it's fine, if it isn't in our favour we should be quiet. We cannot adopt that approach. (Interview with AM, rights-based activist)

Mixing the referential with narratives of human rights may reduce this risk, but according to the view expressed above, Islamic feminists are nevertheless limited in their discourse by the confines of the religious laws.

Rights-based women's groups first organised themselves around the issue of the family law. For more than ten years, until its reform, the *moudawana* defined the organisations and their activities. Proximity work with women victims of violence was closely linked to this advocacy, and case studies and statistics of service users were used as evidence to support the law reform. Faith-based women's organisations followed the lead of the Islamist movements they came from and advocated against any reform of the law. Reform of a law based on Islam through state mechanisms was feared to result in the de-sacralisation of religious texts in general (Sadiqi, 2008).

In the mid-2000s after the family law was reformed, rights-based organisations had to redefine their goals. Many concentrated on teaching the new law to practitioners and citizens as well as on reporting on the implementation of the new *moudawana* and the problems many women were encountering in the courts (Sadiqi, 2008). Support for victims of violence and literacy and professional training, which were always an important part of the women's organisations work, continued throughout. Campaigns are ongoing to introduce a law regarding sexual harassment, increase women's political participation, stop child marriages and labour and to reform the penal code concerning rape, sexual violence, abortion and domestic violence.

Political parity and democracy were important themes to rights-based organisations all through the last decade (Sadiqi, 2008; Salime, 2014). A voluntary quota system in national legislations was introduced in 2007, whereby a separate national list is constituted, consisting of women candidates (Darhour and Dahlerup, 2013). Candidates from this list are not elected, but will be assigned a seat if their party receives enough votes. Few women are placed on the local lists, from which voters choose whom to vote for, and CSOs keep campaigning for better representation of women (Liddell, 2009). Parties are accused of putting forward women without the necessary capacity to take on active political roles as well as marginalising women as soon as they have been elected, as observed by MZ:

> Also there is an obligatory quota that women participate in the political life. The political parties in all of Morocco have taken women…but who are not well trained whether it be on the level of human rights also, and they took women

it's just to add to the number of representatives of each party. But these women, they have exposed these women on the list so that people could give their voice, but after they always have the very marginalised role because they are not trained, most of all. (Interview with MZ, rights-based activist)

One of the interviewees had been nominated for the elections. Because of her activist experience she may have been regarded as having a better capacity to act if elected than many other candidates, as described in the quotation above, however the way in which her nomination took place is an illuminating example of how the quota is applied, as she described:

I even stood in elections. Or in fact it was the [president of the community], who put me on the list without asking me first because he needed two women in order to fill his quotas. In the beginning I was against it, but people told me it could be useful for me. (Interview with KT, village association activist)

Some rights-based organisations offer training to women standing in elections and to those already elected to make up for their lack of experience. Furthermore, some political parties also nominate women from CSOs, as they are often well informed in political decision-making practices (Sadiqi, 2008).

Despite issues of implementation and slowly changing attitudes, work done by women's organisations is paying dividends.

But we can say anyway that in our society there has been change. In our society there has been an opening. The women…it's not like before: they don't dare to speak; they don't dare to criticise; they don't dare to tell their suffering. Now they come to the support centres; they say I have this, I have this, I have this, that's very important. (Interview with BA, rights-based activist)

By knowing their rights and having the confidence to demand them, each woman can contribute to their own emancipation.

Faith-based women's activism

Two main Islamist movements operate in Morocco. The first one is linked to the country's officially recognised political party, Justice and Development (PJD). The second movement, Justice and Spirituality is still officially banned in Morocco, as it refuses to acknowledge the legitimacy of the king. Both movements have their women's organisations, but due to the difference in the movements' political viewpoints the groups do not normally cooperate with each other. The campaigns opposing the *moudawana* reform were exceptions as the movements marched together against the proposed changes and attracted an estimated 200,000 followers to the streets of Casablanca in 2000 (Mir-Hosseini, 2007).

Although all of the faith-based organisations prioritise Islam as the first point of reference in all of their activities, most also incorporate human rights on some level. They may say they are incorporating the 'spirit of human rights' into their framework of Islam. This is often coupled with the defence of human rights as universal, belonging to all and incorporating human values that can also be located within Islam, as LX explained;

> Because there are things we share together: there is citizenship; there is living in peace; there is having the minimum of dignity and rights and feeling like a respected human being. If there is no dignity it is bad. (Interview with LX, faith-based activist)

The very same arguments are also put forward by those rights-based organisations that have opted for a mixed referential incorporating human rights and Islam. Where the two differ, are in cases where human rights, as they are universally recognised, clash with religious texts. In these cases rights-based groups give primacy to human rights, whereas faith-based groups refer to Islam.

> Because the notion of equality in Islam, it is an equality of women and men; a complementary equality: one complements the other. We cannot talk about mechanical equality: woman does the same work as men and men do the same work as women. Anyway the international conventions speak of prohibition of women working at nights; prohibition of women working in mines, so we cannot talk about mechanical equality. There is equality,

but a complimentary equality. We are for equality but we are for a certain, as we say, a certain positive privilege for women, because women aren't obliged to buy whatever, women are the pets of the family because it is men who must bring the necessary to the home. (Interview with BK, faith-based activist)

Seeing the supremacy of Islam as a positive in terms of the meaning it gives to equality allows the activist to dispute that human rights are the only route to women's emancipation. Knowledge of different statues of human rights also allows activists to point out some of the contradictions in human rights, thus defending their positions when tensions between Islam and human rights are presented to them. BK and other faith-based activists' view on equality as complementary is strongly rejected by rights-based activists (Guessous, 2011). It is evident that rights-based activists share what Mahmood (2005b, 5) calls a 'dilemma for feminist analysis': why would any woman want to support an organisation whose ultimate goal is women's subordination to men and a society divided along gendered lines?

Mahmood's (2005b, 14) discussion of Islamic feminism severs the assumed links between agency and subversion, challenging the assumption that anyone with agency will wish to struggle for liberal progressive politics. According to Mahmood (2005b, 14), agency can only be understood and defined within the social context where it operates, and a concept of agency cannot be directly imposed from post-enlightenment Europe to post-colonial Arab Middle East. The ease with which the faith-based activists in Morocco explain their positioning between Islam and human rights points towards a complex and well thought out definition of agency, which recognises emancipation as important but not reducible to western discourses.

An important part of faith-based women's activism is also challenging the patriarchal reading of religious texts. Islamic, or Islamist feminism is connected to the quest by women to reinterpret religious texts and move away from the male interpretation which constitutes the patriarchal rule in society independent of Islam itself (Badran, 2005; Latte Abdallah, 2010). They do not argue that this equals a return to a golden era, where Islam was authentically interpreted. Instead, faith-based activists recognise that patriarchal cultural norms have distorted the view of gender in Islam, and the job of Islamic feminism is to discover the meanings and values that lie behind the male interpretation of the texts (Rhouni, 2011, 77). As LX explains: 'Our jurisprudence is based for however long on a jurisprudence created by,

I mean interpreted; the texts – our texts – were interpreted by men…
They were read with a masculine eye, so certainly women were absent'
(interview with LX, faith-based activist).

Rhouni (2011) describes this hermeneutic activity of redefining the
gender roles in relation to Islam through *ijtihad* – the act of reading
and interpreting religious texts – as 'Islamic gender critique' (Rhouni,
2011, 77). Thus, *ijtihad* becomes understood as a contextual and
deconstructing analysis and a critique of the religious texts rather than
as a search for an existing truth that risks being patriarchal in its essence.

Apart from encouraging *ijtihad* from the women's point of view
and educating women about their rights within Islam, the activities of
faith-based groups do not differ much from rights-based groups. Many
place literacy and professional training at the centre of activities and
encourage women's economic independence (Salime, 2014). There
are also services for women living in difficult situations, but instead
of helping women get through divorce proceedings, as many rights-
based organisations do, the onus is on family unity. The organisations
associated with the official Islamist party PJD are working to improve
political parity, whereas those linked to Justice and Spirituality speak
of democracy as part of a wider, societal process in which women
have an important role to play. Some faith-based organisations are also
concerned about sexual harassment.

Narratives of dichotomy

> There are people who are against everything that is Islamist;
> everything that is PJD, Islamist. Even if you are open, I am
> moderate, I am; not everyone, but certain people. Certain
> people. (Interview with BK, faith-based activist)

An important finding from the empirical evidence is the wide gap
that exists between rights-based and faith-based groups. Guessous
(2011, 174) suggests that the aversion of leftist feminists to faith-based
women's groups is a historically specific reaction dependent on the
view these activists hold of modernity, progress, religion and secularism.
In a study that follows a similar trajectory to this chapter, she traces
this antagonism through a genealogy of events and developments in
Morocco over the past 20 years, such as the *moudawana* reform. During
my research I noticed that this dichotomy is also reproduced in everyday
conversations among activists themselves, and thus reinforced through
their discourse. This is especially true with rights-based activists, whose
criticism of women within the Islamist movements is directed at the

patriarchal structures of these movements: any woman agreeing to work from within such a structure is seen as a hypocrite. This view is defended by their own apparent independence from the political parties from which they originated. Here is one such example:

> And there are, for example, the associations who work, as you said, with referential that is traditional…it is a contradiction with my work because they say to women that they must accept the submission and remain with their husband and after the husband it's the father. (Interview with AE, rights-based activist)

Even when rights-based groups are faced with the actual, and often more nuanced discourses of faith-based organisations, they often refuse to accept these discourses at face value. While rights-based groups wish to present diversity between their positions, similar diversity is not observed when speaking of faith-based groups; rather they are all represented as 'the same', standing for the same political issues.

Faith-based organisations are keener to show their openness, and whereas rights-based organisations may remark on the hypocrisy of a veiled women as an activist after the recorder has been turned off, faith-based groups maintain that veiling and other religious customs are each woman's personal choice and has no effect on the way they will be treated. As LX recounted: '[We work] with women who are members of the movement, with women from outside of the movement, veiled women, unveiled women' (interview with LX, faith-based activist).

Despite this apparent openness towards expressions of personal preferences regarding dress and adherence to other Islamist principles, faith-based activists also differentiate between rights-based and faith-based groups. Although faith-based groups may wish to establish cooperation with rights-based women's CSOs on single issues, they maintain the discursive dichotomy between the values of the different groups.

> The majority of the values, there isn't a problem but sometimes our comprehension, for example, I'll give you an example: equality…certain people said Islam, or your idea of equality; women cannot defend equality because Islam in the inheritance women take less than men. So Islam is for our values on equality between men and women. (Interview with BK, faith-based activist)

BK refers to the fact that according to Sharia law men are entitled to a larger share of inheritance than women. As an Islamist she will not dispute this interpretation, but recognises that rights-based activists see this as an unequal practice and use it as an argument to dispute any claim made from within Islamist discourses on gender equality. To BK the law of inheritance is part of a larger Islamist discourse on equality, whereby men's greater economic responsibility warrants a larger share of inheritance, but this does not diminish the complimentary equality Islam promotes.

At times the rights-based activists' discursive construction of Islamist women activists as 'other' is directed at the politics of Islamist movements and what they see as these movements' deliberate exploitation of religion and traditions to oppress women.

> Moroccan traditions are exploited by the Islamists to keep women in the house and in subordination. This is possible because of illiteracy…But exploitation of traditions and the language of religion is hypocrisy from their part because while they speak against feminism and western values they are happy to use a computer and other technologies that come from the West. (Interview with FA, rights-based activist)

This approach sees Islamist movements as uniform and universally patriarchal, and the women who participate in them as submissive. Mahmood's (2005a) vision of Muslim women's agency as being enacted through something other than the Eurocentric emancipatory project is not acknowledged in this critique. Neither is the diversity of the faith-based women's civil society in Morocco, where economic and political emancipation and education are among the main goals of many faith-based women's groups (Salime, 2014). Faith-based women activists, who wish to challenge the patriarchal Islamist movements from the inside with the help of *ijtihad* are dismissed by rights-based activists as hypocrites. Yet the same rights-based activists are using *ijtihad* and religious referential in their own work. While the dichotomy between rights-based and faith-based women's activism is upheld and reconstructed discursively, the campaigns and narratives produced by the actors often seem more similar than divided.

Similarities across divisions

Although the campaigns focusing on the family law reform positioned rights-based and faith-based women activists at opposing positions politically and socially, since the reform both groups have moved on to campaigns and social projects that have much in common with each other. One such project, which women's CSOs all over Morocco have taken on, is the education of women (Salime, 2014). CSOs provide literacy, language and professional training, such as sewing, cooking and computer literacy. The motivation for such training is also strikingly similar between rights-based and faith-based groups, as evidenced in the two extracts below:

> All development should pass through the education of women, because when we educate a woman we educate the entire family and the children profit from it too. (Interview with LK, faith-based activist)

> The motivation of the association is to give women the opportunity to become economic and social actors. When women have access to money the entire family profits from it. (Interview with AL, rights-based activist)

Both rights-based and faith-based women's CSOs wish to make women independent economic actors. Both also emphasise the importance women's education has for the wellbeing of children and families. Other issues that many faith-based and rights-based groups agree on are political parity and legislation for sexual harassment. There are also important discursive strategies shared by the different organisations.

> So that all those women at one point of their lives have been victims of this kind of behaviour that is immoral, completely immoral and completely humiliating because it touches on the dignity of a woman. (Interview with LM, rights-based activist)

> Because there are things we share together: there is citizenship; there is living in peace; there is having the minimum of dignity and rights and feeling like a respected human being. (Interview with LX, faith-based activist)

For example in the Koran there are a lot of texts that speak of the dignity of men in general, men and women, and at times there are texts that speak even in terms of gender, they address men and they address women. And dignity is an essential principle in the declaration of human rights. (Interview with FM, rights-based activist)

Dignity, as a concept, can bridge the gap between international human rights and local interpretations of equality based on Islam and Moroccan traditions. The word is used strategically by both faith-based and rights-based activists to refer to human rights, Islam and Moroccan culture simultaneously, as it resonates with all three, and establishes a link between the three.

As discussed previously, rights-based and faith-based organisations can be divided by which discourses they prioritise in case the two are found contradictory. When describing their referential, however, it can be difficult to distinguish them.

The referential we have; we work on the rights of women; we are inspired by the values of women's rights on an international level; we are for the improvement of the situation of women and on the other side hoping besides; our Islamic religion and our authentic values of our country Morocco. So we make an equation between the two values: the international values of women's rights and the national authentic values of our society. (Interview with BK, faith-based activist)

I mean we did a re-reading of Islam and the Koran and we concluded that there are texts that are equalitarian with women and there isn't a contradiction; and we thought that even the conventions and international treaties of human rights are a fruit of all civilisation; and including the Muslim civilisations that contributed to...I mean there isn't a contradiction. (Interview with FM, rights-based activist)

There is a long history of positioning rights-based and faith-based women's CSOs in Morocco against each other. This is done by the media, but very importantly also by the women's CSOs themselves. If we put aside the discursively constructed dichotomy between rights-based and faith-based activists and look instead at the issues the organisations campaign for, as well as the motivations, the discourses used to support the campaigns and, in the case of some of the rights-based organisations, even the referential, we can see that in many levels the women's CSOs have more in common with each other than the dichotomised discourses let us believe. The antagonism between the groups, which is not shared to a similar level by political parties from different ideologies, serves to divide the women's movement in Morocco and weaken their important legislative and political campaigns, such as the one to ensure political parity in all decision-making instances. Finding these similarities does not however mean that all the CSOs share priorities and discourses in all instances. Indeed, this would not even be desirable, as too strong a voice leading such activities can mask the needs of those who are outside of the margins. Recognising difference within the women's movement is important, but as the above examples show, it can be done without dichotomising and antagonising discourses.

Why the divided women's civil society is hurting emancipation

Both faith-based and rights-based women's CSOs in Morocco work towards women's political and economic emancipation, but the deep political and ideological divide that exists between them works to marginalise their efforts from national political agendas. While faith-based and rights-based women's groups remain divided, political parties on both sides keep reducing women's political participation to tokenism (Liddell, 2009). Women activists confirm this marginalisation they experience in both political movement and in civil society organisations in Morocco.

> So it's a group of women who found themselves in the structures, the two structures especially UNEM, the National Union of Moroccan Students and the Moroccan Association of Human Rights at the end of the 1970s and the beginning of the 1980s, they realised that the question of women was marginalised in these structures; that in addition to the object of battle that united them with the other activists there was a specificity that concerned their demands as women and there were behaviours, attitudes and ideas that were circulating and that attacked the respect and integrity of women and towards which these structures remained indifferent. (Interview with NR, rights-based activist)

This quote demonstrates that women's civil society was born out of the marginalisation of women's issues and experiences within the structures of the student and human rights movements from which they emerged. The quote below is from a faith-based activist whose organisation is linked to the Islamist party PJD and the interview took place just before the 2011 elections.

> It isn't good enough to have a really democratic parliament. So I am not too optimistic for the elections; but I don't think these elections will have an impact on our activities, I don't think so. Even if we have a parliament that is open; even if we have an Islamist government I am not; I don't think they have an impact on our association because the signs that have been given so far tell me that nothing will change. Nothing will change, or there will be a change of face but no change of heart. (Interview with BK, faith-based activist)

The participant's prediction came true as the party nominated only one woman to the government after their election victory, despite consistently nominating more women in their candidate lists than other parties. Faith-based activists experience the same marginalisation and feel the same urgent need to organise as women in rights-based organisations, however, the effects of the division between the two is having on their possibilities for emancipatory action remains under-analysed. Although the same organisations have worked towards political parity and reinforcing the quota system, the political and ideological affiliations of Islamist women becomes a more important consideration than their sex.

> Yes, but for example, because it's true that [the members of PJD] call themselves democrats, they want parity, but for me parity; when they say they want parity is it going to be the women of PJD who go to the parliament?...it is true that it is democracy but at times we don't know what to do. We have never worked with the Islamist associations nor the other parties, PJD, never. (Interview with AD, rights-based activist)

These reservations do not seem to be experienced by men in the same way. Parti Progress et Socialisme (PPS) (an ex-communist party from which ADFM, the most vehement critics of the faith-based women's groups, emerged as a separate women's organisation in the 1990s (Sadiqi, 2008)) joined the government run by PJD in 2011. Islamist and secular men are thus benefiting from this division within women's civil society, as the voices of the divided interest groups are easier to ignore than would be a more united women's movement.

Conclusion: the need for separate voices

Although rights-based organisations are seen to be part of a united women's movement, the diversity in their referential has been beneficial in 'change[ing] things in favour of women's rights' (interview with NR). The same could apply if faith-based organisations, who share the goals of rights-based organisations, were seen as part of this diverse movement. Indeed, having the voices of faith-based women's organisations in battles such as the one for legislation against sexual harassment and violence against women could help address the conservative opposition to such laws, whereas the rights-based approach considered alongside the religious referential could speak to the modernist fractions of the political elites. Speaking together would allow both approaches to be used simultaneously, while also maintaining the separation between rights-based and faith-based organisations.

The antagonism between rights-based and faith-based women's organisations in Morocco is historically situated in the family law campaign and the state policies of the time in which the Islamist movement was established in order to divide the political opposition to the king, Hassan II (Beau and Graciet, 2006). Such influences are present in many post-colonial feminist struggles, and, as noted by Heng (1997), are haunted by the history of nationalist struggles and the ambivalence of nationalism to modernity. Women's CSOs are left to define the modernities they inhabit in the confines of the political divisions originating from nationalist struggles. Jamal (2005), writing about Pakistan, suggests that Islamic movements present an alternative to the anti-Islam discourse on war on terror and the universalising discourses that equate modernity with secularism. She recommends a conversation between the feminists and the Islamists in Pakistan through exploring 'these contradictory spaces for opportunities, if there be any, for mutual recognition' (Jamal, 2005, 71). Kirmani (2011) notes that in India, Muslim women are often forced to choose between international secular discourses on women and discourses locked in cultural and religious values, without recourse to a hybrid understanding of their identities. In Morocco both rights-based and faith-based groups seem to be promoting a hybrid understanding of women's rights and equality based on human rights as well as Islam and Moroccan culture. Yet despite the similarity of these discourses and the topics campaigned for, faith-based and rights-based groups are unwilling to enter into a conversation with each other.

As the binaries constructed through the identity politics of the different groups are preventing cooperation, we might ask whether cooperation would be made more possible if activists were to adopt a more intersectional lens. Matsuda (1991, 1185) suggests that acknowledging the extent to which our different identities are intertwined might give us a knowledge of self that could allow us to work together, while simultaneously recognising that there may be a time when we must end our coalition in order to preserve our integrity. By avoiding difficult conversations we are ignoring the realities and constraints in the lives of the others, but we lose sight of the ways in which we create our own identities in relation to such perceived otherness. Rhouni (2011) notes that Moroccan women's CSOs have used the *moudawana* as a leverage to define themselves in relation to each other. Now that the CSOs have moved on to more complex issues, where simple identity politics in and religiosity can no longer provide the *raison d'être* of the CSOs, the antagonism between rights-based and faith-based groups is no longer a useful discursive tool. Intersectional thinking, alongside the recognition of the hierarchies that operate in the creation of otherness could make the adoption of strategic essentialism possible. As we compare the language and referential of faith-based and rights-based groups and find several points of convergence, we can conclude that organisations have multiple identities just as individuals do. CSOs' political identity may rest closely within the confines of its originating the political party, but this need not pre-determine the organisation's view-point vis-à-vis religion, use of technology or international human rights conventions.

This chapter has discussed the dichotomies between faith-based and rights-based women's groups in Morocco. The divisions are located within the political context and nationalist struggles, and are thus difficult to overcome, even when CSOs may have the same aims. Concentrating on single issues, recognising the multiple identities of the CSOs and embracing strategic essentialism can allow joint action in the future. While cooperation may be difficult due to the politico-historical origins of the antagonism, women's groups will do well to recognise that the current dichotomy is only serving the male political elites, who are not observing the divisions between socialist and Islamist groups in their exclusion of women from political decision-making.

References

Badran, M, 2005, Between secular and Islamic feminism/s: Reflections on the Middle East and beyond, *Journal of Middle East Women's Studies* 1, 1, 6-28.

Barlas, A, 2005, Globalizing equality: Muslim women, theology and feminism, in F Nouraie-Simone (ed) *On shifting ground: Muslim women in the global era*, New York: The Feminist Press

Beau, N, Graciet, C, 2006, *Quand le Maroc sera islamiste*, Paris: La Découverte

Brand, LA, 1998, *Women, the state, and political liberalization: Middle-Eastern and North-African experience*, New York: Columbia University Press

Cavarero, A, 2000, *Relating narratives: Storytelling and selfhood*, London: Routledge

Cavatorta, F, Dalmasso, E, 2009, Liberal outcomes through undemocratic means: The reform of the *Code de statut personnel* in Morocco, *The Journal of Modern African Studies* 47, 4, 487–506

Danius, S, Jonsson, S, Spivak, GC, 1993, An interview with Gayatri Chakravorty Spivak, *Boundary 2* 20, 2, 24–50

Darhour, H, Dahlerup, D, 2013, Sustainable representation of women through gender quotas: A decade's experience in Morocco, *Women's Studies International Forum* 41, 2, 132–42

Einhorn, B, Sever, C, 2003, Gender and civil society in Central and Eastern Europe, *International Feminist Journal of Politics* 5, 2, 163–90

Guessous, N, 2011, *Genealogies of feminism: Leftist feminist subjectivity in the wake of the Islamic revival in contemporary Morocco*, New York: Graduate School of Arts and Sciences, Columbia University

Hélie-Lucas, M-A, 1987 (1990), Women, nationalism and religion in the Algerian struggle, in M Badran, M Cooke (eds), *Opening the gates: Century of Arab feminist writing*, pp 104–14, London: Virago Press Ltd

Heng, G, 1997, 'A great way to fly': Nationalism, the state, and the varieties of Third-World feminism, in J Alexander, C Mohanty (eds) *Feminist genealogies, colonial legacies, democratic futures*, pp 30–45, New York and London: Routledge

Hitchings, R, 2012, People can talk about their practices, *Area* 44, 1, 61–7

Jamal, A, 2005, Feminist 'selves' and feminism's 'others': Feminist representations of Jamaat-e-Islami women in Pakistan, *Feminist Review* 81, 52–73

Kirmani, N, 2011, Re-thinking the promotion of women's rights through Islam in India, *IDS Bulletin* 42, 1, 56–66

Latte Abdallah, S, 2010, Le feminisme islamique, vingt ans après: économie d'un débat et nouveaux chantiers de recherche, *Critique internationale* 46, 1, 9–23

Liddell, J, 2009, Gender quotas in clientelist systems: The case of Morocco's national list, *Al-Raida* 126/127, 79–87

Lopez Plaza, MA, 1999, Les femmes sur la scène politique, *Confluences Méditerranée* 31, 107–18

Mahmood, S, 2005a, Feminist theory, agency, and the liberatory subject, in F Nouraie-Simone (ed) *On shifting ground: Muslim women in the Global era*, pp 111–52, New York: The Feminist Press

Mahmood, S, 2005b, *Politics of piety: the Islamic revival and the feminist subject*, Princeton, NJ and Oxford: Princeton University Press

Matsuda, MJ, 1991, Beside my sister, facing the enemy: Legal theory out of coalition, *Stanford Law Review* 43, 6, 1183–92

Mernissi, F, 1988, *Doing daily battle: Interviews with Moroccan women*, London: Women's Press

Mernissi, F, 1991, *The veil and the male elite: A feminist interpretation of women's rights in Islam*, Reading, MA: Addison-Wesley Publishing Company

Mir-Hosseini, Z, 2007, How the door of Ijtihad was opened and closed: A comparative analysis of recent family law reforms in Iran and Morocco, *Washington and Lee Law Review* 64, 6, 1499–511

Moghadam, V, 2002, Islamic feminism and its discontents: Toward a resolution of the debate, in T Saliba, C Allen, JA Howard (eds) *Gender, politics and Islam*, pp 15–51, Chicago, IL: The University of Chicago Press

Nash, JC, 2008, Re-thinking intersectionality, *Feminist Review* 89, 1–15

Othman, N, 1999, Grounding human rights arguments in non-Western culture: Shari'a and the citizenship rights of women in a modern Islamic state, in JR Bauer, D Bell (eds) *The East Asian challenge for human rights*, pp 169–92, Cambridge and New York: Cambridge University Press

Pruzan-Jorgensen, J, 2010, Analyzing authoritarian regime legitimization: Findings from Morocco, *Middle East Critique* 19, 3, 269–86

Rhouni, R, 2011, Deconstructing islamic feminism: A look at Fatima Mernissi, in M Badran (ed) *Gender and Islam in Africa: Rights, sexuality, and law*, pp 69–88, Stanford, CA: Stanford University Press

Sadiqi, F, 2003, *Women, gender and language in Morocco*, Leiden: Brill

Sadiqi, F, 2008, The central role of the family law in the Moroccan feminist movement, *British journal of Middle Eastern Studies* 35, 3, 325–37

Salime, Z, 2014, The war on terrorism: Appropriation and subversion by Moroccan women, *Signs* 33, 1, 1–24

Slyomovics, S, 2005, *The performance of human rights in Morocco*, Philadelphia, PA: University of Pennsylvania Press and Bristol: University Presses Marketing

Spivak, GS, 1987, *In other worlds: Essays in cultural politics*, London: Methuen

Tamboukou, M, 2008, Re-imagining the narratable subject, *Qualitative Research* 8, 3, 283–92

Tullis Owen, JA, McRae, C, Adams, TE, Vitale, A, 2009, Truth troubles, *Qualitative Inquiry* 15, 1, 178–200

Young, AE, 2005, *Convincing women: Global rights, local families, and the Moroccan women's rights movement*, PhD thesis, Graduate School of Arts and Sciences, Department of Anthropology, 299, Cambridge, MA: Harvard University.

THIRTEEN

Working within associations: recognition in the public space for women?

Annie Dussuet and Érika Flahault

During the feminist movement of the 1970s, the emergence of the concept of patriarchy as a means of analysing women's experiences (Delphy, 1972) highlighted how the seclusion of women at home (as housewives) contributed to their oppression. As a result, in a context where many women interrupted their working lives when they had young children, having an occupation was considered as a key enabler of emancipation. Since the 1970s, the rate of women's participation in the labour market has grown steadily, especially among the mothers of young children (Maruani and Meron, 2012), so that now, working as an employee is the most common situation for women in France. Women represent 47 per cent, almost half of the workforce: 13.6 million women as of 2012.

In general, this change is seen as a step towards emancipation for women. Because it gives them their own income accessing employment is usually considered to offer women greater freedom in the conduct of their lives compared to women of the previous generation. As their economic autonomy legitimises their participation in public life, their status as citizens is more likely to be recognised and thus, their participation in the public sphere on equal terms with men, which is constitutive of citizenship. However, inequalities between men and women on the labour market remain stark (Milewski, 2005). The general picture shows 'the conjunction of essential social change with the permanence of tough inequalities' (Maruani, 2003, 107).

Within this context, this chapter will consider the role of the voluntary sector in the processes of the emancipation of its female employees. In France, the most common status of civil society organisations (CSO) is the 'association', which is governed by the '1901 Law'.[1] Many women are employed by these associations in France; almost 1.2 million in associations as opposed to 3.4 million in the governmental sector and 4.9 million in for-profit organisations (as of 2001). These associations are, therefore, an important source of employment for women. But does this constitute emancipation? Does employment in an association facilitate access to public space? Or does it function, on the contrary, as a space where women are relegated because of the specific types of jobs available in the sector and lack of recognition that is given to their work?

We first look at forms of women's employment in associations in France. We emphasise that while these jobs are meaningful, they are also of poor quality. Second, we examine the effects of women's employment in associations in terms of emancipation. We show how associations tend to support the sexual division of labour rather than challenge it. This is due to the specifics of the organisation of work in associations, which lead them to deviate from the male standards of employment instituted during the years of economic growth. We therefore conclude that employment in associations may effectively act as substitute private, or domestic spaces, thus limiting rather than enabling women's access to the public sphere.

Women's employment in French associations

In France the non-profit sector includes cooperatives, *mutuelles* and foundations as well as associations, however, associations are the most important organisations within the sector: over 80 per cent of the employees of non-profit sector work in associations (Bisault, 2014).

Associations are very diverse; some are very small, others employ thousands of people. But their main characteristic is the binary nature of their members: some are employees, they earn a salary and are regulated by labour laws; others are volunteers working primarily for personal and moral satisfaction.

As of 2012, 1.77 million employees are working for an association in France. This represents 1.43 million full-time equivalent jobs (FTE) and nearly 10 per cent of total wage employment (ONESS, 2012). However, the significance of these figures must be qualified. To analyse these jobs we face the lack and inadequacy of statistical sources: falling between official job classifications, inadequate categories to describe jobs, a lack of precision in the description of tasks leads to a uniform presentation of these activities (Dussuet and Flahault, 2010a). Furthermore, the predominance of part-time jobs leads to an over-representation of the voluntary sector in employment figures.

Nevertheless associations are significant in terms of women's employment, as women represent 70 per cent of their employees (Tchernonog, 2013), a higher proportion than in the rest of the economy. Women are significantly disadvantaged in the French labour market; they are more likely to be unemployed than men – 9.7 per cent as opposed to 8.8 per cent in 2011 (Morin and Remila, 2013) – although the gap has narrowed. Thus, associations constitute a privileged labour market for women, when other barriers to entry or retention remain a reality (Flahault, 2006).

First, employment in associations is a labour market that is wide open to women with the proportion of women reaching 83 per cent in the field of social action and up to 99 per cent of women in the home care services (Dussuet, 2005). One explanation of the preponderance of women in these jobs is that they are concentrated in areas that are socially assigned to women, often an extension of their household chores: education, health, social action. However, the voluntary sector does provide a gateway to employment, including for those whose employment options are limited, such as those from rural areas. Furthermore, associations also open career opportunities that the for-profit sector does not necessarily offer (ONESS, 2009). Thus, the proportion of women in management positions is a little higher than in for-profit organisations. In particular, the management functions[2] in associations are more likely to be occupied by women (54 per cent) than by men (46 per cent). This is more than in private for-profit companies (29 per cent), and the same as the governmental sector (55 per cent) (ONESS, 2012).

Furthermore, even if those associations are discounted whose primary objective is bringing back to the labour market people who have become distanced from it (referred to as 'work integration'), recent investigations conducted by economists or sociologists show that the non-profit sector seems to be conducive to women's employment. And finally, even though there is still a wage gap between men and women, it is lower (Narcy, 2006) in the non-profit sector than in the for-profit: as of 2013 being 14 per cent of hourly wages in the non-profit sector as opposed to 15.5 per cent in the other sectors (Bailly et al, 2013).

Associations thus appear to offer women a chance to enter the labour market and, at least theoretically, such employment constitutes a way to reach greater autonomy and citizenship. However, it still remains to be investigated whether and if so, under what conditions this integration into employment happens.

Methodology

Research into civil society organisations as employers is recent in France, probably because work in this sector is generally regarded as unpaid volunteering, and because unpaid work is regarded as non-work. Indeed, 84 per cent of French associations operate only through volunteer labour, with no paid employees. Therefore sociologists of politics and of voluntary engagement were the first to analyse these organisations. But associations, notably when they have employees, also play a major role in the economy (providing 8 per cent of the total employment in France (Tchernonog, 2013)) in areas as diverse as education, sports, humanitarian intervention, health and so on. In some areas such as social work, care for children, the elderly or disabled, they play a hegemonic role. Therefore, associations must also be analysed in terms of their economic contribution, especially if we want to understand their role in women's emancipation. On the one hand, we can analyse volunteering as work (Simonet, 2006); on the other, many associations also employ paid staff.

This chapter adopts a sociological approach to work and employment. It is based on a literature review and on data from research projects we carried out in the 2000s. It synthesises the results of several field studies we led or participated in on work in associations in France. Although these studies were not centrally focused on the issue of women's emancipation, they included a lot of highly relevant data, which we analysed thematically through the lens of gender and how it is structured. Since 2010, we have been also engaged in critical quantitative research on the quality of employment in the non-profit sector in which we attempt to measure the influence of gender (Dussuet and Flahault, 2012).

In this chapter, we will use this original data, both qualitative and quantitative, comparing it to that provided by literature, in order to address our question about the extent to which employment in associations contributes to women's emancipation.

A review of the relevant literature

A closer look at the characteristics of jobs offered by the non-profit sector in France, especially those disproportionately occupied by women, reveals that when the indicators of job quality are applied, a grim picture emerges. Most concerning is Devetter's (2010) finding that many of these jobs do not provide a living wage because although legally obliged to pay the hourly minimum salary, so many women work part-time that actual take-home pay is below subsistence level.

Such part-time work is very prevalent in associations, even for management positions. Some of these part-time jobs are even called 'postes annexes' by INSEE and not regarded as 'real' jobs.[3] If we include all positions (*annexes* and *non annexes*), the share of full-time positions is just over 40 per cent while it is 74 per cent in the private for-profit companies and 63 per cent for the public sector. And while these part-time jobs are most prevalent among the auxiliary functions they also represent a large proportion of the staff employed in core activities (Bailly et al, 2012).

Furthermore, women are more often hired on fixed-term contracts (Maisonnasse et al, 2010). Nearly a quarter (24 per cent) of voluntary-sector jobs identified in 2005/2006 are on these fixed-term contracts (as opposed to 8 per cent in general in France); only 65 per cent of jobs are permanent (vs 85 per cent overall) and 11 per cent are made up of casual or temporary work which does not provide the stability considered to be a key element of job quality (Tchernonog, 2013). The high proportion of temporary jobs is partly due to the use of employment opportunities supported by state funding (Hély, 2009). The voluntary sector has allowed experimentation with new forms of employment that do not meet the standards of labour law, in the name of the right to work (Bec, 2007). These temporary jobs are more often offered to women who also appear to have less access than men to permanent contracts (ONESS, 2012).

In summary, the more classic form of employment, that is jobs that are full-time and permanent, is atypical in the voluntary sector; and if the inequality between men and women appears to be less strong in associations, this may not be unrelated to this levelling-down in the conditions of employment.

The higher access of women to management positions in these organisations must also be qualified insofar as the voluntary sector offers proportionally fewer management positions than other sectors. Furthermore, management roles in this context are atypical. They are characterised by having less responsibility (there are fewer employees overall, so executives manage smaller numbers), limited career prospects (the more flattened organisational structures tend to result in career 'peaks' being achieved more quickly) and much reduced job security, as the continuity of funding is never guaranteed.

Even within the voluntary sector only 60 per cent of total wages are paid to women while women represent 70 per cent of voluntary sector employees (ONESS, 2012). Wage levels are also lower than elsewhere: thus the voluntary sector employees receive lower pay compared to other employees about 18 per cent (Legros and Narcy, 2004). The flattening of wage hierarchies particularly penalises the highly qualified, who are paid less than they would be in the market sector. Many associations also fall outside the remit of collective bargaining, as their activities are not classified as belonging neatly to specific professional domains around which such negotiations take place. The presence of unions is particularly weak due to the small size of the vast majority of associations, and there is also a historical distrust on the part of trade union confederations towards the sector. Data generated on wage differentials are calculated on full-time positions, even though, as noted above, in this sector part-time work is much more prevalent. Researchers tend to think in terms of 'theoretical' wages in the abstract, which does not always make much sense for the women in the voluntary sector. Ultimately, the 'real' wage levels observed are low or very low for many women who combine low pay and part-time positions.

To summarise: results from recent research highlight the precarious status, the prevalence of part-time work and the relatively low wages in associations compared with for-profit sector organisations; thus the initial appearance of greater equity between men and women in terms of wages or access to executive status must be qualified. Therefore, does access to employment in associations contribute to women's emancipation?

Findings

More meaningful work but poorer working conditions

When asked about job satisfaction, non-profit sector employees tend to respond by focusing on *dissatisfaction* first, which they quickly however put into perspective by listing their reasons for satisfaction (Dussuet et al, 2007). The reasons given for dissatisfaction are twofold. First, organisational constraints have consequences for working conditions. Associations' lack of financial resources translates into inadequate or obsolete working tools available to employees: for example, one respondent commented that 'offices are too small, we don't have enough funding, we can't help people as much as we would like to' (interview with Caroline, social work). The perpetual quest for new sources of funding means that less time is spent doing the work that they regard as at the heart of their mission. The obligation to work with volunteers multiplies decision-making processes and leads to a 'waste of time' in decision-making: 'working with volunteers has drawbacks, everything takes time. You can't just impose changes, there has to be lots of dialogue, concessions, compromises to make for the volunteers' (interview with Marc, social work). Second, criticisms concern inadequate recognition of the work achieved, of job titles and of the importance of tasks related to the organisations' missions: 'prevention is one of the League's three missions, but it's probably the one that's the least well known within the League, and the least valued by the managers' (interview with Elodie, health work). This lack of recognition may be expressed indirectly through complaints about wages or working time: 'I find that the idea of management and of responsibility isn't well recognised. I don't think we are well paid considering what we take on' (interview with Sonia, manager). The difficulty of maintaining strict limits to working hours is reflected in the increase in overtime, which is rarely paid, sometimes compensated for, but more often ignored and counted as an example of – more or less spontaneous – voluntary commitment over and above the contractual working time.

The interviews highlight an important point, however: the reasons for dissatisfaction appear both fewer and less 'serious' than the satisfaction the employees of associations gain from their work. For a substantial proportion of respondents, these discomforts, especially those related to pay, are downplayed and they highlight the advantages and compensations of what is regarded as the distinctiveness of working in the voluntary sector:

> Yes, working in the voluntary sector makes a difference to me…it's a job that corresponds to values. Personal values, but also the value of placing the person first, the individual, of being there, of being there for someone…which is obviously different to what happens in private companies for instance where you're always trying to make a profit. Personally this is what I need. (Interview with Nathalie, popular education)

In this way we see employees off-setting their dissatisfaction with pay by shifting perspectives. They reject the logic of the market that would judge their wages to be inadequate, relative to the number of hours worked. Instead, they locate their work within a different framework: that of values and social justice, positioning themselves within the 'domestic city', or 'civic city' (Rawls, 1971; Boltanski and Thévenot, 1991). However, the concern must be this shift away from the market logic allows associations struggling with budget constraints to reduce the cost of wages. Respondents speak time and again about the sense of social usefulness, human contacts, autonomy, the variety of roles, a friendly work atmosphere, self-fulfilment. For example: 'The key thing is knowing why I'm doing this job, what it's for. And if it's useful to the people who come to us, but also to the volunteers, who are people too, then that's something I appreciate and that suits me fine' (interview with Marc, social work).

In such conditions it becomes difficult to distinguish between factors relating to the job for which the employee was hired by contract and those characterising commitment: in the voluntary sector, these two frames of experience (Goffman, 1974) seem inextricably intertwined. In associations focused on helping others, proximity is essential: not only do employees know that they are useful, but they know specifically to whom and how. Thus the meaning of work often offsets its monetary aspects, especially when there are interpersonal relationships with the people helped. The market logic is replaced by the logic of gift (Mauss, 1950): being paid less than what they could otherwise hope for becomes acceptable in the name of the relationship with others.

Employees interviewed commented on the good atmosphere in the organisations in which they work. And they seem to attribute these good relationships with colleagues, with interpersonal meetings and cordial – even friendly – relationships to voluntary sector values. 'I'm a people person so this is ideal! I meet people every day, whether they be the job-seekers or the users I go out to meet. And there's the teamwork. That's really great, the girls and I get on really well and that's very important to me' (interview with Caroline, social work). Some even refer to a 'family' atmosphere: 'another difference is the family spirit which there wasn't before in the company I worked for' (interview with Pierre, social work). The possibility of responding to this concern for people is also supported by the autonomy and freedom given, at work, which sometimes open up spaces for innovation and the recognition of inventiveness and creativity. According to these interviewees, the work of voluntary sector employees is not monotonous.

Diversity of tasks, flexibility and freedom of organisation are put forward as assets of the sector, especially in small associations. The recurrence of acknowledgement of this sense of variety also reflects management methods in the non-profit sector: employees are less subject to prescription, their work is less repetitive; they are asked to accomplish a mission rather than fulfil a role. Although employees seem to believe that this is a characteristic of the voluntary sector, Boltanski and Chiapello (1999) argue that it is actually very close to what is also practised in private for-profit companies under the name of management 'by objectives' or 'by project'.

Finally, working in the voluntary sector is seen as a source of self-fulfilment. The grounds for satisfaction are linked to notions of personal development and self-realisation. In carrying out the work itself, voluntary sector employees find reasons to be satisfied with their conditions of employment, even if the latter are objectively worse than in other sectors. It is clear that the work is not considered in the manner of classical economics as a source of alienation but as a way of becoming a rounded fully-fledged human person. This is one reason why, for many respondents, working in the voluntary sector is a choice – a choice, which is not always consciously made but often constructed in the course of the experience. 'I'm in the voluntary sector by choice even though I began there by chance because I couldn't find a job in any other sector' (interview with Isabelle, social work). In this way, working for associations contributes to emancipating women, and perhaps also men, by allowing them to find meaningful employment.

Women's jobs and distinctiveness of the voluntary sector

Notwithstanding the above, when women (and men) seek a job and, ultimately find one in an association, their main goal is generally to earn their living. Although work in the voluntary sector is considered distinctive in terms of being meaningful, employment opportunities are nevertheless to be considered in terms of conventional indicators such as the type of employment contract and working hours. Women can find jobs in associations; but what are their employment conditions?

The major form of precarious employment in this sector is the prevalence of part-time jobs. Of course, one might argue that part-time positions are deliberately chosen by women because they allow them more easily to reconcile family life with work or to spend more time in occupations other than work. This was the case for several of the women we interviewed: 'I do lots of other things…I want to experience other things alongside work' (interview with Catherine, women's rights). However, part-time jobs obviously also provide pro-rata pay: women's own salary is often not sufficient to ensure their independence from a spouse or from the welfare state. Therefore, many women employed in the associations are classified as working poor, unable to meet their needs, although many of them are single parents. This even holds true in the women's rights associations as well as the ones providing care services that we studied: the use of part-time work is frequent, if not systematic.

Many employees told us how they are thus forced to combine several part-time jobs to achieve an adequate income. When they are employed in home care associations working full-time is an exception (more than 75 per cent of employees work part-time). Respondents working in feminist associations illustrate several possible combinations: two part-time jobs in different associations with similar goals in the same area, two part-time jobs in the same association in two different cities, not too far from each other or part-time on two different functions within one association. Such combinations are common but even with two jobs the total working time of employees is overwhelmingly under 30 hours per week.

Despite these poor conditions, we find little challenge of gender inequalities in associations, even in those of a feminist orientation. We suggest that the distinctive characteristics of these organisations may provide one explanation because informal aspects, such as the coexistence of employees and volunteers and the humanistic values they defend, are not neutral in terms of gender.

One distinctive characteristic of the voluntary sector is that there is some blurring of the boundaries between the volunteers and employees, with some tasks being carried out by either, or both. In a crisis period, employment is considered primarily as a cost, so that the proximity and substitutability of employee and volunteer work provides a strong inducement for replacing paid workers with volunteers. Although increasing professionalisation often leads to a clearer distinction between the functions of volunteers and staff, the risk remains. Moreover, the management of associations have often neglected to pay sufficient attention to their responsibilities as employers, their focus being on users and not on those who perform the services.

Furthermore, on the basis of their principles, some organisations refuse to implement a hierarchical structure because they fear that this will inevitably lead to an imbalance of power. For instance, in the feminist network Planning Familial it was regarded as unimaginable to have a director, except when the association has a birth-planning centre (and then the director must be a physician). But this refusal to organise themselves hierarchically may weaken organisations: in comparison with the conditions of employment offered by organisations in other sectors they are often disadvantaged. Precarious employment conditions alongside frequent over-qualification of employees can also be a consequence of applying feminist principles – in the name of emancipation, some feminist organisations avoid reproducing a 'male' bureaucratic division of labour, by promoting a non-hierarchical organisation without experts, more democratic forms for participation of all and the rotation of leadership (Gravel et al, 2007). This can lead to a high staff turnover, which in turn limits the possibilities for developing needed expertise.

Many of these organisations provide services for free or at low prices in order to remain accessible to the poorest populations. As a result they find themselves in the position of seeking funding from various agencies, local communities and decentralised state services. Thus, many CSO executives (volunteers or employees) are torn between the principles of freedom and constant financial concerns. They are forced to look for recurrent funding, leading some to physical and moral exhaustion.

> I still find my job hugely interesting, I believe in the values of the network, I get on very well with the governors and – I believe – with my team, but I'm exhausted by the financial issues, by balancing the books. If I get offered a job whose values I share but where I don't need to deal with the finances, I'll take it straight away! It's really tough to always be on the edge; even though the team is very constructive there always the fear you might have to make people redundant. (Interview with Fanny, women's rights)

If these organisations seem to have escaped the laws of the market, they are nevertheless not exempt from the objectification of activity (through the measurement of outcomes) encountered in commercial organisations and must use instruments that allow such assessment of their activity in order to obtain subsidies. Improving the conditions of employment of employees is hampered by barriers to the formalisation of tasks that stem from the internal functioning and ethos of the voluntary sector.

Due to the limited sources of funding, voluntary sector organisations, including associations, now spend more and more time developing funding bids. They are therefore tied to specific projects that are limited in time, and their finances are weakened, thus making the durability of jobs even more uncertain. Wages account for most of the budgets of these organisations; it could therefore be argued that the poorer conditions of employment are explained by their precarious financial situations. However, it is worth asking whether each is a reflection of the low social recognition accorded to women's work.

Discussion: enabling women's access to public space or supporting the gendered status quo?

Up to this point our analysis of gender has been limited to statements about the employment of women in associations. In this perspective, gender is only regarded as a variable. For us however, a gender approach needs to be more structural (Le Feuvre, 2003). Analysing the potentially emancipatory effects of employment cannot be limited to general considerations about the quality of an abstract, theoretical job, by default 'gender neutral'. Rather, we consider it fundamental to study how forms of employment and work relationships for women in voluntary sector jobs can lead to a change in their place in society, and in so doing deconstruct (or reproduce) the gendered hierarchical structure.

Associations and gendered employment norms

In our societies, the gender structure organises employment differently for men and women by distinguishing tasks, skills and the normal and desirable conditions of employment for both sexes. In recent French social history, two separate periods in time can be considered concerning women's employment in associations.

Until the late 1960s in France, women's relationship to employment was determined by their position in the family life cycle. Their activity rate followed a typical sequence: initially high levels of employment after leaving the educational system, then decreasing rapidly with marriage and childbirth, returning to a second highpoint (lower than the first) and then a gradual diminishing again with the transition to retirement, which occurred earlier for women than for men (Maruani and Meron, 2012). This relationship to employment was closely related to the characteristics of the family structure, male breadwinner model until the early 1970s. Women's jobs were seen as secondary and their remuneration as an extra, secondary wage. In periods of full employment, their return to work was relatively easy, even if the concept of a career was an unattainable ideal. In such a context, the jobs offered by some voluntary organisations seemed particularly well suited to women, even though they represented only a few hours a week and paid very low wages. The suitability of this employment appeared even stronger when the association's jobs corresponded to a role seen as 'female' as in the case of home help services, educational services and community health. Finally, associations' territorial coverage gave them proximity, sometimes being the only provider of jobs available to women in a given area. For example, in home-help associations, domestic cleaning jobs for the elderly represented an opportunity to return to work for women without qualifications. Their experience as housewives and mothers provided multiple expertise and practical knowledge used in this professional position. Thus, gender as a system of normative differentiation played a positive role from the perspective of associations insofar as it ensured their financial stability but it also obscured the inequality that this represented.

Subsequently, however, since the late 1960s, the massive entry of women into wage employment in France has changed social representations in all areas. The new model of working women's lives becomes 'stacking'. In this configuration, part-time jobs may appear to be good jobs for women. Voluntary sector jobs, albeit often part-time and low paying, seem to be particularly suitable for women with family responsibilities, allowing them to reconcile their dual workday. This, at any rate, is the governmental discourse used to justify legislative changes facilitating the use of part-time employment. Faced with the crisis in employment, the part-time female labour force acts as an adjustment variable. In this context, subsidised employment grows in associations with different characteristics and names, but often with the common characteristic of being offered part-time.

In our surveys, the interviewed women often told us that they had chosen their part-time jobs. But this 'choice' can lead them into a vicious circle (Kergoat, 1984): they are better able to manage the combination of work and family duties but this simultaneously maintains, or even increases inequality in the sharing of family responsibilities. Furthermore, these part-time jobs are often essential for women to keep working until retirement age. For example, this elderly carer 'chooses' part-time because full-time is too exhausting to be able to continue working:

> Cleaning, getting in the car, driving to another house, out, in again, it's tiring…And to tell you the truth, out of all the girls, only one does 35 hours. I don't know how she copes. It's a choice, I signed up for 25…usually I'm doing 27–28 hours a week. And you know, if I want more, I just ask them and they write me out a new contract, it's not a problem. But I think it's quite enough! (Interview with Martine, home care)

In summary, associations tend to reproduce gender norms because they offer jobs that correspond to these norms: they are poorly paid, but this is accepted because they are 'women's jobs'.

Lack of recognition devalues associations as well as women's work

An important question is why the associations, which are often led by people espousing humanist and even egalitarian values, do not worry about the quality of women's jobs. Above all, a major explanation for the poor quality of jobs in associations lies in the failure to recognise the work done by their employees. Associations are hegemonic in all sectors related to the provision of care: when it is necessary to take care of others, be it small children, the elderly, chronically sick or socially excluded people who need support in their efforts to rehabilitation, this function is socially assigned to women, both in their own homes and more broadly in society (Tronto, 1993; Molinier, 2013). Thus the dominant presence of women in voluntary sector jobs (and the almost exclusively female presence in some associations, such as those providing home care or women's rights) cannot be explained by the existence of measures intended to help reconcile family and professional lives. We argue that this is clearly due to the sexual division of labour (Héritier, 1996: Kergoat, 2000) and is not specific to the French labour market: in the US similar observations have been made by Albelda et al (2009). Research demonstrates that the tasks usually performed by women are paid less than those assigned to men: they are seen as socially less valuable. In France, Lemière and Silvera (2008), who compared wages for jobs of 'comparable value' show that these low wages are not specific to associations, but are representative of the 'female' sectors, concluding that there is an under-valuation of female jobs. We suggest that this is particularly acute when these jobs correspond to work regarded as a 'female' task, such as care. People who need care are precisely those who are likely to be in a situation of economic dependence; somehow, their 'low value' reflects on those who care for them. Furthermore, the associations of care with maternity are closely coupled. But mothers are supposed to perform their domestic work for their children only for love; being paid for it seems to debase their feelings; 'care workers are implicitly expected to prove their proper motivation by accepting a wage penalty' (England et al, 2002, 457).

In the case of associations, the low value placed on work traditionally carried out by women is further complicated by the fact that activists have long given their time generously, thus implying that quality services can be delivered with very limited resources. However, among the associations analysed in our studies, some have tried to professionalise their employees through recognising the skills and specific training required by their work. In many cases, they have 'invented' new kinds of business, or, more modestly, new ways of working. In these cases associative action has transformed an activity previously carried out on an informal, voluntary, activist or domestic basis into a professionalised occupation, but without the recognition that paying wages transforms the content, while preserving its implementation (Dussuet and Flahault, 2010b).

For example, in the 1940s, family associations invented the idea of the '*travailleuse familiale*' (family worker) who would temporarily replace or supplement domestic work usually carried out free of charge by mothers. These family associations consisted of activists of the Catholic social movement, closest to the labour movement (Loiseau, 1996). For them, the *travailleuse familiale* was neither a servant nor a social worker (Dussuet, 2005). Training was compulsory for the aspiring *travailleuse familiale*, and one innovation of this training was the alternating between institutional training and placements, allowing their socialisation into their work environment. In another sector, since the 1980s, the aim of the Centre d'information des droits des femmes et de la famille (CIDFF) (Information Centre for Women and Families Rights) is to provide legal information about women's rights to a primarily female public in order to allow women to take control of their own situation. This requires proven legal expertise but also a good knowledge of the origins and mechanisms of gender inequality, so as to be able to pick out in all legal texts the items that could be used in an egalitarian perspective. Legal informants employed by this network of associations hold a masters' degree in law, but they must also receive specific training to enable them to act in this capacity. They are therefore not doing exactly the same job as other legal informants working in other organisations.

These are two examples among others of jobs invented by associations: jobs which are mostly held by women, substituting informal work done elsewhere by housewives, volunteers and activists who were unpaid. But here employees perform these jobs, and as they are non-profit organisations, these associations are struggling to pay their employees for their skills. For instance, a woman employed by a CIDFF said:

> Consider that I'm not being paid for what I do, and neither are my colleagues. But I've made this choice of losing something like €350 (a month) because I refuse to spend my whole day at work implementing idiocies set out by people who haven't got a clue. You see, I refused that. (Interview with Elisabeth, women's rights)

The government has been lobbied to recognise these new jobs. The *travailleuses familiales* are a rather successful example of professionalisation: in 1949, a sort of 'licence' (Hughes, 1984) was granted to them by virtue of the requirement to complete training (itself delivered by the voluntary sector) in order to undertake roles partially funded by family benefits (National Fund for Family Allowances (CNAF)). But, in the same sector, organisations employing carers for the elderly have not really succeeded in raising the profile of their employees and distinguishing the provision of services from domesticity (Dussuet, 2010). In 2002, a collective bargaining branch agreement was reached. It distinguished degrees of complexity in interventions narrowly linked to qualification levels, allowing experienced employees and graduates access to a substantially higher pay scale than untrained employees. But public employment policies since 2005 prevented this recognition by blurring the boundaries again, between services for dependent people and domestic services (Jany-Catrice et al, 2009).

Legal informants of the CIDFF provide another example that illustrates the difficulties for voluntary organisations adequately to recognise the level of skill required in their employees' tasks when their activity is not regulated by labour laws. CIDFF employees generally hold a master's degree, the employing organisations, however, are the only guarantors of their competence and the uncertainties organisations face in terms of funding is not conducive to employee claims. The CIDFF example is more recent than the care services, but it suggests that providing information on women's rights does not rank very high in the government's priorities.

The possibility of emancipation for women through voluntary sector jobs appears linked to the economic position of organisations but also to the greater or lesser success of their strategies for professionalisation. This in turn is related to a sector's ability to make itself heard in the public sphere by achieving the power to influence government decisions, both in terms of regulation and funding.

Conclusions

Associations build a 'proximity public space' (Laville and Nyssens, 2001) between the public and private spheres and are a first step towards forms of employment more easily accessible to women than those available in the male dominated public sphere. Between commitment and work, between private and public space, the associations' world appears to be an intermediary space, favourable to women's access to the labour market, including those who are the farthest from it. Thus, associations contribute to the emancipation of women through access to public space. But because of this specific position in the public sphere of work, certain features of associations constitute risk factors for the sustainability and the quality of women's employment. The concentration of associations' activities in sectors exempt from labour law, the onus on humanist values which may lead employees to give a commitment beyond their employment contract, the coexistence of volunteers and employees sometimes involved in the same tasks within the same association, the fragility of the status of employment in many structures, and, more fundamentally, the relationship to work developed by the majority of voluntary sector employees, all these factors weaken employees. It can thus be feared that associations may become a space of relegation, contributing to confining the women they employ to devalued segments of the labour market.

Paradoxically, despite their involvement in the denunciation of gender inequalities, feminist organisations are not an exception in the landscape of voluntary sector jobs. One could suggest that these organisations have failed in their mission and play a cynical game with regard to their employees by affirming goals of equality on the one hand while simultaneously perpetuating the foundations of gender inequality through the jobs offered. However, this critical position seems unfair to the activist administrators, ignoring the context in which they operate, and especially obscuring the significance of the broader inequalities of the context in which they operate. Feminist values in these organisations do not shield them from 'gender effects' in their role as employers. Because they initially focused on the services they provide to users, because these activities were first performed by volunteer activists, because the volunteer activists who take on the employer function in some cases give their time unstintingly, because they do not always distinguish between 'commitment value' and working time, because their activities are about caring, which is difficult to objectify, because they are dependent on uncertain funding, the jobs they offer are typically 'women's jobs'. Thus we find the same elements of job insecurity as in other organisations whose function is to offer 'care', but we can also discern elements that could foreshadow a real professionalisation of care, with a focus on training, combined with an approach to their work that combines care and activism.

The example of feminist associations shows how the ethos of these organisations, conducive to selfless commitment, contributes to the exploitation of their staff. In an overall economic context of job insecurity, many associations appear manipulated by the public authorities. The state withdraws and reduces public employment while promoting competitive funding. Far from being a simple technical operation, contracting with governmental agencies may lead organisations to be funded for fixed-term 'projects' while offering employees permanent contracts, thus resulting in a dangerous imbalance between the sustainability and the quality of their employees' jobs.

Promoting the social recognition of all voluntary sector workers, whether volunteers or employees, requires associations to be as aware of their function as employers and economic actors as they are of their core mission. In this respect, they need to lobby for the acknowledgment of their social utility, and for the acknowledgment that the work they perform is genuine work that needs to be recognised as such, and which requires a decent life for its employees.

Notes

[1] The association is an agreement by which two or more people are sharing, on a permanent basis, their knowledge or activity for a purpose other than sharing profits.

[2] The management functions are twofold in associations: the governing management is made up of unpaid volunteers, the executive management is staffed by wage-earners. Here we consider executive management.

[3] 'A post is considered as non-annexed if the volume of work and the corresponding level of pay are sufficient'" (www.insee.fr/en/methodes/default. asp?page=definitions/poste.htm).

References

Albelda, R, Duffy, M, Folbre, N, 2009, *Counting on care work: Human infrastructure in Massachusetts*, Amherst, MA: University of Massachusetts Press

Bailly, F, Chapelle, K, Prouteau, L, 2012, La qualité de l'emploi dans l'ESS: Étude exploratoire sur la région des Pays de la Loire, *Revue internationale de l'économie sociale* 323, 44–63

Bailly, F, Chapelle, K, Nirello, L, Prouteau, L, 2013, Les écarts de salaires entre hommes et femmes sont-ils plus faibles dans l'ESS?, *Colloque Usages des chiffres dans l'action publique territoriale*, Nantes, 16–18 October

Bisault L, 2014, L'économie sociale, des principes communs et beaucoup de diversité, *Insee Première* 1522, http://insee.fr/fr/ffc/ipweb/ip1522.pdf

Bec, C, 2007, *De l'État social à l'État des droits de l'Homme*, Rennes: Presses universitaires de Rennes

Boltanski, L, Chiapello E, 1999, *Le nouvel esprit du capitalisme*, Paris: Gallimard

Boltanski, L, Thévenot, L, 1991, *De la justification: Les économies de la grandeur*, Paris: Gallimard

Delphy, C, 1972, *L'ennemi principal*, Paris: Maspero

Devetter, F-X, 2010, Définition et analyse des emplois degradés, *Communication aux XXXe journees de l' Association d'Économie Sociale*, Charleroi, www.cresspaca.org/upload/documents/definition-et-analyse-des-122.pdf

Dussuet, A, 2005, *Travaux de femmes: Enquêtes sur les services à domicile*, Paris: L'Harmattan

Dussuet, A, 2010, Un model associatif de régulation du travail? L'example d'associations de service à domicile, *Politiques et management public* 27, 1, 79–96

Dussuet, A, Flahault, E, 2010a, Chiffrage de l'emploi dans les Organisations de l'Économie Sociale en France: une analyse critique, *Cahiers du Cirtes* 5, 279–95

Dussuet, A, Flahault, E, 2010b, Entre professionnalisation et salarisation, quelle reconnaissance du travail dans le monde associatif?, *Formation Emploi* 111, 35–50

Dussuet, A, Flahault, E, 2012, Des emplois soutenables dans les associations? La part du genre, *Cahiers du Cirtes*, special edition 2, 159–72

Dussuet, A, Flahault, E, Loiseau, D, 2007, *Quelle gestion des ressources humaines dans l'économie sociale? Entre bénévolat et professionnalisation, la place du travail dans les associations*, Paris: Rapport DIIESES (Délégation interministérielle à l'innovation et l'expérimentation sociale et l'économie sociale).

England, P, Budig, M, Folbre, N, 2002, Wages of virtue: The relative pay of care work, *Social Problems* 46, 4, 455–73

Flahault, E (ed), 2006, *L'insertion professionnelle des femmes: Entre contraintes et stratégies d'adaptation*, Paris: Presses universitaires de Rennes

Flahault, E, 2013, Le planning familial et la professionnalisation du conseil conjugal et familial: une reproduction de la norme de genre au nom de la subversion?, *Cahiers du genre* 55, 89–108

Goffman, E, 1974, *Frame analysis: An essay on the organization of experience*, New York: Harper and Row

Gravel, A-R, Bellemare, G, Briand, L, 2007, *Les centres de la petite enfance: Un mode de gestion féministe en transformation*, Montréal: Presses de l'université du Québec

Hély, M, 2009, *Les métamorphoses du monde*, Paris: Presses universitaires de France

Héritier, F, 1996, *Masculin/féminin: la pensée de la difference*, Paris: Odile Jacob

Hughes, EC, 1971, *The sociological eye: Selected papers*, New Brunswick, NJ: Transaction Books, 1984

Jany-Catrice, F, Puissant, E, Ribault, T, 2009, Associations d'aide à domicile: pluralité des héritages, pluralité des professionnalités, *Formation Emploi* 107, 77–91

Kergoat, D, 1984, *Les femmes et le travail à temps partiel*, Paris: La Documentation française

Kergoat, D, 2000, Division sexuelle du travail et rapports sociaux de sexe, in H Hirata, F Laborie, H Le Doare, D Senotier (eds) *Dictionnaire critique du féminisme*, pp 35–44, Paris: Presses Universitaires de France

Laville, J-L, Nyssens, M, 2001, *Les services sociaux entre associations, marché et état: l'aide aux personnes âgées*, Paris: La Découverte

Le Feuvre, N, 2003, Le 'genre' comme outil d'analyse sociologique, in D Fougeyrollas, C Planté, M Riot-Sarcey, C Zaidman (eds) *Le genre comme catégorie d'analyse: Sociologie, histoire, littérature*, pp 39–52, Paris: L'Harmattan

Lefebvre, M, 2010, Qualité de l'emploi et hétérogénéité dans le champ des services à la personne: éléments d'analyse à partir des statistiques nationales, *Documents de travail du Centre Lillois d'Etude et de Recherche Sociologique et Economique*, Lille: Université de Lille

Legros, D, Narcy, M, 2004, Différentiel de salaire entre secteur sans but lucratif et secteur privé en France, in D Girard (ed) *Solidarités collectives: Famille et solidarités*, pp 215–230, Paris: L'Harmattan

Lemière, S, Silvera, R, 2008, *Les différentes facettes des inégalités de salaires entre hommes et femmes*, http://rachelsilvera.org/articles/lemiere&silvera%20%sal20GRH.pdf

Loiseau, D, 1996, *Femmes et militantismes*, Paris: L'Harmattan

Maisonnasse, J, Melnik, K, Petrella, F, Richez-Battesti, N, 2010, *Quelle qualité de l'emploi dans l'économie sociale et solidaire? Une perspective plurielle*, Aix-en-Provence: Rapport de recherche pour la Région Provence-Alpes-Côte d'Azur (PACA)

Maruani, M, Meron, M, 2012, *Un siècle de travail des femmes en France*, Paris: La Découverte

Mauss, M, 1950, *Sociologie et anthropologie*, Paris: Presses universitaires de France

Milewski, F (ed), 2005, *Les inégalités entre les femmes et les hommes: les facteurs de précarité*, Paris: La Documentation française

Molinier, P, 2013, *Le travail du care*, Paris: La Dispute

Morin, T, Remila, N, 2013, Le revenu salarial des femmes reste inférieur à celui des hommes, *INSEE première* 1436, www.insee.fr/fr/ffc/ipweb/ip1436pdf

Narcy, M, 2006, *Motivation intrinsèque et équité salariale: une comparaison entre le secteur associatif et le secteur privé*, Thèse de doctorat d'économie, Université Paris 2, Panthéon Assas

ONESS (Observatoire National de l'Économie Sociale et Solidaire), 2009, *Atlas de l'économie sociale et solidaire en France et dans les Régions*, Paris: Conseil National des Chambres Régionales de l'Économie Sociale (CNCRES)

ONESS (Observatoire National de l'Économie Sociale et Solidaire), 2012, *Atlas commenté de l'économie sociale et solidaire,* Paris: Dalloz, Juris-Associations.

Rawls, J, 1971, *A theory of justice*, Cambridge, MA: Harvard University Press

Simonet, M, 2006, Le monde associatif: entre travail et engagement, in N Alter (ed) *Sociologie du monde du travail*, pp 191–207, Paris: Presses universitaires de France

Tchernonog, V, 2013, *Le paysage associatif Français: Mesures et evolutions*, Paris: Juris-Associations-Dalloz

Tronto, JC, 1993, *Moral boundaries: A political argument for an ethic of care*, New York: Routledge

Flexible working practices in charities: supporting or hindering women's emancipation in the workplace

Sally A East and Gareth G Morgan

Flexible working and gender stereotypes

The case for flexible working is inherently linked to the issue of workers needing to balance their commitments as employees with their roles as carers. The case is often made in gendered terms, that it is good for women. So we ask: why women? Why not men as the primary carers? We therefore begin by examining the stereotyping of women and the extent to which such processes are maintained, rather than challenged by HRM (human resource management) policies and procedures.

In 1994 a study by Williams and Best discovered a high degree of agreement across 30 countries with respect to the characteristics associated with each gender group. Male-associated terms included 'aggressive', 'determined' and 'sharp-witted' whereas female-associated terms included 'cautious', 'emotional' and 'warm'. However, according to Schaffer (2004, 322): 'Personality and cognitive differences are far fewer in number than is commonly believed, and, where they do exist, moderate in extent and are quite probably becoming less evident as society redefines the role of the sexes.' And yet, gender-role stereotypes are repetitively portrayed by the media, as well as by parents and teachers (Wober et al, 1987; Hines et al, 2002; Leaper and Friedman, 2007). Favara (2012, 5) confirms that 'gender stereotypes affect both girls' and boys' educational choices' even when choosing a subject: 'girls choose more female than male subjects and the opposite for boys' (Favara, 2012, 23). From a young age, this study suggests, we are passively receptive to the 'accepted' stereotypical roles of women within the home and workplace. Explanations for such behaviour between men and women 'tend to emphasise biological (or other internal) causes, as opposed to social (and other external) causes (individualism)' (Ross, 2010, 764). The recourse to biology tends to be used to reinforce widely held stereotypes regarding the inevitability and unchangeability of gender differences, and thus, continues to contribute to the view that women are inherently suited to the role of primary carer, a view that that follows them into the workplace.

Until the 1980s the common pattern of the UK family employment was predominantly one of men (fathers) working long hours and women (mothers) working in low-paid part-time roles in order to keep the house and look after the children (Dex and Scheibl, 2002). However, the socio-economic and political changes of the intervening decades have seen an increase in the number of women entering the workforce working in both full-time and part-time capacity (see Table 14.1). Moreover, a combined increase in the population of lone mother households, with the consequence that 'women's wages are more important than ever to the family budget' (Family Friendly Working Hours Taskforce, 2010, 19). HRM policies, including flexible working arrangements supported by legislation, have not kept abreast of these changing trends and remain biased towards women, in order to accommodate women's dual role as societal primary carer and employee (Martinuzzi et al, 2011; Grosen et al, 2012).

Table 14.1: Workforce profile of the voluntary sector in the UK (2011)

Workforce		Numbers
UK voluntary sector paid workforce (headcount)		732,000
Gender	Female	501,000 (68%)
	Male	231,000 (32%)
Employment status	Full-time	440,000 (60%)
	Part-time	292,000 (40%)

Source: National Council of Voluntary Organisations (NCVO), 2013

In this chapter, we present findings that suggest that the flexible working policies utilised by medium-sized service providing charities had the effect of reinforcing stereotypical thinking about gender roles, and thus, can be seen as a mode of restricting rather than supporting women (East, 2013). We use the definition of a 'charity' as in the Charities Act 2011 (s.1) (for England & Wales), namely, an institution which is:

- established for charitable purposes only (public benefit); and
- subject to the control of the charity law jurisdiction in England and Wales.

Theoretical models of flexible working such as the 'family-friendly model' (Doherty and Manfredi, 2006, 242) and the 'diversity model' (Kandola and Fullerton, 1994, 7) respectively look to provide 'equity' for women and 'diversity' within the workplace. However, Frank and Lowe (2003) found that flexible working arrangements could be detrimental to long-term career goals and, as a result of gender specific prioritising, may affect more women than men. Cullen and Christopher concluded that 'balancing responsibilities of work and home life is recognised as affecting both men and women; however, maintaining this balance is more problematic for women as women still have the primary child rearing and domestic responsibilities' (Cullen and Christopher, 2012, 70). Furthermore, neither of the models mentioned above appear to be operational within the medium-sized charitable organisations studied (East, 2013).

The implicit assumption that only women can be primary carers and undertake 'domestic responsibilities' draws on arguments surrounding the 'nature versus nurture' debate (Galton, 1876) which concerns the extent to which particular aspects of behaviour are a product of acquired (learnt) or inherited (genetic) characteristics. Nurture, on the other hand, refers to the broad suite of environmental influences (experience). This argument comes into play when considering individuals (women) and whether their behaviour can be separated from the social context (Sameroff, 2010, 13).

The Fawcett Society (2013, 13–15) reminds us that women are in the majority (51 per cent) of the population and yet, power is overwhelmingly concentrated in the minority, men. For example, at the time of writing, out of 22 Cabinet members of the UK government only seven are women, and they argue that women are 'not generally perceived as powerful; this perception filters throughout society, reinforces gendered assumptions and stereotypes of what a leader looks like, and impacts directly on women's power and agency' (Fawcett Society, 2013, 15). Although, the working culture for women has come a long way since the UK's Equal Pay Act 1970, much remains unchanged. Progress towards equality continues to be slow, possibly because women are good at adapting to flexible working and organising their time around work and familial duties. Men are culturally still not expected to step outside their social norms and adapt to life changes (Boundless, 2014).

Why is flexible working important in the charity sector?

To be able to appreciate why flexible working is important within the charity sector, we need to understand the distinctive profile of its workforce. The data presented in Table 14.1 provides a snapshot of the voluntary sector workforce by both gender and employment status (note that the NCVO definition of the 'voluntary sector' does not coincide exactly with the legal definition of a 'charity', but a high proportion of voluntary sector workers are employed in charities). Although the data relates to 2011, the figures do provide appropriate granular detail as compared to the statistical data available on the Charity Commission website, which merely splits the workforce by employees, trustees and volunteers (Charity Commission, 2012).

Interestingly, neither the Charity Commission nor the NCVO provide a further breakdown relating to the split between full-time and part-time employees by gender. Baines (2006, 198) has stated that 'care work is a central concern of most women's professions' and so, 'caring for and about people is generally inseparable within the tasks and goals of this type of work, and is a major source of meaning and job satisfaction'. This theme of care will be discussed again later within the context of familial teamwork; the primary carer role extends not just to the home but to caring for others within the workplace – team, department, organisation and extending to vulnerable clients within the community.

As the statistics demonstrate, women account for a significant proportion of the workforce, dominating both full and part-time domains. As noted above, the initial drive for promoting flexible working was to support women juggling their dual roles as employee and primary carer. However, as we later show, only a 'qualifying employee' within the UK workforce is able to exercise the right to request flexible working arrangements and an employer does not have to grant it (although they do need to give a valid business case for rejection). However, it is unclear whether such provisions help to improve women's position in the workplace and their career development. Houston and Waumsley (2003, 4) conclude that:

> More should be done to establish that flexible working does not necessarily mean poor career prospects. This means making flexible working available at all levels of occupations and challenging the notion that working longer hours means advancement. If this does not happen there is

a risk that flexible working will further segregate men and women in the workforce.

Dex and Scheibl (2002) suggest that unless men overcome their fear of loss of opportunities and promotion, and begin to utilise the family-friendly policies themselves, the gender division will continue to increase, with women taking the majority of part-time and flexible work, and thus, remaining disadvantaged in terms of their career development.

Flexible working was initially presented at the same time as employers were moving increasingly towards individualised contracts and a greater deployment of casual and temporary staff. Thus, trade unions saw flexibility as a major threat to their constituencies and to collectivism (Wilton, 2004, 278). Unions had in the past sought to block the introduction of part-time, temporary and other non-standard employment contracts. In doing so, they could be seen to be acting conservatively, supporting skilled male workers as the employment norm and therefore, perpetuating the cultural perception of women as carers (Bradley, 2009, 93).

While we regard flexible working as an issue for both men and women, the up-take and expansion of organisational policies has been slow, with benefits frequently being only offered to, or taken up by women (Houston and Waumsley, 2003, 1; Grosen et al, 2012, 73). The Trades Union Congress (TUC) (2010, 1) has also more recently embraced flexible working, welcoming the government's proposals for increasing opportunities for both women and men:

> Working parents who are trying to combine a job or career with raising a young family will be relieved that ministers are considering allowing those with children over five the chance to take parental leave...Similarly men who are planning to become fathers in the not too distant future will be pleased that they may have to give their employers less notice to take paternity leave and so spend valuable time with their new families.

There are a number of reasons why the up-take of flexible-working policies may not be successful: first, cultural and behavioural attitudes of both employees and employers; second, flexible working policies may be regarded as likely to increase, rather than decrease gender disparities if implemented; third, policies tend to be aimed solely at women and/or carers; and fourth, the economic consequences (Dex,

1999; Houston and Waumsley, 2003, 45). Millar (2009, 18) and Walter (2010) however, believe that the problems go deeper, with roots in generations of conditioning about women's roles.

As increasing numbers of women enter the labour market, Pocock (2003) argues that with these current patterns of participation in employment and stasis in the domestic relations, roles between men and women, work and care collide. Knowing they have to take on a 'second shift' in the home may account for why women, at least, are happier with shorter working hours (Booth and van Ours, 2005). Better work–life balance might be attained less through flexible working for women but by persuading men to shoulder equitable domestic responsibility. However, the signs for women's equality are not looking good. For example, Australian research revealed that 40 per cent of young males to be 'open minimisers', who plan for their future wives to do all the housework and less than two-thirds of young women expect to share this housework equitably (Pocock, 2006, 143).

As highlighted earlier, the increasing participation of women in the charity labour force has resulted in 'the reality of needing flexibility for childcare or to care for elderly relatives' (Charity Times, 2007). To accommodate these changes, legislation including Employment Act 2006 and Work and Families Act 2006 addressed the right for employees with eldercare responsibilities and for fathers take paternity leave interchangeably with their partners. (In 2014, the right to request flexible working was then extended to *all* employees, regardless of whether or not they had caring responsibilities.)

These changes in legislation should have provided a stimulus for organisations to review their flexible working policies. However, our study found this was not the case with the four medium-sized charities that we studied in depth (East, 2013). Primarily, we found that the HR (human resources) function within these charities could not cope with these changes, either because it was under-developed or under-resourced or because there was no dedicated HR function at all, with HR responsibilities being carried out informally (Cunningham, 2010; see also the Family Friendly Working Hours Taskforce, 2010, 15). Thus, as a result, where legislative changes arise, the changes are either not communicated because they are not understood or they are neglected, because their importance is not appreciated and information is lost because it is not disseminated downwards to junior staff.

Investigation of flexible working in charities

To explore flexible working issues, a study was undertaken to pursue the following research questions: what is understood by the term flexible working within medium-sized charities; what flexible working practices are currently operational within medium-sized charities and what barriers and enablers affect the uptake of flexible-working practices (including funding and line-management) (East, 2013, 21).

We identified a lack of existing research regarding patterns of flexible working in UK charities. Our study focused on medium-sized charities (with an annual income between £500,000 and £5 million) registered in England and Wales. A multi-method approach was used: an initial postal questionnaire to 520 charities regarding their understanding and practices with flexible working was followed by detailed case studies in four charities involving one-to-one semi-structured interviews with staff from across the organisational hierarchy.

One of the questions in the postal questionnaire gave the respondent an opportunity to indicate a willingness to contribute further. The organisations partaking in the second phase were selected from these – they were all service-providing organisations in the field of care and support. Across the four charities, 30 interviews were conducted with a range of individuals ranging from chief executives to operational staff and volunteers. Attempts were also made to speak to trustees (board members) of the charities, but in each case this proved impossible within the timescale available.

The one-to-one semi-structured interviews included both open and closed questions, though the presentation of these was not fixed, in order to achieve a discussion was which as natural as possible and providing the interviewee with virtual vocal space (East, 2013, 90). All interviews were digitally recorded. They were initially transcribed by hand by the researcher with repeated playing where necessary to glean missing words and to note specific nuances such as body language, pauses and other characteristics personal to the interviewee. These hand-written transcription drafts were then dictated back in into Microsoft Word using speech recognition software. The final versions of the transcriptions were uploaded into NVivo (a qualitative data analysis computer software package which is designed to work with rich text-based data where granular levels of analysis are required).

Data analysis and outcomes

The comments and experiences of respondents from both phases of the study were analysed in relation to the three aforementioned research questions (East, 2013, 21). The postal questionnaire incorporated 23 questions and the interviews used 12 semi-structured questions. The postal questionnaire explored the profile of each charity through funding, governance, policies and workforce while the interviews examined flexible working policies and options available, barriers and tensions, communications surrounding flexible-working and whether and how decreasing funding affected the offer and uptake of flexible working. Both men and women were interviewed (6:24 ratio).

The prominent finding was that within the context of formal flexible working policies an informal flexible working model had been established by female junior staff members and was utilised solely by them. Men were less inclined to ask for flexible working, saying that they thought it was for women, as primary carers as compared to men and they generally felt uncomfortable approaching the subject. In contrast, women had asked about flexible working options but had been discretely refused or stalled. Reasons given concerned funding and as stated in the postal questionnaires 'offering part-time working has allowed us to maintain the same number of employees when facing a reduction in funding, without making redundancies'. The senior participants appeared to have a better access to flexible working practices than more junior staff.

It emerged that an informal flexible working model had been established by junior female workers, emerged out of discussions about the rewarding in-house 'family' relationships, and intimate 'team' bonds enjoyed by these female junior staff members, surpassing the immediate concerns of reduced funding. Their philanthropic beliefs, charitable ethos, commitment to each other as well as to the charity gave them the strength and stability to accept change and enabled them to adapt to survive against external influencing factors. Through this ubiquitous 'family' team characteristic, reinforced by volunteer support, and familial oriented language, these distinguishing traits were found to be at the heart of what we term the emergent 'female junior informal flexible working model'.

This informal model was found to have emerged as a result of three main drivers. First, these staff had experienced inconsistent communication and decision-making regarding HRM policies, including flexible working, from line-managers and employers; in contrast, the chief executive officers (CEOs) believed that flexible working options were regularly communicated. Second, instances were found in all organisations of informal HRM agreements between female junior employees and their line-managers. These agreements were dependent upon the working relationship between the employee and their line-manager or employer, and this echoes similar findings by Corby and White (1999), Cunningham (2001) and Yeandle et al (2003). Third, it was found that team-work based on the familial relationships among the predominantly female workforce, together with the habitual informality of operation and understanding of the flexible working concept, led to the development of these patterns of working.

The crux of the model centres on the strong familial ties between fellow female junior staff members. When interviewed, both female junior managers and front-line staff reiterated that their team worked as a 'family' and being a close-knit 'team', 'togetherness' meant that the women worked closely and intimately together – sharing knowledge and covering for each other when fellow team members had to leave earlier to deal with their own personal home-life issues; for example, attending to a poorly child, taking an elderly parent to a hospital appointment or attending a dental appointment. The utilisation of norms such as 'family' and 'togetherness' may have more salience within the team as compared to outside the team culture. This strong working bond is demonstrated by comments such as:

> [We have a] mixed staff, [of] which some have got young children, some have got older children, so it's, we, we [are] normally able to sort it out…cover the service. (Interview with junior female manager–team manager)

Hogg and Vaughan defined group cohesion as 'the way it 'hangs together' as a tightly knit, self-contained entity characterised by uniformity of conduct and mutual support among members' (1998 cited in Gross, 2010, 489). In our interviews we found that this cohesiveness had been strengthened because of the following factors: 1) the similarity of the team members in terms of junior role status, female, similar age and task, with the majority being care-providers; 2) solidarity, cultivated, and nourished through intimate language usage supporting team culture; 3) size and stability – the teams are relatively small and relationships are established, thus further enhancing cohesive strength; and 4) success – the informal model supports individuals while also meeting the group and organisational needs – team members providing cover, supporting others with heavy workloads and so forth.

The following quotes are from two female front-line staff members and a junior manager, respectively:

> Because everyone is so, um [pause], approachable and quite understanding and maybe it's because it's a charity... it works, it works better, like it's almost a give and take. (Interview with female front-line support–employment law advisor)

> You see other people, I guess do it, so I think it's just...over time the more comfortable you get, the more, you know, the more flexible everyone becomes. (Interview with female front-line support–executive assistant)

> For an organisation this size, this small...and it's more hands-on, it's more of a, it's more nurturing as an environment... being so small everyone is aware of everyone's arrangements to, to, to a degree...it should benefit them. (Interview with junior female manager–charity manager)

Throughout the study we noticed the repetitive usage of encouraging, heartening and supportive language and we suggest that this further enhanced the attachments and friendships between the female junior staff, promoting and accentuating these unified intimate bonds. Women participants acknowledged that they are still the primary societal care-providers, as illustrated by a female senior manager who said, 'Unless we stop it, and go more like Sweden, we're never going to get to that equal, um, balance.' In addition, comments from the postal questionnaires revealed support for the idea that women are the primary societal care-provider:

> We are predominantly a female organisation, a lot of who have primary care for their children. (Questionnaire response charity 319)

> We find [the established formal flexible working arrangements] helpful in facilitating different client groups. It also keeps women staff with families. (Questionnaire response charity 317)

Our findings support those of McDonald et al (2005), Eikhof et al (2007), Millar (2009; 2010) and Walter (2010). With the care function being extended from home into the workplace (Baines, 2006) and in particular, to their in-house team, or 'family', this care function further accentuates and promotes the feeling that they are valuable contributors in the delivery of core services, thus increasing their personal self-esteem. Furthermore, we identified a commonly held belief in the synergy between their personal values aligning with those of the organisation:

> [It's] because we have to be so flexible within our work anyway. Um, we're also very caring organisation, so I think the two go hand-in-hand, be[ing] a charity and a caring organisation...our culture. But at the same time, because you give, you get an awful lot back...we're a family. (Interview with CEO)

> [It's] relationships and it's all about the people you work with...with hand on heart that, not one of my staff wouldn't come in and work two hours for somebody that had to, whose child was ill or had to take the child to hospital, carer for somebody that had fallen...you see, we sound like one big family. (Interview with senior female manager–day services manager)

> I think for *me*, because obviously, we're in the carer profession, our profession's *care*...we care about our staff in supporting our, erm, values. (Interview with senior female manager–deputy manager)

> Not, not because it's a charity. But then, it's yeah, it's the culture! (Interview with junior female manager–financial accountant)

Management accepted that employees performed large volumes of unpaid overtime which was 'officially invisible' (Baines, 2004a, 282; 2004b, 22; East, 2013, 196). As noted earlier, there was limited support from HRM: for example, several organisations allowed TOIL (time off in lieu) to be accrued when staff had worked additional hours, but once it reached above a certain level, it would be lost. In addition, findings confirmed that the key employees who undertook 'paid work for an external organisation [in order to keep] the organisation in operation' were female junior staff members (junior managers and front-line workers). The following quote from one of the female junior managers exemplifies and supports Baines' findings (East, 2013, 196):

> Um, sometimes there's clients that need seeing, um, like this evening, I'm going to have to work late because somebody needs something doing. I can't, I can't actually fit it into my working day, um, and that's a real pain in the arse, because I want to go home and cook tea, but at the same time, I've got to do it...we have organisational needs, our clients need to see us...really within office hours, but...(Interview with junior female manager–family mediation worker)

One male CEO stated, 'I would be the first to be told if there were problems', suggesting that senior management were not openly aware of the unpaid overtime being undertaken in order to accommodate heavy workloads and service-user needs at the expense of personal familial time, while remaining 'officially invisible' (Baines, 2004b, 22). This supports the idea that senior management were 'indulging' particular work patterns in which cooperation and loyalty were elicited through a regime of leniency and paternalism (Gouldner, 1954; Burawoy, 1982). The informal flexible working patterns entertained by the female junior staff members were comfortable to senior managers who knew that the work was being delivered, as evidenced in both the postal questionnaire and semi-structured interviews. The work undertaken outside core hours, because 'our clients need to see us' (female junior manager–family mediation worker), was altruistic, emotionally engaging and self-sacrificing.

It could be argued that the junior female staff members were acting professionally and undertaking additional unpaid work through a sense of duty, but the semi-structured interviews provided a granular insight to their rationale and demonstrated the extent to which their commitment was rooted in personal values, bonds with fellow work colleagues and a suite of complex psychological allegiances to both, colleagues, clients and the organisation.

This enhanced the motivation of staff to remain within the charity sector, providing and supporting vulnerable service-users. However, analysing the interviews through Glaserian grounded theory (Glaser and Strauss, 1967) suggesting that the adopted 'family' framework also gave female staff members a degree of work–life balance through flexible working, which in turn meant that they saw the charitable organisation in a positive light, as benefits could be seen for both parties, as the following quotes demonstrate:

Staff are aware we take a positive attitude to flexible working. (Questionnaire response charity 105)

It enables me to spend more quality time with my son...it means I can do breakfast, lunch and dinner...there's a lot of qualities; it improves my work–life balance. (Interview with junior female manager–children centre programme manager)

It gives me a little more freedom...if I think I need to sleep in a little bit more, because I'm tired and I think I would be more productive if I had more sleep...it allows me to be more effective. (Interview with female front-line staff–business manager)

I can do things that I would normally have to take maybe annual leave for. (Interview with female front-line staff–support worker)

This positive perception of the organisation further enriched their work ethic and boosted their sense of self-esteem and of doing something worthwhile (Gallie et al, 1998; Zappala, 2000; Schimel, 2004). Atkinson and Hall (2011) have suggested that flexible working makes employees 'happy' and that there are attitudinal and behaviour links between this happiness and discretionary behaviour, and our interviews give some support for this proposition.

Another important theme that emerged from the data was the utilisation of volunteers in support of staff's flexible working. All categories of interviewees recognised the role of volunteers as 'absolutely wonderful, um, without their commitment, um, life would be extremely difficult' (female CEO). Another female senior manager commented, that 'they support [us] immensely and help us do a lot of things'. A female worker, in a front-line role, said, that 'this place wouldn't run without volunteers. [We] wouldn't be here without the volunteers'.

However, interestingly, many CEOs, senior managers and junior managers rejected the ideas that volunteers had an impact on the flexible working of paid staff, took on paid staff responsibilities or would have an impact on funding. A female CEO commented that the input of volunteers 'helps in the delivery of the work, but not in terms of flexible working'.

By contrast the view of front-line staff regarding the contribution of volunteers was that they 'predominantly use them for, um, staff that we don't, we can't claim time for'. Front-line staff members concluded that 'for me to do my flexible hours, I would first rely on my volunteers' and 'if someone wanted to cut their hours or anything, you could have the volunteers there...to come in and help us out if we needed them to'.

Volunteers were also seen to help with respect to dealing with paid staff responsibilities: 'they can assist to fill the vacancies that we have within a specific project' and deal with work 'that we don't have time to look through' (interview with female front-line worker–executive assistant).

Thus, the interview data demonstrated that volunteers acted as enablers from both a funding and an HRM perspective, being a resource to bridge a gap; thereby, allowing charities to claim against contracts and grants for work carried by non-paid employees, and thereby, also saving on costs. In particular, for front-line staff, this additional resource made it possible for them to enjoy flexible working, knowing that because their work was covered they could come in late or leave earlier to deal with familial and personal matters. A volunteer would undertake a 'bit of reception work, do a bit of typing' (interview with a female volunteer) to provide the necessary cover. This utilisation of volunteers was unofficial and not formally recognised by junior managers and above. However, managers did recognise that heavy workloads were delivered with a limited amount of paid resource, suggesting that they were aware of these practices and were 'turning a blind eye' in order to achieve workloads; such non-disclosure of resources utilised has also been observed by Baines (2004b, 22).

The strength of the familial culture developed within the in-house teams (including the use of volunteers where applicable) has acted as an enabler for female junior staff members to be able to enjoy a degree of flexible working and, concomitantly, a sense of emancipation. So, the informal flexible working model developed by female junior staff has succeeded against the perceived and/or real barriers of line management and allows women to have a degree of control over their work–life balance.

Concluding comments

In examining flexible working practices in charities, our study found that the flexible working concept is broad, complex, intricate and multifaceted. But we need to ask how far these practices that accompany it support or hinder women's emancipation in the workplace.

Emancipation can be described as the liberation from a form of restraint, or from emotional and psychological manacles – whether 'real' or perceived (East, 2013). In the workplace there will always be certain limitations and restrictions either through in-house policies and procedures or through legislative policies such as that of non-smoking within the workplace. Furthermore, specific health and safety guidance needs to be followed for one's personal safety and wellbeing. But whether these are considered as a hindrance or as supportive depends upon one's own life experiences and perceptions, as well as the practices that support them.

The study found a number of extrinsic and intrinsic influencing factors affecting the successful uptake of flexible working, which had an impact, whether direct or indirect, on the degree of emancipation that women enjoy within the charitable workplace (East, 2013). The results are somewhat mixed depending on whether we are considering formal or informal practices, which in turn are dependent upon a number of factors such as seniority and role status.

The CEOs, whether male or female (1:3 ratio among the interview sample), worked at a different pace compared to staff in the rest of their organisations, and together with the freedom to manage their own time supported by technological functionality, not readily available to all staff, were in a position to work from home or a mobile office. Because CEOs operated within a more flexible framework, they responded positively when discussing their own work–life balance and the benefits it provided for their personal family life. Senior managers, although having a good understanding of what options were available in-house, saw in addition that flexible working practices were for the benefit of all employees, not just for women who were juggling employment and caring responsibilities. These senior managers typically held the view that maintaining a work–life balance was primarily an individual concern; a position echoed by authors such as van Wanrooy et al (2013, 33) who write that 'balancing work and family responsibilities [is] the responsibility of the individual employees'. The senior managers appeared to conclude that work–life balance was achievable if an individual managed their own time.

In contrast, junior staff saw flexible working more as a working partnership between employee and employer. It could be argued that formal flexible working practices ideally give employees the necessary support and freedom to accommodate personal familial needs. However, the findings demonstrated that even if formal policies were in place, either women were unable to use them because of workloads and deadlines to meet, or, where they had banked time under TOIL, this was capped and lost if not taken within specified time-periods, or lost because workloads never had the opportunity to utilise to their 'earned' benefit. Therefore, in practice, this equal partnership did not exist. Female junior staff members continued rarely reaped the rewards promised at staff induction and interviews regarding work–life balance.

Our study found, however, that for junior managers and front-line workers informal (rather than formal) flexible working practices were being practised, created by these women to address their own needs and their commitment to the clients whom they supported. Through this approach they achieved a measure of emancipation, which supported both their personal roles as parents/carers and their commitment to their clients in the charity.

The starting point for our research (East, 2013, 54–65) was the increasing numbers of women employed in the charitable sector who bring with them 'the reality of needing flexibility for childcare or to care for elderly relatives' (Charity Times, 2007). As we noted, legislation in the UK has sought to address the needs of all those with caring responsibilities – not just mothers but also fathers and employees with eldercare responsibilities. Further flexibility may emerge as a result of a change in UK employment rights surrounding paternity pay and leave which took effect in November 2014. This change now allows fathers to take one to two weeks paid ordinary paternity leave, and up to 26 weeks additional paternity leave should their partner return to work. This study was concerned with the right to request flexible working arrangements for both men and women, rather than specific issues of maternity and paternity leave, though such changes in legislation can act as a stimulus for organisations to review their policies. However, this finding was not observed in the present study. We speculate that this may be explained by the poorly resourced HR function in these medium-sized charities, which simply cannot cope with these changes.

It was found in both the postal survey and in the case studies that such flexible working policies as existed in these medium-sized charities were rudimentary and biased towards female staff. The policies focused upon women as the primary carers for adults and children and so the theoretical models of flexible working, which have been advanced by other authors, were not wholly supported. The position that 'the underlying rationale [of such policies] is the desire to create "equity" in the allocation of organisational benefits' (Doherty and Manfredi, 2006, 242) was not demonstrated in our findings, that policies were biased towards female staff rather than embracing *all* employees. We note that promoting flexible working to *all* staff allows a charity a greater pool of employees to utilise and thereby, 'understanding there are differences between employees and that these differences, if properly managed, are an asset to work being done more efficiently and effectively' (Kandola and Fullerton, 1994, 7). Diversity incorporates race, disability and other protected characteristics as well as gender, of course, but the study found that an intangible wedge continues to divide men and women. This makes it increasingly difficult, both culturally and socially, for male employees to be accepted as primary carers, while also preventing women from shedding the label of primary carer (Frank and Lowe, 2003).

The female junior informal flexible working model emerged as a result of informal rules being acknowledged and being allowed to continue without HRM policies, including formal flexible working, being regularly promoted or, as one female CEO put it, 'not [being] kept live enough'. So, informal practices crept in and were established. They were sanctioned by line-managers with their predominantly female junior employees and allowed to operate based on trust where 'unofficially, um, you know, I'm trusted, so I start later then, you know, I'm trusted I will work my hours' (interview with female front-line worker). Initially, these informal practices arose depending on the working relationships between employees and line-management, and the importance of this relationship is highlighted in the literature (Corby and White, 1999; Cunningham, 2001; Yeandle et al, 2003). However, depending on the line-managers' behavioural attitude and consistency in decision-making, flexible-working requests might or might not be granted. Hence, against the background of formal flexible working policies, there are acknowledged informal flexible working agreements; female junior employees have developed an informal model which flexes to accommodate the needs of the female junior staff members professionally and domestically.

Again, this informal model is strengthened through the sense of solidarity reiterated and maintained through the use of familial language. This modus operandi gives the female junior staff a degree of emancipation and control as they trust that if they need to deal with an emergency or need personal time, they would have the support of their in-house 'family' to provide the necessary cover. Moreover, front-line staff members have the support of their volunteers who provide yet another tier of requirement if required. This sense of freedom extends further the possibility of emancipation within personal and work arenas.

In summary, female junior staff members have achieved a greater amount of emancipation within the workplace as a result of having the support of each other and, where necessary, volunteers in achieving a flexible working regime. While male junior staff might occasionally be included, the model was clearly female-led and rooted in female employees understanding of their own needs alongside their obligations to charity clients.

Even this limited emancipation is, however, diminished by the fact that female junior staff will strive to ensure that the needs of the service user are met before their own personal needs. Yet psychologically, to some extent emancipation has increased as a consequence of having done something worthwhile (Gallie et al, 1998) and been a valuable contributor to a cause about which that they feel strongly.

The importance of commitment as a resource is acknowledged within the sector: 'It's more than just a job…we are fortunate that the people we employ are passionate about helping people in need. They are motivated by our cause, and not just because it is a job' (Third Sector, 2012, 21). However, our study raises concerns about the extent to which such commitment is relied upon and exploited by senior managers, operating within tight financial constraints. While the informal model developed and maintained by these junior staff provides them with the support they need, by its very nature it is not available to all.

This chapter has demonstrated that the junior female staff, working within the four medium-sized charitable organisations under review, have created an innovative and resourceful informal flexible working model which addresses their personal needs and provides them with a degree of control and freedom, while meeting the needs of the organisation. What makes this model successful is the cohesive, familial, intimate and robust teamwork among the women. Based on our research we conclude that medium-sized charities appear receptive to the ideas of flexible working and yet are not immediately responsive to it and so, the flexible working practices that have emerged are laissez-faire rather than professionally driven. Therefore, informal practices are developed, but they are led by female junior staff members and have the, perhaps unintended, consequence of reinforcing the stereotype of woman as primary carer. The result is that emancipation of women in the charity workplace with regard to flexible working does occur, but the successful implementation of flexible working arrangements and the extent to which they lead to emancipation achieved is driven by them and is thus fragile as a result.

References

Atkinson, C, Hall, L, 2011, Flexible working and happiness in NHS, *Employee Relations* 33, 2, 88–105

Baines, D, 2004a, Caring for nothing: Work organization and unwaged labour in social services, *Work, Employment and Society* 18, 2, 267–95

Baines, D, 2004b, Seven kinds of work – only one paid: Raced, gendered and structured work in social services, *Atlantis* 28, 2, 19–29

Baines, D, 2006, Forum: Quantitative indicators 'Whose needs are being served?', Quantitative Metrics and the reshaping of social services, *Studies in Political Economy* 01/2006, 77, 195–209

Bazeley, P, 2006, The contribution of computer software to integrating qualitative and quantitative data and analyses, *Research in the Schools* 13, 1, 64–74

Booth, AL, van Ours, JC, 2005, *Hours of work and gender identity: Does part-time work make the family happier?*, Canberra: Centre for Economic Policy Research, Australian National University

Boundless, 2014, From birth, children are assigned a gender and are socialized to certain gender roles based on their biological sex, *Gender and Sociology*, www.boundless.com/psychology/textbooks/boundless-psychology-textbook/gender-and-sexuality-15/gender-414/gender-and-sociology-296-12831/

Bradley, H, 2009, Whose flexibility? British employees' responses to flexible capitalism, in EJ Skorstad, H Ramsdal (eds) *Flexible organizations and the new working life: A European perspective*, Farnham: Ashgate Publishing Limited

Burawoy, M, 1982, The written and the repressed in Gouldner's industrial sociology, *Theory and Society*, Special Issue in Memory of Alvin W Gouldner 11, 6, 831–51

Charity Commission, 2012, Charities in England and Wales, www.charity-commission.gov.uk/find-charities/

Charity Times, 2007, Bending the rules, www.charitytimes.com/pages/ct_features/march07/text_features/ct_march07_feature4_bending_the_rules.htm

Corby, S, White, G, 1999, From the new right to new labour, in S Corby, G White (eds) *Employee relations in the public services*, pp 3–25, London: Routledge

Cullen, L, Christopher, T, 2012, Career progression of female accountants in the state public sector, *Australian Accounting Review* 22, 1, 68–85

Cunningham, I, 2001, Sweet charity! Managing employee commitment in the UK voluntary sector, *Employee Relations* 23, 3, 226–39

Cunningham, I, 2010, The HR function in purchaser–provider relationships: Insights from the UK voluntary sector, *Human Resource Management Journal* 20, 2, 189–205

Dex, S, 1999, *Families and labour market: Trends, pressures and policies*, York: Joseph Rowntree Foundation

Dex, S, Scheibl, F, 2002, *SMEs and flexible-working arrangements*, Bristol: The Policy Press and York: Joseph Rowntree Foundation

Doherty, L, Manfredi, S, 2006, Action research to develop work–life balance in a UK university, *Women in Management Review* 21, 3, 241–59

East, SA, 2013, *Flexible-working in charitable organizations: An exploration of barriers and opportunities*, PhD Thesis, Sheffield: Sheffield Hallam University

Eikhof, DR, Warhurst, C, Haunschild, A, 2007, Introduction: What work? What life? What balance? Critical reflections on the work–life balance debate, *Employee Relations* 29, 4, 325–33

Family Friendly Working Hours Taskforce, 2010, *Flexible working: Working for families, working for business*, London: Department for Work and Pensions

Fawcett Society, 2013, *Sex and power 2013: Who runs Britain?*, Centre for Women and Democracy, www.fawcettsociety.org.uk/wp-content/uploads/2013/02/Sex-and-Power-2013-FINAL-REPORT.pdf

Favara, M, 2012, The cost of acting 'girly': Gender stereotypes and educational choices, *Working Paper Series* 36, UniCredit and Universities, Knight of Labor Ugo Foscolo Foundation, http://unicreditanduniversities.eu/uploads/assets/UWIN/WP_Favara_MF.pdf

Frank, KE, Lowe, DJ, 2003, An examination of alternative work arrangements in private accounting practice, *Accounting Horizons* 17, 2, 139–51

Gallie, D, White, M, Cheng, Y, Tomlinson, M, 1998, *Restructuring the employment relationship*, Oxford: Oxford University Press

Galton, F, 1876, The history of twins, as a criterion for the relative powers of nature and nurture, *Journal of the Royal Anthropological Institute* 5, 1876, 391–406

Glaser, BG, Strauss, AL, 1967, *The discovery of grounded theory: Strategies for qualitative research*, New York: Aldine de Gruyter

Gouldner, A, 1954, *Patterns of industrial bureaucracy: A case study of modern factory administration*, New York: The Free Press

Grosen, SL, Holt, H, Lund, HL, 2012, The naturalization of gender segregation in a Danish bank, *Nordic journal of working life studies* 2, 1, 61–79

Gross, R, 2010, *Psychology: The science of mind and behaviour*, 6th edn, London: Hodder Education

Hines, M, Johnston, K, Golombok, S, Rust, J, Stevens, M, Golding, J, 2002, Prenatal stress and gender role behaviour in girls and boys: A longitudinal, population study, *Hormones and Behaviour* 42, 2, 126–34

Hogg, MA, Vaughan, GM, 1998, *Social psychology: An introduction* (2nd edn), Hemel Hempstead: Prentice-Hall/Harvester Wheatsheaf

Houston, DM, Waumsley, JA, 2003, *Attitudes to flexible-working and family life*, York: Joseph Rowntree Foundation

Kandola, R, Fullerton, J, 1994, Diversity: More than just an empty slogan, *Personnel Management*, November, 46–9

Leaper, C, Friedman, CK, 2007, The socialization of gender, in JE Grusec, PD Hastings (eds) *Handbook of socialization: Theory and research*, pp 561–87, New York: Guilford Press

McDonald, P, Guthrie, D, Bradley, L, Shakespeare-Finch, J, 2005, Investigating work–family policy aims and employee experience's, *Employee Relations* 27, 5, 478–94

Martinuzzi, A, Kudlak, R, Faber, C, Wiman, A, 2011, CSR activities and impacts of the retails sector, *Research Institute for Managing Sustainability (RIMAS) Working Papers* 5, Vienna: Vienna University of Economics and Business Administration

Millar, F, 2009, *The secret world of the working mother: Juggling work, kids, and sanity*, London: Vermilion

Miller, F, 2010, How dirty socks kill feminism, *Radio Times*, 6-12 March, pp 16–18

NCVO (National Council of Voluntary Organisations), 2013, *The UK Civil Almanac*, http://data.ncvo.org.uk/a/almanac13/about-the-almanac/fast-facts-2/

Pocock, B, 2003, *The work/life collision: What work is doing to the Australians and what to do about it*, Leichhardt, NSW: Federation Press

Pocock, B, 2006, *The labour market ate my babies*, Leichhardt, NSW: Federation Press

Ross, R, 2010, *Psychology: The Science of mind and behaviour* (6th edn), London: Hodder Education

Sameroff, A, 2010, A unified theory of development: A dialectic integration of nature and nurture, *Child Development* 81, 1, 6–22

Schaffer, HR, 2004, *Introducing child psychology*, Oxford: Blackwell Publishing

Schimel, J, 2004, Why do people need self-esteem? A theoretical and empirical review, *Psychological Bulletin* 130, 3, 435–68

Third Sector, 2012, Charity pulse: Mood of the sector hits a new low, workforce survey finds, www.thirdsector.co.uk/news/1138900/charity-pulse-mood-sector-hits-new-low-workforce-survey-finds/

TUC (Trades Unions Congress), 2010, *TUC welcomes plans to increase flexible-working*, www.tuc.org.uk/workplace/tuc-17456-f0.cfm

Van Wanrooy, B, Bewley, H, Bryson, A, Forth, J, Freeth, S, Stokes, L, Wood, S, 2013, *The 2011 workplace employment relations study: First findings*, London: Department for Business, Innovation and Skills

Walter, N, 2010, *Living dolls: The return of sexism*, London: Virago Press

Williams, JMG, Best, DL, 1994, Cross-cultural views of women and men, in WJ Lonner, RS Malpass (eds) *Psychology and culture*, pp 191–6, Boston: Allyn and Bacon

Wilton, N, 2004, *Chapter 10: Employment relations*, www.sagepub.com/wilton/Chapter%2010%20-%20Employment%20Relations.pdf

Wober, JM, Reardon, G, Fazal, S, 1987, Personality, character aspirations and patterns of viewing among children, Independent Broadcasting Authority Research Department (IBA) *Research Papers*, London: IBA

Yeandle, S, Phillips, J, Scheibl, F, Wigfield, A, Wise, S, 2003, *Line managers and family-friendly employment: Roles and perspectives*, Bristol: The Policy Press and York: Joseph Rowntree Foundation

Zappala, G, 2000, How many people volunteer in Australia and why do they do it?, *Research and Advocacy Briefing Paper*, September, 4, 1–4

Examining and contextualising Kenya's *Maendeleo ya Wanawake Organisation* (MYWO) through an African feminist lens

Anne Namatsi Lutomia, Brenda Nyandiko Sanya and Dorothy Owino Rombo

Introduction

In this chapter *Maendeleo ya Wanawake*, Kenya's oldest registered women's organisation (Wipper, 1975; Akin-Aina, 2011), serves as a point of entry for discussing feminisms in Kenya. The name of the organisation, *Maendeleo ya Wanawake*, directly translates into English as 'women's progress'. Despite the lack of systemic documentation of the organisation's activities (Udvardy, 1998), the historical realities of Kenyan women's work in both private/domestic and public spheres can be understood through this women's organisation, as it has drawn its agenda over time, first from the colonial, then post-colonial governments and finally, from western international donors (Aubrey, 1995). Here, we examine and analyse the success claims and empowerment activities that are attributed to the *Maendeleo ya Wanawake Organisation* (hereafter *Maendeleo*); the improvement of 'the quality of life of the rural communities especially women and youth in Kenya' (*Maendeleo ya Wanawake*, 2015). Given its history, it is intriguing that *Maendeleo* has not been at the forefront of championing women's rights agendas in comparison to younger organisations such as the Federation of Women Lawyers in Kenya (FIDA Kenya), Coalition on Violence against Women Kenya (COVAW-K) or Education Center for Women in Democracy (ECWD). We study *Maendeleo* because it is a prominent organisation. Even though this organisation has been in existence for more than 50 years it is not at the forefront of introducing and advocating for major political reform affecting women. With this in mind, we consider the role that *Maendeleo* played under colonial occupation up to the present day and how their activities have shaped the history of women's rights in Kenya.

We build upon the works of writers, researchers and academics such as Ama Ata Aidoo, Amina Mama, Asenath Bole Odaga, Bessie Head, Grace Ogot, Jane Bennett, Marjorie Oludhe Macgoye, Muthoni Likimani, Nancy Baraza, Pumla Dineo Gqola, Relebohile Moletsane, Sylvia Tamale and Teresa Barnes, among many others, to deploy multiple approaches to understand and give meaning to the experiences of women in both private and public spheres. These approaches allow us to interrogate *Maendeleo*'s work, in its different phases, up to the time of writing this chapter. We consider the intersectional nature of women's lives and interrogate *Maendeleo*'s ability to advance the struggle for female equality and to drive the political and social agendas that create room for many forms of female agency and self-determination (Oyewumi, 2003).

Following a historical content analysis, which explores relevant documents such as colonial government annual reports, historical texts, feminists' documents, relevant research, conference reports and papers, and media, we identify and contextualise the challenges and successes of the organisation. This chapter should be understood as an attempt to further gender justice work in the service of broader civil rights.

The roots of *Maendeleo*

Under British colonial rule Kenyans experienced numerous changes of societal structures and cultures, specifically connected to the imposition of paternalistic ideals that introduced wage labour in the service of the British Empire, and the globalisation of gender norms that were dictated by Victorian Britain. Women were not included or recognised in political life and very rarely occupied leadership positions. They were to be confined to the 'private sphere' (the home) under the rubrics of what McClintock (1995) described as the Victorian 'cult of domesticity'. For women, this meant limited participation in socio-economic and political affairs. This was central to the perpetuation of values of gender and power. These Victorian sensibilities, however, disregarded the political roles played by Kenyan women in pre-colonial and colonial history.[1] Wives of colonial masters and settlers crafted an agenda for the African women that reflected their own understanding of gender roles.

Following the Second World War, the British set up home craft clubs for African women in their African colonies. Kenya, a settler colony, was an exception as *Maendeleo* was set up in place of the home craft clubs (Wipper, 1975; Hansen, 1992). Founded in 1952, *Maendeleo* was embedded in the efforts of European colonial administrators' wives and female missionaries to 'civilise' the Kenyans (Wipper, 1975). *Maendeleo*'s domestic activities included gardening, childcare, basketry, pottery, traditional dancing, literacy classes, sports, clothing, building mud stoves, hygiene and health in the home, recipes or cooking demonstrations, tea parties and talks on current affairs. Neighbourhood clubs were formed throughout the country and members could visit and learn from each other (Wipper, 1975). African Community Development Officers administered these clubs and the patrons were colonial women.

Ironically, *Maendeleo* was founded during a period of cultural and political upheaval surrounding the struggle for independence, in the year when the British colonial government had declared a political state of emergency. According to Wipper (1975), these seemingly contradictory initiatives, that is, the colonial administration's political actions to limit and suppress African liberation struggles and the establishing of *Maendeleo* with its goals 'to promote the advancement of African women and to raise African living standards', are manifested in the incongruent political activities of the nation's oldest women's rights organisation. Other authors have argued that establishing *Maendeleo* was a ploy to give the colonial administration an organisation as a tool to use in fighting the uprising referred to as the Mau Mau rebellion (Aubrey, 1995; Maathai, 2004). Specifically Maathai (2004) observed that the goal was to purposefully distract women from taking part in the struggle for independence and to 'rehabilitate' those who had joined so that they could become collaborators. Through *Maendeleo* and other entities, the colonial government engaged in propaganda programmes, specifically focused on women's unmet needs of education, healthcare, access to clean and reliable water in an attempt to diffuse participation in the Mau Mau rebellion. A large number of black Africans were arrested, detained and interrogated between 1957 and 1960, with many women being imprisoned on prostitution claims (Presley, 1988, 504–5, 512, 513).

The experiences of the Mau Mau and *Maendeleo* are symptomatic of multiple attempts to civilise and subdue the indigenous people. Archival documents from the British colonial administration and media propaganda during the state of emergency rendered freedom fighters as criminals (thus providing justification for actions taken to physically subdue them). *Maendeleo* participated in this cultural subjugation; women, as primary caregivers, were introduced to Victorian ideals with the aim of turning them into 'good citizens according to British standards' (Presley, 1992, 67). After independence *Maendeleo* worked together with the post-colonial government towards a system of social and economic development (called *harambee* or 'pulling together'). Using this model they were able to improve local infrastructure and to acquire wealth such as collectively buying land (Udvardy, 1998).

This complicated relationship between the government and *Maendeleo* continued after political independence, when *Maendeleo*'s agenda was no longer directly driven by British colonial governance and instead, the organisation's focus shifted towards the interests of urban elite women and the ruling party. Although the organisation continued to work with both urban and rural women's self-help groups, the leadership aligned itself with the political elite and isolated rural women (Wipper, 1975). *Maendeleo* then became a platform for women's political activism, while simultaneously working as part of the national government's political machinery, to develop projects collaboratively with communities of women in parts of Kenya. This created political goodwill among women but obscured the longer-term goals of women's legal rights. *Maendeleo*'s cooperation with the one-party political leadership, revealed the complicated dynamics of this women's organisation that were challenged when Kenya became a multi-party democracy. At the time of writing, *Maendeleo* does not have as much political influence as it once did, has reinvented its public image and is now run as a non-governmental organisation (NGO) whose main work focuses on female genital cutting prevention, reproductive rights, gender and governance, women and development and research and development. This phenomenon is rooted in the history of Kenyan women's organisations. Admittedly, post-colonial Kenya saw the proliferation of women's groups that did not work together in solidarity thus leading to a somewhat sustained status quo because the women did selective interrogation of the system and aligned their organisational objectives accordingly.

Reading into *Maendeleo*'s activities

In the 1990s, *Maendeleo ya Wanawake* officially changed its name to *Maendeleo ya Wanawake Organisation*. This decision allowed the organisation, headquartered in Nairobi, to function as an NGO, with satellite offices all over Kenya. In this same decade, *Maendeleo* became one of the few indigenous initiatives in Kenya that is wholly managed by Kenyans.[2] In its current capacity as a women's voluntary NGO, *Maendeleo* is managed by an elected governing body and employed staff. According to official literature and information on its website

(*Maendeleo ya Wanawake*, 2015) the organisation has branches in every district of the country, more than 25,000 group affiliates and, over 3 million individual members; this represents a huge increase since its inception when, in 1954 there were approximately 300 clubs and a membership of 37,000 with 12 European and two African Home Craft Officers in charge (Wipper, 1975). Since then, *Maendeleo* has developed strategic plans targeted at the concerns of women with low socio-economic status. These plans have been focused on healthcare, economics and environmental concerns.[3]

The organisation's website currently reports that they are maintaining the following programmes:[4] first, engaging in the empowerment of women by enhancing women's, girls' and youth economic empowerment through creating awareness, education and information on income generating activities.[5] Second, they are increasing girls' access to education through girls' clubs, which provide counselling for girls and training for teachers. The girls are also encouraged to run income-generating activities through these clubs. Third, *Maendeleo* raises awareness through civic education, democratic rights and campaigning for an increase in the number of women in legislative and civic leadership positions. Finally, *Maendeleo* is involved in environmental legislation, in various capacities[6] (*Maendeleo ya Wanawake*, 2015).

Maendeleo records several achievements including the following: fighting for the rights of women and children, petitioning the government to review the measures taken against rape victims and violence against women and children, participating in the task force reviewing laws relating to women and children. It also boasts of being instrumental in the democratisation process, as many of the women who are current leaders have been directly or indirectly supported by virtue of experience gained while being a member of *Maendeleo* (*Maendeleo ya Wanawake*, 2015). *Maendeleo* therefore serves as proxy for politicians to achieve their goals, such as being elected by the votes of women under the banner of the organisation. However, the organisation's efforts to assist and advocate for women to secure leadership positions have not been deliberate.

Maendeleo is also actively involved in initiating alternative rites of passage to replace female genital cutting, within communities that practice the rite and for whom it has cultural significance (*Maendeleo ya Wanawake*, 2015). One such initiative is known as *Ntanira Na Mugambo* ('circumcision through words') which was developed in collaboration between *Maendeleo*, the local community and an international organisation called Program for Appropriate Technology in Health (PATH).[7] In this alternative rite, communities are educated on the biological and psychological consequences of female genital cutting on women's health and quality of life. This current project relies on establishing what Chelala (1998) describes as a new rite, a hybrid of the traditional practice, consisting of a week of seclusion, where the girls are taught basic anatomy and physiology, sexual and reproductive health, hygiene, gender issues, respect for adults, development of self-esteem and how to deal with peer pressure.

Challenges of *Maendeleo ya Wanawake*

Despite achieving some successes and launching important initiatives, *Maendeleo*'s replacement of European women with African women in leadership positions after independence was not free from elitism. The new leaders were usually related to the political elite and therefore this raises the question of whether or not their agendas were the interest of the rural woman, the largest population of women in the country. What was witnessed in the organisation was a shift in representation, with the change of leadership effectively foreclosing the voices of rural women, due to class and educational differences. Kabeer (2005) explains that 'efforts to create an increase in political or organisational participation of women at the local level have tended to favour the participation of elite women who are no more likely to represent the interests of poor women just by the fact of being female' (Kabeer, 2005, 17). With the new changes, the fledgling organisation's leadership was consumed with fundraising and promoting international contacts. In terms of community work, *Maendeleo* was mostly engaged in advocating women's equality in legislation and charitable activities such as donating clothes, food and medicine to the needy in the capital city. These activities were however limited to Nairobi, rural women were ignored. Consequently, these rural women complained that the government and the national executives of *Maendeleo* were indifferent to their problems (Wipper, 1975). Nonetheless, these rural women, having little choice, remained members of *Maendeleo*.

The government continuously praised *Maendeleo* and allowed community development workers to work with local groups, however they were not supportive in responding to training needs or providing travelling funds to the rural areas (Wipper, 1975). The relationship between the government and *Maendeleo* was delicate. *Maendeleo* depended on the government for facilities and personnel. The government on the other hand, stressed that *Maendeleo* was an autonomous entity, and insisted that it should be self-supporting; yet when the leaders of *Maendeleo* acted autonomously by expressing views that did not sit well with the government they were berated and told not to make political statements (Wipper, 1975).

In 1987, the ruling party, Kenya African National Union (KANU), decided to work with *Maendeleo* as part of its policy of recruiting of women voters. This collaboration essentially strengthened the party's reach in rural areas where *Maendeleo* had a strong membership base. KANU's support led to some confusion, as it was unclear whether KANU–*Maendeleo* was autonomous from the other women's wing of KANU.

In the years following, *Maendeleo* continued to be an influential organisation, with members of its leadership receiving presidential nominations to legislative and parastatal positions. Women members living in rural areas were important as their votes helped secure KANU projects and agendas. In short, *Maendeleo* acted in a similar way to a political party.

During this period, Kenyan feminists and women's rights activists participated in and contributed to two major international movements: the first, being the UN Decade for Women Conference in Nairobi, in which many women from the rural areas attended and participated in a lot of the activities along with other women from all over the world.[8] Second, as a follow-up to the conference, *Maendeleo* established a more diverse delegation that represented the nation at the UN Beijing Conference ten years later. However, after Beijing, efforts to execute proposals from the agenda were met with great resistance. Media and political statements reported legislators stating that women from organisations such as *Maendeleo* and FIDA Kenya were lesbians[9] and divorcees with ideas that would mislead Kenyan women and this functioned as a conversation stopper for changes from Beijing at the parliamentary level.

Nairobi, 'the unfinished agenda' and African feminisms

Nairobi welcomed thousands of women to the planned activities surrounding the Third Women's Conference to review and appraise the achievements of the UN Decade for Women (1975–85), and Forum '85, a parallel meeting organised under the leadership of Dame Nita Barrow[10] and Kenyan activists, academics, non-governmental and government agencies. Forum '85 was hailed as a pivotal political moment for Third World feminisms as well as a site where feminists nurtured developing transnational solidarities. Here in our analysis we use *Maendeleo*, because of its long legacy of engagement and national influence, to help us assess the legacy of the UN meeting and the accompanying Forum '85 in Kenyan women's participation in global discourses about political activism, identity formation, knowledge and cultural production. The July 1985 Nairobi meeting was host to over 14,000 women; 'the largest gathering of women in history' (O'Barr et al, 1986, 584). Prior to the arrival of the women from over 100 countries in the world, there was great anticipation of the significance of Forum '85. Barbadian Dame Nita Barrow, the chair of the organising committee predicted that 'you will see something that is not a conference but an encounter, a happening…a meeting of the minds of women' (Smolowe, 2005).

Accounts following the meeting confirmed Barrow's prediction. Nairobi was significant for a variety of reasons. As a location, Nairobi brought women from all over the world to Africa and, with African women's involvement in the planning process there was a shift in the understanding of power. Scholars who were present spoke about Nairobi as being significant because 'it was here, unfettered by formal responsibilities, that feminists openly expressed ideas, analysed experiences, and set forth expectations for the future' (O'Barr et al, 1986, 584).

The Nairobi Forum was defined by feminist scholars as a significant moment which ushered in transnational feminism as well as the development of a more complex understanding of global feminism, acknowledging 'the need to live with differences among women while building on the communalities of the female experience' (O'Barr et al, 1986, 585). In essays following the event Angela Davis, Beverly Guy-Sheftall and Amrita Basu described the space and dialogue that Nairobi provided. Davis discussed how Nairobi provided a social space where diasporic women and other women of colour met to explore 'the global socio-historical conditions of…oppression and [build] new bridges' (Davis, 1990, 111). Forum '85 served as an opposition to capitalist exploitation, patriarchal subjugation and racist oppression. Particularly for black women, this was a site where women from all parts of the diaspora could rethink their understanding of blackness/ notions of authenticity or exclusion and work towards a more critical view of patriarchy, capitalism and racism in postcolonial and post-slavery societies. Documents emerging from the meeting showed that women began embracing a transnational feminist framework, although this was beneficial only as an egalitarian space for resistance against oppression. Guy-Sheftall's (1986) descriptions of the opening ceremonies revealed the transnational solidarities that were already in place. She wrote of an opening speaker invoking the US black civil rights call 'We women shall overcome' as a reminder of the importance of the civil rights movement in the fight for women's rights, as well as its continuing impact on black people around the world (Guy-Sheftall, 1986, 597). However, she similarly positions the deliberations in Nairobi as a re-assertion that even while women shared experiences based on gender identity, they should not and cannot be perceived to be a monolithic group.

Maendeleo and the feminist agendas

It was within this same decade that *Maendeleo* was co-opted by KANU, the ruling political party of the time. The political dynamics of Kenya have had a detrimental impact on the feminist agenda for all women in Kenya, regardless of class, race or ethnicity. Indicators of women's wellbeing, including access to education, healthcare, wealth and the like, show national and regional disparities between men and women and also between women from different regions. Although the first African leader of *Maendeleo*, Phoebe Asiyo, declared that the transition in leadership from white women to African women would enable the organisation to be more relevant to the needs of African women, Aubrey (1995) observed that rural-based African women continued to be marginalised. Thus the prevailing political agenda of those in power over *Maendeleo* and the divide across ethnic, class, gender and international interests ensured that *Maendeleo* was limited in its ability to articulate and work towards any specific, far-reaching feminist agenda with a national perspective.

Furthermore, *Maendeleo* didn't alter its historical focus on domesticity; instead the organisation introduced technology to facilitate women to do their chores more expediently. *Maendeleo* didn't address domestic work as a labour concern and as integral to economic activity; rather domestic work was considered to belong purely to the private sphere. Improving women's domestic work was thus understood to be a service to capitalism. However, if providing assistance to expedite women's chores could be considered a feminist goal, then *Maendeleo* did achieve this in selective regions such as the Central and Eastern Provinces.

Some rural Kenyan women maintained that *Maendeleo* did not have the structures in place that are conducive to promoting women's issues (Udvardy, 1998). Aubrey's research (1995) also uncovered negative sentiments regarding the role of *Maendeleo* in promoting women's rights; interviewees observed that politicians both in the colonial and post-colonial governments had influence over the organisation. Aubrey (1995) also added that its involvement in donor driven activities also added to the unpopularity of *Maendeleo* because the proposed programmes did not meet the needs of the women they served.

The subaltern speaking?

In our attempts to understand the marginalised rural and the poor women who *Maendeleo* had a mission to serve, and how it failed them so significantly, we draw on Gayatri Chakravorty Spivak's ground-breaking and incisive essay, *Can the subaltern speak?* (1988). In this essay Spivak argues that for the subaltern[11] to be heard, she must develop and adopt western ways of knowing, reasoning and understanding. Spivak posits that as the intellectual field uses the language of the centralised in western thought, the subaltern can never express her own reasoning, forms of knowledge and understanding or logic. Thus, the intellectual is complicit in the creation of the Other as a shadow of the Self. As a way out of this impasse Spivak offers the processes of text deconstruction as a 'safeguard' to combat the repression or exclusion of 'alterities' (radical 'Others' to the dominant world view); stressing that deconstruction's concentration on the 'violence' of hierarchical binary oppositions (between male and female, the West and the rest, and so forth) creates space for the movement from literary theory to radical politics. To truly engage with the subaltern, the intellectual would need to de-centre herself from the position of expert, and privilege the voice of the subaltern in the dominant discourse.

What is important is that Spivak (1988) cautions against the misconception that the subaltern is part of a homogeneous, or essentialist group. For this reason, she rejects the hope that political movements can unite the subaltern group. She challenges such essentialist thinking[12] by proposing that those who romanticise the subaltern are trapped in a reproduction of the very colonialist discourses they critique. Based on the premise that identity is relational, rather than essentialist, she calls for the creation of strategic alliances among women, acknowledging that such claims may themselves be frames around essentialist constructions. Other feminist scholars, such as Chandra Mohanty and Omofolabo Ajayi-Soyinka, consider how to combine solidarity and cultural specificity at the same time. Since feminist philosophies tend to vary and have a wide range of concerns, one must take into account the particularities of a given group of feminists, feminisms and the experiences of specific communities. In this regard, Ajayi-Soyinka states that 'aside from the basic common objectives of feminism to end the oppression, powerlessness, and patriarchal exploitation of the women, each feminist must identify, define and adopt strategies of resistance within its cultural confines' (Ajayi-Soyinka, 2003, 168). This prescription doesn't preclude 'sisterhood' or solidarity, rather, it suggests encompassing global encounters with empire alongside culturally specific struggles to move away from what Mohanty terms 'a cross-culturally singular, monolithic notion of patriarchy or male dominance [that] leads to the construction of a similarly reductive and homogeneous notion of...third world difference' (Mohanty,1988, 63).

Appropriating these conceptualisations of subalterneity, alongside the importance of cultural specificity and solidarity, provides us with analytical tools to consider *Maendeleo*'s roots and vision and gives rise to important questions. Should those who create a feminist organisation come from the same cultural group as its members? Is it important for the leadership of feminist organisations to be representative of its members and their lived experiences? In what ways is *Maendeleo*'s varied history relevant to its current organisational goals? Can an organisation whose foundation was determined by imperialist agendas, such as the need to 'civilise' become transformational without radical structural changes?

We refer to Spivak again to underscore the experiences of rural women and *Maendeleo ya Wanawake*. We suggest that Spivak would regard the rural women who were affiliated to *Maendeleo* as 'foreclosed' and in her research Wipper (1975) identifies a numbers of ways in which such foreclosure occurred. First, rural women complained about not receiving information and visits from the headquarters. Second, in a subsequent interview, a rural-based woman said that the leaders speak but do not act. Third, another woman pointed out that the organisation only becomes active at the time of elections when it warns the rural women to be careful in choosing their leaders. And fourth, Tom Mboya, who was then a Minister, in a speech criticised the educated women who did not want to associate with the rural women but pursued the company of the European and Asian women. Mboya stated that 'these women are not even one generation removed from a rural background, but the distance they have travelled in putting it behind them suggests just how quickly the upwardly mobile can begin to lose touch with their origins and become engrossed in the peripheral tasks of office' (Mboya cited in Wipper, 1975, 116).

It is our proposal that some of the rural women who are members of *Maendeleo* epitomise the subaltern, as conceptualised by Spivak (1999) as an individual who is oppressed and without lines of social mobility. Cleaver (2002) similarly described the subaltern rural women as a marginalised group that is structurally excluded (by barriers of time, health, money) or excluded through fear of speaking in public and perceived lack of education. Within *Maendeleo* we can see how this subaltern status is perpetuated even through programmes such as PATH or the *Maendeleo* development of an alternative ritual to female genital cutting. The community members do have a voice in the programme because they identify the girls, participate in the training for family life education (FLE), send them into seclusion and agree to be present during the coming of age ceremony to play the various roles that they would have played if the girls were to go through the female genital cutting ritual (Chege et al, 2001). However, while this attempt by *Maendeleo* to give the community a voice in this project can be said to be an act of making the native informant relevant, it cannot be said to be making the subaltern speak while *Maendeleo* and PATH hold power as the funders and agenda setters of the programme.

So, we return to Spivak's question: can the subaltern speak? We agree that the subaltern can only speak when they are in power. This is not to minimise the efforts of *Maendeleo* in eradicating female genital cutting. Through this programme *Maendeleo* is addressing real concerns of rural women, yet this does not automatically mean that they are given decision-making power.

The colonialist roots of *Maendeleo,* and its relationships with government and rural woman are important areas for analysis given that it has provided a platform for elite women to speak on behalf of underprivileged women. In more recent years, *Maendeleo* has started foregrounding rural women's agendas as do more avowedly feminist organisations: through raising consciousness and empowering women. In short, *Maendeleo* can be described as constrained by its history even as it attempts to put feminist principles into actions, albeit with limited autonomy and capacity.

In summary, our analysis of the activities of *Maendeleo,* as seen through a gendered lens suggests the following observations: first, the organisation, from its inception, has had a history of disconnection between its elitist leadership and the rural membership (Nzomo, 1989). Second, its activities appear secondary to the primary purpose of serving the colonial and post-colonial governments to meet their political goals. For example, the colonial government used *Maendeleo* to reduce the powers of Mau Mau and the post-colonial government has used the organisation to gain political mileage with members as voters/supporters of political parties. Third, *Maendeleo*'s past over-reliance on international donors meant that its programmes, agendas and interventions have been centred on the project of the donors thus de-centring the community's priorities in some circumstances.

Championing women's rights under different rubrics: activists, feminists and womanists

'For African women, feminism is an act that evokes the dynamism and shifts of a process as opposed to the stability and reification of a construct or framework... Feminism is structured by cultural imperatives and modulated by ever-shifting local and global exigencies' (Nnaemeka, 2004, 378). African feminists have developed different approaches to articulate and protect different aspects of women's rights. In embracing diversity, some African feminists such as Nnaemeka have proposed a model they call 'nego-feminism', emphasising the processes of negotiating for their rights. In order for any African feminist organisation to have a national impact, there needs to be some degree of consensus about certain shared experiences of women that jeopardise their wellbeing. For example, we may learn from western feminists who established such a consensus in the 1920s on the need to improve maternal and child health, safe working environments and compulsory education for children and they worked together, even though they were from distinct socio-political groups, to influence legislation to meet these goals (Bogenschneider, 2006). Such solidarity is lacking in *Maendeleo*, instead we observe pockets of ethno-geopolitical regions with better outcomes for women.

Tamale (2006) has identified certain weaknesses with the feminist movement in Africa. Tamale (2006) suggests that there is a tendency to practice feminism as a career or a source of income while lacking passion and choosing not to work in alliances with others. Although in Kenya the Bill of Rights provides a broad range of protection to all, including women, children in Kenya have been granted additional policies to protect their rights, which has not happened to women (Rombo et al, 2013). Baraza (2009) argued that western donors' interests are likely to be instrumental in determining the progress of specific public policies that address women's issues in both private and public spheres, implying a lack of indigenous influence on governance and notwithstanding the fact that successful policy implementation requires a culture and civil society that embraces the ideology behind that policy and translates it into practice.

Learning from the challenges and weaknesses of *Maendeleo* as an organisation with a feminist agenda, we argue that a feminist organisation should not be part of the political system. The prevailing political contexts have had significant influence on the agendas, processes and outcomes for *Maendeleo*. Under the one-party government, *Maendeleo* lost the supposed autonomy it had under colonial rule and overtly performed as a state-run and state-led entity. Akin-Aina (2011) argues that *Maendeleo* is not unique, similar phenomena have been observed in many leaders and members of women's organisations in Africa. She writes that 'in the post-independence era however, women's groups were perceived as having lost their autonomy and as mere puppets of state machinery' (Akin-Aina, 2011, 4). Muthoni Wanyeki made the related point that women's organisations in Africa face conceptual and ideological challenges due to the assumption that 'working on gender and women's human rights presupposes a shared vision of African women's development, equality and other human rights. This assumption is false, and is further buttressed by persisting and misleading perceptions of African women's organisations and their leaders as being "elite" and "urban"' (Wanyeki, 2005, 108).

Women's experiences and outcomes are shaped by their context. We argue that in Kenya, the context is highly determined by ethno-geopolitical regimes, which have led to the violation of basic rights nationally. Additionally, regional disparities are also evident. A feminist agenda would therefore need to take into account the disparate history, geography and political/ethnic realities. Besides forming common goals to meet the national agenda, specific strategies (policy and practice) to address disparities and diversity would be prudent. A gender divide that already exists in Kenya can be bridged through lobbying and creating allies among men and other emerging minorities and the lesbian, gay, bisexual, transgender, queer and intersex (LGBTQI) communities. The ethnic divide also challenges feminists' agendas. We advocate for the adoption of solidarity through sisterhood models as being a fruitful way for women who are in closer proximity to power, such as highly educated women and political leaders, to work towards the achievement of agendas that shift these unequal structures of power in order to improve the lives of those who lack structures that facilitate quality living.

In any women's rights organisation, goal setting and implementation is influenced by its understanding of feminism. Feminism is a heterogeneous category and African feminisms are certainly not monolithic. Akin-Aina describes African feminism as 'multifaceted, multipurpose, and reflects the diverse nature of feminist organising, practice and scholarship on the continent' (Akin-Aina, 2011, 69). Wanyeki (2005) also observes an emerging, but conflicted feminism focusing on African women's bodily integrity, autonomy and choice, with respect to reproductive and sexual rights. With the diversity of feminisms in Kenya, we argue that clearly defined goals and agendas can only emerge from understanding similarities in the experiences of women in order to resist the crippling effects of patriarchy. Ultimately, a focus on women's rights underscored by legal and human rights may offer one way to bridge these divergent feminist agendas and form alliances between women's organisations.

A call for solidarity

In her article 'African feminism: How should we change?' (2006) Ugandan feminist Sylvia Tamale points out that African feminists struggle with self-identification due to negative associations that the label provokes. For example, Akin-Aina (2011) states that in Kenya women who identify themselves as feminists are considered to be against African culture as well as anti-religious and anti-men.[13] In response, Tamale argues for women to 'embrace the F-word' (feminism) and shift away from the more inclusive, but less focused rhetoric of 'gender activist' terminology. Other challenges Tamale identifies include the lack of passion in some feminists who consider feminism as a career and not a personal and political reality that encompasses their lives. She links this professionalising of feminism to the regimes of NGO funding alongside the institutionalisation of gender justice work. Tamale therefore urges African feminists to engage in politics, openly declare their political agenda and draw inspiration from the feminist adage that the personal is political and the political is personal. Still, Tamale (2006) illuminates that the gap between feminist theory and praxis (often attributed to the increasing distance between the academy and activist practitioners) has two consequences: the lack of social transformation and the neglect of research into indigenous feminist theory.

We observe that sympathy, solidarity and empathy is necessary, especially with rural women who have been disenfranchised by women's rights organisations such as *Maendeleo*. As an example of what such sympathy and solidarity can mean in practice, we refer to the work of Eleanor Preston-Whyte. Preston-Whyte (1976) explored the relationship between black domestic workers and their white employers in two sections of Durban, South Africa, during apartheid. She concluded that the lower-income, more politically conservative employers were more intimate, familiar and maternal towards their black servants compared to those living in the higher income, politically more liberal neighbourhood. She further states that what brought the white and African women together was the shared social environment, the validation of each other's problems and that they offered each other genuine sympathy in times of crisis and insecurity. While acknowledging the differences that exist between Kenyan women as well as Kenyan feminisms, we argue that through genuine sympathy, commonalities that transcend geo-ethnicity and class can be applied to include rural women who continue to be marginalised.

Conclusion

Maendeleo, although not a specifically feminist organisation at its inception, nonetheless epitomises the struggle that feminists' movements and organisations in developing countries face, as they negotiate the patriarchal societies in which they are situated. As we have shown, *Maendeleo* has struggled to include both rural and poor urban women: in short, *Maendeleo* has had limited success in the emancipation of women and work because the way that it works reinforces gender norms which cripple, limit and obstruct women from securing better lives. Since Forum '85, there have been significant advancements made among Kenyan women such as introducing laws and legislations that protect women's rights, provide access to land, healthcare and legislation. However, whether these new laws and regulations are going to be implemented remains to be seen. It is ironic that Kenyan women were central in championing discourses and strategies towards gender justice and equality in Forum '85, yet there is still little political participation (as marked by women in leadership positions) when compared to other East African countries who have a larger representation of women in their elective political leadership, for example, Rwanda, Uganda and Tanzania currently respectively have 56.3 per cent, 31 per cent and 30 per cent (Kamau, 2010).

A similar point can be made about the levels of feminist scholarship about Kenya. Although Kenya's economic, socio-political and cultural significance on the continent can't be disputed, scholarship on Kenyan feminisms and the grassroots activities is limited. Some scholars, such as Kanogo (1987) who has written on the Mau Mau Rebellion, Shaw (1995) who studies gender, class and racial issues in the country, and Hay (1976) who conducted a study among Luo women in colonial Kenya, have managed to excavate women's histories and reveal identity politics and agency among Kenyan women, in ethnic contexts. Other scholars such as Oruka (1990) and Cohen and Atieno-Odhiambo (1999) have applied gender as a category of analysis in their research and have included questions relating to gender in their fieldwork. However, Kenya's participation in the African feminist academic space still lags behind Ghana, Nigeria, Uganda and even South Africa (who did not participate in Forum '85 because of being still under the apartheid regime). And so, while the documented history and analysis of Kenyan women's experiences and African feminisms has been limited, it will be exciting to see what may emerge during the next decade.

Notes

[1] Makeri was appointed 'Chief' of Weithaga Location by the British in 1902 where she was a member of the council of elders, which was usually reserved for men (Wanyoike, 2002, 28–29, 35–40). Nyanjiru was regarded as the mother of female political protest among women of the central province of Kenya (Ogot, 1993, 524). Women also served in the Mau Mau political movement as recruiters, organisers, spies and soldiers. These women also smuggled arms, food, clothing and medicine to the guerrilla army, which completely transformed their political roles (Ogot, 1993, 524).

[2] Even though *Maendeleo* is autonomous it is still dependent on donors in the western world and this dependency means that projects of choice cannot be pursued, they have to align themselves with themes like the Millennium Development Goals or are absorbed in political agendas.

[3] The causes and the consequences or effects include: HIV/AIDS, maternal child health/family planning (MCHIFP), cervical cancer prevention, malaria prevention and control, civic education and leadership, economic empowerment, agriculture, energy and environmental conservation.

[4] *Maendeleo's* work is in light with the targets set by the United Nations Millennium Development Goals. *Maendeleo* has opened Information Communication Centres and trained 139 women in eight provinces. This project is meant to avail new technologies, information and communication to communities. Essentially these skills are meant to give the women confidence to participate in social life on equal terms with men as leaders and informed citizens. It also aims to encourage women's groups to work together to identify and address the common issues that face them in relation to poverty eradication.

[5] *Maendeleo* lobbies banks for credit facilities for women. The women secure the loans and engage in activities such as hand looming and make shirts, table runners, mats and scarves.

[6] Similar to the Greenbelt movement, *Maendeleo* has tree nurseries for women's groups all over Kenya.

[7] PATH is an international NGO whose aim is to improve the health of women and children in developing countries. This programme was implemented in 1990 following years of basic research into genital mutilation, studying the cultural norms and expectation surrounding and arising from its practice. Initially implemented in one community, the alternative rite has now been carried out in 13 communities in rural Kenya. The young women spend a week receiving counselling and life skills training. At the end of the week they celebrate their 'coming of age' day. Since this project was started, about 300 women have been initiated.

[8] Although this process was transformative, there was much criticism about how local women were treated in comparison to their international counterparts, with limited access to hotels and agenda setting at the main conference.

[9] The use of sexuality in this case was a derogatory term that was meant to dissuade 'good women' (read: hetero-normative daughters and wives) from participating in women's rights activities.

10 Following Forum '85, the NGO Planning Committee produced a report documenting its activities.
11 Gramsci uses the term 'subaltern' in the literal sense referring to non-commissioned military troops who are subordinate to the authority of lieutenants, colonels and generals in the *Prison Notebooks*: 1, 48 and 54. In later notes, he uses the term figuratively in non-military instances, with regard to positions of subordination of lower status. He writes, 'Subaltern classes are subject to the initiatives of the dominant class even when they are in a state of anxious defence' (Green, 2002, 1–2).
12 According to Webster's Dictionary essentialism is the practice of regarding something (such as a presumed human trait) as having innate existence or universal validity rather than as being a social, ideological or intellectual construct.
13 This does not mean that Kenyan women do not participate in activities that interrupt patriarchal systems. Kenyan women participate in everyday feminisms such as #mydressmychoice protests that took place in various major towns of Kenya and on the internet following the undressing of women in Nairobi.

References

Adawo, L, Gikonyo, LW, Kudu, RM, Mutoro, O, 2011, *History of feminism in Kenya*, www.nawey.net/wp-content/uploads/downloads/2012/05/History-of-Feminism-in-Kenya.pdf

Akin-Aina, S, 2011, Beyond an epistemology of bread, culture and power: Mapping the African feminist movement, *Nokoko*, Fall, 2, http://carleton.ca/africanstudies/wp-content/uploads/Nokoko-Fall-2011-3-Sinmi.pdf

Ajayi-Soyinka, O, 2003, Negritude, feminism, and the quest for identity: Re-reading Mariama Bâ's 'So long a letter', in AU Azodo (ed) *Emerging perspectives on Mariama Ba. Postcolonialism, feminism, and postmodernism*, Trenton: Africa World Press, www.academia.edu/556896/Negritude_Feminism_and_the_Quest_for_Identity_Re-Reading_Mariama_Bâs_So_Long_a_Letter

Ajayi-Soyinka, O, 2005, Transcending the boundaries of power and imperialism: Writing gender, constructing knowledge, in O Nnaemeka (ed) *Female circumcision and the politics of knowledge: African women in imperialist discourses*, pp 47–77, Westport, CT: Praeger

Aubrey, L, 1995, *The politics of development cooperation African, NGOs and their relational environment: A study of Maendeleo ya Wanawake, Kenya*, Dissertation, Columbus, OH: Ohio State University

Baraza, N, 2009, Family law reforms in Kenya: An overview, presentation at Heinrich Böll-Stiftung, paper presented at the foundation's Gender Forum in Nairobi, 30 April

Bogenschneider, K, 2006, *Family policy matters how policymaking affects families and what professionals can do* (2nd edn), Mahwah, NJ: Lawrence Erlbaum Associates

Chege, JN, Askew, I, Liku, J (nd) *An assessment of the alternative rites approach for encouraging abandonment of female genital mutilation in Kenya*, Population Council, www.popcouncil.org/uploads/pdfs/frontiers/FR_FinalReports/Kenya_FGC.pdf

Chelala, C, 1998, An alternative way to stop female genital mutilation, *The Lancet* 352, 9122, 126

Chege, JN, Askew, I and Liku, J, 2001, *An assessment of the alternative rites approach for encouraging abandonment of female genital mutilation in Kenya*, Kenya: Population Council, www.popcouncil.org/uploads/pdfs/frontiers/FR_FinalReports/Kenya_FGC.pdf.org

Cleaver, F, 2002, *Masculinities matter! Men, gender and development*, New York: Zed Books

Cohen, D, Atieno-Odhiambo, ES, 1999, *Siaya: The historical anthropology of an African landscape*, pp 85–110, Athens, OH: Ohio University Press

Davis, A, 1990, *Women, culture and politics*, New York: Vintage Books

Green, M, 2002, Gramsci cannot speak: Presentations and interpretations of Gramsci's concept of the subaltern, *Rethinking Marxism* 14, 1–24

Guy-Sheftall, B, 1986, Reflections on Forum '85 in Nairobi, Kenya: Voices from the International Women's Studies Community, Signs: *Journal of Women in Culture and Society*, 587–99

Hay, MJ, 1976, Luo women and economic change during the colonial period, in N Hafkin, EG Bay (eds) *Women in Africa: Studies in social and economic change*, pp 87–109, Stanford, CA: Stanford University Press

Hansen, KT, 1992, White women in changing world: Employment, voluntary work, and sex in post-World War II Northern Rhodesia, in N Chaudhuri, M Strobel (eds) *Western women and imperialism*, pp 247–68, Bloomington, IN: Indiana University Press

Kabeer, N, 2005, Gender equality and women's empowerments: A critical analysis of the Third Millennium Development Goal, *Gender and Development* 13, 1, 13–24

Kamau, N, 2010, *Women and political leadership in Kenya: Ten case studies*, Nairobi and Berlin: Heinrich Böll Stiftung

Kanogo, T, 1985, *Squatters and the Roots of Mau Mau, 1905–1963*, in N Chaudhuri, M Strobel (eds) *Western women and imperialism*, pp 247–68, Bloomington, IN: University Press

Maathai, W, 2004, *The Greenbelt movement: Sharing the approach and the experience*, New York: Lantern Books

McClintock, A, 1995, *Imperial leather: Race, gender and sexuality in the imperial contest*, London: Routledge

Maendeleo ya Wanawake, 2015, *Maendeleo ya Wanawake*, www.mywokenya.org

Mohanty, CT, 1988, 'Under Western eyes': Feminist scholarship and colonial discourse, *Feminist Review* 30, Autumn, 61–88

NGO Planning Committee, 1985, *Forum '85 final report: Nairobi, Kenya*, New York: International Women's Tribune Centre (IWTC)

Nnaemeka, O, 2004, Nego feminism: Theorizing, practicing, and pruning Africa's Way, *Signs: Journal of Women in Culture and Society* 29, 2, 357–85

Nzomo, M, 1989, The impact of the Women's Decade on policies, programs and empowerment of women in Kenya, *Issue: A Journal of Opinion* 17, 2, 9–17

O'Barr, JF, Tinker, I, Hultman, T, Gaidzanwa, R, Guy-Sheftall B, Callaway, H, Basu, A, Bernstein, A, 1986, Reflections on Forum '85 in Nairobi, Kenya: Voices from the international women's studies community, *Signs: Journal of Women in Culture and Society* 11, 3, 584–608

Ogot, BA, 1993, Reviewed works: Marshall S Clough. Fighting Two Sides: Kenyan chiefs and politicians, 1918–1940; CA Presley. Kikuyu women, the Mau Mau rebellion, and social change in Kenya, *The Journal of African History* 34, 3, 522–4

Oruka, O, 1990, *Sage philosophy: Indigenous thinkers and modern debate on African philosophy*, Leiden and New York: EJ Brill

Oyewumi, O, 2003, Introduction: Feminism, sisterhood and other foreign relations, in O Oyewumi (ed) *African women and feminism: Reflecting on the politics of sisterhood*, pp 1–24, Trenton, NJ and Asmara, Eritrea: African Worldwide Press

Presley, CA, 1988, The Mau Mau rebellion, Kikuyu women, and social change, *Canadian Journal of African Studies/La Revue canadienne des études africaines* 22, 3, 502–27

Presley, CA, 1992, *Kikuyu Women, the Mau Mau rebellion, and social change in Kenya*, Boulder, CO: Westview Press

Preston-Whyte, E, 1976, Race attitudes and behavior: The case of domestic employment in White South African homes, *African Studies*, 35/2, 71–90

Rombo, DO, Wilson, SM, Oseland, LM, 2013, Public policy and families in Kenya, in M Robila (ed) *Handbook of family policy across the globe*, pp 31–46, New York: Springer

Shaw, C, 1995, *Colonial inscriptions: Race, sex, and class in Kenya*, Minneapolis, MN and London: University of Minnesota Press

Sita R, 1992, 'Education Eve': The women's club movement and political consciousness among rural African women in Southern Rhodesia, 1950–1980, in K Tranberg Hansen (ed) *African encounters with domesticity*, pp 195–217, New Brunswick, NJ: Rutgers University Press

Smolowe, J, 2003, Kenya: A global feminist critique, *Time*, www.time.com/time/magazine/article/0,9171,1048368,00.html

Spivak, GC, 1988, Can the subaltern speak?, in C Nelson, L Grossberg (eds) *Marxism and the interpretation of culture*, pp 271–313, Urbana, IL: University of Illinois Press

Spivak, GC, 1999, *A critique of post-colonial reason: Toward a history of the vanishing present*, Cambridge, MA: Harvard University Press

Tamale, S, 2006, African feminism: How should we change?, *Development* 49, 1, 38–41

Udvardy, ML, 1998, Theorizing past and present women's organizations in Kenya, *World Development* 26, 9, 1749–61

Wanyeki, ML, 2005, The African women's development communication network (FEMNET): Experiences of feminist continental organizing, *Feminist Africa* 4, 4, 105–15

Wanyoike, MW, 2002, *Wangu wa Makeri*, Nairobi and Kampala: East African Educational Publishers

Wipper, A, 1975, Women in Africa. The *Maendeleo ya Wanawake* Organisation: Co-optation of leadership, *African Studies Review* 18, 3, 99–120

SIXTEEN

Organising for emancipation/ emancipating organisations?

Jenny Onyx, Christina Schwabenland, Chris Lange and Sachiko Nakagawa

Introduction

In this final chapter we reflect on what the various contributions in this anthology have to tell us about the current state of women's activism around the globe, and to what extent social movements and more formally organised civil society organisations (CSOs) have been effective in responding to the challenges of achieving women's emancipation. With a century of feminism behind us, we would expect to find major improvements in women's rights and wellbeing, and strong support from the many CSOs that exist to enable them to achieve their aspirations. That is not always what we have found. Hence, we return to the key problematic that runs through the anthology: do CSOs contribute to women's emancipation or do they merely reinforce the status quo? We begin by considering the questions we identified, drawing on Fraser's (2013) understanding of emancipation as both an aspiration and a position from which to locate and resist domination, in whatever form it takes. We ask what differing understandings of emancipation inspire the activists recorded here. We then ask where domination is located in these accounts and how it is resisted. Following this analysis we move on to a more measured review of the roles of organising and organisations. We see three alternative ways of framing these; organisations as a means to an end, organisations as the manifestation of alternative/feminist values and organisations as themselves, locations of systemic domination. The chapters in this anthology have provided examples of all of these. We conclude with some comments on the insight we have gained through our engagement with these authors and their research.

Differing understandings of emancipation

The first clear message that emerges from these studies is that women's activism is alive and well in many parts of the globe. We see major and concerted campaigns against women's oppression in Italy, Russia, France, Uruguay and Nigeria in particular. Some of these campaigns are continuations of longstanding feminist demands and concerns that have been documented over the past century in countries of 'the North'. In Portugal we see women from a very marginalised group, the Roma, beginning to organise together (Chapter Eleven). We see women working together everywhere, both internally and across organisations to offer support to each other, both formally and informally. We also see creative use of social media in many countries to bring people together and reach out to each other across the globe.

We also, however, see contradictions and tensions emerging with regard to the different ways in which emancipation is understood and acted upon. Phillips' chapter (Chapter Two), highlights one of the most significant differences: whether emancipation can be achieved through an accumulation of individual endeavours and struggles or whether it requires the kinds of systemic changes that can only be achieved by people working together in solidarity. Her contribution could be interpreted as an attempt to discover how deeply neoliberalism, with its celebration of the individual, has really taken root in the women's organisations which she surveyed. Understood in this way, her results give us some encouragement; for example, in the existence of a substantial, if not a majority voice that is critical of the more instrumental and individualist approach of the third United Nations Millennium Development Goal (MDG 3) and that, as she concludes, 'A clear message from women's NGOs is that the transformations required for gender equality must occur at a structural level; all women must have equal rights that are inclusive of human, civil, political, legal, social, welfare and economic rights' (Philips, Chapter Two). However, speaking from the Kenyan experience, Lutomia et al (Chapter Fifteen) reframe this argument, noting that where feminist organisations have been coopted into the political system this has led to the professionalising of feminism as it becomes more incorporated in NGO work. Such developments serve to alienate feminist organisations' actions from the grassroots and from those most vulnerable to domination.

The clearest example of differing understandings of emancipation is that explored by Lounasmaa (Chapter Twelve) in which the rights-based and Islamic faith-based organisations in Morocco share many aspirational goals and yet are motivated by very different 'referentials' (her expression); with the rights-based organisations drawing on an, arguably, more westernised understanding of rights while the faith-based organisations take their inspiration for women's emancipation from interpretations of Islam. Her chapter is very timely, as the re-emergence of the importance of religion within the public sphere (Schwabenland, 2015) is placing such differing understandings of emancipation onto the central stage. These differences are profound at the level of ideology, with the 'separate but equal' approach relying on a more essentialist understanding of gender (women's role being domestic and nurturing), thus challenging so much of (largely western) feminist theory that proceeds from the view of gender as socially and not biologically constructed. However, at a more practical level, Lounasmaa's chapter also offers some possibilities for hope because she identifies many shared aims and aspirations around which such groups could coalesce, even if only in the short term.

Locations of domination: emancipation as a standpoint

Nancy Fraser writes that the struggle for emancipation 'intersect[s] with another struggle, [that] between protection and de-regulation' (Fraser, 2013, 240). Her helpful insight is that domination is to be resisted wherever it is found, and that significant dynamics within *both* of the 'great' institutions of the state and market are inimical to women's wellbeing. She argues that many feminists, already very aware of the domination inherent in statist models of social protection, have been seduced by the freedoms offered (at least rhetorically) by the market, and that this has, at least until recently, blinded us to their more repressive aspects. However, we should also be alert to the marginalising dynamics inherent in *all* forms of organising, including deep-seated cultural mores underpinning both the market and the state. Nor can we exclude the repressive aspects of organisations, including CSOs themselves. Organising works through creating dynamics of inclusion and exclusion, and it is in this terrain that we also need to direct our critique. We therefore understand domination (and resistance) as occurring in multiple sites and in overlapping and contradictory ways.

Both *La Barbe* (Chapter Six) and *Se Non Ora Quando?* (Chapter Three) were founded, in part, out of outrage at political representations of women, from those of the socialist presidential candidate Ségolène Royal in France and the then capitalist prime minister of Italy, Silvio Berlusconi, who was convicted of child prostitution (although the conviction was later overturned on appeal). While feminists have long resisted the use of images of women, usually highly sexualised, to sell products or services, these political representations are more complex as their influence is much more pervasive. Furthermore, the increasing importance of social media (particularly where Berlusconi owns much of the popular media) gives this form of domination a particularly sinister salience. We might also locate Keyhan's study of Hollaback! here because street harassment is, at least to some extent, given its 'oxygen' through such sexualised images of women which contribute to what she terms a 'culture of permissiveness' (Chapter Four).

Hinterhuber and Fuchs (Chapter Five) suggest that Pussy Riot locate their critique in the nexus of political, cultural and religious domination. The context of their study is one in which the level of democratic engagement in Russia is seen to have fallen, the state has become increasingly authoritarian and gender segregation has increased again. Within this context the role of the Russian Orthodox Church is critical – from a position of near extinction during the Soviet period the church is now highly popular and its leadership has been very supportive of the Putin government. Their study is particularly interesting in Fraser's terms because here it is the *intersection* between market, state and civil society (in the form of the church) that has created a situation in which women are increasingly marginalised.

Hildwein, from France (Chapter Six) provides the only study represented here in which the focus is primarily on the market, and in particular, large corporations, *La Barbe*'s activism being aimed directly at the boardroom. Pousadela's study in Uruguay (Chapter Seven) focuses on the relationship between CSOs and the state, in the struggle for legalised abortion, and the importance of legislation as the most basic guarantor of rights. However, neither study takes an uncritical stance on civil society, with each commenting on significant divisions between actors in the wider movements in which they are located. For example, in Uruguay, much of the struggle devolved around the conflict between feminist organisations and the Catholic church.

Acey's study of women's environmental and social activism in the Niger Delta (Chapter Eight) is an interesting attempt at what Fraser describes as a 'triple movement': an analysis that challenges a positional duality of state versus market. Her focus on the nexus between the political and commercial interests that have led to the degradation of the Niger Delta, and its implications for the lives of women, highlights the complexities of these systemic inter-relationships.

Finally, we have several studies in which dominating dynamics are located *within* civil society itself. Both Rego, speaking of the Roma in Portugal (Chapter Eleven) and Tanaka, speaking of trafficking survivors in Nepal (Chapter Nine) express reservations about the impact of 'top-down' CSOs that are not member controlled, and Lounasmaa, in the Moroccan context, highlights the ways in which unquestioned allegiance to dogma can weaken and fracture solidarity.

How is domination to be resisted and emancipation achieved through organising?

Alongside accounts of traditional models of activism, we also see newly emergent forms of resistance. Hollaback!'s use of social media, for example, goes beyond that of mobilising support: by putting women who have experienced street violence in touch with each other the internet facilitates Hollaback!'s intervention strategies (Keyhan, Chapter Four). Women gain confidence and begin to transform their sense of self, from victim to survivor. Hollaback! and *Se Non Ora Quando?* (Elia, Chapter Three) can be regarded as very postmodernist organisations, adopting virtual forms of organising in order to intervene at the level of identity formation.

La Barbe (Hildwein, Chapter Six) similarly, responds to the absence of presence (of women in the corporate boardroom) by adopting a Butlerian strategy of parody. In her discussion of drag, Butler comments that 'the parodic repetition of "the original" [in this case the adopting of false beards] reveals the original to be nothing other than a parody of the *idea* of the natural and the original' (Butler, 1999, 41, her emphases).

Pussy Riot's performance (Chapter Five) of their 'Punk Prayer', and in particular their choice of location and their incorporation of Russian sacred music and theology can also be understood as an attempt to disrupt the taken-for-granted by re-presenting these elements in a form that is both shocking and beautiful. These organisations are working at the level of culture formation: challenging oppressive aspects of culture by disruption and subversion. *La Barbe*'s focus is quite specific, but that of Pussy Riot is very diffused – they aim to open up a space for resistance rather than mobilising around a specific platform or set of desired outcomes.

In their analyses both Hildwein, and Hinterhuber and Fuchs concentrate on the forms of protest rather than their impact. In fact, discussion of their 'successes' is largely absent. We can read these chapters as themselves acting to disrupt the more neoliberal structuring of accountability in which problem identification leads to proposed solution/intervention, which necessarily leads to a discussion of impact and resulting change. No such easy, or formulaic closure is available in these chapters, in which success can only really be understood as, in *La Barbe*'s case, the speeding up of the moment of recognition that men-only Boards are insupportable, or for Pussy Riot, in the international support that forced Putin's government to release Nadezhda Tolokonnikova and Maria Aljochina from prison, thus creating a new form of democratic accountability.

Lounasmaa, in Morocco, and Pousadela, in Uruguay, both demonstrate in their analyses the importance of activists coming together to create a synthesis (however provisional and temporary) of rights-based approaches and more radical perspectives. Pousadela presents this struggle as at the centre of a 'culture war' invoking science, religion and human rights discourses for legitimacy. Lounasmaa, however, argues that the divisions between these groups in Morocco have weakened their potential to campaign for lasting change.

Acey's detailed analysis of the extent to which women have become empowered in Nigeria through their participation in CSOs and networks synthesises radical and liberal approaches, recognising the opportunities that women have taken while also highlighting the need for longer-term, more transformational change in which justice becomes a political, ecological and gendered discourse (Acey, Chapter Eight). In these accounts emancipation is presented as neither simply an individual concern, nor primarily structural, but both – structural change that doesn't work for individuals is merely a new tyranny but individual empowerment without structural change is selfish and limited. This is not an endorsement of neoliberal meritocracy. Hollaback! captures this perfectly: individual emancipation is advanced through shared solidarity which in turn challenges structures of patriarchal ideology.

Do CSOs reinforce or challenge the status quo?

The key problematic that this anthology has attempted to explore is the role that organising and organisations play in the struggle for women's emancipation. We regard organisations as sites of contested values and conflictual dynamics, the focus of coercive pressures from the environments in which they are situated. Consequently, there is no simple answer to this question as organisational actors experience multiple pressures and tensions. Yet organising is essential for the pursuit of aspirations. As noted above, we think it is helpful to reflect on organising from three different perspectives: organisations as a means to an end, organisations as the manifestation of alternative values and finally, organisations as means of domination. We now consider each of these in turn.

Organisations as a means to an end

The majority of the authors in the first section of the anthology treat organisations as relatively unproblematic, although noting that dissent can occur between members and between different parts of the organisation that can have negative consequences for the fulfillment of desired goals. Elia, for example, refers to the tensions between the promoters and locally-based organisers of *Se Non Ora Quando?* (Chapter Three) and Keyhan's chapter also identifies the challenges in managing a global movement from a western base (Chapter Four). Lutomia et al's case study of *Maendeleleo ya Wanawake*, Kenya's oldest women's organisation (Chapter Fifteen) interrogates its role in achieving women's emancipation. The authors are highly critical, arguing that the organisation's limited success can be attributed primarily to its close connections with ruling elites and distance from the lived experiences of rural, poor women.

We also see new models of organising under discussion here, however. Tavanti et al propose that what they term 'meso' level organisations (Chapter Ten) may be uniquely able to provide a channel for the exchange of cultural norms between the diaspora communities and organisations working in the homeland in the context of the relationships between the Somali diaspora settled in the United States and grass roots organisations working in Somalia. These intermediary organisations are currently playing an important role in providing resources; arguably, however, their potential role in terms of providing a channel for the exchange of cultural norms may be more problematic and carries the risk of replacing one form of dominance with another. However, Tavanti et al argue that meso-level organisations are well placed to manage these bridging processes, carrying as they do, deep understandings of both cultural contexts. This is an important study because it focuses on the increasingly prevalent international relationships between home and diaspora.

Hollaback! also represents a twenty-first century model of activism against street violence (Keyhan, Chapter Four), organising primarily through the internet, exposing women's experiences through blogs and embracing technological innovations in order to provide support on an individual level, rapid mobilisation around local issues and analysis at an international level. Keyhan notes that the 'unbounded nature of street harassment thus calls for a similarly unbounded response; one that can adapt and respond to the behaviour in a collaborative but expansive way' (Keyhan, Chapter Four). These examples highlight the importance of creating alternative institutional forms that demonstrate some congruence with the issue being pursued. As new forms of oppression emerge new forms of resistance are needed.

Organisations as embodiments/manifestations of values

Similarly, the idea that methods of organising should reflect the founding values is an important theme in feminist activism (Bordt, 1990; and introduction to this volume; Schwabenland, 2006). Tanaka analyses one such model (Chapter Nine) the 'incubator' role played by the Women's Rehabilitation Centre (WOREC) to CSOs that mobilise around women's issues, and concentrates specifically on a network of survivors of human trafficking. The activities of WOREC in supporting a wide network of smaller NGOs is conceptualised through the metaphor of the incubator which evokes 'feminine' connotations of nurturing (see Hopfl, 2003, for a discussion of the 'maternal' in organisation theory). Tanaka's chapter is redolent with such discourse: WOREC refers to one of the CSOs it supports as a 'younger sister' also invoking the metaphors of family and *maita* or 'home' (Tanaka, Chapter Nine). Her research suggests that this is a highly successful model which offers an interesting alternative to the more traditional, and arguably 'masculine' organisational imaginaries.

Similarly, Rego's chapter (Chapter Eleven) on the organising models of the Portuguese Roma women she studied also invoked the 'family' metaphor, suggesting that the forms of organising adopted had to be congruent with Roma community cultural mores. She observes, however, that the boundary between family and organisation was at times hard to discern.

The pressures on collectivist and non-hierarchal forms of decision-making are also discussed in Hinterhuber and Fuchs' chapter on Pussy Riot (Chapter Five), noting the tensions that emerged between the two members of the group who had served prison sentences and the others, who had not. Elia's analysis of *Se Non Ora Quando?* (Chapter Three) similarly identifies the struggles the movement has faced in operationalising its core values of solidarity and inclusivity. Lutomia et al (Chapter Fifteen) highlight important, and unresolved, questions. They ask whether those who create a feminist organisation should have the same identity as the members and whether it is important for the leadership of feminist organisations to be representative of its members and their lived experiences. In the example of Kenya's *Maendeleo*, can an organisation whose agenda relies on colonial mores, such as 'civilising', be transformational without radical structural change?

Organisations as instruments of domination

Finally, a number of critical examples emerge from these chapters. First, the tensions between different types of organisations, mentioned by Lutomia et al above, resonate in other chapters as well. For example, Rego (Chapter Eleven) suggests that the small, informal associations, initiated and headed by Roma women, have emerged more in spite of, than because of the initiatives of the bigger, capacity building organisations, of which she is highly critical. Lounasmaa's chapter on the divisions between faith- and rights-based women's organisations in Morocco, argues that the conflicts between them are resulting in the marginalisation of both groups from influence in national political processes. Although acknowledging that both faith- and rights-based organisations are often campaigning around very similar issues and shared concerns Lounasmaa concludes that women's civil society 'is divided even when all agree' (Lounasmaa, Chapter Twelve).

Two final studies take up a different theme, that of the internal dynamics of CSOs. Dussuet and Flahault (Chapter Thirteen) ask whether CSOs in France, despite their avowed commitment to women's emancipation, actually provide more empowering models of employment. They note that more women are employed in CSOs than in other sectors but they examine the nature of the jobs available to women, their recognition and status and the terms and conditions of employment available and highlight some disturbing questions about whether the overall impact is to maintain women's inequality rather than to challenge it. While acknowledging that for many women the CSO sector is experienced as a good place to work, primarily because of its more humanist values, they note that '"feminist values" do not protect [organisations] from the "gender effects"' inherent in their roles as employers (Dussuet and Flahault, this volume). Even more concerning, they suggest that women implicitly collude in their own marginalisation in these organisations by their very allegiance to the 'values' which render their disadvantaged situation more palatable to them.

Similarly, East and Morgan continue the debate about the extent to which the CSO sector is an empowering place to work through their survey of flexible working practices in medium-sized, service-providing charities in the UK. The authors conclude that in this sector as in others, formal policies tended to maintain, rather than challenge the 'woman as carer' stereotype. They uncovered examples of female junior staff developing innovative ways of working that were more successful and these were based on cohesive, intimate and robust team-work among women staff. This, however, was informal and was dependent on women showing solidarity towards each other *despite*, rather than because of, the more formal processes, and their chapter reveals a very worrying lack of such formal supportive policies (Chapter Fourteen).

Feminism as a global social movement?

We now return to our initial problematic: to what extent have social movements and more formally organised CSOs been effective in responding to the challenges of achieving women's emancipation? First, we ask to what extent these organisations form part of a global social movement. Some of the cases are more clearly linked to global movements than others. Perhaps the clearest example is that of the Uruguayan women's movement to legalise abortion (Chapter Seven) which received ongoing international support for the campaigns. Hollaback! (Chapter Four) also clearly refers to a global campaign against street violence, although in both cases, many of the actual strategies and actions were local.

Does this matter? We recognise the importance of women organising locally to take action on the issues that concern them, and in the ways that are most culturally appropriate to their specific context. We also acknowledge the damage that has been done by probably well-intentioned, but condescending initiatives imposed by the west. However, we are also concerned that such actions will necessarily have limited effect unless they are able to contribute to a wider movement.

We noticed that no reference was made, in any of the chapters, to the work of DAWN (Development Alternatives with Women for a New Era). DAWN is a network of feminist scholars, researchers and activists from the economic south working for economic and gender justice and sustainable and democratic development. DAWN provides a forum for feminist research, analyses and advocacy on global issues (economic, social and political) affecting the livelihoods, living standards, rights and development prospects of women, especially poor and marginalised women, in regions of the south. Through research, analyses, advocacy and, more recently, training, DAWN seeks to support women's mobilisation within civil society to challenge inequitable social, economic and political relations at global, regional and national levels, and to advance feminist alternatives (www.dawnnet.org).

Since its founding in 1984, the network has become a significant voice in the development of south feminist analyses in gender and development and a key player in global feminist forums (Mayo, 2005). DAWN has had some remarkable achievements. However, it has had little immediate or obvious effect on the cases explored in this anthology. And almost all of our cases are focused on the urgency of solving immediate and local, or national issues.

The second question we need to consider is what has prevented the achievement of major improvements in women's rights and wellbeing. One suggestion can be found in social movement theories, and particularly the 'political process' approaches to understanding social movements (Mayo, 2005). This strand of theorising emphasises the structures of political opportunity as these affect social movements. These refer both to existing and emergent socio-economic and political cleavages but also to the opportunities that these provide for action. Such opportunities tend to be cyclical according to the cycles of oppression and liberalisation that occur in the wider socio-political environment. We note, of course, that such opportunities have decreased in many contexts in recent years – as the case of Pussy Riot (Chapter Five) illustrates.

The CIVICUS[1] *State of civil society report* for 2015 comments that:

> In 2014, there were significant attacks on the fundamental civil society rights of free association, free assembly and free expression in 96 countries. Threats to civil society emanate from both state and non-state actors that benefit from perpetuating governance failures and denying human rights; including corrupt politicians, unaccountable officials, unscrupulous businesses and religious fundamentalists. New attempts are underway, even by democratic states, to roll back long-established human rights norms, which are described as obstacles to national development and security, while critical voices are conflated with terrorism. Hostility to civil society is becoming normalised, and CSO energy is being forced into fighting existential threats. (http://civicus.org/index.php/en/media-centre-129/reports-and-publications/socs2015)

It is within this context that we should assess the success or otherwise of those CSOs reported in this anthology. From these accounts of current and concerted activism we see that many are responding to newly emerging forms of gender oppression. *Se Non Ora Quando?* is partly a new response to old concerns in Italy. But it is also a response to rapidly escalating cultural shifts in modern politics and the media which overwhelmingly objectify and denigrate women's bodies as sexual objects to be exploited at will. This level of public exploitation goes beyond anything seen in recent history in Europe. Pussy Riot is a dramatic response to a rapidly increasing silencing of women's voices in Russian politics and the church, a sad loss of the relatively high visibility of professional women during the Soviet era. The tales of oppression and increased burden on women in the Delta region of Nigeria speak of loss of livelihood and environmental destruction affecting women in fundamental ways thanks to the unethical and at times illegal action of oil companies, and corrupt government practices. The position of women in the oil rich Delta region, a region of Africa which had about the best hope of full economic and social development, instead of benefiting from the new wealth, has significantly deteriorated. But in rich as well as poor countries, there has been a global escalation of urban street harassment of women, as documented by Keyhan. Much of this street harassment has long existed under the radar. But its effects can be very serious indeed, affecting women's sense of decency and respect, their capacity to move freely in the city, and increasingly their personal safety. The levels of street attacks on women appear to be growing exponentially.

What is responsible for this expanded oppression of women? Always the state is implicated, but usually in support of powerful interest groups. Clearly the dominance of the market and development capitalism has been a factor. But behind all the cases presented are deep-seated cultural practices, traditional norms and values that have always subordinated women but which now find a new use and rationale in the hands of those in power as a form of justification and punitive control over women's choices and actions.

Given that in many parts of the globe, conditions for women have deteriorated, what then are the opportunities for action? What kind of strategies are most likely to have a positive impact?

Current strategies for action

We have identified four quite different approaches that these organisations have taken. All have made significant improvements to women's position, but all have met considerable, though different challenges.

The first approach is best illustrated by Tanaka's explication of women's NGOs as incubators to develop leadership skills for socially excluded women in Nepal. These are directed specifically at the large number of women who have been trafficked and sold, usually for sexual or menial labour in neighbouring India. The practice is not new, but the response is. As these women are gradually returning to their place of birth, they find themselves isolated, scorned and discriminated against in Nepal. Identity-based feminist organisations, newly formed by and for these women, enable them to develop a more positive self-identity, and a collective voice to demand their rights. We may call this the *'picking up the pieces' approach*, working with those women who are the most obvious victims of oppressive practices, and helping them gain a voice and improved conditions. A similar approach is illustrated in the case of the Roma women of Portugal. These organisations can and do use their work as a basis to launch campaigns against the prevailing hegemony, to change legislation, to improve work and housing opportunities, to try to change attitudes. But they cannot change the underlying causes of that oppression: they can only assist women to deal with it.

The second approach that may be taken is to try to *work within the existing cultural practices* and political structures to modify those practices that are most likely to oppress or disempower women. This appears to be the most prevalent strategy in Africa and the Middle East. In Islamic countries that means, for many, accepting the dominant laws of Islam, Sharia law, but working within that framework to try to reinterpret the core statutes that are used to oppress women. It means accepting the traditional role of women as mothers and housewives, but providing better rights within that role, for example by better education, or by stopping the excesses of genital mutilation. The seven chapters that form the second section of our anthology illustrate three difficulties with this position. First, despite their 'softly softly' approach, they may still be seen as a threat to the status quo. Second, and at the same time, a few high profile feminist advocates may be co-opted into the existing political hierarchy, and in the process lose the will to challenge practices that threaten their own material advantage. Both these reactions are evident in Kenya's Maendeleo organisation. A third difficulty faced by these same organisations is that they also face challenges from other forms of more radical feminism of the 'north'. African or Islamic feminism must be different they argue, and must operate within the existing cultural and religious context in which they are embedded. From a global feminist viewpoint, this strategy may at best lead to some sort of 'empowerment' but never real emancipation, as Ruth Phillips argues in her global overview.

The third approach that is well evidenced in the first section of this book is to *directly challenge the dominant cultural regimes* in the most dramatic and sophisticated way possible. In fact this is the single most defining feature of the difference between the cases in section one and those in section two of this book. The strategies make use of drama and humour and are able to attain high media profile, as witnessed by Pussy Riot, and *Se Non Ora Quando?* The capacity to directly challenge dominant cultural practices appears to be limited to advanced economies which can appeal to democratic traditions. The most effective strategies are those which deliberately break the law or at least entrenched cultural practices…such as women wearing beards invading corporate all-male board meetings…or young women making pop music in an orthodox cathedral. Such tactics challenge formal authority, and are likely to be stopped by the police, or lead to imprisonment as in Russia, or to being killed. Such direct challenges to powerful entrenched interests are dangerous. They resonate the first wave of feminism in England in the 1920s in which brave suffragettes faced humiliation and imprisonment to achieve the vote. Such strategies, though dangerous, are more likely to be successful in the long run, but only if there is sufficient momentum to continue for long periods against entrenched opposition.

The fourth approach occurs in post-industrial economies where sufficient feminist liberation has already occurred such that more women are employed and may now *work in organisations of their choice*, using preferred feminist practices. There are two such cases identified here, one in England (East and Morgan) and one in France (Dussuet and Flahault). Both cases report modern, flexible, family-friendly work practices, that attract women who wish to do meaningful work, in collaborative workplaces with flexible conditions that allow them to juggle family and work commitments. Many women are happy with this arrangement. However, as both cases illustrate, they also generate continued disadvantage for women, with low wages, insecure tenure and few career advancement opportunities. It is as if these organisations perpetuate women's disadvantage by their very success. Women remain entrenched in low paid, insecure, poorly recognised employment. Much is gained, but much remains the same.

Given that these CSOs are operating under difficult socio-political conditions, it is not surprising that there often develops ideological conflict between feminist groups over strategy. The strongest identification of this is in Lounasmaa's case of women's activism in Morocco. Those who wish to work within Islamic principles to achieve women's empowerment are in direct and open conflict with those who wish to challenge existing power structures. Both often campaign for the same ends, such as education for women, but refuse to acknowledge or work with those of a different orientation, and so the total effort becomes fractured and less effective. Such conflict becomes more entrenched and also leads to less effective outcomes when a feminist organisation becomes allied to a particular political party, as is illustrated in both Morocco and Kenya. In both cases, the alliance with a political party appears to be a rational strategy in terms of larger political support for feminist reforms. However, the danger occurs when inevitably the feminist issues are dominated by party ideology and masculinist power interests, as illustrated by the pro-abortion campaign in Uruguay. Keeping the feminist cause away from political interests is however easier said than done. Not only is it tempting to accept political patronage, but political parties are likely to attempt to infiltrate or co-opt the feminist movement for their own political gain, as illustrated by the *Se Non Ora Quando?* movement in Italy.

This raises the question of what is the best organising strategy: top down or bottom up? Is there any role for the state in the struggle for women's emancipation? Clearly the state is implicated in virtually all cases of oppression. Equally clearly, full emancipation cannot occur without significant changes in legislation and the implementation of that legislation, both responsibilities of the state. So the state needs to be persuaded to be responsive to women's demands. Can the state also take a more direct initiating role? One case in point is that of the Roma in Portugal. Raquel Rego illustrates the state's attempt to stimulate the development of Roma women's organisations. So far there has been mixed success, given that they are working directly against prevailing Roma cultural rules which require women to marry and bear children while very young, and in which virtually all decisions are made by men. In the case of Nepal, the NGO acts as incubator for the development of fledgling identity-based feminist organisations, in which the relationship moves from sponsor to partner as the new organisation gains in strength and capacity. In this case the NGO is acutely aware of the importance of remaining separate from the state, but also from powerful international NGOs that may impose their own conditions. The case of the Somalia diaspora argues that both a top down and a bottom up approach need to occur in tandem if any real change is to occur. What appears to be clear from all cases is that women's own voices must be represented in some form. Philanthropy may bring temporary relief, some "empowerment" but no lasting or real change or emancipation.

It is also clear, however, that support from the state is 'necessary but not sufficient'. The deep-rooted cultural practices and beliefs referred to by so many of the writers here demonstrate the limits of the state – for example, FGM (female genital mutilation) is against the law in several African countries (and many western ones as well), yet the practice continues. If there are lessons to be learned from the most recent period of feminist activism it is that hard won victories can be overturned, oppression can be reasserted in hitherto unexpected forms and locations, a new generation of activists can be encouraged and enthused. Progress is not linear; eternal vigilance is always required. New models of resistance will continue to be necessary. We all owe it to our embattled sisters to continue the struggle.

Note

[1] CIVICUS is the major international infrastructure organisation for civil society.

References

Bordt, R, 1990, How alternative ideas become institutions: the case of feminist collectives, *Program on Nonprofit Organizations (PONPO) working paper 159*, New Haven, CT: Yale University

Butler, J, 1999, *Gender trouble: Feminism and the subversion of identity*, New York: Routledge

Civicus, 2015, *State of civil society report;* http://civicus.org/index.php/en/media-centre-129/reports-and-publications/socs2015

DAWN (Development Alternatives with Women for a New Era), 2015, www.dawnnet.org/feminist-resources/about/main

Fraser, N, 2013, *Fortunes of feminism: From state-managed capitalism to neoliberal crisis*, London: Verso

Hopfl, H, 2003, Maternal organization: Deprivation and denial, *Interpreting the maternal organization*, pp 1–12, in H Hopfl, M Kostera (eds) London: Routledge

Mayo, M, 2005, *Global citizens: Social movements and the challenge of globalization*, London: Zed Books

Schwabenland, C, 2006, *Stories, visions and values in voluntary organisations*, Aldershot: Ashgate

Schwabenland, C, 2015, Discursive strategies for mapping the terrain between the sacred and the profane, *Culture and Organization* 21, 1, 59–77

Index

Page references for notes are followed by n

activities 324–6
challenges 326–7
and feminist agendas 329–30
roots 322–4
subaltern 330–2
Magar, V 28
Mahilako Nimti Mahila Manch see
  WOFOWON
Mahmood, S 264, 267
Makeri 337n
Malamut, AB 81
Maloney, W 9
Mama Cash 191
Manfredi, S 314
marketisation 11–12
Maruani, M 277
Marx, Karl 127
Mary, Mother of God 101–2
materialist feminism 124, 127–30
Matsuda, MJ 273
Mau Mau 323, 332, 337n
Mayo, M 4, 5, 9–10
Mboya, Tom 331
media
  Italy 51, 52–3
  Russia 90, 91, 94
  Se Non Ora Quando? 56, 59–61, 66
MediaZona 96
Medical Union of Uruguay (SMU) 141,
  142
Mernissi, F 255
meso-level policies 210, 211–12, 219–21,
  222–9, 349
Meuser, M 91
Mexico City 74
Meyer, IH 79
micro credit 10, 29
micro-level policies 210
Middle East 31
  Somali diaspora 218
Millar, F 304
Millennium Development Goals
  (UNMDGs) 25, 27–8, 40–1, 172,
  211, 212, 227, 337n, 344
Millett, Kate 100
mirror 117, 118, 130
Mitterand, François 126
Moghadam, V 260
Mohamed, Khadra 223
Mohammed V 256
Mohammed VI 256
Mohamud, Hassan Sheikh 210
Mohanty, Chandra 330, 331
Monteiro, Francisco 245
Moroccan Association of Human Rights
  270
Morocco 255–6, 258, 272–3, 344–5,
  347, 348, 351, 356–7

divisions hurting emancipation 270–2
faith-based women's activism 263–5
narratives of dichotomy 265–8
rights-based women's activism 259–62
similarities across divisions 268–70
women's activism history 256–7
Mouvement de Libération des Femmes
  (MLF) 121, 127
Movement for the Emancipation of the
  Niger Delta (MEND) 161, 171
Mujica, José 142, 148
Mulligan, D 8
multinational oil companies (MNOCs)
  157, 161–2, 169, 176, 354
Muraro, Luisa 61–2

N

Nadotti, M 62
Nagel, U 91
Nairobi 327–9
Naked Option, The 162
não cignao see Roma
National Alliance of Women Human
  Rights' Defenders (NAWHRD)
  197–8, 200, 202
National Coordination of Organisations
  for the Defence of Reproductive
  Health 141, 142, 145
National Council of Voluntary
  Organisations (NCVO) 300, 302
National Network against Trafficking of
  Women and Girls (NNTWG) 194–5
National Pastoral Work with Gypsies
  240, 242, 245
National Union of Moroccan Students
  (UNEM) 270
National Women's Commission (NWC)
  197
nego-feminism 333
Nentwich, JC 6
neoliberalism xix, 9–12, 347
  and civil society organisations 4, 25,
  41, 344
  Eastern Europe 103
  and empowerment 27, 29
Nepal 186–203, 346–7, 350, 354–5, 357
  CSOs, NGOs and IBAs 187–9
  Shakti Samuha 191–6, 198–201, 203
  WOFOFON 196–7, 198–201, 203
  WOREC 186–7, 189–91, 197–203
Nepali Congress 194
Netherlands 214
Network of Women's Health of Uruguay
  138
new social movements approach 4, 5
NGO Federation of Nepal (NFN) 195
NGOisation 25